BUSINESS ECONOMICS IN A RAPIDLY-CHANGING WORLD

UNDERSTANDING RISK

CONTRIBUTIONS FROM THE JOURNAL OF RISK AND GOVERNANCE

BUSINESS ECONOMICS IN A RAPIDLY-CHANGING WORLD

Additional books in this series can be found on Nova's website under the Series tab.

Additional e-books in this series can be found on Nova's website under the e-book tab.

GLOBAL ECONOMIC STUDIES

Additional books in this series can be found on Nova's website under the Series tab.

Additional e-books in this series can be found on Nova's website under the e-book tab.

BUSINESS ECONOMICS IN A RAPIDLY-CHANGING WORLD

UNDERSTANDING RISK

CONTRIBUTIONS FROM THE JOURNAL OF RISK AND GOVERNANCE

MATTHIAS BECK
EDITOR

nova publishers
New York

For permission to use material from this book please contact us:
Telephone 631-231-7269; Fax 631-231-8175
Web Site: http://www.novapublishers.com

Library of Congress Cataloging-in-Publication Data

Understanding risk : contributions from the Journal of risk and governance / editor, Matthias Beck.
pages cm
Includes index.
ISBN 978-1-62618-686-6 (hardcover)
1. Risk management. 2. Financial risk. 3. Risk. 4. Corporate governance. I. Beck, Matthias, 1964- II. Journal of risk and governance.
HD61.U535 2013
658.15'5--dc23
2013014137

Published by Nova Science Publishers, Inc. † New York

CONTENTS

PREFACE

During recent years, news headlines have been rife with criticisms of the risk management practices of public and private sector entities. These criticisms have often been accompanied by calls for greater transparency in the way government entities manage risks and communicate dangers to the public. Similarly, in the private sector, the internationalization of economic activity has heightened concerns over the potential adverse implications of mismanagement and financial scandals, and has led to calls for greater regulation and supervision. While the responses of public sector agencies and private sector actors to these challenges have differed, they share a common acknowledgement that effective governance relies on the pro-active identification, assessment, and management of risks as well as appropriate regulatory frameworks.

This edited book covers a number of divergent topics illustrating the emergence of several novel themes in the area of economic and social risk. As a commonality, these novel themes relate to the growing complexity in which human activity in this late stage of capitalist development is embedded. This risk-generating complexity, in turn, can be observed at several levels, including workplace hazards, governance problems within the private sector or within the intersection of private and public, and in relation to the economic risks faced by larger entities such as individual countries.

Chapter 1 - The study investigates the information content of insider trading transactions employing different signal definitions. Using directors' open market dealings during the period 1999-2000 for FTSE100 companies and new extensions of the event study methodology, the evidence suggests directors have, and trade on, price-sensitive private information and, thus, attain short-term abnormal returns. The study finds that the market perceives such transactions as price sensitive signals. Selling signals are assimilated by the market later than buying signals but create greater market reaction, particularly when the signal is reinforced by the trades of more than one director.

Chapter 2 - This chapter examines the determinants of corporate social disclosure (CSD) using a sample drawn from environmentally sensitive industries. It extends the traditional literature in two respects. First, it is international in scope, examining the accounting disclosure responses of Multinational companies to the pressures implied by the nature and scope of their operations. Second, variables measuring political risk and social development are developed so that these pressures can be measured, thereby introducing new dimensions to the literature. In common with previous studies, financial risk, size and other control variables are included. The relationships are tested econometrically utilising regression techniques not previously applied in the CSD literature but nonetheless more generally appropriate when using count dependent variables. Their results suggest that managers feel an unequal sense of responsibility to different constituencies and their disclosure priorities are determined by stock market accountability, lobbying power of their domestic audience and the political risk of their activities rather than the impact of their activities in countries of operation.

Chapter 3 - The credit crisis that commenced in 2007 has created significant economic uncertainty and prompted major debates about the future of capitalism. This chapter utilises Mary Douglas's cultural theory of risk to examine the crisis. It is argued that since the 1980s the individualistic culture has been the dominant form and inherent within the individualistic culture is a persistent shortsightedness. This myopia created a vulnerability to the financial crisis. This may appear paradoxical given that an individualistic culture has a primary focus upon financially-related risks and this contradiction is also explained.

Further, it is suggested that the severity of the crisis has created such a significant threat to the individualistic culture that this has intensified debates as to the most appropriate societal form. The eventual result of these highly vociferous cultural dialogues will potentially have major impacts upon key issues such as risk and regulation.

Chapter 4 - This chapter seeks to address how political risk influences behaviour, in particular rent seeking behaviour. Such risk is important in many industries, which poses challenges both for policy makers and economic agents.

This chapter studies how political uncertainty affects rent seeking, and what level of political uncertainty is "optimal" for society. The authors find that under some conditions, a higher level of political uncertainty might be beneficial to discourage rent seeking. On the other hand, high risk aversion among the agents decreases the optimal level of uncertainty, as risk averse agents suffer a greater loss in utility from a high uncertainty. It is possible to find several areas where this analysis is relevant. For instance, in fisheries, increasing uncertainty about whether or not to implement (or extend) a pay-back scheme will reduce the incentive for fishermen to overinvest in vessels.

Chapter 5 - In this chapter, the authors examine the level of disclosure on corporate governance practices among the biggest companies (in terms of market capitalization) in the top five emerging markets Brazil, China, India, Korea and Russia in the time period 2007-2008 and its effects on performance and profitability. Reviewing the *UNCTAD* (2008) report on corporate governance disclosure in emerging markets and testing it against financial indicators and theories the authors find that – ceteris paribus – the rate of disclosure: (1) is higher for companies in Brazil and India compared to Russia and Korea; (2) is higher for companies operating in financial services compared to other sectors; (3) correlates positively with return on equity; (4) does not affect market valuation; (5) increases with the legal environment; (6) increases with the market infrastructure. The results of this chapter support theoretical arguments that corporate governance disclosure increases performance, measured by return on equity. However, it disproves theories that find a positive correlation with market valuation, measured by price to book ratio. A country's government environment – especially legal and market infrastructure - highly affect the companies' rate of disclosure which then increases profitability. To policy makers and practitioners, the results suggest that corporate governance should be monitored. Good legislation and a market environment free from corruption are essential for corporate governance disclosure to be efficient.

Chapter 6 - This study presents findings from a series of interviews with Risk Managers and/or Chief Risk Officers from major Malaysian companies about the prerequisites for the effective implementation of Risk Management programmes. The interviews highlight the importance of a number of factors, including: a strong commitment from the Board of Directors and Management in general, a desire for an appropriate risk culture, the development of formal Risk Management frameworks and policies, a recognition of the importance of risk communication, the appointment of a Chief Risk Officer (CRO) and the development of a complementary system of internal audit.

Chapter 7 - The policy of key international organisation continues to be informed by the assumption that Foreign Direct Investment (FDI) has an unambiguously positive effect on recipient nations. However, there is increasing evidence that, on a global scale, increased trade and investment flows from rich to poorer nations have not contributed to a convergence of levels of income and well-being. This is particularly apparent in the context of former Soviet states, many of which continue to experience a decline, in both relative and absolute terms, in per capita GDP alongside a diminution in the life expectancy of their populations. Examining data on FDI received by former Soviet States from 1997 to 2005, this chapter notes, firstly, that these investments have been concentrated on a few, typical natural-resource-rich states. Secondly, it observes that even these resource-rich countries experienced massive fluctuations in terms of the amounts of FDI they received over this time period. Lastly, the chapter examines the impact of FDI on a number of country risk indicators via a pooled regression model which includes data for twelve former Soviet countries, namely the Central and Eastern European States of Belarus, Moldova, Russia, and Ukraine, and the Central Asian Republics of Armenia, Azerbaijan, Georgia, Kazakhstan, Kyrgyzstan, Tajikistan, Turkmenistan and Uzbekistan. This analysis indicates that FDI has either a marginally negative effect on individual country risk measures such as in the case of 'Overall Country Risk', or significantly negative effects as in the case of 'Economic Risk' and 'Legal Risk'. The chapter concludes that there is a strong case for questioning the existing orthodoxy which argues that problems of transition can be overcome via increased FDI and which continues to advise former Soviet states to pursue foreign capital at all cost.

Chapter 8 - Following the collapse of the Soviet Union in 1991, the newly independent oil-rich country of Kazakhstan has become a major recipient of foreign direct investment (FDI). Although international organisations such as the IMF and UNCTAD have claimed that FDI can be considered as an engine in the transition from state socialism and as a powerful force for integration of this region into the global economy, this investment also poses significant risks to Kazakhstan. These risk fall into two broad categories. The first category can be broadly described as issues associated with the "resource curse" or the "Dutch disease". The term Dutch disease describes a situation where booming demand in oil exporting countries due to high oil revenues leads to shift of an economy's productive resources from the tradeable sector to the non-tradeable sector. The second category is associated with the over-dependency of oil exporting countries on a relatively small number of large multinational corporations (MNCs). This over-dependency can lead to a situation where licenses and concessions are granted at less favourable conditions than if they were auctioned in an efficient market. Examining the licensing policy of the Kazakhstani Energy and Mineral Resource Ministry, this chapter notes that the latter issue of over-dependency has become less of a risk due to deliberate efforts to diversify investment relationships. Notwithstanding this situation there is some evidence that it remains diilfcult for oil exporting nations such as Kazakhstan to ensure that oil revenues are channeled into sustainable economic development.

Chapter 9 - This chapter examines the relationship between concepts of MNE bargaining power and broader concepts of political power. It notes that the analysis of MNE bargaining power presents a number of puzzles from the perspective of political theory. These puzzles arise, in part, from the fact that the overlap between traditional concepts of MNE bargaining power and broader concepts of political power is only a partial one. Despite these problems, it is suggested that political- theory-based approaches can add realism to our understanding of bargaining power.

Chapter 10 - The management of public sector risk is increasingly seen as a priority area of UK government policy. This has been highlighted recently by the Prime Minister Gordon Brown who stated that "the issue of public risk is one of the most challenging areas of policy-making for any government" (Strategic Risk, 2008). In response to these challenges, the UK Prime Minister has appointed a new body - the Risk and Regulation Advisory Council (RRAC) which is tasked with improving the way risk to the public is understood and managed. One area of particular concern with regard to the governance of public sector risks involves projects procured via the Private Finance Initiative (PFI). These projects involve long-term contracts, complex multi-party interactions and thus create various risks to public sector clients. Today, most PFI actors acknowledge the potentially adverse effects of these risks and make an effort to prevent or mitigate undesirable results. As a consequence, issues of risk allocation, risk transfer and risk management have become central to the PFI procurement process. This chapter provides an overview of the risk categories and risk types which are relevant to the public sector in PFI projects. It analyses risk as a feature of uncertain future project-related events and examines potential pitfalls which can be associated with PFI risk management on the basis of a case study of a high-profile PFI hospital in Scotland. The chapter concludes that, despite the trend towards diminished risk profiles during the operational phase, the public sector continues to be exposed to significant risks when engaging in PFI-based procurement.

Chapter 11 - The UK government introduced the Private Finance Initiative (PFI) and, latterly, the Local Improvement Finance Trust (LIFT) in an attempt to improve public service provision. As a variant of PFI, LIFT seeks to create a framework for the effective provision of primary care facilities. Like conventional PFI procurement, LIFT projects involve long-term contracts, complex multi-party interactions and thus create various risks to public sector clients. This chapter investigates the advantages and disadvantages of LIFT with a focus on how this approach facilitates or impedes risk management from the public sector client perspective. Their chapter concludes that LIFT has a potential for creating additional problems, including the further reduction of public sector control, conflicts of interest, the inappropriate use of enabling funds, and higher than market rental costs affecting the uptake of space in the buildings by local health care providers. However, there is also evidence that LIFT has facilitated new investment and that Primary Care Trusts (PCTs) have themselves started addressing some of the weaknesses of this procurement format through the bundling of projects and other forms of regional co-operation.

Chapter 12 - During the past twenty years, the UK has relied heavily on Public-private Partnerships (PPP) and especially the Private Finance Initiative in the procurement of infrastructure and services. Discussing the causes of the credit crunch and its effects on PPP, this chapter notes that the provision of new public sector infrastructure and related services has been adversely affected by the impact of the credit crunch on Private Finance Initiatives (PFIs). These problems have arisen primarily from the unwillingness of commercial banks to replace collapsed PFI bond financingunless new PFI contracts reduce financial risks; which, in turn, is likely to increase the cost of these projects to the public sector. Additional financial strains have arisen for the UK government from the need to bail out collapsed PFI projects. Overall the authors find evidence that the UK commitment to PFI has not only increased immediate fiscal pressures on the UK when these have become least palatable, but has also created fiscal vulnerabilities at local and national levels which are likely to hamper the country's ability to launch counter-cyclical responses to the ongoing crisis.

Chapter 13 - A central tenet of the risk society thesis is that, in today's world, individuals are required by the State to take on far greater responsibility for their own welfare provision. The present wave of NHS reforms have systematically moved risk away from the State and towards not only individuals (Beck, 1992; Giddens, 1994), but also to the public, private and not-for-profit organisations that now provide healthcare in the UK, and to the managers and doctors within them. This chapter examines the process by which this has happened, particularly since 1997, exploring the ways that risk has passed away from the state. It is argued that the State has created national bodies such as the Healthcare Commission and National Institute for Clinical Excellence (NICE) which have little independence from government in practice, but which allow the current Labour government to argue that they are not making contentious decisions concerned with treatment regulation and inspection. As well as this, the health service can be conceptualised as inverting the settlement upon which the NHS was created in 1948, moving from a system of central accountability but local paternalism, to central paternalism but local accountability (Greener and Powell, 2008). Organisational risk has therefore passed from the State to local organisations, especially in relation to NHS budgeting, and at the same time the State has managed to achieve unprecedented operational control over the NHS through its use of performance management. This process is exemplified by the Public Finance Initiative (PFI), which should be regarded as transferring risk between the public and private sectors, and needs to be assessed in terms of the relative capacities of each of those sectors to manage that risk (Asenova and Beck, 2003).

Chapter 14 - The chapter explores arsenic as an active ingredient in the cycle of dipping substances used to control sheep parasites in the UK in the 19th and 20th centuries. Technological optimists prevailed over a small number of prudent decision-makers in agriculture and used untested, unknown, suspect or even known carcinogens such as arsenic for supposed economic gain and, at the same time, marginalised worker health. Early unsuccessful efforts were made by some in industry to apply the precautionary principle primarily for consumer protection reasons; but action only occurred when 'better' products appeared on the markets. A similar pattern was to be repeated in later decades with other active ingredients. The risks were inevitably almost always born by the farm worker and small farmer. Sheep dipping demonstrated cyclical developments depending on which risks were assessed and what political and economic pressures were at work. Such pressures included perceived economic gains as well as compulsory regulatory dipping controls. Meanwhile, the evidence base of toxicology and occupational medicine developed in particular ways, whereby different adverse health effects of arsenic sheep dip were documented at different time periods. Focusing on the uneven and cyclical nature of these processes, this chapter highlights how the dominance of chemistry over the biological and medical disciplines ultimately led to a neglect of the subtle and chronic effects of arsenic dips on human health. The chapter concludes by drawing potential lessons from these developments.

Chapter 15 - Global occupational health history contains numerous cases of employees who worked in hazardous industries, contracted work-caused or work related diseases and who were then neglected and abandoned when those industries closed. Often decades pass before agreement is reached among scientists and civil servants about the causation, impact and compensation of such diseases although a range of risks may well have been identified and control standards set. Evidence may exist, rarely recognised or used by official sources, that employees recognised some of the occupational diseases they faced with sentinel events indicating possible disease causation or the specific causes prior to the scientific community either investigating, revealing or agreeing that such diseases existed.

This health study was organised and carried out by former employees of one plant, now closed, and their representatives. 162 questionnaires from a survey were collected and analysed from former plant workers on selected ill-health reported and primarily relating to respiratory, cardio-vascular and mental health functions as well as recorded angiosarcoma cases. The survey revealed under-reported and unrecorded illnesses in the ex-workers that were associated with VCM in the scientific literature since the 1970s. The chapter also documents working conditions using papers and reports from the ex-employees. Government departments at the time of the study such as the HSE (Hereafter Health and Safety Executive: the UK enforcement body on occupational health and safety) and Department of Work and Pensions (DWP) did not and still do not appear to offer coordinated and comprehensive support to those who later develop diseases that may be caused or related to their past work.

Chapter 16 - Nurses working in services for people with mental health problems are twice as likely to be assaulted as nurses working in general hospital settings (Health Care Commission 2007). The emergence of the issue of violence towards nurses as a social problem has however been accompanied by a contest to date unexamined, between conflicting 'frames' of the problem, which this chapter seeks to make transparent. Two distinct 'master' frames are discussed the 'individualising' and the 'co-creationist'. It is concluded that the influence of these frames has influenced the nature of responses to the problem but the recent dominance of the individualising frame is being challenged by the emergence or perhaps re-emergence, of the ideals and values of the therapeutic community.

Chapter 17 - In the aftermath of the World Trade Center (WTC) conflagration in 2001, a debate began about the role of fire-retardants. Some commentators argued that the decision to dispense with asbestos during the construction of the Twin Towers played a key role in their subsequent collapse. It was further argued that the disaster was a consequence of the 'asbestos hysteria' that had supposedly gripped New York in the 1960s and 1970s. This article, based on contemporary documents and recent investigations of 9/11, shows that there is no evidence linking asbestos (or the lack of it) to the collapse of the Towers and that the debate about asbestos in the WTC has been largely 'manufactured'.

Chapter 18 – In Norway, recent health political documents adhere to the idea of rendering patients and health professionals equal. In this article, discussions between health workers, lay representatives and academic actors concerning equality within patient education is investigated. The aim of the article is to reveal how health professionals cope with the idea of equality that in many ways seams impossible to practice.

The discussions were analyzed in a theoretically informed inductive process inspired by grounded theory. A theoretical framework based upon Brunsson's organized hypocrisy and Habermas' division between system and lifeworld guided the analysis. Three categories of double-bind situations originating from the demand for rendering lay representatives and health professionals equal were identified: considering knowledge payment and collaboration.

The dilemmas are coped with by decoupling those values evoked when attuning to the health care system, and those values evoked when attuning to patient education as practice. The article concludes that the decoupling between idea and practice is made possible by equality being an idea in the system world and a practice in the lifeworld. This nails equality to the lifeworld and makes it fragile to quality assurance.

Versions of these chapters were also published in *Journal of Risk and Governance,* Volume 1, Numbers 1-4, published by Nova Science Publishers, Inc. They were submitted for appropriate modifications in an effort to encourage wider dissemination of research.

EDITORIAL

Matthias Beck

During recent years, news headlines have been rife with criticisms of the risk management practices of public and private sector entities. These criticisms have often been accompanied by calls for greater transparency in the way government entities manage risks and communicate dangers to the public. Similarly, in the private sector, the internationalisation of economic activity has heightened concerns over the potential adverse implications of mismanagement and financial scandals, and has led to calls for greater regulation and supervision. While the responses of public sector agencies and private sector actors to these challenges have differed, they share a common acknowledgement that effective governance relies on the pro-active identification, assessment, and management of risks as well as appropriate regulatory frameworks.

This edited book draws and articles which appeared in the "Journal of Risk and Governance." The "Journal of Risk and Governance" is a new interdisciplinary peer-refereed publication that focuses on the intersection of risk and governance research in its broadest sense. The focal point of this Journal is on the growing body of research that views risk management not as a discrete expert activity, but rather as an integral part of socio-economic governance. In adopting this focus, JRG places a key emphasis on the historical, conceptual, cultural, societal, and economic contexts in which risk management and regulation take place. In terms of substantive areas, JRG invites contributions in a broad range of fields including business, economics, finance, sociology, public policy, health, and environmental studies, provided that these contributions address aspects of risk regulation or governance.

Within this broad disciplinary matrix, the Journal seeks to further the understanding of:

- how corporate and government entities (central, state, local government units and agencies) respond to, manage, and seek to prevent disasters and crises;
- how these entities regulate and control risks;
- how risks, disasters, and crises affect these institutions in terms of their institutional make-up, resourcing, and strategic outlook; and
- how corporate and government entities respond to regulatory demands.

This edited book includes articles from the first issues of JRG. Although covering a number of divergent topics, these articles illustrate the emergence of several novel themes in the area of economic and social risk. As a commonality, these novel themes relate to the growing complexity in which human activity in this late stage of capitalist development is embedded. This risk-generating complexity, in turn, can be observed at several levels, including workplace hazards, governance problems within the private sector or within the intersection of private and public, and in relation to the economic risks faced by larger entities such as individual countries.

Section A:

Corporate Governance and Risk Management

In: Understanding Risk
Editor: Matthias Beck

ISBN: 978-1-62618-686-6

Chapter 1

SIGNALLING CHARACTERISTICS AND INFORMATION CONTENT OF DIRECTORS' DEALINGS ON THE LONDON STOCK EXCHANGE

Moh'd Ajlouni[1] and J. Steven Toms[2,*]

[1]Department of Banking and Finance, Faculty of Economics and Administrative Sciences, Yarmouk University, Irbid, Jordan

[2]The York Management School, University of York, York, , UK

ABSTRACT

The study investigates the information content of insider trading transactions employing different signal definitions. Using directors' open market dealings during the period 1999-2000 for FTSE100 companies and new extensions of the event study methodology, the evidence suggests directors have, and trade on, price-sensitive private information and, thus, attain short-term abnormal returns. The study finds that the market perceives such transactions as price sensitive signals. Selling signals are assimilated by the market later than buying signals but create greater market reaction, particularly when the signal is reinforced by the trades of more than one director.

INTRODUCTION

Cumulative evidence from prior studies offers strong evidence that directors' trading in the shares of their own firm conveys significant market sensitive information. The method of defining the signal has an important impact on the conclusion drawn [Gregory et al. (1997)]. However, relatively little is known about the differential effects of the signalling methods available to directors to communicate such information. The contribution of the study is to employ several signals definitions to give insights into the information content of insider transactions, and also the timing with which the market reacts to such signals. Prior UK

* E-Mail: st27@york.ac.uk.

insider trading based literature defines the event in a number of ways. These are the *net value* or value of shares traded per month referred to hereafter as a Quantified Signal (QS), the *net number* of inside trades per month referred to as a Multiple Signal (MS), or the *net transaction type*, *i.e.* buy or sell, per month referred as Single Signal (SS). Using daily data, this event study updates prior UK research and extends it by systematically comparing the strength of all three signal definitions.

The findings generally confirmed expectations about the information content of directors' trades. Specifically, there is strong evidence of abnormal returns following buying transactions and some evidence for selling transactions. Also different signal definitions produce different results in terms of the sign, level, and significance of return. Consistent with the Efficient Market Hypothesis (EMH), our results show that the market reacts significantly earlier to successive signals (MS and QS) than SS. Overall, these findings demonstrate that directors' trading in the UK has significant incremental information content.

The reminder of the paper is organised as follows. Section 2 reviews the relevant literature, while section 3 presents (a) the methodology used and develops the main hypotheses of the study and (b) provides a description of the data used to test the hypothesis. Section 4 discusses the empirical findings, and Section 5 concludes the study.

INSIDER TRADING AND MARKET REACTION

Share price reaction to insider trading has produced a large, empirically dominated literature which has established some consistent facts about return behaviour following insider trading. Table 1 provides an overview of prior event studies, including the event definition used, method of measurement of abnormal returns, and results.

Table 1 (columns 1-3) show that insider-trading is under-researched in the UK compared with the USA and that the UK studies are relatively old and do not necessarily reflect current regulatory and market conditions. For example, Hillier and Marshall (2002a), which is the most recent study, used 1991-1997 data (column 4). Column (5) states the type of *securities* investigated; *i.e.* ordinary shares (OS) and/or executive share options (ESO). Only Gregory et al. (1994) uses ESO in addition to the OS and this study follows the literature and investigates only OS. Again, as in previous studies [Friederich et *al.* (2002) and (1999), Gregory et al. (1997) and (1994), Hillier and Marshall (2002a, b), King and Roell (1988) and Pope et al. (1990)], we concentrate on director's dealings rather than other classes of insider listed in column 6.

The most important contrast between this study and the prior literature follows from the *event definition*. Such a definition is an important factor in conducting the event test. It can be seen, however, that there is no consensus among the prior literature regarding definition of the event (column 7). Column (8) reports the number of *transactions* (buy and sell) in the sample. Given the data availability and the breadth of the market, *i.e.* number of securities listed in the market, it is obvious that the US literature typically uses larger number of transactions than the UK. Column (9) indicates the *frequency of the data* used while column (10) states the length of the *event window(s)*. Clearly, these two columns are associated with each other. When the frequency of the data used is monthly, the length of the event window examined is in monthly terms. One exception is Hillier and Marshall (2002/a) who used monthly data and daily event windows. Another exception is Givoly and Palmon (1985) who used daily data and accumulated it monthly. Column (11) and (12) refer to the *model* used in computing the expected return and the *tests of significance employed to detect type I error*, respectively. The majority of the literature used Sharpe's (1964)-market model (MM) to measure the expected return. Because the intercept term of the MM can impound abnormal returns, particularly in the period of the event window (Pope et al. 1990, p.366), this study uses a CAPM formulation.

A summary of this extensive body of empirical evidence shows that insider trading transactions yield significant and persistent cumulative abnormal returns CARs, as summarised in column 13, across different countries, markets, time intervals, transaction type and type of trader. The signal (column 7) is typically defined in terms of the dates of insider trading transactions. However, such a signal might also be defined in terms of number of transactions, volume, value, or number of insiders traded within the event date.

The empirical literature highlights two anomalies in the behaviour of abnormal returns. These are first persistency over time [1977 – 1997 in the UK and 1950 – 1997 in the USA]. Second buy portfolios dominate sell ones in terms of both rate of return and significance of such returns [Aboody and Lev (2000), Chang and Suk (1998), Friederich et al. (2002), Givoly and Palmon (1985), Gregory et al. (1994), Hillier and Marshall (2002/a), King and Roell (1988), Pettit and Venkatesh (1995), Roth and Saporoschenko (1999) and Seyhun (1986)]. Given the various non-profit reasons for insider trading, which usually prompt sell transactions, for example liquidity motives, the second anomaly is reasonable. All UK studies reported that over a period of up to two years insider trading buy transactions tended to outperform significantly. Using daily data, Friederich et al. (2002) and (1999) and Hillier and Marshall (2002/a) report significant abnormal returns (AR) over 8 days after the event, while Gregory et al. (1997), using monthly data, document significant CARs of 3.18%, 3.54%, 4.80%, and 4.80% of buy transactions over 3, 6, 12, and 24 months, respectively. Similarly, Chang and Suk (1998), Seyhun (1986) and Givoly and Palmon (1985), of the USA studies, reported significant CAR of buy portfolios over 1, 2, 3 and 12 months. Insider trading sell transactions, on the other hand, indicate contradicting results. Of the UK literature, Friederich et al. (2002) and (1999), Gregory et al. (1997), Hillier and Marshall (2002/a) and Pope et al. (1990) found significant abnormal losses over 3, 6, 12, and 24 months. While Gregory et al. (1994) provided indistinguishable from zero CARs during the transactions' month and insignificant losses thereafter. King and Roell (1988) found positive but insignificant abnormal returns over a period of up to one year. Except for Finnerty (1976b), the USA studies reported similar insignificant losses to those of the UK's.

Many of these results are based on certain methodological assumptions and the current study examines the robustness of previous findings with reference to the most important aspects. These are (A) the signal definition and date, (B) the length of the event window used, and (C) the significance of the results and each is discussed in turn.

Gregory et al. (1997), Hillier and Marshall (2002/aandb), King and Roell (1988), Lorie and Niederhoffer (1968) and Pettit and Venkatesh (1995) used this definition, as well, but with monthly event windows. In fact, Gregory et al. (1997) did not report the exact event date, instead using the end of the month or last transaction's date within a month, and Pettit and Venkatesh (1995) used January of each calendar year to cumulate the abnormal returns for each security.

Table 1. Summary Review of Empirical Literature on Defining the Event, Measuring Abnormal Returns, and Reporting the Results

1	2	3	4	5	6	7	8		9	10	11	12	13	
Country	*Study*	*Market*	*Test Period*	*Type Of*	*Type Of*	*Signal Definition / Signal Date*	*No. of Signals*		*Data*	*Event*	*E (R)*	*T-Test*	*Results*	
	Year of Publication			*Security*	*Insiders*		*Buy*	*Sell*	*Freq-cy*	*Windows*	*Model*	*Model*	*Buy*	*Sell*
UK	Friederich et al. (2002) and (1999)	LSE	10/1986 - 12/1990	OS	Directors	Net Quantity of SharesTraded (QS)	1702	1268	Daily	-20 to +20 days	MM	BW1985, Boehmer et al. (1991) and Corrrado (1989)	-AR (-20 to -1)* +AR (0 to 8)* +CAR (0 to 20)	+AR (-20 to -1) -AR (0 to 8) +CAR (0 to 20)
	Hillier and Marshall (2002/a)	LSE	17/9/1991 - 31/3/1997	OS	Directors	Net Trading (buy - sale) (QS)	1841	2145	Monthly	-120 to +120 days	MM	Boehmer et al. (1991)	-CAR (-40 to -1)* +AR (0) +AR (1 to 3*)	+CAR (-40 to -1)* +AR (0) - AR (1 to 3*)
	Hillier and Marshall (2002/b)	LSE	1/1/1992 - 31/12/1996	OS	Directors	No. of Trades Around Interim & Final Earnings Announcent / No. of All Trades in the Year. (SS) Interim and Final Announcement Periods Compared With Other Periods.	1215	930	Daily	-120 to +120 days around announce-ment date	MM	Boehmer et al. (1991)	Buy > Sell in the Event Period and B=S in other periods. B/S in Event > B/S in Other Period.	B interim > B final, S interim < S final, B interim > S interim, Directors Buy (Sell) After (Before) Poor (Good) Stock Performance.
	Gregory et al. (1997)	LSE	1/1986 - 12/1990	OS	Directors	(1) Net Value of Shares Bought/Sold in a Month (QS)	3722	3034	Monthly	3, 6, 12, 24 month	MM	DW1983	+CAR (3,6,12,24)*	-CAR (3,6,12,24)*
						(2) Net Number of Deals (Buy/Sell) in a Month > 2 (QS)	1380	973					+CAR (3,6,12,24)*	-CAR (3,6,12,24)*

1	2	3	4	5	6	7	8		9	10	11	12	13	
Country	*Study*	*Market*	*Test Period*	*Type Of*	*Type Of*	*Signal Definition / Signal Date*	*No. of Signals*	*Data*	*Event*	*E (R)*	*T-Test*	*Results*		
						(3) Net Value of Shares Bought/Sold in a Month > £10k, > £100k, & £1m (QS)	1826, 368, 55	2376, 1051, 179					+CAR (3,6,12,24)* +CAR3,6,12	-CAR (3,6,12,24)* -CAR (3,6)*
	Gregory et al. (1994)	LSE	1/1984 – 12/1986	OS & ESO	Directors	Net Value of Shares Bought/Sold in a Month (QS)	613	1040	Monthly	0, 1, 3, 6, 12, 24 month	MM	DW1983	s1: +CAR 3* 12* s2: +CAR (1,3,6,12)*	S1&s2&s3 +CAR 0, -CAR 1, 3, 6, 12, 24
	Pope et al. (1990)	LSE	4/1977 – 12/1984	OS	Directors	Net Number of Buyers (Sellers) In a Month > 2 (MS)	275	289	Monthly	6 month	MM	BW1980	+CAR0* +CAR(1to6)	+CAR0 -CAR(1to6)*
	King and Roell (1988)	LSE	1/1986 – 8/1987	OS	Directors	Transaction Type / Publication Date in FT (SS)	31	84	Monthly	1,3,12 month	MAR & RAR	Std. Error	+AR (1,3,12)*	+AR 1,3,12
	Year of Publication			Security	Insiders		Buy	Sell	F-eq-cy	Windows	Model	Model	Buy	Sell
USA	Aboody & Lev (2000)	NYSE	1/1985-12/1997	OS & SSC	Officers	Transaction Type/ (SS)Transaction Date R&D and (No R&D)	7027 (17124)	18255 (21585)	Monthly	Trnsct To SEC filing	MAR	N/R	+AR3% (0.9%)	-AR0.5% (-0.1%)
	Roth & Saporos-chenko (1999)	NYSE	1993-1995	OS	Officers/Directors	Transaction Type / (SS) Publication Date of Purchases	142	0	Daily	-14 to +14,252 d	MAR	BW1985	+CAR0*	N/R
	Chang & Suk (1998)	NYSE	8/1988 – 12/1990	OS	Officers/Directors	Transaction Type / (SS)Transaction, Filing, & Publication Dates	330	377	Daily	-19to22 day	MM	DW1983	+CAR +1to+3*	-CAR +1to+3
	Yermack (1997)	AMEX	1992/1993 & 1993/1994	ESC	CEO	ESO Award Date (SS)	620		Daily	-20 to +20 day	MM	DW1983	At -20d, 47.6% +CARs, 0d 48.1%, 15d 53.1%*, 20d 54.5%*,	30d 55.4%*, 40d 55.7%*, and at 50d 57.4%* CAR are + and = 2%

Table 1. (Continued)

1	2	3	4	5	6	7	8		9	10	11	12	13	
Country	*Study*	*Market*	*Test Period*	*Type Of*	*Type Of*	*Signal Definition / Signal Date*	*No. of Signals*	*Data*	*Event*	*E (R)*	*T-Test*	*Results*		
	Year of Publication		Security	Insiders		Buy	Sell	Freq-cy	Windows	Model	Model	Buy	Sell	
	Pettit & Venkatesh (1995)	NYSE&AMEX	1/1980 – 8/1987	OS	Officers/ Directors	Value(Number) of Net Purchases (QS)	30000	70000	Monthly	3years (12m*3)	MM	Parametric &Non-Test	+CAR0* (CAR0)	N/R
	Rozeff & Zaman (1988)	NYSE	1/1973 – 12/1982	OS	Officers/ Directors	3 Insiders Buy (Sell) With No One Sells Monthly (MS)	365	333	Monthly	12 months	MM	Jaffe1974	-AR1* +AR3,6,12	N/R
	Seyhun (1986)	NYSE	1975 – 1981	OS	Officers/ Directors	Number of Buyers-Sellers Monthly (Last Deal Date) (MS)	6244	8839	Daily	-200 to 300 d	MM	DW1983	+CAR 1 to 300*	-CAR 1 to 300
	Givoly & Palmon (1985)	AMEX	1973 –1975	OS	Officers/ Directors	Transaction Type / Transaction Date (SS)	1118	413	1month = 20 day	0- 239 days	MM	N/R	+CAR 1*2*3*	-CAR1, +CAR2to12
	Finnerty (1976)a	NYSE	1971	OS	Officers/Directors	# Insider *{(Volume sold –Volume bought) / Volume holding} > 0=Sell,<0=Buy (MS)	282	572			MDA	N/R	YES	YES
	Finnerty (1976)b	NYSE	1/1969 – 12/1972	OS	Officers/ Directors	Transaction Type / Transaction Date (SS)	9602	21487	Monthly	11 momths	CAPM	N/R	+AR (1,3,4,5,6,10)*	-AR (0to4)* 6* (8to11)*
	Jaffe (1974)a	NYSE	1962 – 1968	OS	Officers/ Directors	#Buyer > # Seller = Buy Month / Publication Date (MS)	466	486	Monthly	8 months	CAPM	N/R	+CAR1*2* 8*	N/R
	Lorie & Niederhoffer (1968)	NYSE	1/1950- 12/1960	OS	Officers/ Directors	#Buy - #Sell, Volume buy-Volume sell / Last Deal in Month, (QS)	3973	3277	Monthly	6 months	% Price / Market	N/R	YES	YES

1	2	3	4	5	6	7	8		9	10	11	12	13	
Country	*Study*	*Market*	*Test Period*	*Type Of*	*Type Of*	*Signal Definition / Signal Date*	*No. of Signals*	*Data*	*Event*	*E (R)*	*T-Test*	*Results*		
	Year of Publica-tion	Security	Insiders	Buy	Sell	Freq-cy	Win dows	Model	Model	Buy	Sell			
Austral	Arnand et al. (2002)	ASX	N/R	OS	Directors	ASX Announcement Day of Insider Trading (Called Signal G) [Directors have to disclose within 14 days] (SS)	380	186	Daily	-10 to +20 days	MM and MAR	N/R	-10d -AR*, 0d -AR, 1d - AR, 2d -AR, 6d -AR*, 10d -AR	-10d +AR*, 0d -AR, 1d -AR*, 2d - AR, 6d - AR, 10d - AR*
Norway	Eckbo & Smith (1998)	OSE	1/1985 – 12/1992	OS	Officers/ Directors	Number of Buyers-Sellers Monthly (Last Deal Date) (MS)	N/R	N/R	Monthly	7 months	MM	N/R	NO	NO
Spain	Brio et al. (2002)	MSE	1/1992 – 12/1996	OS	Directors & Large Sharehoders	Buy or Sell (SS)	589	406	Daily	-80 to +10 days	MM & CARCH MM	DW1980 & CARCH Test	CAR(0,1) +, (1,15) +, (15,32) +, (1,60) +	CAR(0,1) +*, (1,15) - *, (15,32) +, (1,60) +

Notes: abbreviations used in the table.

* = Significant rate of return,%Price/Mrkt = Changes in security prices relative to the market, AMEX = American Stock Exchange, AR = Abnormal returns, ASX = Australian Stock Exchange , BEO = Exercised ESO, held not sold, BW1980 = Brown and Warner's (1980) t-test formula, BW1985 = Brown and Warner's (1985) t-test.

CAPM = Capital Asset Pricing Model, CAR = Cumulative Abnormal Returns, CARCH = Constrained ARCH, CEO = Chief Executive Officer, d = Day, DW1983 = Dodd and Warner's (1983) t-test formula, E (R) = The model used to estimate the Expected Return, ESO = Executive Share Options, LSE = London Stock Exchange, m = Month, MAR = Market Adjusted Return, MDA = Multiple Discriminant Analysis, MM = Market Model, MS = Multiple Signal, QS = Quantitative Signal, MSE = Madrid Stock Exchange, N/R = Not Reported, NYSE = New York Stock Exchange, OS = Ordinary Shares, OSE = Oslo Stock Exchange, R & D = Research and Development, RAR = Risk Adjusted Return, SEC = Securities Exchange Commission, USA, SS = Single Signal.

[The literature are listed according to the country/market of investigation and date of publication, where the most recent is listed first]

The second definition is the net transaction *value* (or volume) during a calendar month, referred to here as QS. Friederich et al. (2002), Gregory et al. (1997) and (1994), Hillier and Marshall (2002/b), Lorie and Niederhoffer (1968), and Pettit and Venkatesh (1995) used this sort of signal. Using monthly data places a limitation on interpretation because it does not take into account the market's daily reaction to the signal during the event month. The current study overcomes the problem by using daily instead of monthly-quantified signals. The third definition is the net number of insider trades during a calendar month, referred to here as MS. Eckbo and Smith (1998), Finnerty (1976a), Pope et al. (1990), Rozeff and Zaman (1988) and Seyhun (1986) used this signal. The approach suffers from the same limitation as the use of monthly data and event windows. To overcome this limitation the average daily abnormal returns for each transaction-day during the calendar month can be employed.

Table 1 shows that the event window ranges from one month to 36 months, for monthly data, and from one day to 300 days, for daily data. However, most literature reported sub-windows within a wider window. All UK studies and most of the US studies used monthly data. McWilliams and Siegel (1997) indicate that a longer window is more likely to incorporate other confounding events, but none of the Table 1 studies literature control for such effects.

It is assumed in the literature that the event date is identified with certainty. However, it is difficult to identify the exact date in practice. Approaches include collecting event dates from the Saturday section of the *Financial Times* [King and Roell (1988)], LSE's *Official Weekly Intelligence* [Pope et al. (1990)], from the *Insider Trading Spotlight* weekly section of the *Wall Street Journal* [Chang and Suk (1998) and Roth and Saporoschenko (1999)], or from the SEC's *Official Summary* [Jaffe (1974)]. In such cases, one cannot be certain if the market were informed prior to publication. An event date for the insider, is therefore not typically an event date for the market. The common approach to handle the matter of uncertain event date is to expand the event window, whilst controlling for other event effects, which has not been utilised in the prior UK literature.

It can be seen from column 12 of Table 1 that different significance tests are used. Dodd and Warner's (1983) *t*-test formula is most common [for example, Brio et al. (2002), Chang and Suk (1998), Gregory et al. (1997) and (1994), Seyhun (1986) and Yermack (1997)]. While Brown and Warner's (1985) is used by two studies [Friederich et al. (2002) and Roth and Saporoschenko (1999)] and Brown and Warner's (1980) is used by one UK study [Pope et al. (1990)]. The difference between these formulas is the standardisation process employed. This study follows Dodd and Warner's (1983) *t*-test, because it is assumed that events are firm specific with cross-sectional independence, but also reports Brown and Warner's (1985) t-test to test the sensitivity of the assumption.

METHODOLOGY, DATA AND EMPIRICAL TESTS

Methodology and Hypotheses

The event is defined as a firm's director buying or selling his firm's ordinary shares on transaction date (t_0). However, the transaction must be reported to the LSE within seven days and also the major source, the *Financial Times*, publishes such news every Saturday, embedding delays in disclosure to the market. Moreover, since market makers widen the bid/ask spread to reduce their potential risk/loss arising from information uncertainty implied by directors dealing [Chung and Charoenwong (1998), Chakravarty and McConnell (1997) and Seyhun (1986)]. This process may imply adjustments in share prices between the transaction date and the disclosure date. This study extends the event window long enough to accommodate these effects, whilst avoiding the problem of confounding effects of longer event windows.

The data set consists of specific transactions, including multiple transactions by a director on the same date. The initial sample was filtered to attain a defined SS event for equally weighted portfolios, according to the following procedures. (i) multiple, but similar type of, transactions (e.g. buy) of a given director at the same day are considered one (buy) transaction in the (Buy) portfolio. The volumes of these transactions are also summed. (ii) Multiple, but similar type, transactions (*e.g.* buy) by different companies' directors on the same day are considered one (buy) transaction in the (Buy) portfolio. Again the volumes of these transactions are also summed, and the number of directors is reported. (iii) Multiple, but different types, transactions (*e.g.* buy and sell) of a given director on the same day are considered one transaction. However, the volumes of these transactions are differenced. If the volume of the buy (sell) transactions is more than that of sell (buy), then such transaction is considered as a buy (sell) transaction in the Buy (Sell) portfolio, and the number of buying directors (selling) is reported.

MS is defined as the number of a firm's directors trading in their own firm's securities within a calendar month. The defined SS sample, mentioned above, is used to construct a multiple signal sample, according to the following steps. (i) For each calendar month, firm-level signals with only one director transaction are excluded from the sample. (ii) All the firm's directors' transaction within a calendar month are summed together to form a multiple signal for each firm-month. (iii) The number of directors and volume of shares traded for each firm-month multiple signal are summed and (iv) then abnormal returns are calculated for each transaction within the firm-month and the average is then computed.

A quantified signal (QS) is defined in terms of volume of shares traded in each transaction (Kyle, 1985). The SS sample defined above is used to construct a quantified signal sample, according to the following procedure. (i) Each portfolio is sorted by net volume of each transaction, (ii) four quartiles for each portfolio are identified according to volume of shares traded per deal and four sub-portfolios in order of descending volume are then constructed, QS1, QS2, QS3, and QS4.[1] The difference between an SS portfolio and QS is thus in terms of the volume of transactions. SS consists of all deals regardless of their volume, whilst QS consists of those deals within certain volume ranges, according to the specified quartile.

Sharpe's (1964) simple Market Model (MM) expresses the actual rate of return (R) on the security (i) at time (t) as a function of market return, in the context of past time series (t-L2 to t-L1), such that:

[1] In addition, the quantified signal is defined in terms of the median of the volume of shares traded in each deal. That is the 50% percentile of each portfolio. Since the size of directors trading volume within each portfolio is highly varied, viz. insignificant arithmetic mean, an alternative definition is employed to overcome the size variance problem. This is the ratio of each transaction-security volume to the total volume traded in that security per day. In other words, the ratio of net volume traded by directors per security-transaction/total volume traded of that security per day (NV/TV). Then the median of the ratio's transaction(s) is (are) identified and considered as a stand-alone portfolio for each buy or sell.

$$R_{it} = \alpha_i + (\sum_{t=t-n}^{t=n} \beta_{it} * R_{mt}) + \Omega_{it} \quad (1)$$

where α is the intercept term, β the systematic risk of security i, and Ωit is the error term, with ΣΩit = 0. This equation indicates that the actual return can be measured by regressing (t-n) lagged, (t+n) leading days or months, and contemporaneous (t) market rate of returns (Rm) on observed security returns. The validity of the MM depends on satisfying three conditions. (1) The sum of the residuals should equal to zero, ΣΩit = 0, (2) there is no significant correlation between the residuals (Ωit) and the market return (Rmt), and (3) the sum of the differences between the average residuals (AΩi) and residuals (Ωit) should equal to zero, i.e. ΣΦit = 0. That is:

$$A\Omega_i = \Omega_{it} + \Phi_{it}$$

Thus

$$\Phi_{it} = A\Omega_i - \Omega_{it} \quad (2)$$

If these conditions satisfied, the MM parameters can be used in the two-factor *ex-ante* CAPM to calculate the *expected rate of return* [E(Rit)] as:

$$E(R_{it}) = R_{ft} + \beta_{iK} * (R_{mt} - R_{ft}). \quad (3)$$

where Rf is the rate of return on a risk-free security, βik is Dimson's beta (1979), where the sum of Beta's of the lagged, leading, and contemporaneous regressions of MM equals to ($\sum_{t=t-n}^{t+n}$ βit). Then, the *ex-post* CAPM is re-stated to calculate the expected rate of return [E(Rit)] as

$$E(R_{it}) = \alpha_i + R_{ft} + \beta_{iK} * (R_{mt} - R_{ft}) \quad (4)$$

In this equation, β is obtained by summing the slope coefficients from the MM (equation 1), and α and β are estimated for a given security for the *conventional prior window*. That is 200 trading days from preceding 250 trading days of the test period. Since the test period, in which abnormal returns are measured should be completely separate from the estimation period, the MM parameters used in line with events occurring in one period are estimated from data on a previous period (Givoly and Palmon, 1985). Specifically, a 50 day exclusion period is used to take into account the assumption that insiders may trade following a period of abnormal performance by the company (Gregory et al., 1994).

The abnormal rate of return (ARit) is the difference between the actual and expected rates of return on the security at time (t) calculated during the event window (t0 to t+T).

$$AR_{it} = \varepsilon_{it} = R_{it} - E(R_{it}) \tag{5}$$

The simple arithmetic mean of all signals abnormal returns (ÁRt) at any point of time during the event window is:

$$\overline{AR}_t = \frac{1}{N} * \sum_{i=1}^{N} AR_{it} \tag{6}$$

where (N) is the number of sample securities at time (t). The *cumulative abnormal rate of returns* (CART), of all securities during the event window t+T, is measured as:

$$CAR_T = \sum_{t=0}^{t+T} \overline{AR}_t \tag{7}$$

where (t+T) is the length of the event window. The null hypothesis is H0: CAR ≤ 0 (CAR ≥ 0) for buy (sell) portfolios, and the alternative hypotheses, if H0 is rejected, are: H1: CART > 0 for the "Buy" portfolios, and CART < 0 for the "Sell" Portfolios. This study follows Dodd and Warner (1983) t-test (hereafter DW1983). That is:

$$t - value = \overline{SCAR_T} * \sqrt{N}.. \tag{8}$$

where T is the length of the event window, and N is the number of the securities in the portfolio, and ŚCARt is the cross-sectional average standardised cumulative abnormal return. In addition, we report that of Brown and Warner (1985) (hereafter BW1985). That is:

$$t - value = \frac{1}{\sqrt{N}} * \sum_{i=1}^{N} SAR_{i,t+T} \cdots \tag{9}$$

However, accepting or rejecting the null hypothesis will be based upon the DW1983 formula.

Data and Empirical Tests

The sample firms consists of all of the FTSE 100 companies experiencing directors' trading in their firms' ordinary shares during the period 1/5/1999-1/7/2000 (hereafter called the *sample period*), collected from the *Hemscott.NET's* website[2]. The initial sample consists of 1200 transactions (96,245,713 shares). This resulted in a sample of 665 transactions, of which 508 are transactions in 13,683,912 shares of directors buying their firm's ordinary

[2] Unlike in the US, there is no institutional agency to record, update and maintain such transactions in the UK, such as Centre for Research on Security Prices (CRSP). Hemscott is a public shareholding investment company, URL: www.hemscott.com.

shares (Buy Portfolio), and 157 transactions (19,842,685 shares) selling ordinary shares (Sell Portfolio).

All securities in the FTSE100, with continuous daily trading were chosen. Of the FTSE100 securities, 96 securities satisfied this condition. Market-based data, for each firm during the period 1/1/1997-1/1/2001 was collected from *Datastream*. These are (1) the share's daily return index (RI), (2) the daily FT All Share return index (FTALLSH) and (3) daily UK Treasury Bond benchmark (UKTB). FTALLSH is used as the market portfolio's return, despite the sample's securities being the FTSE 100. Many securities exited from the FTSE100 and others entered during the period 1997-2000. So the FTSE100 does not represent all securities in the sample at many points of time, but the FTALLSH does. The UKTB return index is assumed to be a risk-free security.

There are three reasons for selecting the security' return index, instead of the share prices used in prior literature. (i) Security returns are complete and scale-free summary of the investment opportunity, (ii) security returns have more attractive statistical properties than prices, such as stationarity (Campell et al., 1997, p.9), and (iii) *Datastream*'s security return indices are computationally more efficient with respect to adjustments for dividends and capital changes than share prices.

Table 2 provides descriptive statistics for the returns of the 96 firms. It shows that, on average, the daily return during the MM estimation period (16/6/1998-23/3/1999) is 0.11%, with standard deviation of 0.0286. The FTALLSH return index is lower (0.03%) with (0.0130) standard deviation. To test the assumption of normality of the indices' time-series distribution a one-sample Kolmogorov-Smirnov (Lilliefors significance correction) (K-S) test was conducted. None of the RI's showed a significant departure from normality. The mean studentised range of the returns is 0.2123 for the 99% fractile, which indicates that the sample is normally distributed. Other indicators, such as the average time-series skewness (0.2983) and kurtosis (3.3904), support this conclusion. The percentile figures are not affected by the observed skewness of return index distribution. These provide further evidence on the RI's. The median, for example, shows average RI's of -0.02%, compared with 0.00% of market return index.

The bi-variate *Pearson's* correlation between each security's return index (RI) and the market return index (Rm) during the estimation period and the test period shows statistically significant strong association between security return indices and the market return index during both periods. On average, the correlation during the estimation period (46.22%) is slightly more than that during the test period (31.92%). These results justify the use of MM for estimating each security's alpha and beta. The CAPM is used to estimate the security's expected return. The CAPM captures additional factors that explain the security's return, the risk-free portfolio (Rf) and the security's risk premium, *i.e.* $[\beta i^*(Rm - Rf)]$.

The overall statistical properties for each of securities return indices (RI's) and market return index during the test period (1/4/1999-31/8/2000) provide a similar picture as during the estimation period per Table 2. The average daily RI's of 96 securities of FTSE100 during the test period (0.10%) is very close to that of the estimation period, with similar standard deviation (0.0290). The market returns index is higher slightly than the estimation period (0.04%) with standard deviation 0.0100.

The empirical tests are mainly based on equation (5) above. Firstly, daily percentage changes of security's return index are calculated for sample's securities, FTALLSH return index, and UKTB benchmark, during the period -250 day to -50 days of the sample period.

That is from 16/6/1998 to 23/3/1999 (the estimation period). Equation (1) is used to estimate the intercept term α and systematic risk β of a security, by regressing the market return at time t, to the security's return during the estimation period[3]. Table 2 shows that, of 96 securities' β, 94 are significant at < 5%. In Table 2, the sum of the residuals of each security is equal to zero, the mean residuals of the whole sample equal to zero, the sum of the differences between the average residuals (AΩi) and (Ωit), equation (4) of each security in the sample are zero. There is no significant correlation between the market return (Rmt) and each security's residuals (Ωit). Thus the data are heteroscedasticity-free and the error term is unit normally distributed.

The possibility of overlaps in successive abnormal returns within the event windows was investigated. The correlation coefficient of cross-sectional dependence between subsequent abnormal returns during the event window, *viz.* t0 to t+12, as well as other windows, are computed and found very weak. This is a result of weak form market efficiency, in which security returns follow a random walk.

The *ex-post* CAPM, equation (4), is used to calculate the expected return on security (i) at time (t) during the test period 1/4/1999 to 31/8/2000. Table 2 summarises the results. On average, the expected return on FTSE100 is 0.12% compared with 0.05% on risk-free security and 0.04% on market portfolio. The abnormal return (ARit), equation (5), is calculated for the test period 1/4/1999 to 31/8/2000. The abnormal returns for each SS, MS, and QS signals are computed according to equation (5)[4]. Then the average for each signal-portfolio is calculated following equation (6). To examine the statistical significance of the mean standardised AR during the event period, the test statistics are computed according to DW1983. Since the alternative hypotheses have one-way directions, *viz* positive for buy portfolios and negative for sell portfolios, a one-tailed test is used. Finally average abnormal returns for each SS, MS, and QS signal-portfolio are accumulated during the event window and test statistics calculated according to BW1985.

EMPIRICAL RESULTS

In this section, results in relation to the benchmark signal definition (SS) and other signals (MS and QS) defined above are discussed. Firstly, empirical results arising from different signal definitions are examined, then the portfolios' performance in relation to the research hypotheses are examined.

---

[3] For a sub-sample, each of the market index return at time –15, -7, 0, +7, +15 days is regressed on the security's index return at time t. Then the coefficients of variation from each regression equation are summed. The result then is compared with the initial regression coefficient. The findings are almost the same, with only slight differences. However, the Adjusted R-Square of the initial regression MM improves significantly. The sample securities are correlated weakly, but significantly, with FTALLSH at time 0. However, this becomes rather weak but negatively insignificant at time -7 +7, and +15.

[4] As well as the signal defined by the median of the transaction's volume and that of the ratio of NV/TV, as explained in footnote 2 above.

Abnormal Returns of Different Signals

Table 3 reports ARs, standard deviation, and test-statistics for the event window. A notable difference is between buy and sell portfolios. Significant positive ARs for the buy portfolios tend to cluster in the t+5,t+8 window, as expected. At t+5, t+6 and t+8 all signal definitions for the buy portfolio have similar signs to the SS. It is more difficult to interpret t+7 as the AR for SS happens to be very close to zero. For t+5, t+6 and t+8 8/18 (11/18) individual ARs are significant at the 5% (10%) level. In contrast for the sell portfolios significant negative returns tend to cluster in the t+1, t+2 window and 5/12 (6/12) individual ARs are significant at the 5% (10%) level. All but one portfolio has a negative sign (QS3 in t+1).

Cumulative Abnormal Returns of Different Signals

Table 4 states the results for each signal-portfolio. As can be seen the buy portfolio becomes significant at the 10% level on the 6th day (CAR(SS) = +0.83%) and at the 5% level on the 8th day (+1.29%). The sell portfolio becomes significant on the 11th and 12th days at 5% and 1% (CAR= -1.44% and -2.16%, respectively). The apparent early reaction for the sell portfolio at t+1, t+2 noted above is therefore not sustained, whereas the buy portfolio does experience sustained ARs from t+6 onwards. There is little evidence that the volume of transactions produce differing reactions. Although buy QS2 has earlier and more significant returns, there is no pattern consistent with increasing volume through QS1 to QS4. However, the sell MS portfolio has a noticeably earlier reaction than the SS portfolio, reaching 10% significance at t+6 and 5% at t7. In the t+6, t+12 window the MS CARs are of consistently higher magnitude than SS. Also the QS1 portfolio becomes significant at t6 and whilst this is not sustained until t+11, t+12, the magnitude is greater than the other volume based portfolios in the t+6,t+12 window.

Portfolio Performance

Taking into consideration the above empirical findings, it is reasonable to conclude that none of other signal definitions (MS or any of QS) have shown significantly consistent results with previous literature, or in comparison with the primary signal definition used in this study (SS). Therefore, the empirical findings will be explained mainly by SS results. Figure 1 shows that CARs of buy and sell ordinary shares portfolios are in line with expectations[5].

The results (Table 4) show that CARs of directors buying their firm's ordinary shares is significantly positive (using DW1983 and BW1985 t-tests) at the end of the assumed day of disclosure (t+6 = 0.83%) as well as at the end of the event window (t+12 = 1.02%). None of the returns are significant during the first six days (t0 to t+5) and this finding is consistent with the event definition. Hence the market recognises directors trading, and reflects the signal as soon as it has been disclosed. Since it was not possible to specify the exact date of

[5] CARs produced by other signals show similar trend.

Table 2. Statistical Properties of FTSE100 Securities' Parameters Used in the Event Test

Item (Period)	N Of Firms	Range	Min	Max	Mean	Mean Std Error	Std. Deviation	Variance	Skewness Stat. Std Error		Kurtosis Stat. Std Error	
Return (16/6/98-23/3/99)	96	0.2123	-0.0978	0.1145	0.0011	0.0021	0.0287	0.0009	0.298	0.178	3.390	0.353
Beta (16/6/98-23/3/99)	96	0.7290	0.0710	0.8000	0.4623	0.0164	0.1607	0.0258	-0.15	0.246	-0.53	0.488
Alpha (16/6/98-23/3/99)	96	0.0177	-0.0036	0.0141	0.0008	0.0002	0.0022	0.0000	2.93	0.246	14.42	0.488
F-Value (16/6/98-23/3/99)	96	352.56	1.0000	353.56	72.854	6.4964	63.651	4051.52	1.54	0.246	3.09	0.488
DW (16/6/98-23/3/99)	96	1.4190	1.2910	2.7100	1.8954	0.0221	0.2163	0.0468	0.55	0.246	2.49	0.488
R-Square Adjusted (16/6/98-23/3/99)	96	0.6380	0.0000	0.6380	0.2351	0.0152	0.1485	0.0220	0.55	0.246	-0.48	0.488
MM Residuals (16/6/98-23/3/99)	96	0.1833	-0.0831	0.1002	0.0000	0.0018	0.0242	0.0006	0.334	0.172	3.541	0.342
E(R) =CAPM (1/4/1999-31/8/2000)	96	0.0428	-0.0198	0.0230	0.0012	0.0004	0.0075	0.0001	0.022	0.127	0.033	0.253
Return (1/4/1999-31/8/2000)	96	0.2483	-0.1087	0.1396	0.0010	0.0015	0.0288	0.0009	0.416	0.127	3.971	0.253
Abnormal Return (1/4/1999-31/8/2000)	96	0.2548	-0.1119	0.1429	-0.0002	0.0016	0.0301	0.0010	0.450	0.127	3.494	0.253

Table 3. Average Abnormal Returns and Test Statistics during the Event Window

AR	N	t0	t+1	t+2	t+3	t+4	t+5	t+6	t+7	t+8	t+9	t+10	t+11	t+12
Buy(SS)	295	-0.0001	0.0016	0.0005	0.0007	-0.0011	0.0033	0.0035	0.0000	0.0046	-0.0014	0.0008	-0.0019	-0.0002
T-Value		0.1611	1.4623*	0.1768	0.3604	-0.5851	2.2515**	2.1577**	-0.1569	2.9689*	-1.2490*	0.6795	-1.1816	0.0348
Buy(MS)	103	0.0001	0.0007	-0.0031	0.0003	-0.0017	0.0026	0.0054	-0.0027	0.0062	-0.0019	0.0013	-0.0015	0.0034
T-Value		0.2356	0.2713	-1.527*	0.2138	-0.3656	1.3629*	2.0705**	-1.2577	2.3898***	-1.0715	0.4667	-0.6321	1.6151*
Buy(1QS)	74	-0.0040	-0.0013	0.0014	0.0018	0.0002	0.0008	0.0029	-0.0022	0.0012	0.0002	0.0021	-0.0035	0.0026
T-Value		-1.4446*	-0.5203	0.6229	1.0357	0.2800	0.3893	1.2168	-1.0805	0.0978	0.0306	0.3633	-1.2609	0.7674
Buy(2QS)	73	0.0041	0.0057	0.0016	-0.0014	0.0005	0.0059	0.0026	0.0011	0.0034	-0.0045	-0.0033	-0.0021	-0.0056
T-Value		1.5665*	2.7324***	0.1694	-1.0679	0.4005	1.9336**	0.9033	0.6506	1.2562	-1.9008	-0.9912	-0.6880	-1.9904
Buy(3QS)	74	0.0032	0.0004	0.0011	0.0032	-0.0008	0.0025	0.0039	0.0034	0.0054	-0.0051	0.0027	-0.0040	-0.0018
T-Value		1.0515	0.2784	0.5094	0.8524	-0.6156	0.6054	0.8621	1.0956	2.0527**	-1.4668	1.1951	-1.0763	-0.5457
Buy(4QS)	74	-0.0038	0.0015	-0.0021	-0.0010	-0.0043	0.0040	0.0045	-0.0022	0.0083	0.0036	0.0017	0.0019	0.0040
T-Value		-0.8536	0.4409	-0.9129	-0.1121	-1.2227	1.5978*	1.2940*	-0.9473	2.5565***	0.8671	0.7847	0.6781	1.8137**
Sell(SS)	95	0.0091	-0.0006	-0.0084	-0.0015	0.0019	-0.0033	-0.0043	-0.0001	0.0007	0.0024	-0.0038	-0.0066	-0.0072
T-Value		2.4141	-0.4179	-3.2754***	-0.6983	0.5687	-0.9590	-1.1586	0.2095	0.1602	0.5285	-1.4554*	-1.6828**	-1.7788**
Sell(MS)	34	0.0087	-0.0160	-0.0107	0.0038	-0.0006	-0.0054	-0.0053	-0.0026	-0.0024	0.0021	0.0065	-0.0046	-0.0080
T-Value		0.9311	-2.9920***	-2.0606**	0.7311	-0.2474	-1.2239	-0.3947	-0.5072	-0.4748	0.0196	1.0595	-0.5548	-1.1538
Sell(1QS)	24	0.0001	-0.0042	-0.0151	-0.0029	0.0054	-0.0123	-0.0031	0.0064	0.0054	0.0005	-0.0114	-0.0096	-0.0066
T-Value		0.0376	-0.8062	-3.0592***	-0.6093	0.6643	-2.1990**	-0.2333	1.2653	0.9679	0.0190	-2.2165**	-1.8549**	-0.9964
Sell(QS2)	23	0.0060	0.0009	-0.0076	0.0063	0.0043	-0.0015	-0.0065	-0.0065	-0.0092	-0.0041	0.0048	0.0090	0.0000
T-Value		0.4100	-0.3441	-1.1480	1.2171	0.5355	-0.2120	-0.6174	-1.4686*	-1.8761**	-1.1288	0.6868	2.0088	0.0183
Sell(QS3)	24	0.0150	0.0142	-0.0078	-0.0056	0.0022	0.0038	0.0019	0.0022	-0.0014	0.0042	-0.0079	-0.0096	-0.0103
T-Value		2.8139	2.1260	-1.6094*	-1.1774	0.1466	0.7929	0.2039	0.3343	0.2041	1.1250	-1.5049*	-1.5898*	-1.2791
Sell(QS4)	24	0.0151	-0.0132	-0.0032	-0.0033	-0.0040	-0.0030	-0.0095	-0.0027	-0.0076	0.0088	-0.0007	-0.0158	-0.0115
T-Value		1.5501*	-1.8144**	-0.7240	-0.7941	-0.2037	-0.2944	-1.6713*	0.2549	0.9832	1.0075	0.1221	-1.8913**	1.2837

Notes: (SS) indicates the Single Signal definition of the event, (MS) represents the Multiple Signal, (QS1) to (QS4) denotes the First to Fourth Quartile Quantitative Signal; (N) represents the number of signals (transactions) in each portfolio; and (***) denotes one tailed significance at 1%, (**) 5%, and (*) 10%.

Table 4. Cumulative Abnormal Returns and Test Statistic, During the Event Window

CAR	N	t0	t+1	t+2	t+3	t+4	t+5	t+6	t+7	t+8	t+9	t+10	t+11	t+12
Buy(SS)	295	-0.0001	0.0015	0.0020	0.0026	0.0015	0.0048	0.0083	0.0083	0.0129	0.0115	0.0123	0.0104	0.0102
T-Value		-0.0209	0.2871	0.3818	0.5105	0.2984	0.9334	1.6137*	1.6203*	2.5108***	2.2309**	2.3895*	2.0203**	1.9867**
Buy(MS)	103	0.0001	0.0008	-0.0023	-0.0020	-0.0037	-0.0011	0.0043	0.0016	0.0078	0.0058	0.0071	0.0057	0.0091
T-Value		0.0165	0.0948	-0.2655	-0.2360	-0.4343	-0.1313	0.5017	0.1833	0.9079	0.6847	0.8354	0.6639	1.0655
Buy(1QS)	74	-0.0040	-0.0053	-0.0039	-0.0021	-0.0019	-0.0011	0.0018	-0.0004	0.0009	0.0011	0.0032	-0.0002	0.0024
T-Value		-0.3849	-0.5147	-0.3745	-0.2006	-0.1850	-0.1067	0.1771	-0.0351	0.0854	0.1059	0.3140	-0.0234	0.2295
Buy(2QS)	73	0.0042	0.0100	0.0115	0.0101	0.0107	0.0165	0.0191	0.0203	0.0237	0.0192	0.0159	0.0138	0.0082
T-Value		0.4011	0.9562	1.1082	0.9770	1.0300	1.5959*	1.8502**	1.9585**	2.2873**	1.8555**	1.5344*	1.3312*	0.7926
Buy(3QS)	74	0.0032	0.0037	0.0048	0.0080	0.0072	0.0097	0.0136	0.0170	0.0224	0.0172	0.0200	0.0160	0.0142
T-Value		0.3153	0.3581	0.4643	0.7759	0.7029	0.9429	1.3241*	1.6558*	2.1773**	1.6790**	1.9457**	1.5588*	1.3803
Buy(4QS)	74	-0.0038	-0.0023	-0.0044	-0.0054	-0.0097	-0.0057	-0.0012	-0.0034	0.0049	0.0085	0.0101	0.0121	0.0161
T-Value		-0.3704	-0.2199	-0.4282	-0.5264	-0.9451	-0.5577	-0.1170	-0.3307	0.4786	0.8264	0.9872	1.1762	1.5696*
Sell(SS)	95	0.0091	0.0085	0.0000	-0.0014	0.0005	-0.0028	-0.0071	-0.0071	-0.0064	-0.0040	-0.0078	-0.0144	-0.0216
T-Value		0.9987	0.9357	0.0055	-0.1574	0.0547	-0.3048	-0.7801	-0.7882	-0.7094	-0.4400	-0.8607	-1.5927**	-2.3867*
Sell(MS)	34	0.0087	-0.0073	-0.0181	-0.0143	-0.0147	-0.0202	-0.0255	-0.0281	-0.0305	-0.0285	-0.0219	-0.0265	-0.0345
T-Value		0.5723	-0.4848	-1.1938	-0.9441	-0.9824	-1.3363	-1.6852*	-1.8574**	-2.0152**	1.8789**	-1.4479*	-1.7492**	-2.2763**
Sell(1QS)	24	0.0001	-0.0041	-0.0192	-0.0221	-0.0167	-0.0290	-0.0321	-0.0257	-0.0204	-0.0199	-0.0312	-0.0409	-0.0475
T-Value		0.0044	-0.2272	-1.0632	-1.2238	-0.9259	-1.6070*	-1.7809**	-1.4253*	-1.1286	-1.0799	-1.6710*	-2.1712**	-2.5153*
Sell(QS2)	23	0.0060	0.0069	-0.0008	0.0055	0.0098	0.0083	0.0018	-0.0047	-0.0139	-0.0180	-0.0133	-0.0043	-0.0043
T-Value		0.3239	0.3739	-0.0408	0.3007	0.5318	0.4513	0.0958	-0.2566	-0.7544	-0.9772	-0.7192	-0.2309	-0.2325
Sell(QS3)	24	0.0150	0.0292	0.0214	0.0158	0.0179	0.0218	0.0236	0.0259	0.0245	0.0287	0.0208	0.0112	0.0094
T-Value		0.3296	1.6182	1.1364	0.8735	0.9932	1.2060	1.3107	1.4345	1.3580	1.5593	1.1304	0.6090	0.0511
Sell(QS4)	24	0.0151	0.0019	-0.0013	-0.0047	-0.0087	-0.0117	-0.0212	-0.0239	-0.0163	-0.0075	-0.0082	-0.0240	-0.0355
T-Value		0.8360	0.1045	-0.0723	-0.2572	-0.4790	-0.6473	-1.1757	-1.3252*	-0.9024	-0.4054	-0.4434	-1.3005	-1.9271**

Notes: (SS) indicates the Single Signal definition of the event, (MS) represents the Multiple Signal, (QS1) to (QS4) denotes the First to Fourth Quartile Quantitative Signal; (N) represents the number of signals (transactions) in each portfolio; and (***) denotes that the Cumulative Abnormal Return (CAR) is significant at 1%, (**) significant at 5%, and (*) at 10%.

the disclosure for each transaction the results indicate that it takes, on average, seven working days to disclose the directors trading, at which time the market significantly reflects the new information.

Further tests indicated a longer window might be useful for this type of portfolio. For longer event windows, higher values are found. For example, CAR after 20 days of the transaction date (t0 to t+19) is 2.29% significant[1]. And that for 50 days (t0 to t+49) is 3.21% significant[2]. Also, CAR for 60 days is 3.57% significant[3]. Taking the presumed disclosure date (t+6) as the event date, the results show that the null hypothesis is still rejected, and that the level of CAR is magnified up until t+60.

It is possible that insiders might disclose their price-sensitive, inside, information privately. Chakravarty and McConnell (1999) and (1997) and Meulbroek (1992), for example, investigated illegal insider trading, where insiders revealed their private information to others (tippee). This issue is investigated by extending the event window to include six days before the event date. However there were no significant ARs or CARs during this period.

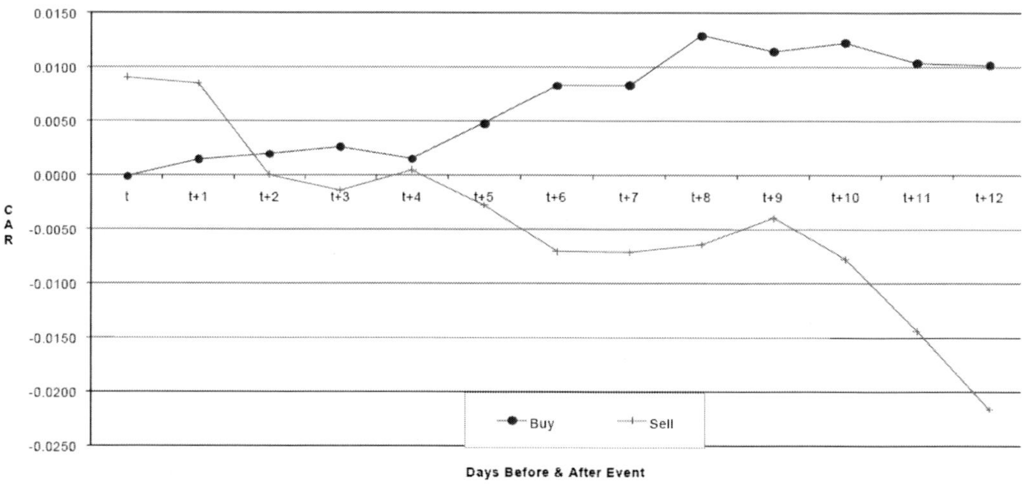

Figure 1. Single Signal CAR of FTSE100 Directors Buying and Selling Portfolios During the Event Window.

CARs of directors selling their firm's ordinary shares at the presumed day of disclosure (t6) are insignificant (-0.71%) but significant at the end of the event window (t+12) (-2.16%). CARs during longer event windows are examined and found to be significantly and negatively big enough to indicate that directors avoid abnormal losses by selling their shares. For example, CARs for the event windows (t0 to t+19), (t0 to t+49), and (t0 to t+59) are -3.06%, -3.42%, and -9.13% respectively. The longer the event window the more CAR becomes negative. Likewise, CARs during the event windows (t0 to t+21, t+22, and t+60) are all significant at 1%.

[1] By DW1983 and BW1980 at 1%, and by BW1985 at 10%.
[2] By DW1983 at 1% and BW1980 at 5%.
[3] According to BW1985 at 5%.

Robustness Checks

In order to test whether directors trading abnormal return was a result of other key firm events, each of the buy and sell portfolios were partitioned according to whether or not a director traded in the 13 days (the length of the event windows) after any key firm announcement (such as interim or annual earnings announcement, first or third quarter results or primary or annual results). The portfolios containing confounding events were much smaller, and in any case their separation had no impact on the patterns observed above.

It is possible that most of the abnormal returns earned by director dealings might in fact be due to the firm size effect, where information in small firms would be at a premium as the disseminate of information is less frequent [see, for example, Gregory et al. (1994) and (1997) and Hillier and Marshall (2002/a)]. To test this, the Lakonishok et al. (1994) model was used in which the abnormal return is computed as:

$$AR_{it} = R_{it} - R_{j(i)t} \cdot \qquad (10)$$

where [$R_{j(i)t}$] is the group control portfolio, defined as follows. Firstly the market capitalisation group at the end of previous year is identified for each firm/stock in the sample. Then the firms in the sample-year (1999 and 2000) are split into two: those firms with market capitalisation below the average market capitalisation (72 firms in 1999 and 74 firms in 2000 in group G1) and those above the average market capitalisation (24 firms in 1999 and 22 firms in 2000 in G2). The average market capitalisation of the firms in the sample was £10,439m at the end of 1998 and £12,934m at the end of 1999. The average for G1 in 1999 (2000) was £4,444m (£28,426m) and for G2 was £5,696m (£37,279m), respectively.

There are two size control portfolios used. Each of which consists of equally weighted group to which firm (i) belongs at the beginning of each year. Here, the all-buy-transactions or sell portfolio differs from the single signal buy or sell portfolio because of different benchmarks used to compute the abnormal returns. The overall mean of the abnormal returns of group 1, computed according to equation 16 above, is 0.01% (0.06% in 1999 and 0.00% in 2000) and that of group 2 is 0.00% (0.00% in 1999 and 0.00% in 2000). These figures support the earlier findings that the abnormal returns earned from director trades are not due to market movements but from the information content of their trades.

Following Gregory et al. (1997), and for the purpose of estimating the DW1983 test statistic, the variance of (AR_{it}) is calculated on post-signal data. The results of CAR defined by the simple size adjusted return from Lakonishok et al. (1994) are presented in Table 5, which summarizes the complete set of CARs and t-statistics.

In general the signal imparted by directors' trades is much stronger for small firms (G1) in terms of magnitude and significance. Abnormal returns for G1 buy portfolios are higher in all cases. Similarly for the sell portfolios subsequent losses are smaller with the exception of the t6 to t12 event window. In addition, G1's CAR at the end of longer event windows still dominates that of G2. For instance, G1 CARs (t0 to t+60) and (t+6 to t+60) are 8.63% and 7.26%, respectively, are much higher than corresponding values in G2 (1.94% and 1.54% respectively). For the overall buying (selling) portfolio, which consists of both groups' transactions, the results of the firm-size model [All Buy (Sell) portfolio in Table 7] support the single signal market-model reported in Table 4, particularly in terms of the sign and significance. However, they are varied in terms of the level of abnormal return (loss) earned (avoided). Such variation, however, is expectedly due to the firm size, which supports the hypothesis of the firm-size model. For example, CAR of All-Buy (Sell) firm-size portfolio at (t0 to t+60) is significantly positive (negative) 5.80% (-8.46%) more than 1.02% (-2.16%) of the single signal market-model. Also, that of firm-size portfolio at (t+6 to t+60) is 4.84% (-8.36%) more than 0.54% (-1.89%) of single signal market-model.

Table 5. Firm Size Effect: Cumulative Abnormal Returns during Different Event Windows/For Buy and Sell Size-Adjusted Portfolios during 1999 and 2000

CAR during Different Event Windows	Buy Portfolios			Sell Portfolios		
	G1 N=189	G2 N=102	All N=291	G1 N=68	G2 N=25	All N=93
-30 to +60 days	2.68 %	0.14 %	1.60 %	6.25 %	-4.01 %	1.70 %
T-Statistics	*1.3740*	*0.0610*	*1.2303*	*2.2063***	*-0.5874*	*0.7501*
-6 to +12 days	2.15 %	%1.07	1.70 %	-0.47 %	-3.81 %	-1.16 %
T-Statistics	*2.3246****	*1.0391*	*2.7572****	*-0.3598*	*-1.7007*	*-0.9088*
0 to +12 days	3.65 %	1.74 %	2.84 %	-3.06 %	-4.86 %	-3.43 %
T-Statistics	*4.7562****	*2.0381***	*5.5787****	*-2.8577****	*-2.8161****	*-3.4414****
0 to +60 days	8.63 %	1.94 %	5.80 %	-4.85 %	-10.56 %	-8.46 %
T-Statistics	*5.2435****	*1.0471*	*5.2903****	*-2.090***	*-2.6568****	*-3.8624****
+6 to +12 days	2.27 %	%1.34	1.88 %	-3.64 %	-2.15 %	-3.33 %
T-Statistics	*4.3640****	*3.9173****	*5.4266****	*-5.0047****	*-2.1342***	*-5.0384****
+6 to +60 days	7.26 %	1.54 %	4.84 %	-5.43 %	-7.85 %	-8.36 %
T-Statistics	*4.6511****	*0.8727*	*4.6516****	*-2.4647****	*-2.1338***	*-4.0586****

Note: (1) (***) Significant at 1% or less, and (**) Significant at 5% or less.
(2) T-Statistic is computed according to modified DW1983, equations 8 and 9.

SUMMARY AND CONCLUSION

The study examined short-term profitability of FTSE100 directors' trading in their own firm's ordinary shares in 1999 and 2000, employing an event study methodology to measure CARs, using different signal definitions. Using the simple MM's parameters in the CAPM, our results of buy and sell portfolios are similar to those obtained by previous literature using the same methodology.

Employing different signal methodologies revealed marginal differences with some interesting specific aspects. First, multiple signals make little difference to buy transactions over and above the impact of the single signal. For sell transactions on the other hand multiple signals amplify the abnormal return and have an earlier impact. The likely explanation for this difference is that the market is undecided as to whether an individual sell transaction is motivated by the individual director's need for liquidity, so that a subsequent signal from another director adds credibility. There is no such reinforcement required in the case of buy transactions. Also the lack of pattern in the volume based portfolios suggests that transaction size does not ad weight to the signal.

Directors' trades in their firm's shares are confirmed to be significantly profitable from t6. Therefore directors have inside price-sensitive information that the market does not and the market perceives directors' trading as a signal. Directors' buying indicates good news and, hence, increases the share price. As directors' selling represents a bad news, the share price falls. Employing SS with daily data produces not only significant results, but also higher rates of return. Figure 2 shows the annualised CARs[4] for this research and comparable studies.

As in other research there are positive and significant returns for the buy portfolio comparable to recent surveys [Friederich et al. (2002) and Hillier and Marshall (2002/a)] and somewhat higher than earlier studies [Gregory et al., (1997), Gregory et al. (1994), Pope et al., (1990)]. The differences are more striking for the sell portfolios which in this research have annualised CARs close to 50%, which are more than double the highest comparable result [Friederich et al., (2002)]. Much depends on the interpretation of the large losses in the sell portfolio at t11 and t12 (Table 4 and figure1), during which time the sell portfolio CARs out-strip the corresponding CARs for the buy portfolio. As suggested above, the market seems slower to react to sell transactions when conveyed via a single signal and awaits further confirmatory transactions. The t11 and t12 CARs may therefore be incorporating a 'catch-up' element that otherwise as in the buy portfolio would have begun at t+6. The annualised multiple signal abnormal return is therefore even higher (74.75%) and the divergence from prior studies even greater. It seems possible that prior studies have under-estimated the reaction to sell transactions through reliance on single signals. On the other hand it is possible that 1999 and 2000 were atypical years and retesting would confirm similar results to the prior literature. Further research is needed in this respect.

The robustness checks confirmed that the abnormal returns earned by FTSE100 directors are due only to the information content of their trades but not to occurrence of other events. Also there are very significant size effects. Directors of small firms earned (avoided) significantly more returns (losses) than their counterparts in larger firms, particularly in the long-term (short-term) event windows. These empirical findings support prior literature in this respect [see, for example, Friederich et al. (2002), Gregory et al. (1997) and Hillier and Marshall (2002/a)]. A likely reason is that because smaller firms are less well monitored by market analysts and investors, signals from directors' transactions have greater information content.

The empirical results of this study, in addition to other UK literature, show clearly that the stock exchange is significantly inefficient in terms of the strong level of market efficiency. The evidence for semi-strong market efficiency is also weak. The availability of abnormal returns to outsiders following the publicly known information, *viz.* insiders' transactions can be seen as a direct test to the semi-strong level of market efficiency. The empirical results indicate that abnormal returns can be earned by outsiders' imitating insiders' transactions.

In summary, the empirical results clearly and significantly reject the null hypothesis that directors trading in their own company's securities are not profitable. Instead they suggest the alternative hypotheses that directors buying portfolios achieve positive abnormal returns and those of selling ones avoid negative abnormal returns to a greater degree, particularly where

[4] The annual CAR is computed by multiplying CAR at the end of the event window with the number of intervals (event windows) within a working days-year (260 days). That is: CAR*(260/12).

informed as multiple signals through the actions of more than one director and where the firm is small.

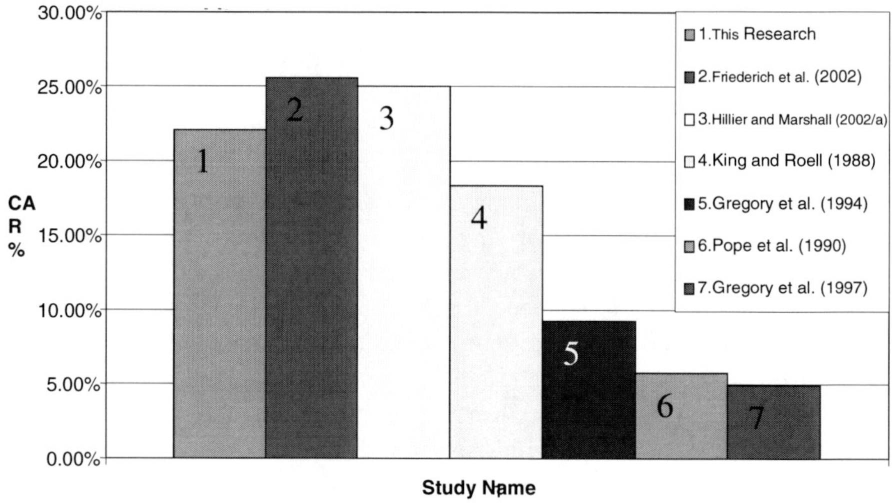

Figure 2A. Comparison of CARs of Buy Portfolio by UK.

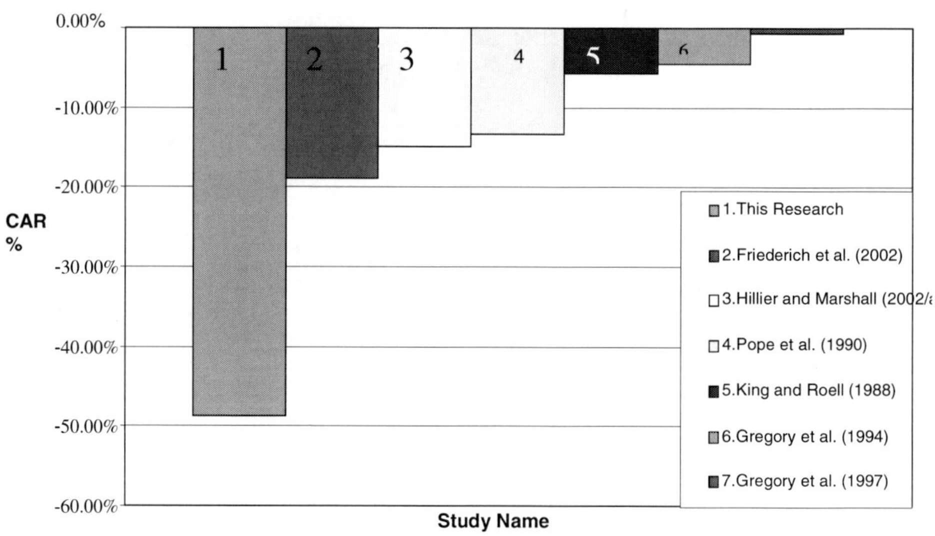

Figure 2B. Comparison of CARs of Sell Portfolio by UK.

REFERENCES

Aboody, D., and Lev, B. 2000. Information Asymmetry, RandD, and Insider Trading. *Journal of Finance* 55(6): 2747-2766.

Arnand, A., Brown, P., Watson, I. 2002. Directors' Trades As Signals of Their Firms' Future Financial Performance: Evidence From the Australian Share Market, A Working Paper

Presented (by Brown) in the British Accounting Association Conference, Held in Jersey During the Period 3-5/4/2002.

Brio, E.B., Miguel, A., Perote, J. 2002. An Investigation of Insider Trading Profits in the Spanish Stock Market. *The Quarterly Review of Economics and Finance,* 42: 73-94.

Brown, S.J., Warner, J.B. 1985. Using Daily Stock Returns: The Case of Event Studies. *Journal of Financial Economics*, 14: 3-31.

Brown, S.J., Warner, J.B. 1980. *Measuring Security Price Performance. Journal of Financial Economics,* 8: 205-258.

Campbell, J.Y, Lo, A.W., MacKinlay, A.C. 1997. *The Econometrics of Financial Markets.* Princeton University Press.

Chakravarty, S.. McConnell, J.J. 1997. An Analysis of Prices, Bid/Ask Spreads, and Bid and Ask Depth Surrounding Ivan Boesky's Illegal Trading in Carnation's Stock. *Financial Management,* 34(2): 18-34.

Chakravarty, S.. McConnell, J.J. 1999. 'Does Insider Trading Really Move Stock Prices? *Journal of Financial and Quantitative Analysis,* 34(2): 191-209.

Chang, S., Suk, D.Y. 1998 Stock Prices and the Secondary Dissemination of Information: The Wall Street Journal's "Insider Trading Spotlight" Column. *The Financial Review,* 33: 115-128.

Chung, K.H., Charoenwong. C. 1998. Insider Trading and the Bid-Ask Spread. *The Financial Review*, 33: 1-20.

Dimson, E. 1979. Risk Measurement When Shares Are Subject To Infrequent Trading. *Journal of Financial Economics*, 7: 197-226.

Dodd, P., Warner, J.B. 1983. On Corporate Governance: A Study of Proxy Contests. *Journal of Financial Economics*, 11: 401-438.

Eckbo, B.E., Smith, D.C. 1998. The Conditional Performance of Insider Trades. *The Journal of Finance,* 53(2): 467-498.

Finnerty, J.E. 1976a. Insiders' Activity and Inside Information: A Multivariate Analysis. *Journal of Financial and Quantitative Analysis,* 11(2): 205-215.

Finnerty, J.E. 1976b. Insiders and Market Efficiency. *The Journal of Finance,* 31(4): 1141-1148.

Friederich, S., Gregory, A., Matatko, J., Tonks, I. 2002. Short-Run Returns Around the Trades of Corporate Insiders on the London Stock Exchange. *European Financial Management,* 8(1): 7-30.

Friederich, S., Gregory, A., Matatko, J., Tonks, I. 1999. Stock Price Patterns Around the Trades of Corporate Insiders on the London Stock Exchange. *Discussion Paper* 332-09/1999, Financial Markets Group, London School of Economics, 38p.

Givoly, D., Palmon, D. 1985. Insider Trading and the Exploitation of Inside Information: Some Empirical Evidence. *Journal of Business,* 58(1): 69-87.

Gregory, A., Matatko, J., Tonks, I. 1997. Detecting Information from Directors' Trade: Signal Definition and Variable Size Effects, *Journal of Business, Finance and Accounting,* 24(3/4): 309-342.

Gregory, A., Matatko, J., Tonks, I., Purkis, R. 1994. UK Directors' Trading: The Impact of Dealings in Smaller Firms. *The Economic Journal,* 104: 37-53.

Hemscott.NET, PLC. (2000), *'www.hemscott.com'*, 2nd Floor, Finsbury Tower, 103-105 Bunhill Row, London, EC1Y 8TY, England, UK, Tel: 020-7496-0055, Fax: 020-7847-1719.

Hillier, D., Marshall, A.P. 2002a. The Market Evaluation of Information in Directors' Trades. *Journal of Business, Finance and Accounting,* 29(1): 77-110.

Hillier, D., Marshall, A.P. 2002b. Are Trading Bans Effective? Exchange Regulation and Corporate Insider Transactionss Around Earnings Announcements. *Journal of Corporate Finance*, 89: 393-410.

Jaffe, J.F. 1974. Special Information and Insider Trading. *Journal of Business*, 47: 410-428.

King, M., Roell. A. 1988. Insider Trading. *Economic Policy*, 7: 163-193.

Kyle, A.S. 1985. Continuous Auctions and Insider Trading. *Econometrica,* 53(6): 1315-1335.

Lakonishok, J., Schleifer, A., Vishny, R.W. 1994 Contrarian Investment, Extrapolation, and Risk. *Journal of Finance,* 49: 1541-1578.

Lorie, J.H., Niederhoffer, V. 1968. Predictive and Statistical Properties of Insider Trading. *The Journal of Law and Economics,* 11: 35-53.

McWilliams, A., Seigel, D. 1997. Event Studies in Management Research: Theoretical and Empirical Issues. *Academy of Management Journal*, 40: 626-657.

Meulbroek, L.K. 1992. An Empirical Analysis of Illegal Insider Trading. *Journal of Finance,* 47(5): 1661-1699.

Pettit, R., Venkatesh, P.C. 1995. Insider Trading and Long-Run Return Performance. *Financial Management,* 24(2): 88-109.

Pope, P.F., Morris. R.C., Peel, D.A. 1990. .Insider Trading: Some Evidence on Market Efficiency and Directors' Share Dealings in Great Britain. *Journal of Business, Finance and Accounting,* 17(3): 357-380.

Roth, G., Saporoschenko, A. 1999. The Informational Effects of Large Insider Stock Purchases. *Managerial Finance,* 25(1): 37-48.

Rozeff, M., Zaman, M.A. 1988. Market Efficiency and Insider Trading: New Evidence. *Journal of Business,* 61(1): 25-44.

Seyhun, H.N. 1986. Insiders' Profits, Costs of Trading, and Market Efficiency. *Journal of Financial Economics*, 16: 189-212.

Sharpe, W.F. 1964. Capital Asset Prices: A Theory of Market Equilibrium Under Conditions of Risk, *Journal of Finance,* 19(3): 425-442.

Yermack, D. 1997. Good Timing: CEO Stock Option Awards and Company News Announcements. *Journal of Finance*, 52(2): 449-476.

In: Understanding Risk
Editor: Matthias Beck
ISBN: 978-1-62618-686-6

Chapter 2

ASYMMETRIC RESPONSE: EXPLAINING CORPORATE SOCIAL DISCLOSURE BY MULTINATIONAL FIRMS IN ENVIRONMENTALLY SENSITIVE INDUSTRIES

***J. Steven Toms*[1,*] *and John Hasseldine*[2]**
[1]The York Management School, University of York, York, UK
[2]Nottingham University Business School, Jubilee Campus, University of Nottingham, Nottingham, UK

ABSTRACT

This paper examines the determinants of corporate social disclosure (CSD) using a sample drawn from environmentally sensitive industries. It extends the traditional literature in two respects. First, it is international in scope, examining the accounting disclosure responses of Multinational companies to the pressures implied by the nature and scope of their operations. Second, variables measuring political risk and social development are developed so that these pressures can be measured, thereby introducing new dimensions to the literature. In common with previous studies, financial risk, size and other control variables are included. The relationships are tested econometrically utilising regression techniques not previously applied in the CSD literature but nonetheless more generally appropriate when using count dependent variables. Our results suggest that managers feel an unequal sense of responsibility to different constituencies and their disclosure priorities are determined by stock market accountability, lobbying power of their domestic audience and the political risk of their activities rather than the impact of their activities in countries of operation.

* E-mail: st-27@york.ac.uk.

INTRODUCTION

Why do large Multinational firms make corporate social disclosures (CSDs) in their annual reports? Two possible hypotheses are explored in this paper. First, the 'benign' managerialist hypothesis that the firms are essentially enlightened oligarchies, which recognise their social and environmental impact and their associated responsibilities and make appropriate disclosures. At the centre of this argument is the notion that CSD arises from an ethical code which is espoused by the senior management of the firm and is transmitted 'top down' as a matter of policy. If the benign hypothesis were true, it would be expected that the CSD response would be proportionate to the international scope of the firm's activities.

An alternative second hypothesis is that firms have no such ethical code and that managers merely respond to market, social and political pressures when making CSDs. According to this hypothesis, CSDs reflect differential political, regulatory and lobbying power in different countries. Where these powers are the strongest, the firm makes greater CSDs in response, notwithstanding the objective level of environmental impact in that country. Where powers are weaker, for example in unstable and underdeveloped countries managers face less direct pressure to make CSDs. Actual disclosures may in these circumstances be aimed at the governments and public where the corporation is domiciled, particularly where political, regulatory and lobbying systems are well-developed. If this is so, then managers are motivated to make CSDs as an 'asymmetric response' to the asymmetric power and influence produced by the ownership of resources and differential patterns of regulation.

Such an asymmetric response hypothesis is suggestive of two further detailed relationships. First, CSDs, like other accounting disclosures, are responses to the requirements of shareholders. As a powerful interest group, shareholders demand, and managers supply, non-financial as well as financial information as part of a risk management process designed to mitigate political risks. Consequently, a second relationship is that CSDs will be made for the benefit of the domestic population rather than for the benefit of populations impacted by the firms' overseas operations. A corollary is that CSDs inculcate a sense in domestic populations that their domiciled corporations are much more socially responsible than they actually are.[1]

It should be noted that in setting up these hypotheses, the study differs from previous theoretical literature in important respects. The next section outlines these differences and reviews the prior empirical literature. Section three sets out the data and model to test the benign and asymmetric response hypotheses. Section four analyses the results. Section five draws conclusions and discusses the implications of the support for the asymmetric response hypothesis.

[1] This aspect of the asymmetric response hypothesis is similar to the 'Maginot' hypothesis (Glasbeek, 1988; Wolfson and Beck, 2005), where, like the French fortifications of 1940, CSDs create a false sense of security.

PRIOR STUDIES OF THE DETERMINANTS OF CSD

The purpose of the paper is to conduct an empirical test of the null benign hypothesis and the alternative asymmetric response hypotheses as introduced above. There is currently little recent evidence in favour of either hypothesis or indeed on the relationship between international activity and CSD in general. In recent studies the firm's country of origin (Newson and Deegan, 2002) and associated cultural differences contribute to differences in practice (Adams, 2002).[2] Even so, of the large recent empirical literature on the determinants of CSD (for recent reviews, see Newson and Deegan, 2002; Brown and Fraser, 2006), the overwhelming majority is country specific (for example Deegan and Gordon, 1996; Deegan et al. 2002; O'Dwyer, 2002; Cho et al. 2006). Gray et al's (2001, p.332) suggestion that 'it is increasingly clear that social and environmental disclosure varies according to country.... Whether, however, any putative relationship between disclosure and corporate characteristics could be expected to exhibit itself consistently across different countries has not been examined systematically', therefore remains an important motivation for further research.

Country specific studies have adopted two distinct approaches. First, there have been *economic* studies which have explained CSD in terms of national stock market reaction and associated accounting metrics (Aerts et al. 2008). Second, CSD has been related to the *social context* in which firms operate. In these approaches, either the economic relationship between the firm's management and shareholders is extended to include social and environmental interests as part of a wider definition of the firm's stakeholders, or CSD is seen as a process of legitimating the firm's activities in the eyes of society. To explain the differences between the approaches used in the current paper and the previous economic and social context studies, each aspect of the prior literature is now discussed in turn.

Economic studies have suggested that the stock market acts as an important source of demand for CSD information. Content analyses of website disclosures (Jose and Lee, 2007) and surveys of stock market participants have tended to conclude that CSDs are of moderate relative importance (Belkaoui, 1984; Benjamin and Stanga, 1977; Chenall and Juchau, 1977; Firth, 1979; Epstein and Freedman, 1994) while other ranking studies undertake surveys of potential users to indicate their needs and demands for social information (e.g., Buzby and Falk, 1979; Belkaoui, 1980; Dierkes and Antal, 1985). These studies find CSD to be of importance to users, and, in some cases, at least equally important as financial items of disclosure. More recently, Deegan and Rankin (1997) asked respondents to consider whether different decisions would be made depending on the availability of CSD, finding that environmental disclosures are important and material to investors. From an agency theory perspective, as shareholders become aware of the effect of social and environmental performance of the firms in which they invest, managers will emphasise social and environmental performance by disclosing social and environmental information in the annual reports (Ness and Mirza, 1991). Other studies (Milne and Chan, 1999, Murray et al., 2006) however, suggest investors largely ignore narrative social disclosure, whilst Toms (2002) and Hasseldine et al. (2005) find that specific, auditable, and quantitative disclosures are more useful in building corporate social reputation.

[2] Where the literature on voluntary disclosure includes international comparison, studies have focused on areas besides CSD, for example intellectual capital (Brennan, 2001, and Bozzolan et al., 2003). For an exceptional example, see Guthrie and Parker (1990)

To compound the problems of interpreting their mixed empirical results, these studies are often either mis-specified, under-theorised, fail to discriminate between hypotheses (Gray et al., 1995a; Tilt and Symes, 1999; Milne, 2002; Al-Tuwaijri et al. 2004) or, lacking an international dimension, too limited in scope. In general, they are unable to accommodate structural conflicts of interest and inequalities (Tinker et al., 1991). Specifically for the purposes of the current study, if the demand for CSD is expressed only as a function of stock market calculation, although stock market participants may reflect social and political pressures in their valuations, the influence of these wider pressures cannot be quantified or differentiated from the underlying financial value of the disclosure. As the scope of international activity expands, it is expected that the firm faces greater pressure to disclose from a wider range of international financial institutions whose expectations may be complementary. At the same time, the political and social pressure for disclosure will potentially increase and these must be differentiated for the purposes of empirical testing.

Legitimacy theory offers a potential solution to the under-theorisation of the economics-based studies. It is founded on the notion of a social contract (Dierkes and Antal, 1985; Gray et al., 1995b) and the dimensions of such a contract potentially increase as the firm diversifies its activities internationally. Accordingly, CSD is sometimes seen as a response to threats to the organisation's legitimacy (Deegan et al. 2000; Deegan, 2002). CSD may also be seen as a tool for establishing, protecting or repairing the legitimacy of the organisation in that they may influence public opinion and public policy (Patten, 1991; Cho and Patten 2007) and reduce political, social and economic exposure and pressure (Deegan and Rankin, 1997). Additionally, legitimation through CSD may play a part in influencing the policy process by shaping social and environmental standards, as suggested by Patten (1992: 472).

From the description of these studies, it can be seen that legitimacy theory is potentially nested within the benign hypothesis, as managers seek to fulfil their side of the social contract. The same might be said of ethical perspective stakeholder theory, in which all stakeholders (both primary and secondary) have a right to be provided with information about how the organization is impacting on them, through pollution, community engagement and so on (Deegan, 2000). For Lindblom (1994) the purpose is to influence 'relevant publics'. If a Multinational corporation begins to exploit the natural environment of an underdeveloped country, it follows that the members of that society become a 'relevant public'. However, it seems equally likely that the firm will not seek to manage its relationship with this 'public' if it has underdeveloped political organisation, regulation and lobbying institutions. Some studies have noted the selective nature of corporate legitimation and find that in situations of conflicting interests, organisations attempt to communicate legitimating characteristics to the most important relevant public and to ignore less important publics (Neu et al., 1998; Oliver, 1991). Acceptance of differential importance provides potential support for the asymmetric response hypothesis, and how 'most important' is defined and measured is very important for empirical testing.

Some of the answer is provided by stakeholder theory. According to this perspective, a stakeholder's power to influence corporate management is viewed as a function of the stakeholder's degree of control over resources required by the organization (Ullmann, 1985). There is some empirical support for stakeholder theory (Roberts, 1992, Neu et al. 1998; Magness 2006), but these results need extending. In the existing literature, stakeholders groups are seen as spatially undifferentiated, for example 'shareholders', 'employees', 'publics'. A Multinational company is very likely to deal with more than one national group of shareholders for example. Moreover, in the international context especially, there is no necessary correlation between resource control and CSD because societies in possession of crucial resources, such as oil, are missing other necessary conditions for CSD to occur, for example developed stock markets and structures of political accountability. Meanwhile the absence of such structures may increase the perception of political risk in countries where investment finance is sourced, thereby creating an asymmetric demand for CSD in other locations. In summary therefore the asymmetric response hypothesis offers a refinement of stakeholder theory and the possibility of extending it for the purposes of empirical testing.

Although the stakeholder and legitimacy approaches have achieved significant results, due to the theoretical overlaps discussed above it is not clear how the approaches compare and which of explanation is the more robust. In order to assess this, and the relative importance of stakeholder groups, the approach adopted in this study is to quantify the economic, social and political variables. Whilst this allows us to see the relative performance of these variables in testable models, a limitation is that it does not provide any generalisable test of stakeholder theory or legitimacy theory, nor offer comparable results to prior studies which have used qualitative approaches, although such results may be complementary to their principle findings. The study below is nonetheless important, since it is the first to simultaneously quantify economic, political and social variables in this fashion. In selecting the oil industry as its principal focus, it provides a useful case study of an environmentally sensitive industry operating in highly differentiated international social and political contexts.

HYPOTHESES, DATA AND VARIABLES

Hypotheses

According to the benign hypothesis, managers feel a sense of social responsibility which applies equally to the citizens of the countries in which they conduct their activities. As a company expands its scope of operations, the benign hypothesis predicts that the scope of the annual report also expands to accommodate the new arrangements of social accountability. If the benign hypothesis is true, CSD will be positively related to the number of countries of operation.

According to the alternative asymmetric response hypothesis, managers apply CSD where they are forced to do so by financial, political and social pressures. They will make differential disclosures reflecting inequalities in lobbying power between countries and between types of institution. For example where political institutions are underdeveloped, managers are less likely to adopt CSD in response to pressures in that country. To test the asymmetric response hypothesis three proxies are developed to measure financial, political and social accountability, derived respectively from stock market data, indices of political risk and social development.

Data

The sample comprises 87, 22 and 16 companies from the global Oil and Gas, Chemicals and Transportation industries, respectively. Consistent with Alciatore et al. (2004) oil is the primary focus of the study and the chemical and transportation sub-samples were chosen as reference group comparators of firms also engaged in environmentally sensitive activities, but without the evident political pressures associated with oil extraction (Jenkins and Yakovleva, 2006). The dataset is based on year 2000 and the sample of oil and gas production companies was obtained from a population of 1841 oil and gas production companies (as listed on the Wood Mackenzie database). Of these firms, the substantial majority did not have stock market quotations and were therefore excluded from the study. Eliminating other firms with missing data left a sample of 87. Therefore, most abandoned companies happened to be not listed in the stock market or they are only listed once in the best situations. Generally speaking, excluded companies were smaller and less Multinational in scope, which also reduces their potential relevance to the study. The information available for the remaining companies allowed the quantification of the number of countries where a company has oil and gas reserves and the commercial value of these reserves. The sample of 87 oil companies represents 5.54% of the population, and covers US$607,982m commercial reserves, or 72.85% of the population's commercial reserves.

Model Tested

The model tested in the paper can be summarised as follows:

$$CSD = \beta 0 + \beta 1NOC + \beta 2SMQ + \beta 3CONRISK_i + \beta 4ESI + \beta 5FRISK\ \beta 6SIZE + \beta 7\ IND + \varepsilon$$

where,

CSD = Corporate Social Disclosure;

$\beta 0$ = intercept;

$\beta 1$ to $\beta 7$ = coefficients of slope parameters;

NOC = the number of countries of operation for each company;

SMQ = the number of foreign stock market quotations;

$CONRISK_i$ = the unweighted average political risk of the countries in which firm i operates expressed as a percentage where 0% = minimum degree of risk and 100% = maximum risk;

ESI = the unweighted average environmental sensitivity index (ESI) of the countries in which firm i operates expressed as a percentage where 0% = minimum degree of sensitivity and 100% = maximum sensitivity;

FRISK= the total financial risk measured by the standard deviation of stock returns for the year 2000;

SIZE = a control variable that proxies for corporate size and is measured by the natural logarithm of sales turnover;

IND = the industry classification dummy variable, CHEM = chemical industry firm, OIL = oil industry firm; TRANS = transport industry is used as a reference group; and

ε = error term.

Dependent Variable

CSD as an empirical variable is defined as all the information produced by corporate management in the annual report regarding the interaction between the organisation and its physical and social environment, including issues such as those relating to human resources, community involvement and the natural environment. This study adopts the annual reports as the source of CSD data. The annual report is a statutory, accessible corporate document which speaks about the organisation as a whole, is widely used in prior research (Deegan and Rankin, 1997 Gray et al., 2001; Wiseman 1982: 55) and is viewed as credible by user groups (Tilt, 1994).

Content analysis is used to measure CSD as it has been widely adopted in previous social responsibility disclosure studies (Hackston and Milne, 1996). To facilitate the completion of the content analysis, an interrogation instrument, checklist, and decision rules were developed. The sentence was used as the unit of coding. Reliability was assessed using two rounds of pre-testing by three coders. The two pre-testing rounds produced increasingly convergent views as to what constituted a CSD sentence, and led to the formulation of several decision rules and amendments to the initial checklist.

Two measures of CSD were used. CSD is the total number of sentences and CSDP is the average number of sentences per page, using an approximation to page measurement from the sentence-coded data (after Hackston and Milne, 1996). The central assumption underlying the choice of dependent variable is that expanded disclosures in the Annual Report are complements rather than substitutes, and CSD is the measure that captures this. Therefore, in the regression analysis CSDP is primarily a robustness check on the main model.

Independent Variables

Number of countries (NOC) is used as a measure of the degree of Multinationality (extent of Multinational operations) and the MNC's power and is the principal variable used to test the benign hypothesis, where, if true, a positive relationship with CSD is expected. Belkaoui (2001) measures the level of Multinationality by the ratio of foreign profits / total profits and the number of countries in which the company operates. Meek et al. (1995) measure Multinationality as a ratio of sales from outside the MNC's home country to total sales. For this study, because expansion into a new country creates a new social responsibility relation and therefore a potentially new accountability relation, number of countries of operation is used and was directly obtained for each company from its annual report.

The number of stock market quotations (SMQ) is used to examine whether financial market pressure contributes a proportionate increase in CSD. This variable is used to test whether or not such listings create financial pressures for more disclosure over and above the mere scope of international operations suggested by the benign hypothesis. A positive relationship between CSD and SMQ would provide support for the asymmetric response hypothesis. The number of stock listings for the sampled companies was obtained from *Datastream*. Listings on more than one stock exchange in any given country are counted as one listing for purpose of this study. This is because, the stock exchanges in one country usually share the same working environment and thus add nothing to the study that aims to investigate the effects of foreign multiple listing. Additionally, only those stock listings occurring before April 2001 are included in the study. Hackston and Milne (1996) provide some evidence that dual and multiple overseas listings may be associated with greater social disclosure. Cooke (1989, 1992) finds an international listing effect on general voluntary accounting disclosures for Swedish and Japanese companies, respectively and Gray et al. (1993) find the same for their sample of U.S., U.K. and Continental European MNCs.

Country risk (CONRISK) is a proxy for political stability. The study uses the International Country Risk Guide (ICRG) risk rating system to assign a numerical value (risk points) to a predetermined range of risk components, according to a preset weighted scale, for each country covered by the system. Each scale is designed to award the highest value to the lowest risk and the lowest value to the highest risk. The country risk variable refers to different risk aspects of countries where MNCs operate. The country risk measure is used twice in the study as a measure of both the countries' of origin and the countries' of operation political systems (coded [CONRISK(O)] and [CONRISK], respectively). For each sample company the average political risk for all the countries in which the firm operates was computed. In line with the assumption under the benign hypothesis that social responsibility to new publics creates complementary lines of accountability, simple averages were used so that each country carries an equal weighting. The total was then subtracted from 100%, so that firms with operations typically in higher risk countries have higher CONRISK scores.

The Environmental Sustainability Index (ESI) is used to proxy for social development. A high score indicates a high level of development and associated social and environmental regulation. The ESI has been used to proxy for country environmental risk in other contexts (Sandrea, 2003), but not to date in accounting research. The measure includes different areas such as the environmental system (urban air quality, water quantity and quality, land, biodiversity) in the country, environmental stresses on the system such as air pollution, water pollution/use, ecosystem stress, waste/consumption, and population, human vulnerability and public health, the social and institutional capacity (their science/technical capacity, rigorous policy debate, environmental regulation and management, tracking environmental conditions, and the public choice failures), and the overall country's global stewardship (its ability to participate in efforts to conserve international environmental resources, and its impact on global commons). For each sample company the average ESI for all the countries in which the firm operates was computed. In similar fashion to the CONRISK variable above, ESI is used twice in the study as a measure of both the countries' of origin and the countries' of operation environmental sensitivity (coded [ESI(O)] and [ESI], respectively). Again, the assumption is that under the benign hypothesis social responsibility to new publics creates complementary lines of accountability, so again simple averages were used so that each country carries an equal weighting. The total was then subtracted from 100%, so that firms with operations typically in socially underdeveloped countries have higher ESI scores.

Financial risk (FRISK) is included in the study as a risk variable in parallel with CONRISK and ESI. It is assumed that if corporate managers engage in CSD in response to widening their scope of operations or exposure to political and social risk then financial risk will also form part of their risk management strategy. Financial risk is computed as the standard deviation of monthly stock returns which was calculated from the share prices for the year 2000 and obtained from the *Datastream* database for each of the sample companies.

Control Variables

A number of studies have examined whether industry sector is able to explain CSD, so controlling for industry membership in the regressions is potentially important. Hackston and Milne (1996) report that disclosures are higher in, what they classify as, high profile industries while Ness and Mirza (1991) found this relationship holds specifically for the oil industry. On the other hand, Cowen et al. (1987), Adams et al. (1995) and Freedman and Jaggi (1986) find that specific areas of disclosure are related to industry sector. Cowen et al. (1987) find that the industry helps to explain energy and community disclosures whilst Adams et al. (1995) conclude that industry sector explains some environmental and some employee disclosures. The sample contains companies from three industries, shown under the IND grouping variable. They are Chemicals (CHEM), Oil (OIL) and Transport (TRAN). Each is chosen for the relative environmental sensitivity of its activities. TRAN is used as a reference group so that the differential effects of CHEM and OIL can be assessed in the analysis.

An association between company size and CSD has been demonstrated in a number of empirical studies (Belkaoui and Karpik, 1989; Cowen et al., 1987; Kelly, 1981; Patten, 1991, 1992, Trotman and Bradley, 1981). Although size appears to be the most consistently reported as having a significant association with CSD, not all CSD studies have supported a size-disclosure relationship, where, for example, Roberts (1992) found no relationship in a US sample. Similarly, in New Zealand, Ng (1985) failed to support hypothesised association between company size and CSD practices. These inconsistencies might reflect differences in the countries of study or even the nature of sampled companies (local, Multinational, or a mix of the two types). Corporate size is measured in different ways in the prior CSD literature such as by the natural logarithm of book value of total assets (Singhvi and Desai, 1971; Patton and Zelenka, 1997; Inchausti, 1997), by the market value of equity (Lang and Lundholm, 1993), the natural logarithm of turnover (Belkaoui and Karpik, 1989; Patten, 1991; Roberts, 1992). In this study SIZE is the natural logarithm of the turnover, being the most popular measure of corporate size in the past research of CSD.

ANALYSIS

Descriptive Statistics

Summary descriptive statistics are reported in Table 1. Preliminary exploration of the data revealed a number of problems. As the dependent variable CSD is a count measure, the most important issue was model specification. As is typical of such data the standard deviation is high relative to the mean. However all companies in the sample made some disclosure and there was no limit on the right hand side of the distribution. Therefore the dependent variable CSD was transformed into a categorical variable CSD1 taking a value of 1 if CSD>0 and CSD<=20; 2 if CSD>20 and CSD<=39; ... 5 if CSD >80. The effect of this transformation was to reduce the standard deviation in relation to the mean (Table 1, Panel A). For the same reasons a similar transformation was applied to CSDP, using cut points at CSDP>0, 1, 2, 3, and >4 to create a new categorical variable CSDP1.

Table 1. Descriptive Statistics and Correlation Matrix

A: Variable descriptives

Variable	Mean	Std. Dev.	Min	Max	Swilk
CSD	64.544	61.356	1	258	0.000
CSDP	3.093	2.976	0.040	12.320	0.000
CSD1	2.838	1.732	1	5	0.033
CSDP1	2.862	1.579	1	5	0.272
ESI	50.568	9.937	25.570	77.260	0.808
ESI_O	35.295	9.370	19.530	62.440	0.000
CONRISK	28.119	6.022	17.1	45.58	0.083
CONRISK_O	19.261	6.965	9.500	52.500	0.000
CHEM	0.185	0.390	0	1	
OIL	0.685	0.466	0	1	
SIZE	6.433	1.051	3.580	8.380	0.000
FRISK	0.120	0.050	0.020	0.300	0.000
NOC	17.855	22.541	2	150	0.000
SMQ	2.298	1.385	1	9	0.000

B: Correlations	CSD1	CONRISK	CONRIS~O	ESI	ESI_O	CHM	OIL	SIZE	FRISK	NOC	SMQ
CSD1	1.000	0.215	-0.103	0.105	-0.068			0.466			
CONRISK		1.000	0.254	0.618	0.147			0.125			
CONRISK_O			1.000	0.324	0.627			-0.024			
ESI			0.345	1.000	0.474			0.258			
ESI_O			0.528	0.493	1.000			0.200			
CHEM	0.294	-0.064	-0.112	0.185	0.179	1.000					
OIL	-0.193	0.192	0.190	-0.078	-0.224	-0.705	1.000				
SIZE						0.153	-0.210	1.000			
FRISK	-0.461	-0.115	0.114	-0.047	0.021	-0.081	0.117	-0.371	1.000		
NOC	0.385	0.420	0.123	0.435	0.246	0.225	-0.228	0.578	-0.364	1.000	
SMQ	0.361	0.158	-0.018	0.144	0.009	0.264	-0.185	0.231	-0.259	0.280	1.000

As can be seen from Table 1, the effect of these transformations was to reduce the standard deviation relative to the mean. To accommodate the categorical dependent variable, ordered probit specification was used.

A second problem was the influence of outlying observations in the regression residuals in tests of the full model. Royal Dutch Shell had a particularly disproportionate influence and was removed from subsequent regressions in which the sample size is reported as 124. Cook-Weisberg tests indicated the presence of heteroscedasticity in the residuals, so robust standard errors were used in all models tested (White, 1980). Finally, as can be seen from Table 1 Panel B there was significant cross correlation between several of the independent variables. The CONRISK and ESI variables both measure the general level of development to some extent and therefore some correlation is to be expected. Multicollinearity was dealt with by sequential variable omission and by using stepwise model building.

Discussion of Results

Panel A of Table 2 reports the results of six models using CSD1 as the dependent variable. NOC was insignificant in all models tested, including model 1a which offers a specific test of the benign hypothesis. Although NOC always has a positive coefficient, there is no evidence that as the firm diversifies its operations, managers feel any obligation to open up new lines of reporting and accountability to the public in the affected countries.

Model 2a adds the SMQ variable which is highly significant in this and all subsequent models tested. Looking at the results in models 1a-6 inclusive it can be seen that the SMQ variable dominates the NOC variable. International diversification of financial accountability therefore dominates the diversification of operating activity as a determinant of CSD. In addition, the marginal effects are much greater. On average, the firms were operating in 18 different countries but had only two stock market quotations. Marginal effects analysis shows that an additional stock market quotation increases CSD by around 25%.

The introduction of CONRISK and ESI variables into the analytical models illustrated their differential effects.[1] CONRISK had a higher coefficient in all models in which it was tested compared to CONRISK(O). In contrast, ESI(O) had a higher coefficient and was more significant than ESI in all models. In all models CONRISK (including CONRISK(O)) and ESI (including ESI(O)) variables have positive and negative signs respectively. As expected, exposure to political risk increases CSD whilst relative social underdevelopment reduces it. Model 3a summarises the main results from tests using permutations of these variables.

Models 4 and 5 show the differential impacts of ESI and ESI(O), confirming the latter variable to be more influential. These results suggest that political risk in the destination country and social development in the home country condition the level of CSD. Because CSD is explained more strongly by the level of social development in the Multinationals' own country, rather than in the country of operation, the benign hypothesis is rejected. Managers do not provide equal accountability to the people of the different countries in which they operate. Managers seem to be giving precedence to publics that can exert more influence

[1] On average a sample company's engagement in international activities increased its exposure to political risk by 46% and to environmental sensitivity risk by 43% (based on the ratios of CONRISK/CONRISK(O) and ESI/ESI(O) respectively in table 1.

on them and but they feel nonetheless obliged to respond to the increased political risk overseas through increased CSD. These results provide support for the asymmetric response hypothesis.

Table 2. Regressions on Corporate Social Disclosure

A: Dependent variable = CSD1

	Model					
	(1a)	*(2a)*	*(3a)*	*(4)*	*(5)*	*(6)*
NOC	0.005	0.003	0.002	0.004	0.004	
SMQ		0.282***	0.256***	0.262***	0.279***	0.251***
CONRISK			0.033**			0.061***
CONRISK (O)						0.032**
ESI					-0.016*	-0.033**
ESI(O)			-0.027**	-0.023**		-0.029**
FRISK	-7.620***	-6.955***	-6.679***	-6.643***	-6.992***	-7.846***
CHEM	0.934**	0.742**	0.770**	0.812**	0.871**	0.943**
OIL	0.368	0.278	0.117	0.276	0.364	
SIZE	0.516***	0.486***	0.521***	0.523***	0.520***	0.597***
Psuedo R^2	0.154	0.179	0.199	0.190	0.185	0.216
Chi Sq	58.290	83.620	75.420	76.880	81.430	97.350
N	124	124	124	124	124	124

B: Dependent variable = CSDP1

	Model					
	(1b)	*(2b)*	*(3b)*	*(7)*	*(8)*	*(9)*
NOC	0.006	0.004	0.004	0.004	0.005	
SMQ		0.279***	0.268***	0.254***	0.278***	0.262***
CONRISK			0.005			
CONRISK_O				0.046***	0.026**	0.049***
ESI					-0.018*	
ESI_O			-0.010	-0.033**		-0.035**
FRISK	-5.543***	-4.681**	-4.428**	-5.531**	-5.653**	-5.941***
CHEM	0.969***	0.745**	0.759**	0.884**	0.929**	0.637***
OIL	0.493	0.415	0.387	0.302	0.464*	
SIZE	0.501***	0.476***	0.491***	0.537***	0.524***	0.548***
Psuedo R^2	0.133	0.158	0.161	0.174	0.168	0.171
Chi Sq	56.010	81.320	79.830	85.910	83.690	79.770
N	124	124	124	124	124	124

Significance levels.

*** $p < .01$.

** $p < .05$.

* $p < .10$.

Based on White's (1980) heteroscedastic consistent standard errors.

Model 6 reports a stepwise forward selection model using a 0.2 significance level for variable addition. The model confirms the positive relationship between CSD and the two CONRISK variables and the negative relationship with the two ESI variables. In view of the high correlation between CONRISK and ESI and CONRISK(O) and ESI(O) respectively (Table 1), the t-statistics for individual variables must be treated cautiously.

FRISK had a consistently high and negatively significant coefficient. The volatility of the firm's stock therefore seems to act as a strong constraint on CSD. There may be two reasons for this. First, where firms have a high level of combined operating and financial risk, they may be reluctant to disclose details of other aspects of their activities in case the market's perception of their riskiness increases further. Second, the volatility of their stock price may reflect their relatively narrow range of international activities which in itself reduces the necessity for disclosure. The interpretation of this variable is not central to the main objectives of the current paper, but in view of these findings is nonetheless a subject of potential further research.

Dealing with the control variables in turn, the industry control variables showed that whereas oil and transport firms were indistinguishable from one another, firms in the chemical industry make significantly more CSD. Finally, the SIZE variable was positive and significant in all models tested showing strong support for the common finding of a strong relationship between size of firm and CSD.

Panel B of Table 2 shows the results of similar models using CSDP as the dependent variable. Models 1b, 2b and 3b correspond exactly to the same numbered models in Panel A. Also, as in Panel A, model 9 reports the results of a stepwise forward selection model using a 0.2 significance level for variable addition. The results for models 1 and 2 respectively were very similar. Using the alternative dependent variable the result for NOC remains the same. In model 3b neither CONRISK nor ESI(O) were significant, in contrast to model 3a. In other words, these factors promote an increase in absolute quantity of disclosure (model 3a) but not an increase in the prominence of CSD as a reported issue relative to other disclosures (model 3b). A possible reason is that because disclosures are being made primarily for the consumption of stock market participants and the domestic audience, managers consider the quantity of information to be sufficient, and do not privilege CSD at the expense of other disclosures. As models 7 and 8 in Panel B suggest, they are more likely to do this where CONRISK(O) is high. Again in these models ESI(O) has a larger coefficient and is more significant than ESI, suggesting support for the asymmetric response hypothesis consistent with the Panel A results. Results for control variables are qualitatively similar to Panel A.

CONCLUSION

This paper extends prior literature on CSD determinants in two ways. First, it uses a sample of multinational firms in environmentally sensitive industries to examine their accounting disclosure responses to the pressures implied by the nature and scope of their operations. Second, the paper includes two hitherto unexamined variables measuring political risk and social development in order that these pressures can be measured and their effects directly tested.

The benign hypothesis, which assumes corporate control by enlightened oligarchs of managers, who apply similar standards of social accountability to different groups of people across the globe, is rejected. The alternative asymmetric response hypothesis is favoured by the evidence presented above. According to this hypothesis, the domestic public is comforted by the presence of impressively detailed CSDs in annual reports but is in ignorance of the true threat presented by corporate activities internationally. Meanwhile in countries where environmental protection is weak, local populations are all too well aware of the impacts of corporate activity but lack the defence mechanisms offered by CSD in more developed countries. As the survey results show, whatever the conscience of an individual manager, collectively managers are motivated by the need to satisfy the requirements of stock market participants first, their domestic public second and the people affected by their international activities last. To the investor in the developed world, this 'Maginot' of CSD offers scant protection from the changes in material conditions that necessarily follow from the exploitation of the world's resources by oil companies and others, and like the French generals of 1940 they will find that whilst paying attention to their neat line of forts, everything else was being lost.

REFERENCES

Adams, C.A., Hill, W.Y. and Roberts, C.B. 1995. *Environmental, Employee and Ethical Reporting in Europe*. London, ACCA.

Adams, C.A. 2002. Internal Organisational Factors Influencing Corporate Social and Ethical Reporting, *Accounting, Auditing and Accountability Journal*, 15(2): 223-50.

Aerts, W., Cormier, D. and Magnan, M. 2008. Corporate Environmental Disclosure, Financial Markets and the Media: An International Perspective, *Ecological Economics*, 64(3): 643-659.

Alciatore, M., Dee, C. and Easton, P. 2004. Changes in Environmental Regulation and Reporting: The Case of the Petroleum industry from 1989 to 1998, *Journal of Accounting and Public Policy*, 23(4): 295-304.

Al-Tuwaijri, S., Christensen, T. and Hughes, K. 2004. The Relations among Environmental Disclosure, Environmental Performance, and Economic Performance: A Simultaneous Equations Approach, *Accounting, Organizations and Society*, 29(5/6): 447-472.

Belkaoui, A. 1980. The Impact of the Disclosure of the Environmental Effects of Organizational Behaviour on the Market, *Financial Management*, 5(4): 26-31.

Belkaoui, A. 1984. *Socio-Economic Accounting*. Connecticut, Quorum Books.

Belkaoui, A. 2001. Level of Multinationality, Growth Opportunities, and Size as Determinants of Analyst Ratings of Corporate Disclosures, *American Business Review*, 19(2): 115-120.

Belkaoui, A. and Karpik, P.G. 1989. Determinants of the Corporate Decision to Disclose Social Information. *Accounting, Auditing and Accountability Journal*, 2(1): 36-51.

Benjamin, J.J. and Stanga, K.G. 1977. Differences in Disclosure Needs of Major Users of Financial Statements, *Accounting and Business Research*, (Summer): 187-192.

Brown, J. and Fraser, M. 2006. Approaches and Perspectives in Social and Environmental Accounting: An Overview of the Conceptual Landscape, *Business Strategy and the Environment*, 15: 103-117.

Buzby, S.L. and Falk, H. 1979. Demand for Social Responsibility Information by University Investors, *The Accounting Review*, 54(1): 23-37.

Chenall, R.H. and Juchau, R. 1977. Investor Information Needs: An Australian Study, *Accounting and Business Research,* 27(Spring): 111-119.

Cho, C. and Patten, D. 2007. The Role of Environmental Disclosures as Tools of Legitimacy: A Research Note, *Accounting, Organizations and Society*, 32(7/8): 639-647.

Cho, C., Patten, D. and Roberts, R. 2006. Corporate Political Strategy: An Examination of the Relation between Political Expenditures, Environmental Performance, and Environmental Disclosure, *Journal of Business Ethics*, 67(2): 139-154.

Cooke, T.E. 1989. Disclosure in the Corporate Annual Reports of Swedish Companies, *Accounting and Business Research*, (Spring): 113-124.

Cooke, T.E. 1992. The Impact of Size, Stock Market Listing and Industry Type on Disclosure in the Annual Reports of Japanese Listed Corporations, *Accounting and Business Research*, 22(87): 229-237.

Cowen, S.S., Ferreri, L.B. and Parker, L.D. 1987. The Impact of Corporate Characteristics on Social Responsibility Disclosure: A Typology and Frequency-Based Analysis, *Accounting, Organizations and Society*, 12(2): 111-122.

Deegan, C. and Gordon, B. 1996. A Study of the Environmental Disclosure Policies of Australian Corporations, *Accounting and Business Research*, 26(3): 187-199.

Deegan, C. and Rankin, M. 1997. The Materiality of Environmental Information to Users of Annual Reports. *Accounting, Auditing and Accountability Journal*, 10(4): 562-83.

Deegan, C. 2000. *Financial Accounting Theory.* Sydney, McGraw-Hill.

Deegan, C., Rankin, M and Tobin, J. 2002. An Examination of the Corporate Social and Environmental Disclosures of BHP from 1983-1997: A Test of Legitimacy Theory, *Accounting, Auditing and Accountability Journal*, 15(3): 312-43.

Dierkes, M. and Antal, A.B. 1985. The Usefulness and Use of Social Reporting Information, *Accounting, Organizations and Society*, 10(1): 29-34.

Epstein M.J. and Freedman, M. 1994. Social Disclosure and the Individual Investor, *Accounting, Auditing and Accountability Journal,* 7(4): 94-109

Firth M. (1979). 'The Impact of Size, Stockmarket Listing and Auditors on Voluntary Disclosure in Corporate Annual Reports'. *Accounting and Business Research,* Autumn: 273-280.

Freedman, M. and Jaggi, B. 1986. An Analysis of the Impact of Corporate Pollution Disclosures Included in Annual Financial Statements on Investment Decisions, *Advances in Public Interest Accounting*, 1: 193-212.

Glasbeek, H. 1988. The Corporate Social Responsibility Movement: The Latest in Asymmetric response Lines to Save Capitalism, *Dalhousie Law Journal*, 11: 363-402.

Gray, R., Bebbington, K.J. and Walters, D. 1993. *Accounting for the Environment: The Greening of Accountancy*. London, Paul Chapman.

Gray, R., Kouhy, R. and Lavers, S. 1995a. Corporate Social and Environmental Reporting: A Review of the Literature and a Longitudinal study of UK Disclosure, *Accounting, Auditing and Accountability Journal*, 8(2): 47-77.

Gray, R., Kouhy, R. and Lavers, S. 1995b. Methodological Themes: Constructing a Research Database of Social and Environmental Reporting by UK Companies. *Accounting, Auditing and Accountability Journal*, 8(2): 78-101.

Gray, R., Javad, M., Power, D.M. and Sinclair, C.D. 2001. Social and Environmental Disclosure and Corporate Characteristics: A Research Note and Extension, *Journal of Business Finance and Accounting*, 28(3): 327-356.

Guthrie, J. and Parker, L.D. 1990. Corporate Social Disclosure Practice: A Comparative International Analysis. *Advances in Public Interest Accounting*, 3: 343-352.

Hackston, D. and Milne, M.J. 1996. Some Determinants of Social and Environmental Disclosures in New Zealand Companies. *Accounting, Auditing and Accountability Journal*, 9(1): 77-108.

Hasseldine, J. Salama, A. and Toms, J.S. 2005. Quantity versus Quality: The Impact of Environmental Disclosures on the Reputations of UK plcs, *British Accounting Review*, 37(2); 231-248.

Inchausti, B.G. 1997. The Influence of Company Characteristics and Accounting Regulation on Information Disclosed by Spanish Firms, *European Accounting Review*, 6(1): 45-68.

Jenkins, H. and Yakovleva, N. 2006. Corporate Social Responsibility in the Mining Industry: Exploring Trends in Social and Environmental Disclosure, *Journal of Cleaner Production*, 14(3/4): 271-284.

Jose, A. and Lee, S. 2007. Environmental Reporting of Global Corporations: A Content Analysis based on Website Disclosures, *Journal of Business Ethics*, 72(4): 307-321.

Kelly, G.J. 1981. Australian Social Responsibility Disclosure: Some Insights into Contemporary Measurement, *Accounting and Finance*, 20(2): 97-107.

Lang, M. and Lundholm, R. 1993. Cross-Sectional Determinants of Analyst Rating of Corporate Disclosure, *Journal of Accounting Research*, 31(2): 246-271.

Lindblom, C. 1984. The Accountability of Private Enterprise: Private - No Enterprise – Yes, in Tinker A. (ed.) *Social Accounting for Corporations*. New York, Marcus Weiner.

Magness, V. 2006. Strategic Posture, Financial Performance and Environmental Disclosure: An Empirical Test of Legitimacy Theory, *Accounting, Auditing and Accountability Journal*, 19(4): 540-563.

Meek, G.K., Roberts, C.B. and Gray, S.J. (1995). 'Factors Influencing Voluntary Annual Report Disclosures by U.S., U.K. and Continental European Multinational Corporations'. *Journal of International Business Studies*, 26(3): 555-573.

Milne, M.J. and Chan, C.C. (1999). 'Narrative Corporate Social Disclosure: How Much of Differences Do They Make to Investment Decision-Making'. *British Accounting Review*, 31: 439-457.

Milne, M.J. 2002. Positive Accounting Theory and Social Disclosure Analyses: A Critical Look, *Critical Perspectives on Accounting*, 13: 369-395.

Murray, A. Sinclair, D. Power, D. and Gray, R. 2006. Do Financial Markets Care about Social and Environmental Disclosure? *Accounting, Auditing and Accountability Journal*, 19(2): 228–255

Ness, K.E. and Mirza, A.M. 1991. Corporate Social Disclosure: A Note on a Test of Agency Theory'. *British Accounting Review*, 23(3): 211-18.

Newson, M. and Deegan, C. 2002. Global Expectations and their Association with Corporate Social Disclosure Practices in Australia, Singapore, and South Korea, *International Journal of Accounting*, 37, 183-213.

Neu, D., Warsame, H. and Pedwell, K. 1998. Managing Public Impressions: Environmental Disclosures in Annual Reports, *Accounting, Organizations and Society*, 23(3): 265-82.

Ng, L.W. 1985. Social Responsibility Disclosures of Selected New Zealand Companies for 1981, 1982 and 1983. Occasional Paper, No. 54, Palmerston North, Massey University.

O'Dwyer, B. 2002. Managerial Perceptions of Corporate Social Disclosure: An Irish Story, *Accounting, Auditing and Accountability Journal*, 15(2): 406-436.

Oliver, C. 1991. Strategic Responses to Institutional Processes, *Academy of Management Review*, 15: 145-179.

Patten, D. 1991. Exposure, Legitimacy, and Social Disclosure, *Journal of Accounting and Public Policy*, 10: 297-308.

Patten, D.M. 1992. Intra-industry Environmental Disclosure in Response to The Alaskan Oil Spill: A Note on Legitimacy Theory, *Accounting, Organizations and Society*, 17(5): 471-475.

Patton, J. and Zelenka, I. 1997. An Empirical Analysis of the Determinants of the Extent of Disclosure in Annual Reports of Joint Stock Companies in the Czech Republic, *The European Accounting Review*, 6(4): 605-626.

Roberts, R.W. 1992. Determinants of Corporate Social Responsibility Disclosure, *Accounting, Organizations and Society*, 17(6): 595-612.

Sandrea, R. 2003. Upstream Opportunity Index Assesses EandP Investments, *Oil and Gas Journal*, 19(May): 18-22.

Singhvi, S.S. and Desai, H.B. 1971. An Empirical Analysis of the Quality of Corporate Financial Disclosure, *The Accounting Review*, 46(1): 129-138.

Tilt, C.A. 1994. The Influence of External Pressure Groups on Corporate Social Disclosure: Some Empirical Evidence, *Accounting, Auditing and Accountability Journal*, 7(4): 47-72.

Tilt, C.A. and Symes, C.F. 1999. Environmental Disclosure by Australian Mining Companies: Environmental Conscience or Commercial Reality? *Accounting Forum*, 23(2): 137-155.

Tinker, T., Lehman, C., and Neimark, M. 1991. 'Falling Down the Hole in the Middle of the Road: Political Quietism in Corporate Social Reporting'. *Accounting, Auditing and Accountability Journal*, 4(2): 28-54.

Toms, S. 2002. Firm Resources, Quality Signals and the Determinants of Corporate Environmental Reputation: Some UK Evidence, *British Accounting Review*. Vol.34, pp.257-282.

Trotman, K.Y. and Bradley, G.W. 1981. Association Between Social Responsibility Disclosure and Characteristics of Companies. *Accounting, Organizations and Society*, 6(4): 355-362.

Ullmann, A. E. 1985. Data in Search of a Theory: A Critical Examination of the Relationships among Social Performance, Social Disclosure and Economic Performance of US Firms, *Academy of Management Review*, 10(3): 540-557.

White, H. 1980. A Heteroskedasticity-Consistent Covariance Matrix Estimator and a Direct Test for Heteroskedasticity, *Econometrica*, 48(4): 817-838.

Wiseman, J. 1982. An Evaluation of Environmental Disclosures made in Corporate Annual Reports, *Accounting, Organizations and Society*, 7(1): 53-63.

Wolfson, C. and Beck, M. 2005. The International Oil Industry. in Wolfson, C. and Beck, M (eds.) *Corporate Social Responsibility Failures in the Oil Industry,* New York, Baywood.

In: Understanding Risk
Editor: Matthias Beck
ISBN: 978-1-62618-686-6

Chapter 3

CULTURAL THEORY OF RISK AND THE CREDIT CRISIS

***Philip M. Linsley*[*,a] *and Alexander P. Linsley*[b]**
[a]The York Management School, The University of York, Heslington, York, UK
[b]Merton College, University of Oxford, UK

ABSTRACT

The credit crisis that commenced in 2007 has created significant economic uncertainty and prompted major debates about the future of capitalism. This paper utilises Mary Douglas's cultural theory of risk to examine the crisis. It is argued that since the 1980s the individualistic culture has been the dominant form and inherent within the individualistic culture is a persistent shortsightedness. This myopia created a vulnerability to the financial crisis. This may appear paradoxical given that an individualistic culture has a primary focus upon financially-related risks and this contradiction is also explained.

Further, it is suggested that the severity of the crisis has created such a significant threat to the individualistic culture that this has intensified debates as to the most appropriate societal form. The eventual result of these highly vociferous cultural dialogues will potentially have major impacts upon key issues such as risk and regulation.

INTRODUCTION

'Over the ten years that I have had the privilege of addressing you as Chancellor, I have been able year by year to record how the City of London has risen by your efforts, ingenuity and creativity to become a new world leader. So I congratulate you Lord Mayor and the City of London on these remarkable achievements, an era that history will record as the beginning of a new golden age for the City of London.

* Corresponding author. Tel.: +44 1904 43 4107; *Email address:* pl521@york.ac.uk.

And I believe the lesson we learn from the success of the City has ramifications far beyond the City itself - that we are leading because we are first in putting to work exactly that set of qualities that is needed for global success:

openness to the world and global reach,
pioneers of free trade and its leading defenders,
with a deep and abiding belief in open markets, … and
a basic faith that from wherever it comes and from whatever background, what matters is that the talent, ingenuity and potential of people is harnessed to drive performance.

And I believe it will be said of this age, the first decades of the 21st century, that out of the greatest restructuring of the global economy, perhaps even greater than the industrial revolution, a new world order was created.'

Speech by the Chancellor of the Exchequer, the Rt. Hon. Gordon Brown, to Mansion House, June 2007

Two months after Gordon Brown paid the above tribute to the City of London the inter-bank lending markets ceased functioning, resulting in a funding crisis at the UK bank, Northern Rock. Disclosure of the Northern Rock funding difficulties by a television journalist employed by the BBC resulted in depositors queuing to withdraw cash and led to the Bank of England being compelled to supply emergency funding to Northern Rock in September 2007 to suppress this run on the bank (Bank of England, 2009). The press reports and television images of lines of Northern Rock customers waiting for branches to open to withdraw their cash mark the onset of the credit crisis.

Subsequently, other banks have received substantial support from governments with the Bank of England stating that if "all the facilities offered by central banks and governments were fully called upon, the scale of support to banking systems in the United Kingdom, the United States and euro area would exceed US$14 trillion" (Bank of England, 2009, p. 20).

The ensuing crisis has been characterized by uncertainty as economies have gone into recession (Stewart, 2009a), unemployment has increased sharply (see for example Bureau of Labor Statistics, 2009), and comparisons have been drawn with the Great Depression (Arner, 2009). Additionally, the current form of capitalism has come under intense scrutiny resulting in fundamental debates as to how societies should be constructed and taking in issues such as trust, risk, regulation and financial liberalisation (see for example, Barber, 2009).

The banking community has been singled out as having a dominant role in causing the crisis and the actions of senior bankers such as Sir Fred Goodwin (ex-Chief Executive of RBS) have been severely criticised (McIntosh, 2009). However, there is a wider context to the financial crisis and it incorporated elements such as bankers' bonus payments, securitisation of debt, credit default swaps, risk management practices, underwriting standards and the role of regulators (see for example, G20, 2008). These facets of the crisis initially appear relatively distinct as they relate to disparate topics of employee motivation, financial innovation, control systems and regulation. However, in this paper we contend that by drawing on cultural theory of risk[1] as developed by the anthropologist Mary Douglas the

[1] Hereafter referred to as cultural theory.

different elements of the crisis and the debates about the future of capitalism can be seen to be connected.

Douglas has developed a particular account of cultural theory which uses a grid-group framework to connect social structures and worldviews, and using Douglas's typology of social structures we can understand the crisis as a phenomenon borne out of a prevailing individualistic[2] worldview. Importantly, it will be argued in this paper that inherent within the individualistic culture is a persistent shortsightedness that created a vulnerability to the financial crisis. This is notwithstanding the paradox that an individualistic culture has a primary focus upon financially-related risks. It is also suggested that the severity of the crisis has created such a significant threat to the individualistic culture that this has intensified debates as to the most appropriate societal form. The eventual result of these highly vociferous cultural dialogues will potentially have major impacts upon issues such as risk and regulation.

The paper is structured as follows. The next section discusses the key facets of Douglas's cultural theory and the grid-group model, and includes an explanation of the features of the four types of culture. An account of the shift from a hierarchical to an individualistic culture during the 1970s and early 1980s is then provided. The authors then argue that the individualistic culture and the financial crisis are connected through a myopia that is intrinsic to the individualistic culture. Finally, conclusions are drawn concerning the implications of the different types of culture and the possibility of future crises.

The Development of Cultural Theory and the Grid-Group Model

The Underpinnings of Cultural Theory

Douglas developed and refined her notion of cultural theory over a substantial period and commencing with ideas of pollution as expressed in the mid-1960s in Purity and Danger (1966). As an anthropologist researching 'primitive societies' she identifies the fundamental role of pollution rituals as devices for preserving the current societal structure and for reducing the likelihood that actors in that society will behave in ways that may destabilise the existing societal order. Pollution rituals associated with the body (for example, rituals concerning foods that may or may not be eaten) are considered especially important and, because the body is symbolic of society, these rituals and customs are symbolic expressions of more generalized anxieties about the tainting of the social group (Douglas, 1970). Importantly, these rituals are (unarticulated) fears concerning the potential breaching of societal boundaries. Thus they are associated with issues such as who may become a member of the society, how to guard the boundaries against those who are deemed unsuitable as members of the society and how to identify and eject existing members of the society who are threatening the current way of life.

Hence, these beliefs are fundamentally associated with the maintenance of the social order and demarcate behaviours that are acceptable from those that represent a threat or

[2] It is important to note that Douglas's conception of the term 'individualistic' differs from how it has been used by, for example, Oliver Williamson. Douglas's conception is explained further in the next section of the paper.

danger to that order. The establishment of moral conventions enables the society to set up 'punishment' systems that can warn off those actors who may potentially transgress and via their behaviours undermine the current pattern of social relations.

Therefore, a major contention of Douglas's cultural theory is that "danger and risk are social constructions with different social structures causing different risk perceptions" (Linsley and Shrives, 2009, p. 495). That is, the risks that any particular society will focus upon are those that potentially threaten the extant configuration of social relations. This idea of "selective attention to risk" (Wildavsky and Dake, 1990, p. 43) applies equally to 'modern' and 'primitive' societies. The only difference being that modern' societies such as the USA and the UK now use the term 'risk' as a secular substitute for the term 'sin'.

Grid-Group Model

Douglas subsequently develops these initial ideas by identifying and classifying social relations through the creation of a grid-group model (see for example, Douglas 1978, 1986, 1989, 1990, 1992, 1994, 1995, 2003, 2004; Douglas and Wildavsky, 1982). This two-dimensional matrix distinguishes four cultural typologies in the following manner.

The group aspect of the model concerns the strength of allegiance that an individual actor has to fellow members of that society. If the individual is highly committed to other group members and places the aims of the group above their own aims then this denotes a high group state. Conversely, if the individual feels little loyalty to other members of the society and considers their own goals and objectives to be of greater importance than the group's goals then this would be categorized as a low group state (Douglas, 1978). The grid dimension of the model concerns the degree of freedom that an individual has over their choice of social role. If the society allows for minimal selection of one's role in society then this represents a high grid state. For example, gender or race may be a constraint or impediment to self-selecting one's social role (Rayner, 1992). In a low grid society then there are few restrictions upon social roles and individuals can freely choose who they might wish to collaborate with. Consequently, this grid-group model results in four types of culture; hierarchical, egalitarian, individualist and fatalist (see figure 1).

Douglas's grid-group model has been criticized as lacking subtlety and oversimplifying how patterns of social relations really are. However, it is important to note that the two dimensions are continuous and do not simply comprise two states. Its value is as a device that can assist us in comprehending how alternative worldviews are the product of societal structures. Cultural theorists such as Douglas are very aware that any given society may not be *wholly* individualistic or *wholly* egalitarian, but to examine societies in a meaningful manner requires typologies to be established (Thompson and Ellis, 1997). The number of typologies that one should create is contentious but Douglas argues that societies have a proclivity to lapse into one of these four forms as they have a relative stability.

Further, within any given society there will be a tension as cultures vie with one another for dominance. In this way there are always ongoing cultural dialogues as to what form of social relations should be favoured albeit with the dominant worldview influencing the cultural bias displayed at any given time (Douglas, 2004). This notion of cultural dialogues is important in that it also indicates that free will is not absent under cultural theory. The presence of a particular pattern of social relations in a society does not imply that all individuals will behave alike in that society or that any given individual will confine their membership to groups of a particular cultural type. Hence, Douglas's earlier static view has been replaced by a dynamic view of how individuals might move across societies and cultures (Douglas, 2004: Rayner, 1992).

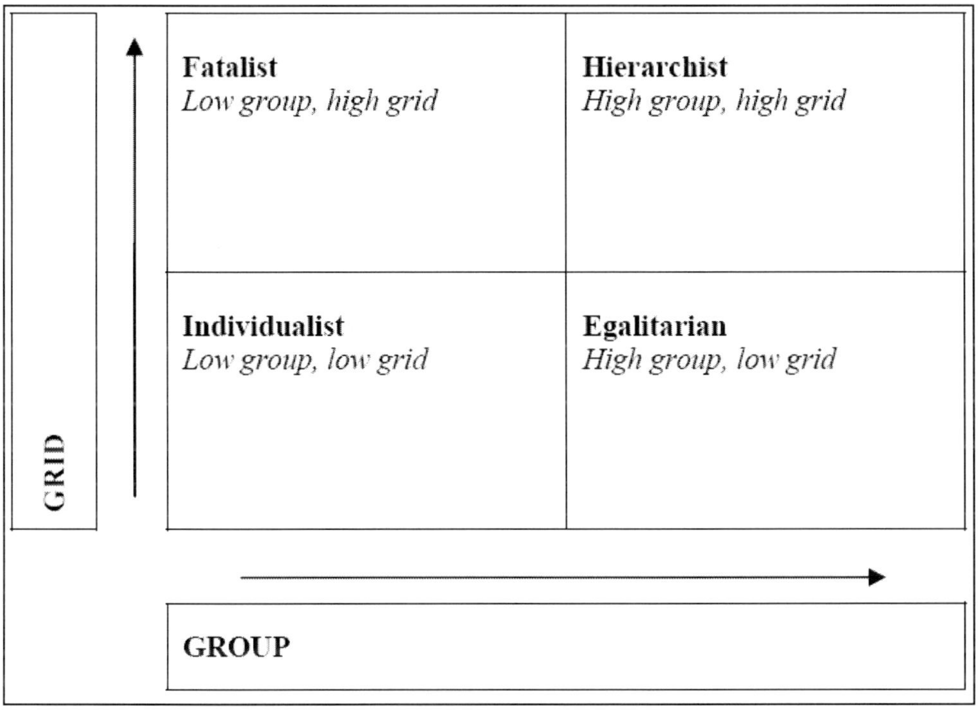

Figure 1. Grid-group model.

The Four Cultural Typologies

The hierarchical (high grid-high group) form of society comprises clearly delineated boundaries. The external (high group) boundary partitions societal actors from alien outsiders who potentially threaten the border. Limitations upon social roles are present in this type of society; hence the internal (high grid) boundary is also clearly distinguished. Tradition and respect for authority are features of a hierarchical society and abnormal or anomalous behaviour deemed unacceptable. Bureaucratic rules are important as they can regulate actions and maintain strong justice systems that will impose admonitory punishments upon insiders who violate boundaries (Heap and Ross, 1992). The verdicts of professional experts would not be questioned in such a society as this would threaten to undermine the high grid-high group form of social relations.

An individualistic (low grid-low group) culture is largely devoid of internal and external boundaries. There is no commitment to others in the society and the individuals may associate with whoever they choose. This is an entrepreneurial society where free-market ideas are espoused and individuals have "a propensity to collaborate with other individuals when gains can be made from such alliances" (Linsley and Shrives, 2009, p. 495). This materialistic type of society is highly competitive and individuals who fail to thrive cannot expect to find others will aid them. The individualist will allege there is parity of opportunity but, in reality, this does not hold and societal members will seek to establish advantages through whatever means they can.

The third cultural form is the (low grid-high group) egalitarian society. In common with the hierarchical society it shares a strong (high group) external boundary, but the low grid state indicates there is a freedom to self-select social roles. Loyalty to the group is of the utmost importance and individual goals must be subservient to the group's goals. Disloyalty is an odious 'sin' and will likely result in severe punishment or permanent ostracism from the group. The egalitarian society is disposed towards ideas of equality and justice, and often considers broader society as harbouring many ills. The social relations of religious sects and environmental groups have been identified as egalitarian (Rayner, 1992).

The (low group-high grid) fatalist cultural type consists of individuals who have highly restricted social mobility and no feeling of kinship with others. This is an unenviable position to be in as the fatalist is an outcast who has little scope to determine their own fate. They are affected by risk, but powerless to impose any control over their destinies.

Hierarchical and individualistic groups are considered to be at the 'Center' (Douglas and Wildavsky, 1982). This is because of the significant political and economic power they possess, and this power is intensified if they choose to collude and work together. The primary risks and dangers these cultures are focused upon differ dependent upon their grid-group configuration (Douglas and Wildavsky, 1982). The hierarchical society is concerned with crime and foreign confrontations or hostilities as these risks threaten the internal and external boundaries respectively. Status in an individualistic culture is derived from material success and it is therefore concerned about risks that adversely impact upon financial wealth. Additionally, as its foundations are rooted in the free-market system it is also concerned about risks to the exchange system (Douglas, 1978). Egalitarian groups lack the power of the hierarchical and individualistic cultures and are on the 'Border' (Douglas and Wildavsky, 1982). They may goad and antagonise hierarchical and individualistic organizations as this helps maintain group cohesion through identifying the 'Center' as malevolent, immoral, inequitable and the like. By contrast, the powerlessness of the fatalists often results in their being excluded from the typology (Tansey and O'Riordan, 1999).

The Move From Hierarchy to Individualism at the Outset of the 1980s

It has been emphasised that in any society the four types of culture can exist alongside each other. Cultural dialogues occur as the supporters of the different typologies endeavour to convince others of the superiority of their cosmology for "culture … (is) … an ongoing, never resolved argument about rightness of choice" (Douglas, 1994, p. 260). Thus in any society a particular culture may have greater influence but it may also be superseded over a period of time. Heap and Ross (1992) have proposed that in the UK and USA an individualistic culture has gained ascendancy over a hierarchically-based culture in recent times. The key point in this cultural shift can be traced to the period beginning at the outset of the 1980s and with causes of the shift traceable to events occurring in the 1970s.

Thus in the USA in the 1970s significant negative factors such as the 1973 oil price shock, the demise of the Bretton Woods Agreement, de-industrialization, rising unemployment and economic decline caused US citizens to question the efficacy and rightness of the current order (Fraser, 2005). In part this order was associated with Roosevelt's New Deal which as a response to the Great Depression had brought about, for example, The Glass-Steagall Banking Act and the alphabetical agencies (Brogan, 1999). In the USA the economic difficulties of the 1970s came to be seen as following from increasing US government regulation of business (Gersemann, 2004). Political and social debates about the merits of a deregulated enterprise society relative to a welfare society therefore became prominent. In the UK severe economic difficulties were also an important feature of the 1970s culminating in 1978-1979 with the so-called 'Winter of Discontent' characterised by a series of workers strikes. Consequently in the UK similar deliberations about the merits and demerits of government interference in the marketplace came to the fore.

President Reagan (1981-1989) in the USA and Prime Minister Thatcher (1979-1990) in the UK were subsequently voted into power having espoused free market principles and following their respective elections these principles were enacted with measures including: reducing taxation, curbing social welfare, deregulating markets, privatizing public entities and lowering government spending (Gersemannn, 2004; Heywood, 2003). This "capitalist version of liberation theology … (that) gathered momentum throughout the dolorous 1970s … (and) combined reverence for the free market with resentment of state interference" (Fraser, 2005, p. 477) is an exemplar for a pro-competition individualistic culture based upon material acquisition. Thus an individualistic culture came about because a sufficient number of individuals were convinced this was the right choice.

The modification of culture in wider society during the 1980s and 1990s had a substantial impact upon business organizations in the UK and USA. Hendry (1999) discusses how the previously well established hierarchical arrangement of firms promoted a situation where the strong sense of group facilitated the management and regulation of the workforce. As these firms pursued profits they were also engaged in sustaining a market (individualistic) culture and hence there was the potential for a destructive tension between individualistic and hierarchical value systems to arise. However, in the years prior to the economic difficulties of the 1970s a reciprocity existed as employees considered the firm a source of comparative job security and the provider of a defined role within the firm and society. Thus this tension was dissipated whilst employees felt looked after by the firm. As the economic problems of the 1970s escalated and firms' managers began downsizing and re-structuring in a more focused pursuit of profit then employees felt that their prior allegiance to the firm was no longer warranted. At this point employee commitment had to be obtained through individualistically-based appeals to self-interest largely predicated upon materialistic reward systems.

The central argument of this paper is that the current financial crisis can be attributed to the dominance of the individualistic culture following the cultural turmoil of the 1970s and this is discussed in the next section of the paper.

THE FINANCIAL CRISIS AND CULTURAL THEORY

The financial crisis has been attributed to the search for higher returns on the part of banks and related financial institutions leading to credit indiscipline particularly in respect of the US subprime mortgage market and leveraged buyout market (IMF 2007; IOSCO, 2008;

G20, 2008). The factors that have been identified as the principal causes of the crisis are: weak underwriting standards, inadequate risk management practices, the innate complexity of financial transactions and structures, and incentive structures encouraging the pursuit of short-term gains (Arner, 2009; IMF, 2007; IOSCO, 2008: G20, 2008; Crouhy et al., 2008).

The Individualistic Culture, Wealth Acquisition and Democracy

Subprime lending to individuals with flawed credit histories and near-prime lending to individuals with less serious credit quality problems had been occurring pre-2000, but grew substantially during the period from the outset of the 2000s through to 2006 (Mayer et al., 2008). For example, there were approximately 1.45 million subprime mortgage loan originations and 0.92 million mortgage near-prime loan originations for near-prime loans in 2006, with growth rates of 33.6% and 203.1% respectively in originations over the period 2003 to 2006 (Mayer et al., 2008). The growth in nonprime lending, which carries greater risk due to the higher probability of default, resulted from financial institutions relaxing underwriting standards to gain increased shares of the market (IOSCO, 2008).

The individualistic culture has a central focus upon the acquisition of wealth as this is the primary measure of success. Therefore, it was inevitable that underwriters would seek new opportunities as this was a means of further enriching the firms they worked for and, ultimately, themselves. The individualistic culture embraces a belief in free markets that is wholly accepting of competition and motivated by the pursuit of profit. The sale of subprime and near-prime mortgage loans was just another business prospect that required risks to be taken. This is a natural progression as within an individualistic culture it is the upside of risk that is emphasised as it presents the possibility of improved returns.

A less obvious aspect of the move into selling greater numbers of subprime and near-prime mortgage loans is associated with the connection between the individualistic culture and democracy. Linsley and Shrives (2009) state that "the low grid-low group individualistic society *suggests*, although it does not actually create, a democratic arrangement that has an inherent appeal because of the message it communicates … (and) … implies an equality of opportunity exists for anyone wanting to pursue success" (p. 499). This particular notion of equality is what Gordon Brown is alluding to in his Mansion Speech when he states that, "a basic faith that from wherever it comes and from whatever background, what matters is that the talent, ingenuity and potential of people is harnessed to drive performance" (Brown, 2007). Consequently, selling a vision of home ownership to individuals who had previously not had the possibility becomes relatively easier when an underlying core tenet of a society is that all members of the group are able to participate in the acquisition of this primary symbol of wealth. Concomitantly, this tying together of democracy and the individualistic culture implies that if you are already a home owner then trading up to a larger, more expensive property is possible as well as desirable.

It has been suggested that the increase in default rates on mortgage loans occurred because of the complexity of the products that were being offered and hence there was a lack of consumer understanding (Mayer et al., 2008). An alternative interpretation, drawing upon cultural theory, is that the providers of mortgage loans were creating products (such as short-term hybrids or so-called 'teaser' rate mortgages) which played upon this idea of equality of opportunity and its intrinsic message that all members of the individualistic culture could participate in home ownership. This is not to suggest that the concern of the providers of mortgage loans was to democratize home ownership; rather this represented a market opportunity that was personally beneficial to the providers of mortgage loans. In retrospect the question has been asked, whether it was appropriate to sell such loans? However, within the individualistic culture the nature of transactions is that they occur for reasons of personal gain and there is acceptance that any party to a transaction has to look after their own interests.

Financial Risk, Threats to the Exchange System and Myopia

A further aspect that assisted in selling this vision of home ownership to individuals who signed contracts on these subprime and near-prime mortgage loans concerns the idea of risk in individualistic societies. It has been explained that the key risk focus in this type of culture is economic or financial risk. It is likely that these risks were largely invisible to individual home buyers because of the strong upward trend in house prices through to 2005. For example, the SandP/Case Shiller Composite-20 Index[3] rose continuously from January 2000 to July 2006 recording an overall increase of 106% over this period (SandP/Case Shiller Index, 2008). The general macroeconomic background of low interest rates and low unemployment rates (Mayer et al., 2008) would have also contributed to this sense of economic risks being relatively immaterial. Compounding this would have been the tendency for individualistic societies to look ahead across only a short time horizon. Consequently, a favourable outlook for the future was anticipated by borrowers of mortgage funds and only token attention was paid to financial risk.

Contemporaneously, the risk focus of the providers of mortgage loans would have been affected by the benign economic climate and this myopic tendency. It may be questioned why they did not consider the sustainability of this strategy of selling nonprime mortgage loans. These mortgages carry a greater risk of default and it might have been foreseen that a relaxation of underwriting standards could not only affect the near-prime market but also threaten to impact on the exchange system. The latter would be of considerable importance as the individualistic culture is at risk of being usurped by another culture if the market system ceases to function effectively. Again, it is the problem of myopia that can explain this difficulty as this form of culture is not only myopic "to larger effects ... (but) ... foresees danger from the individual perspective" (Douglas, 1994, p. 66). Thus, individuals pay attention to those risks that may have a direct effect upon their personal wealth position. Therefore, it is probable underwriters will have focused primarily upon ensuring they complete mortgage transactions as this maintains or enhances their personal incomes. They are less likely to have considered the wider picture and to have thought about how their individual acts might impinge upon the wider market system within which they operated. In the wider context of the credit crisis banks generally have been criticised for having incentive structures that encouraged short-term risk taking (Stewart, 2009b); but in an individualistic culture this is inevitable and simply an extension of what has already been stated concerning the providers of mortgage loans. It can appear surprising that individualistic short-sightedness operates in this manner but it has been observed in respect of other incidents that have

[3] This Index measures changes in the value of residential properties across 20 regions in the USA.

endangered the exchange system under an individualistic culture. For example, Linsley and Shrives (2009) have provided a cultural theory-based explanation of why several potential warning signs in respect of Enron's earnings were ignored.

Risk Management, Complex Financial Transactions and Patrolling the Margins

The risk management practices of banks have often been considered well developed (Bessis, 2002) and yet reports post-crisis suggest that there were inadequacies in the risk management control systems that were partly responsible for the problems that arose (see for example IOSCO, 2008). In part managing risk was a difficult task because of the complexity of the financial transactions that were occurring including securitisation and the use of credit derivatives (Murphy, 2009), and thus the two aspects of risk management and financial structuring have connections.

Broadly, securitisation is the process whereby money is raised through issuing bonds which are backed by a group of assets such as a bank's mortgage portfolio (Murphy, 2009). This potentially diversifies risk for the bank whilst also freeing up capital (IOSCO, 2008). It has already been stated that risk is a natural feature of the landscape for the individualist who sees it as a means for providing potential returns. Consequently, risk is not to be feared as such, but managed to one's advantage. Through securitisation the banks could focus on their "core competencies ... originating loans and servicing them" (Murphy, 2009, p. 17). The capital released could then be used to create more profits under this Originate to Distribute Model (ODM). Thompson (1992) explains that individualist organisations have a risk handling style that can be summarised as "acceptance and deflection" (p. 200). Thus, for the banks as individualistic organizations the use of securitisation (for example, through the issuance of mortgage backed securities) was also a means of transferring (deflecting) risk through to another party. Once the risk was transferred on then it was for the other party to consider how to deal with the risk.

The banks were also able to shift unwanted risk through the use of credit derivatives. Thus, credit default swaps transferred the risk of default to another party providing protection in the event of the original borrower defaulting and moving risk around was commonplace. The individualistic view of the world is "cornucopian (skill-controlled) and '(i)f you can do it, it's natural'" (Thompson, 1992, p. 202). Thus, although the markets for credit derivatives and securitisation grew to immense proportions[4] the individualistic culture of the banks would imply that they would have been accepting of this. That is, it would likely be considered 'natural' to shift risk and to assume that there would be a 'natural' equilibrium overall in respect of the risk to the banking and financial system. Thus, it is not complacency as such that would hold with regards to risk and risk management, but a confidence that in the normal course of events balance occurs and stability is in-built.

This is not to say that some intervention may not be required to ensure that agency and asymmetric information problems are confronted. The individualist is not gullible or naïve

[4] For example, the credit derivative market is estimated to have a worth approaching $50 trillion and in 2006 $3 trillion of asset backed securities were issued in comparison to approximately $1 billion issued in 2002 (Murphy, 2009).

and is aware that others may try to gain at their expense. Consequently, there is need for gatekeepers to verify information and the like. Examples of gatekeepers include auditors who verify the financial report by attesting to its truthfulness and hence aid investors to know that directors are fulfilling their stewardship role. In the case of securitisation the credit ratings agencies had the role of verifying the risks that were attached to the loan portfolios being securitised.

In terms of cultural theory gatekeepers patrol "margins (which) are those points in a society that are particularly vulnerable to risks and dangers" (Linsley and Shrives, 2009, p. 502). The ratings agencies have been criticised for not being assiduous enough in patrolling the borders with concerns expressed about conflicts of interest (Arner, 2009). A particular concern was that the ratings agencies were paid by the issuers of the securities and it is possible to see that, in an individualistic culture, the agencies might act in their own interests (to gain payments from issuers) rather than acting impartially. This is because the "form of culture ... directly affect(s) the practice adopted" (Linsley and Shrives, 2009, p. 503). It would be wrong to single out the ratings agencies as the sole gatekeepers who had a role in the crisis. For example, auditors (as mentioned above) and regulators also had a gatekeeping function to perform that may have been weakened because of the individualistic culture.

Conclusion

At the outset of the article it was explained that in August 2007 a liquidity crisis occurred as banks stopped lending to each other. The freezing up of the inter-bank lending market was a colossal shock to the financial community. Individualists consider resources as abundant (Thompson, 1992) and this includes supplies of capital. With the onset of the credit crisis came headlines such as:

> "Backlash grows over bonuses for culprits of disaster" (Bowers , 2008)
> "The voices in G20's chorus of protest" (Vulliamy and Rogers, 2009)
> "The closing of the Thatcher era" (Rachman, 2009)
> "It's got so horrible that we ought to be revolting" (Caulkin, 2009)

These headlines are not just indicative of the magnitude of the crisis but also signify the scale of the threat to the individualistic worldview. In a case such as Enron the repercussions were largely confined to a small and very distinct group of people; namely, ex-employees who suffered greatly as they lost their jobs and 401(k) pension plans became worthless (Linsley and Shrives, 2009). However, as this credit crisis has unfolded the repercussions have been pervasive. Mortgage defaulters have become homeless (Burkeman, 2009), significant jobs losses have been occurring and for those remaining in employment there is a general feeling of insecurity. Additionally, the need for governments to provide additional capital to banks has created a sense of uncertainty as to whether savings are safe.

In an individualistic system where failure is considered an individual weakness and there is little assistance afforded to those who do not succeed then it is unsurprising that dialogues have opened up as to whether the individualistic pattern of social relations is appropriate. Additionally, it offers an opportunity for those whose worldview is not individualistic to try to persuade disillusioned individualists (or ex-individualists who may have 'fallen out of the system' through unemployment or homelessness and become fatalists) to swap allegiance. This is a particularly good opportunity for egalitarian groups to seek new recruits. These egalitarian groups have different agendas that may be, inter alia, political, environmental or religious (Vulliamy and Rogers, 2009) but what they have in common is they offer the possibility of belonging to an activist group where loyalty is valued (and required) and the injustices of the outside world are a prime focus.

The difficulty this presents for governments and business is that these groups are at the 'Border' and, if they are successful in their recruitment, threaten the individualistic and hierarchical cultures at the 'Center'. Consequently, politicians and business have to be seen to be acting forcefully to address key concerns. It is to be expected that debates will centre around issues such as regulation, expertise and risk and in a manner that highlights the differences in the worldviews of the different cultural types. Hierarchists will wish to see a return to greater regulation and to emphasise the need for expertise in the running of financial institutions; to revive trust in the financial system they will assert that strong controls are needed to manage risk. Individualists will wish to perpetuate self-regulation and will argue that the individual is best able to manage resources effectively. Egalitarians will place less emphasis on regulation than on everyone committing to working together to create a better world believing the approaches of both the hierarchists and the individualists to be flawed.

The individualistic culture is currently under threat and cultural theory suggests that any society under threat will act to preserve the current order. It is too early to know whether its actions will be sufficient to ward off the danger it currently faces, or whether a different worldview and pattern of social relations will prevail. The crisis and responses to the crisis are still ongoing and future research projects will need to make this assessment with the benefit of hindsight. It is also important to note that whichever worldview triumphs, cultural dialogues will continue as to what social form is most apt.

REFERENCES

Arner, D. W. 2009. The global credit crisis of 2008: causes and consequences. *AIIFL Working Paper No. 3.* Available at: http://papers.ssrn.com/sol3/papers.cfm?abstract_id=133074 (accessed 19 June 2009).

Bank of England, 2009. Financial Stability Report, June, Issue 25.

Barber, L. 2009. Capitalism redrawn. Financial Times, May 12, 2009, 3.

Bessis, J. 2002. *Risk management in banking*. Chichester: Wiley.

Bowers, S. 2008. Backlash grows over bonuses for culprits of disaster. *The Guardian, September,* 26: 37.

Brogan, H. 1999. *The Penguin History of the USA*. London: Penguin.

Brown, G. 2007. Speech by the Chancellor of the Exchequer, the Rt. Hon. Gordon Brown MP, to Mansion House. Available at: http://www.hm-treasury.gov.uk/press_68_07.htm (accessed 11 May 2009).

Bureau of Labor Statistics, 2009, Employment situation summary, July 2009. Available at: http://www.bls.gov/news.release/empsit.nr0.htm (accessed August 1 2009).

Burkeman, O. 2009. Out in the open: recession exposes America's homeless underclass. *The Guardian*, March 27, 2009.

Caulkin, S. 2009. It's got so horrible that we ought to be revolting. *The Observer,* January 1, 2009.

Crouhy, M. G., Jarrow, R. A. and Turnbull, S. M. 2008. The subprime credit crisis of 07. Available at:http://papers.ssrn.com/sol3/papers.cfm?abstract_id=1112467andrec=1and srcabs=133074 4 (accessed 19 June 2009).

Douglas, M. 1966. *Purity and danger: An analysis of concepts of pollution and taboo.* London: Routledge and Kegan Paul.

Douglas, M. 1970. *Natural symbols*. London: Barrie and Rockliff.

Douglas, M. 1978. Cultural bias. *Royal Anthropological Institute*, Occasional Paper 35. Republished in *In the Active Voice* (1982). London: Routledge and Kegan Paul, 183-254.

Douglas, M. 1986. *Risk acceptability according to the social sciences*. London: Routledge and Kegan Paul.

Douglas, M. 1989. The background of the grid dimension. *Sociological Analysis 50, 2,* 171-76.

Douglas, M. 1990. Risk as a forensic resource. *Daedalus 119, 4,* 1-16.

Douglas M. 1992. The person in an enterprise culture. In S. H. Heap, and A. Ross, *Understanding the enterprise culture: themes in the work of Mary Douglas* (41-62). Edinburgh: Edinburgh University Press.

Douglas, M. 1994. *Risk and blame: essays in cultural theory*. London: Routledge.

Douglas, M. 1995. Converging on autonomy: anthropology and institutional economics. In Williamson, O. E. (Ed.). *Organization theory: from Chester Barnard to the present and beyond* (98-115). Oxford: Oxford University Press.

Douglas, M. 2003. Being fair to hierarchists. *University of Pennsylvania Law Review 151, 4,* 1349-70.

Douglas, M. 2004. Traditional culture: let's hear no more about it? In V. Rao, and M. Walton (Eds.). *Culture and public action* (pp. 85-109). Stanford: Stanford University Press.

Douglas, M. and Wildavsky, A. 1982. *Risk and culture: an essay on the selection of technical and environmental dangers*. London: University of California Press.

Fraser, S. 2005. *Wall Street – A cultural history*. London: Faber and Faber.

Gersemann, O. 2004. *Cowboy capitalism – European myths, American reality*. Washington: Cato Institute.

G20 2008. Declaration of the summit on financial markets and the world economy, *G20,* November 15, 2008. Available at: http://www.g20.org/Documents/g20_summit_declaration.pdf (accessed 18 June 2009).

Heap, S. H. and Ross, A. 1992. Introduction: Mary Douglas and the enterprise culture. In S. H. Heap, and A. Ross, *Understanding the enterprise culture: themes in the work of Mary Douglas* (1-18). Edinburgh: Edinburgh University Press.

Hendry, J. 1999. Cultural theory and contemporary management organization. *Human Relations,* 52, 5, 557-77.

Heywood, A. 2003. *Political Ideologies*. Basingstoke: Palgrave MacMillan.

IMF 2007. Global Financial Stability Report -Financial Market Turbulence: Causes, Consequences, and Policies, IMF, October 2007.

IOSCO 2008. Report on the subprime crisis. *Technical Committee of the International Organization of Securities Commissions,* May 2008.

Linsley, P. M. and Shrives, P. J. 2009. Mary Douglas, risk and accounting failures. *Critical Perspectives on Accounting,* 20, 4, 492-508.

Mayer, C. J. Pence, K. M. and Sherlund, S.M. 2008 The Rise in Mortgage Defaults, Finance and Economics Discussion Series Working paper 2008-59, Federal Reserve Board, Washington, D.C. 2008-59.

McIntosh, L. Anti-capitalist group boasts of attack on Sir Fred Goodwin's home. *The Times*, March 25, 2009.

Murphy, D. 2009. *Unravelling the credit crunch.* Abingdon: CRC Press.

Rachman, G. 2009. The closing of the Thatcher era, *The Financial Times*, April 28, 2009.

Rayner, S. 1992. Cultural theory and risk analysis. In S. Krimsky and D. Golding (Eds.). *Social Theories of Risk* (83-115). Westport: Praeger.

SandP/Case Shiller Index (2008). Available at:http://www2.standardandpoors.com/portal/site/sp/en/us/page.topic/indices_csmahp/0,0,0,0,0,0,0,0,0,5,1,0,0,0,0,0.html (accessed 1 July 2009).

Stewart, H. 2009a. This is how we let the credit crunch happen Ma'am. *The Observer*, July 26, 2009.

Stewart, H. 2009b. Darling to clamp down on bonuses. *The Observer*, July 5, 2009.

Tansey, J. and O'Riordan, T. 1999. Cultural theory and risk: a review. *Health, Risk and Society,* 1, 1, 71-90.

Thompson, M. 1992. The dynamics of cultural theory and their implications for the enterprise culture. In S. H. Heap, and A. Ross, *Understanding the enterprise culture: themes in the work of Mary Douglas* (182-202). Edinburgh: Edinburgh University Press.

Thompson, M. and Ellis, R. J. 1997. Introduction. In Ellis, R. J. and M. Thompson, *Culture matters – essays in honor of Aaron Wildavsky* (pp. 1-18). Boulder, Colorado: Westview Press.

Vulliamy, E. and Rogers, R. 2009. The voices in G20's chorus of protest. *The Observer*, March, 8, 2009.

Wildavsky, A. and Dake, K. 1990. Theories of risk perception: who fears what and why? *Daedalus,* 119, 4, 41-60.

In: Understanding Risk
Editor: Matthias Beck
ISBN: 978-1-62618-686-6

Chapter 4

REGULATIONS, RISK, AND RENT SEEKING BEHAVIOUR

Ole Jakob Bergfjord[1,*] and Urs Steiner Brandt[2]
[1]Bergen University College, Norway
[2]Department of Environmental and Business Economics,
University of Southern Denmark, Denmark

ABSTRACT

This paper seeks to address how political risk influences behaviour, in particular rent seeking behaviour. Such risk is important in many industries, which poses challenges both for policy makers and economic agents.

This paper studies how political uncertainty affects rent seeking, and what level of political uncertainty is "optimal" for society. We find that under some conditions, a higher level of political uncertainty might be beneficial to discourage rent seeking. On the other hand, high risk aversion among the agents decreases the optimal level of uncertainty, as risk averse agents suffer a greater loss in utility from a high uncertainty. It is possible to find several areas where this analysis is relevant. For instance, in fisheries, increasing uncertainty about whether or not to implement (or extend) a pay-back scheme will reduce the incentive for fishermen to overinvest in vessels.

INTRODUCTION

In an important early paper, Kydland and Prescott (1977) analysed regulators' best strategies, laying the foundations for a large branch of literature concluding that, to minimise negative side effects, regulators should try to stick to objective rules and limit their own ability to deviate from these rules in the future. The applications for this approach seem endless. Kydland and Prescott used patent policy as an example. Policy makers have incentives to promote research by offering patents (i.e., monopolist profit) to inventors, yet

* E-mail: ojb@hib.no.

once the invention is made, they have incentives to open the market for normal competition to maximise the social benefit from the invention. Other important applications have been central bank policy (e.g., Barro and Gordon, 1983) and environmental policy (e.g., Gersbach and Glazer, 1999).

These areas seem far from natural resource economics, yet we see similar problems where commitment to rules or objectives does not necessarily solve the problem in agriculture, fisheries, and aquaculture. A commonly debated problem today is CO_2 emissions and quotas. Future quotas are bound to be affected, one way or the other, by current emissions. Hence, the regulations here create counter-productive incentives, i.e., to increase emissions before the quotas are introduced, in order to increase one's own share of the quotas in the future (e.g., Brandt, 2002).

An important area for these types of problems is fisheries. Each year, the EU Commission sets total allowable catches (TACs) for the maximum quantity of different species of fish that is allowed to be caught the following year. These TACs are allocated among member states as national quotas. When setting the size of the TAC, the EU Commission bases its decision on the advice from two expert committees, namely the internal Scientific, Technical and Economical Committee (STECF) and the International Council for the Exploration of the Sea (ICES). One year TACs implies a lot of uncertainly for the fishermen, e.g., given that investment in boats and equipment are long terms investment.

Uncertainty is further increased by ineffective (and to some extent unpredictable) enforcement effort. In the UK, for example, the Court of Justice ruled against the UK in 1999 and 2002 for infringements on the grounds of failure to carry out inspections and close fisheries once the catch quota had been taken. According to Nello (2005), too few EU inspectors without sufficient legal powers had to enforce legislation and proposals to increase the authority and the size of the EU supervision unit were generally rejected by the Council of Ministers.

For our study, it is particularly interesting that some future quotas for individuals/vessels are based on their past or current catches. To maximise future quotas, fishermen have incentives to maximise their current catch, thus effectively reducing the future stock. Also, governments have introduced buy-back programs for vessels to reduce the overcapacity in some fisheries. If fishermen expect that such programs might be repeated, they have incentives to invest in capacity today, thus undermining the objective of the program. This mechanism is probably one of the reasons why such programs have been less successful than expected (Wenninger and McConnell, 2000; Clark et al., 2005). These situations, at least at first sight, provide reasons to question whether governments should always try to reduce risk as this would seem to encourage rent seeking efforts. This is in a sense the main problem we will study in this paper.

Also in other, related industries we see similar problems. In aquaculture, there seem to be expectations that the government will bail out large producers in case of a crisis due to overproduction and low prices. If this expectation is widespread, it will lead to decreased risk aversion, higher investment and increased probability of a crisis. This is the same known moral hazard problem we have seen in banking in recent years – confidence that government in the end will bail out the large players gives these incentives to take on more risk, thus increasing the risk of a crisis.

In agriculture, we see the same pattern. In many countries, the industry is characterised by overproduction and (decreasing) subsidies, and to improve their bargaining position, farmers could have incentives to over-invest or otherwise act against the objectives of the policy maker. Again, we get the impression that rent seeking becomes easier and more profitable when the industry agents have high confidence about the government's future actions. Many of these examples are just anecdotal evidence to motivate the study of a link between political uncertainties and rent seeking. Nevertheless, they still suggest that the costs from rent seeking can be defined more broadly, such that they include all costs to society arising from "sub-optimal" regulation, where the non-optimality is caused by interference of potential stakeholders in the process of determining regulation.

From the literature we know that regulatory interference (and expectations thereof) can have negative side effects, both for individuals and for society at large, which consequently has led to the result that regulators should follow certain rules of thumb (as outlined by Kydland/Prescott) to reduce these side effects. The recommendation of Kydland/Prescott implies that political induced uncertainty should be reduced to a minimum. However, compared to the above results, this paper shows that political uncertainty, under certain conditions, can have a welfare increasing effect, since it reduces wasteful rent seeking effort. If increasing political uncertainty reduces costs to society by reducing rent seeking effort more than it increases costs to society from larger political uncertainty, then a positive level of political risk is desirable.

To understand this result, we have to look at rent seeking. Rent seeking is a common problem in most situations with regulation and regulatory risk. Rent seeking could be defined as actions with the purpose of influencing or taking advantage of regulatory decisions - actions that are both socially inefficient and would not be undertaken without the possibility of gaining from the regulations. These gains could come in the form of granted monopoly power, quotas or other benefits, or in the form of political decisions considered helpful for the rent-seeker.

In food production, it is easy to think of various kinds of rent seeking behaviour. In fisheries, the main issue is quotas. Rent seeking behaviour could be undertaken to increase one's own quota, compared to other competing fishermen, other vessel types, quotas of other species, and quotas in other countries. In aquaculture, rent seeking behaviour could be used for obtaining production licenses at good locations, or in the fight for favourable trade agreements. In many countries, agriculture is particularly prone to rent seeking behaviour, as a very large share of farmers' income comes from various forms of direct subsidies, grants and transfers from the government.

The theoretical literature on the economics of rent seeking is large and growing – see e.g. Lockard and Tullock (2001) for a review. One of the fundamental results is that firms will undertake rent seeking behaviour/lobbyism to maximise their expected utility. That is, they will spend resources on rent seeking behaviour as long as the expected utility of the investment is positive.

Tullock (1967) and Posner (1975) point out that becoming a monopolist is a competitive activity and hence the expected profit from obtaining the monopoly is zero. The mechanism is that each firm invests in rent seeking to the point where the last dollar spent equals the improved probability of obtaining the rent. The idea is that in order to obtain or maintain a monopoly (defend its position), it is necessary to engage in rent seeking expenditures. Total rent dissipation occurs when competition for rents is perfectly competitive. (In the words of Hillman (2003): "With complete dissipation, we can measure the social cost of rent seeking by the value of the rent that was the price in the rent seeking contest."). Other analysis suggests that the level of rent dissipation depends on types of assumptions. For our purpose, Boyce (1998) provided an analysis of rent seeking for a number of natural resources, concluding that a rent seeking model might be chosen over an open-access model because full rent dissipation will be more difficult.

Less work has been done on the *risk*[1] carried by the regulated firms and industries. Regulations and expected regulations might lead to changed decisions, but usually, one does not know whether or how the regulations will change in the future. On the one hand, this risk implies a cost for businesses. First, obviously, compared to the situation with certainty, they will make wrong/unprofitable decisions on a certain percentage of all occasions. Also, the presence of risk implies a direct loss of utility, as decision makers must be assumed to be risk averse. Some studies (e.g., Flaten et al., 2005 and Bergfjord, 2009) indicate that such regulatory risk is important for producers.

As the review above suggests, both rent seeking and political uncertainty have large potential consequences. One could arguable that political uncertainty is a necessary condition for rent seeking, and hence that too much political uncertainty leads to undesirable rent seeking. On the other hand, we will argue that total political certainty might not be optimal either. This could also increase rent seeking, thus implying some kind of trade-off between political uncertainty and rent seeking. Hence, it is interesting to study how this link works, and more normatively, what can be done to improve the regulations. These are the topics for the rest of this paper.

Some prior work has been done in this area. Most directly related to our problem are the papers of Hillman and Katz (1984); van Long and Vousten (1987); Konrad and Schlesinger (1997); Cornes and Hartley (2008); Yamazaki (2009); and Treich (2009), all of which analyse various types of rent seeking games with risk averse agents. Their general result, with different generality and under different assumptions, is that risk and risk aversion typically decreases rent seeking efforts. Among the related literature, Murphy et al. (1993) find that rent seeking has a negative effect on growth and investment, whereas Brunetti and Weber (1998) and references therein conclude that political uncertainty has a negative effect on investment. Skaperdas and Gan (1995) study how risk aversion affects the different agents' chances of winning a rent seeking contest and find that under limited liability, the more risk averse agent will always have a higher chance of winning. Otherwise, risk aversion will have no or ambiguous effects on the chance of winning. Finally, Bramoulle and Treich (2004) studied how uncertainty influences welfare and behaviour in the game of global pollution, and obtained the result that emissions will be lower with high uncertainty due to risk aversion and that uncertainty can in fact have a positive impact on the welfare of the risk averse polluters.

The rest of the paper is organised as follows: Section 2 presents the basic model, while section 3 introduces political risks. Section 4 presents the main result that under certain condition a positive level of political risk is optimal, and section 5 concludes the paper.

[1] In a Knightian sense (Knight, 1921), some of the issues we are discussing are primarily "risky", whereas others are primarily "uncertain". However, as the distinction between the two seems to be vague (if existent at all) in the modern literature, we do not differentiate between these terms.

MODEL

Assume n identical rent seekers who are equipped with the following utility function, which measures the expected utility for an individual from engaging in rent seeking activity:

$$U_i = p_i(x_i)\cdot u_i(R+I_i-x_i)+(1-p_i(x_i))\cdot u_i(I_i-x_i) \quad [1]$$

where I_i is the initial wealth of rent seeker i, p_i is the probability of "winning" for rent seeker i, i.e., that the rent seeking effort proves successful, R is the "prize" for successful rent seeking, and x is the rent seeking cost. All rent seekers solve the program:

$$\max_{x_i} U_i = p_i(x_i)\cdot u_i(R+I_i-x_i)+(1-p_i(x_i))\cdot u_i(I_i-x_i) \quad [2]$$

This approach makes it very complicated to derive the analytical result we are looking for.

We assume a simplification of this utility function given by

$$U_i = p_i(x_i)\cdot u_i(R+I_i)+(1-p_i(x_i))\cdot u_i(I_i)-x_i \quad [3]$$

That is, we let the utility function be quasi linear in x_i. Given this, we do not take into consideration how changes in x_i affects marginal utility, which is to say that we neglect the income effect coming from changes in x_i. Rather, we focus on the effect on the probability of winning of a change in x_i. This approach can be justified by assuming that x_i is (very) small compared to total welfare of the agents, which is usually the case.

Taking the other rent seekers' investments as given, this gives the following first order condition for optimal rent seeking behaviour of rent seeker i:

$$\frac{\partial U_i}{\partial x_i} = \frac{\partial p_i(x)}{\partial x_i}\cdot[u_i(R+I_i)-u_i(I_i)]-1=0 \quad [4]$$

We apply a commonly used contest success function (CSF), first used by Tullock (1980). A Contest Success Function (CSF) states each player's probability of winning as a function of all players' rent seeking effort, such that increased effort of one agent enhances its probability of winning. We here assume the following a linear technology:

$$p_i = \frac{x_i}{x_i+\sum_{j\neq i}^{n} x_j} \quad [5]$$

where n is the number of rent seekers. Due to the symmetry, we get the following expression (suppressing the subscripts for convenience):

$$\frac{\partial p}{\partial x} = \frac{1}{x} \cdot \frac{n-1}{n^2}. \qquad [6]$$

Substitute this into the above expression for $\partial U_i / \partial x_i$ and solving for the optimal level of rent seeking yields:

$$x^* = \frac{n-1}{n^2} \cdot [u(R-I) - u(I)] \qquad [7]$$

Hence, without any uncertainty about the size of the price, we get the following expression for the optimal level of rent seeking:[2]

$$\frac{\partial x^*}{\partial n} = (\frac{n^2 - 2n(n-1)}{n^4}) \cdot [u(R-I) - u(I)] < 0 \text{ for } n > 2. \qquad [8]$$

Introducing Risk

It has been shown by Hillman and Katz (1984) and Konrad and Schlesinger (2000) that risk aversion always leads to lower investment in rent seeking. The latter paper makes a distinction between rent seeking, where the investment affects the chance of winning, and rent augmenting, where the investment increases the potential price, and the picture is more ambiguous. We will focus on the first case, in which the investment increases the chance to win.

With risk averse agents the result is that higher risk aversion (or, as in our case, higher political uncertainty) leads to less rent seeking. However, higher risk (and/or risk aversion) also leads to less utility derived from any particular situation.

Hillman and Katz (1984), made an early contribution to the literature on risk and rent seeking, and Long and Vousten (1987) used their result to model the effect of uncertainty on rent seeking under certain realistic assumptions. The first assumption is that the rent to be achieved is relatively small compared to other wealth among the agents. While it is easy to imagine situations where this is not the case, in most cases, the rents related to any one particular investment are relatively small, as larger rent seeking scenarios often an be deconstructed into several smaller problems. The second assumption is that the number of potential rent seekers should be large. This is reasonable in most situations. Finally, the third assumption is that the prize has a fixed size, but that there is uncertainty about the share each rent seeker will receive. Given this, a smaller share of the rents are dissipated, and rent seeking decreases in risk aversion and variance, indicating that variance should be kept high to reduce social waste, as briefly mentioned by Long and Vousden. However, this ignores the effect on rent seekers.

[2] When talking about no risk here, we refer to a situation where no uncertainty about the size of the price from winning the contest exists. For the individual rent seeker, it still remains uncertain whether or not he/she wins the price, as described by the contest function.

To find the "optimal" level of political uncertainty, we would hence have to ask ourselves:

(1) Should all rent seeking efforts be considered waste, or only a percentage of them? We do not study this in detail, but it seems clear that the damage to society from $1 of rent seeking investments might differ between different situations.
(2) For what level of variance σ in the prize R will the benefits (smaller loss to society) be equal to the loss to rent seekers in terms of lost utility?

To study these questions further, we build on the general model from the previous chapter, and introduce political uncertainty to the model. It is assumed that the political uncertainty affects the prize (R). For this, assume that R is uniformly distributed over the range $[R^L, R^H]$, such that $E[R]=(R^L+R^H)/2$.

Now introduce a political uncertainty parameter $I_{PU} \geq 0$ where $I_{PU}=0$ implies no uncertainty and the political risk is increasing in I_{PU}.[3]

Consider the situation where:

$$\frac{\partial E[R]}{\partial I_{PU}}=0,\ \frac{\partial R^L}{\partial I_{PU}}<0,\ \frac{\partial R^H}{\partial I_{PU}}>0 \text{ and } \frac{\partial^2 R^H}{\partial (I_{PU})^2}=-\frac{\partial^2 R^L}{\partial (I_{PU})^2},$$

that is, a change in the political risk does not change the expected value of the prize, but changes the variance.[4] The utility function in the presence of uncertainty is now:

$$u_i = p_i(x)\cdot[p^L\cdot u(R^L(I_{PU})+I_i)+p^H\cdot u(R^H(I_{PU})+I_i)]-(1-p_i)u(I_i)-x_i \quad [9]$$

It follows that the optimal rent seeking as derived in equation 1 can be re-written as:

$$x^* = \frac{n-1}{n^2}\cdot[\ p^L\cdot u_i(R^L(I_{PU})+I_i)+p^H\cdot u_i(R^H(I_{PU})+I_i)]-(1-p_i)u(I_i) \quad [10]$$

and

$$\frac{\partial x^*}{\partial I_{PU}} = \frac{n-1}{n^2}\cdot[p^L\cdot\frac{\partial u_i}{\partial R^L}\cdot\frac{\partial R^L}{\partial I_{PU}}+p^H\cdot\frac{\partial u_i}{\partial R^H}\cdot\frac{\partial R^H}{\partial I_{PU}}] \quad [11]$$

[3] See Brunetti and Weder (2002), where different types of uncertainties are described.

[4] It follows that $\sigma^2(R)=\frac{1}{2}\sum_{R_i=\{R_L,R_H\}}(R_i-\bar{R})^2$, such that $\frac{\partial \sigma^2}{\partial I_{PU}}>0$.

Note that it must be that $\frac{\partial p_i(x)}{\partial I_{PU}} = 0$ because n is unchanged, and the relative contribution of the contenders also is unchanged.

It follows that, by using the assumption:

$$\text{that} - \frac{\partial R^L}{\partial I_{PU}} = \frac{\partial R^H}{\partial I_{PU}} \qquad [12]$$

It follows that:

$$sign\{\frac{\partial x^*}{\partial I_{PU}}\} = sign\{p^L \cdot \frac{\partial u_i}{\partial R^H} - p^H \cdot \frac{\partial u_i}{\partial R^L}\} \qquad [13]$$

Finally, given the assumption about the uncertainty:

$$\frac{\partial^2 x^*}{\partial (I_{PU})^2} = \frac{n-1}{n^2} \cdot [p^L \cdot \frac{\partial u_i}{\partial R^L} \cdot \frac{\partial^2 R^L}{\partial (I_{pu})^2} + p^L \cdot \frac{\partial^2 u_i}{\partial R^L \partial I_{pu}} \cdot \frac{\partial R^L}{\partial I_{pu}} + p^H \cdot \frac{\partial u_i}{\partial R^H} \cdot \frac{\partial^2 R^H}{\partial (I_{pu})^2} + p^H \cdot \frac{\partial^2 u_i}{\partial R^H \partial I_{pu}} \cdot \frac{\partial R^H}{\partial I_{pu}}] \qquad [14]$$
$$= \frac{n-1}{n^2} \cdot [p^L \cdot \frac{\partial^2 u_i}{\partial R^L \partial I_{pu}} \cdot \frac{\partial R^L}{\partial I_{pu}} + p^H \cdot \frac{\partial^2 u_i}{\partial R^H \partial I_{pu}} \cdot \frac{\partial R^H}{\partial I_{pu}}].$$

Since

$$p^L \cdot \frac{\partial u_i}{\partial R^L} \cdot \frac{\partial^2 R^L}{\partial (I_{pu})^2} + p^H \cdot \frac{\partial u_i}{\partial R^H} \cdot \frac{\partial^2 R^H}{\partial (I_{pu})^2} = 0 . \qquad [15]$$

It follows that

$$\frac{\partial^2 x^*}{\partial (I_{PU})^2} \gtreqless 0, \qquad [16]$$

depending on the size of P^L and P^H (Note that for $P^L = P^H$, $\frac{\partial^2 x^*}{\partial (I_{PU})^2} < 0$).

There are now two types of costs that the regulator has to consider when choosing the optimal level of political uncertainty. We use the standard result from microeconomics that the risk premium is positive if the agent is risk averse and increasing with the risk of the lottery. The behavior of the regulator is assumed to minimise the total costs coming from rent seeking, $n \cdot x^*(I_{PU})$, and the cost associated with risk averse agent action under uncertainty, measured by the total risk premium, $n \cdot \Pi(I_{PU})$ such that the costs that the regulator minimises are given by:

$$C(I_{PU}) = n \cdot x^*(I_{PU}) + n \cdot \Pi(I_{PU}), \qquad [17]$$

First order conditions for optimal choice political uncertainty:

$$\frac{\partial C(I_{PU})}{\partial I_{PU}} = n \cdot \frac{\partial x^*(I_{PU})}{\partial I_{PU}} + n \cdot \frac{\partial \Pi(I_{PU})}{\partial I_{PU}} = 0 \qquad [18]$$

Given the way political risk has been defined, it follows that:

$\frac{\partial \Pi(I_{PU})}{\partial I_{PU}} > 0$, and $\frac{\partial^2 \Pi(I_{PU})}{\partial (I_{PU})^2} > 0$. Moreover, as already derived, $\frac{\partial^2 x}{\partial (I_{PU})^2} = 0$.

With $I_{PU} \geq 0$ as defined above, it follows that the condition for the interior optimum is given by:

$$\frac{\partial^2 C(I_{PU})}{\partial (I_{pu})^2} > 0 \text{ and } \frac{\partial C(I_{PU})}{\partial (I_{PU})} = 0 \text{ for } I_{PU} \in \mathbb{R}_+. \qquad [19]$$

For the following, it is convenient to be more precise about the range of the political uncertainty parameter, I_{PU}. There might be several reasons why policy makers cannot freely change I_{PU}, or there might be bounds on I_{PU} (see also the discussion below). To capture this, let $I_{PU} \in [\underline{I}_{PU}(z); \overline{I}_{PU}(z)]$, where z is a vector of exogenous restrictions (conditions that restrict) on the range of the political uncertainty.

Because $x^*(I_{PU})$ is linear in I_{PU}, while $\Pi(I_{PU})$ is convex and increasing in I_{PU}, it is possible to identify a number of case to describe the optimal choice of I_{PU}.

(1) It is optimal to choose $I^*_{PU} > 0$ following the rule $\frac{\partial C(I^*_{PU})}{\partial I_{PU}} = 0$,

$$\text{if } \left|\frac{\partial x^*(I_{PU})}{\partial I_{PU}}\right|_{I_{PU}=0} > \left|\frac{\partial \Pi}{\partial I_{PU}}\right|_{I_{PU}=0} \text{ for } I^*_{PU} \in [\underline{I}_{PU}(z); \overline{I}_{PU}(z)]. \qquad [20]$$

(2) It is optimal to choose $I'_{PU} > 0$ where $I'_{PU} = \arg\min C(I_{PU})$ s.t. $I_{PU} \in [\underline{I}_{PU}(z); \overline{I}_{PU}(z)]$ if $\left|\frac{\partial x^*(I_{PU})}{\partial I_{PU}}\right|_{I_{PU}=0} > \left|\frac{\partial \Pi}{\partial I_{PU}}\right|_{I_{PU}=0}$ but

$$I^*_{PU} \notin [\underline{I}_{PU}(z); \overline{I}_{PU}(z)]. \qquad [21]$$

(3) It is optimal to choose $I_{PU} = 0$, if

$$\left|\frac{\partial x^*(I_{PU})}{\partial I_{PU}}\right|_{I_{PU}=0} \leq \left|\frac{\partial \Pi}{\partial I_{PU}}\right|_{I_{PU}=0}. \qquad [22]$$

We can identify three cases. Conventional wisdom suggests that reducing risk increases welfare. The first case, however, shows under what conditions an increase in the political risk increases welfare, when taking into consideration that increases in political risk reduces other types of distortions, in this case distortions from wasteful rent seeking activity. Such a case is shown in figure 1.

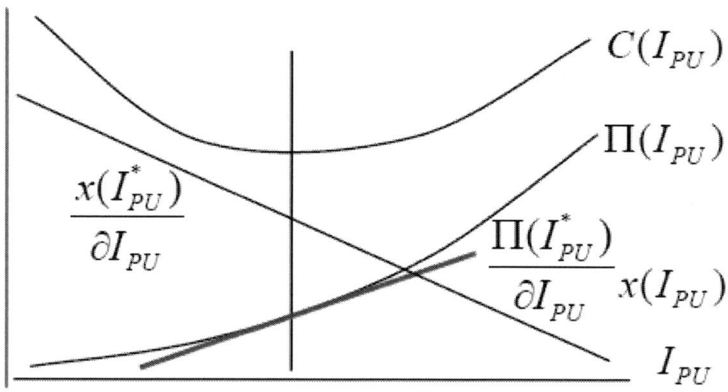

Figure 1. Choosing the level of political uncertainty I_{pu} that minimises the total costs C(I_{pu}).[5]

If we focus on situations where the first condition holds, this gives us the following comparative static result:

1. The more rent seeking decreases with increased political risk, the more "beneficial" is political risk (all else equal)
2. The more risk averse agents are, the more damaging is the political risk

The reason for 1) is that when the gain from an increase in I_{PU} increases in terms of reduced rent seeking, then, all else being equal, it is optimal to provide more political risk. The reason for 2) is that when the costs from increasing I_{PU} increase, it is optimal to provide less political risk. This could be due e.g., to an increase in the agents' risk aversion, since higher risk aversion means larger $\frac{\partial \Pi}{\partial I_{PU}}$ (for the same level of I_{PU}).

[5] In the figure, it is assumed that $\partial^2 x(I_{PU}) / \partial(I_{PU})^2 = 0$.

In the second case, it is also optimal to increase the political uncertainty. Although it cannot be excluded theoretically, one obvious bound could be that $R_L(I_{pu}) \geq 0$, i.e., a negative prize should not be possible. The possible restrictions and interpretations of I_{PU} are discussed further in the next section.

Finally, there are situations like the third case, where it is optimal to keep the political uncertainty as low as possible. This will happen in situations where the gain from increasing political uncertainty in terms of reduced rent seeking outlets cannot fully compensate for the higher loss in terms of increased risk premium, even for small levels of political uncertainty.

IMPLICATIONS

Having obtained these results, the next question is what implications they have for both policy makers and agents.

The variable to be controlled by policy makers here is I_{PU} - the level of political risk. Ideally, this uncertainty level should be kept at an optimal level, given the gains and losses outlined above. Obviously, other factors will also influence the chosen level. In particular, one might think that the need for future flexibility will always push up the political uncertainty. It is not possible, nor desirable, for a government to eliminate all political risk by stating that "No matter what happens in the future, we have set out this set of rules, and they will be kept like this forever." However, this can be taken into account when calibrating I_{PU}, such that $I_{PU} = 0$ is interpreted as "minimum political uncertainty, given these constraints". Also, changing the level of political uncertainty involves transaction costs. These are mainly ignored in our analysis, but it is clear that these could be substantial in real life, meaning that the optimal frequency and magnitude of such deliberate changes to the political uncertainty are likely to be relatively small.

Given all of this, it seems reasonable to assume that policy makers should try to set I_{PU} such that society's costs from political risk areminimised[6]. In practice, a precise adjustment of I_{PU} is of course impossible, but a reasonable rule of thumb is that efforts should be made to reduce uncertainty where I_{PU} is higher than optimal, whereas uncertainty could be introduced in various ways in situations where I_{PU} is too low.

To view the political uncertainty as a control variable to be "manipulated" by the government and not a fixed parameter that ought to be as low as possible is a new approach compared to most earlier literature. Our assumption that the level of uncertainty can be manipulated with great ease and precision is of course a simplification, but we argue that the government in fact should have considerable action space. If the present level of uncertainty is deemed to be too high, the government has several instruments available to decrease the risk. In some countries, a strengthened legal system might be necessary, including new laws limiting future government interference and more independent courts and judges. In other

---

[6] Here, we assume that politicians act rationally on society's behalf, and not rationally on their own personal or party's behalf.

countries, all it takes to decrease the perceived political uncertainty may be rhetorical changes, for instance by emphasizing political and regulatory stability as important objectives. Other measures include different insurance schemes, longer term contracts and longer term budgeting.

If the present level of uncertainty is deemed to be too low, some of the measures above could of course be reversed. Legislation could be changed to increase future flexibility; the rhetorical focus could be moved from stability to flexibility etc. In situations where the rent seeking efforts are likely to be pure losses to society, more uncertainty and less rent seeking is, *ceteris paribus,* likely to be beneficial to society. One example of this can be found in NILF (2006), which indicates that the total investment in Norwegian agriculture was at its lowest around the vote about Norwegian membership in the European Union – the result of which had large implications for future policy in Norway. As these investments on average yield very low or negative returns, this political uncertainty is likely to be beneficial to society both through reduced rent seeking and directly through reduced investment.

If we continue with this example, farmers are on the other hand typically quite risk averse (Flaten et al., 2005). This implies that increased uncertainty will be relatively costly for them in terms of utility. This utility loss will thus to some extent outweigh the social benefits from the increased utility.

If we study fishing and fish-farming, some of the "input variables" are different, yet the fundamental problem is the same. Fish farmers and fishers seem to be considerably less risk averse than farmers (Bergfjord, 2009; Eggert and Martinsson, 2004). This implies that the social cost of high uncertainty is less in these industries, and that, *ceteris paribus*, the optimal level of political uncertainty is higher.

Some of the political risk will be exogenous to the decision maker. This could for instance be the perception of legislation from the EU, or new international treaties. In such cases, it might be optimal for the national decision maker to counteract this by regulation of other types of risks to reduce the overall cost of society from such exogenous shocks.

CONCLUSION

In this paper, we have studied the link between political risk and rent seeking behaviour. In a simple model, we show that under some conditions (low risk aversion, high social costs of rent seeking) some political uncertainty is beneficial to society, as it reduces the agents' optimal level of rent seeking efforts. Political uncertainty will, however, always impose a cost on (risk averse) agents by lowering their utility.

We assume that governments to some extent can control the level of political uncertainty, either by committing to future actions or, more subtly, by always acting in accordance with the agents' expectations. Even though it might be impossible to exactly calculate the optimal uncertainty level in every situation – and even more so to actually reach it – this means that governments should be aware of this trade-off. In situations where agents are risk averse, and rent seeking is uncommon and/or not very costly to society, governments should try to eliminate as much of the political uncertainty as possible. On the other hand, if rent seeking is common and costly, and agents are more risk-tolerant, reducing the political uncertainty might in fact reduce the total social benefits. In terms of robustness, the main mechanism behind our argument is that the rent seekers will invest as long as the net benefit from doing so is positive. Given risk aversion, when uncertainty is increased, rent seeking investments will be reduced as net benefit is reduced. In this respect, our result is robust since any mean-preserving but risk enhancing situation will imply a reduction in (wasteful) rent seeking investment. Konrad and Schlesinger (1997) find that rent aversion unambiguously reduces rent seeking expenditures in a competitive market, but this result is not necessarily robust when agents are acting strategically.

At this stage, it is also worthwhile to point out possible extensions and further research. While our model simply assumes that the political uncertainty affects the variance of the prize, it would be interesting to explore situations where the political uncertainty affects other variables, for instance the probabilities of winning, the number of contestants, the size of the prize, or some combination of these. Although the general trade-off between risk and rent seeking would remain the same, the models and specific results would provide additional insights about the robustness of our results in this paper. Additionally, using different assumptions and comparing the normative model results with actual behaviour from both regulators and agents could give new knowledge about how political uncertainty in reality affects rent seeking, i.e., which of our assumptions are closest to reality.

Finally, it is clear that uncertainty in these situations in reality goes both ways. Governments impose uncertainty on (potential) rent seekers through their policies, but the uncertainty for rent seekers also introduces uncertainty for the government as to how common rent seeking will be, which in turn makes it more difficult for governments to implement optimal policies. We have only studied the uncertainty imposed by government on rent seekers, and an interesting extension could be to include the risk faced by governments in a similar model.

Our paper addresses both the issue of rent seeking and the direct cost to society from (political) risk. By properly manipulating the political risk, the overall cost to society from such risk is minimised. Ideally, since the decision maker addresses two distinct problems, a first best policy would involve using two distinct instruments. That is, if there existed a policy that could be optimally tailored toward the rent seeking problem, then it logically follows that the political risk should be set to zero. However, it is difficult to find such instruments for at least two reasons. First, it is difficult to restrain rent seeking without compromising the benefits from a free competitive market, and secondly, it is, as noted by e.g., Hillman (2003), difficult to observe rent seeking activity directly.

Finally, it is worth pointing out that most of the situations where rent seeking is a problem, and where some positive level of political risk could be beneficial, are a result of underlying problems. These could be "natural" causes of a market failure (for instance, well defined property rights to fish would solve some of these problems within fisheries, yet such rights are difficult to establish). Other such problems are policy created because other objectives have been considered more important than pure economic considerations. For instance, rent seeking would be less common in agriculture without subsidies, and less common in aquaculture if trade was free. While Kydland and Prescott (1977), stated that rules are better than discretion, one could hence say that our proposition is that discretion (uncertainty) in some cases might be better than bad rules.

REFERENCES

Barro, R.J. and Gordon, D.B., 1983. A Positive Theory of Monetary Policy in a Natural Rate Model, *Journal of Political Economy*, 91(4): 589-610.

Bergfjord, O.J., 2009. Risk perception and risk management in Norwegian aquaculture, *Journal of Risk Research*, 12(1): 91-104.

Boyce, J.R., 1998. Rent seeking in natural resource quota allocations, *Public Choice*, 96: 271-94.

Bramoullé, Y. and Treich, N., 2004. Can Uncertainty Alleviate the Commons Problem?, *Working Paper, LEERNA-INRA, University of Toulose*, France.

Brandt,U.S., 2002. Actions prior to entering an international environmental agreement, *Journal of Institutional and Theoretical Economics,* 158: 695-714.

Brunetti, A. and Weber, B., 1998. Investment and Institutional Uncertainty: A Comparative Study of Different Uncertainty Measures, *Weltwirtschaftliches Archiv,* **134:** 513–33.

Clark, C.W., Munro, G.R., and Sumaila, U.R., 2005. Subsidies, buybacks and sustainable fisheries, *Journal of Environmental Economics and Management*, 50: 47-58.

Cornes, R. and Hartley, R., 2008. Risk aversion in symmetric and asymmetric contests, *University of Manchester Economics Discussion Paper, EDP-0806.*

Eggert, H. and Martinsson, P., 2004. Are Commercial Fishers Risk-Lovers?, *Land Economics*, 80 (4): 550-60.

Flaten, O., Lien, G., Koesling, M., Valle, P.S. and Ebbesvik, M., 2005. Comparing risk perceptions and risk management in organic and conventional dairy farming: empirical results from Norway, *Livestock Production Science*, 95: 11–25.

Gersbach, H. and Glazer, A., 1999. Markets and Regulatory Hold-Up Problems, *Journal of Environmental Economics and Management*, 37: 151-64.

Hillman, A.L., and Katz., E., 1984. Risk averse rent seekers and the social cost of monopoly power, *The Economic Journal*, 94: 104-10.

Hillman A.L, 2003. *Public Finance and Public Policy: Responsibilities and Limitations of Government*, Cambridge University Press, Cambridge.

Knight, F.H., 1921. *Risk, uncertainty and profit*, University of Chicago Press, Chicago.

Konrad, K.A. and Schlesinger, H., 1997. Risk Aversion in Rent seeking and Rent-Augmenting Games, *The Economic Journal*, 107: 1671-83.

Kydland, F.E. and Prescott, E.C., 1977. Rules rather than discretion: the inconsistency of optimal plans, *Journal of Political Economy*, 85: 473-91.

Lockard, A.A. and Tullock, G., 2001. *Efficient Rent seeking: Chronicle of an Intellectual Quagmire*, Kluwer Academic Publishers, Boston, USA.

Long, N.V. and Vousden, N., 1987. Risk averse rent seeking with shared rents, *The Economic Journal*, 97: 971-85.

Nello, S.S., 2005, *The European Union: Economics, Policies and History*, McGraw- Hill Education, Berkshire, UK.

NILF, 2006. http://www.nilf.no/Totalkalkylen/Bm/2006/BMposter/BM_R_340A.shtml.

Posner, R.A., 1975. The social costs of monopoly and regulation *Journal of Political Economy,* 83: 807-27.

Riley, J.G., 2000. Asymmetric contests: A resolution of the Tullock paradox. In Howitt, P., de Antoni, E., and Leijonhufvud, A. (eds), *Money, Markets, and Methods: Essays in Honour of Robert W. Clower*. Edward Elger, Cheltenham.

Skaperdas, S. and Gan, L., 1995. Risk Aversion in Contests, *The Economic Journal,* 105: 951-62.

Treich, N., 2009. Risk aversion and Prudence in Rent seeking Games, *Discussion paper.*

Tullock, G., 1967. The welfare costs of tariffs, monopolies and theft *Western Economic Journal,* 5: 224–32.

Weninger, Q. and McConnell, K.E., 2000. Buyback programs in commercial fisheries: efficiency versus transfers, *Canadian Journal of Economics*, 33(2): 394-412.

Yamazaki, T., 2009. The uniqueness of pure-strategy Nash equilibrium in rent seeking games with risk averse players, *Public Choice*, 139(3): 335-42.

In: Understanding Risk
Editor: Matthias Beck
ISBN: 978-1-62618-686-6

Chapter 5

CORPORATE GOVERNANCE DISCLOSURE AND ITS EFFECTS ON PERFORMANCE AND PROFITABILITY

***Tristan Nguyen*[1] *and Natalie Djodat*[2]**
[1]Department of Economics, WHL Graduate School of Business and Economics, Hohbergweg Lahr/Schwarzwald, Germany
[2]Former Researcher with the United Nations Conference on Trade and Development, Palais des Nations, Geneva, Switzerland

ABSTRACT

In this paper, we examine the level of disclosure on corporate governance practices among the biggest companies (in terms of market capitalization) in the top five emerging markets Brazil, China, India, Korea and Russia in the time period 2007-2008 and its effects on performance and profitability. Reviewing the *UNCTAD* (2008) report on corporate governance disclosure in emerging markets and testing it against financial indicators and theories we find that – ceteris paribus – the rate of disclosure: (1) is higher for companies in Brazil and India compared to Russia and Korea; (2) is higher for companies operating in financial services compared to other sectors; (3) correlates positively with return on equity; (4) does not affect market valuation; (5) increases with the legal environment, (6) increases with the market infrastructure. The results of this paper support theoretical arguments that corporate governance disclosure increases performance, measured by return on equity. However, it disproves theories that find a positive correlation with market valuation, measured by price to book ratio. A country's government environment – especially legal and market infrastructure - highly affect the companies' rate of disclosure which then increases profitability. To policy makers and practitioners, the results suggest that corporate governance should be monitored. Good legislation and a market environment free from corruption are essential for corporate governance disclosure to be efficient.

---

[1] Prof. Dr. TRISTAN NGUYEN is chairholder at the Department of Economics, WHL Graduate School of Business and Economics, Hohbergweg 15-17, 77933 Lahr/Schwarzwald, Germany, e-mail: tristan.nguyen@whl-lahr.de.
[2] NATALIE DJODAT, M.Sc., B.A., worked as a researcher at the United Nations Conference on Trade and Development, Palais des Nations, Geneva, Switzerland, in 2008.

Keywords: Corporate governance, disclosure, emerging markets, transparency, price to book ratio, return on equity, governance environment

Corporate Governance and Performance

Corporate governance refers to the structures and relationships that determine the way in which an enterprise is controlled, administered or directed. A wave of corporate scandals in recent years (*Enron*, *WorldCom*, *Parmalat…*) has shown how important good corporate governance is. Some economists (*Diamond* and *Verrecchia*, 1991) suggest that greater disclosure of corporate governance lowers information asymmetry and estimation risk. Corporate governance disclosure should improve financial performance and raise investor confidence. Thus, firm performance and governance should be well communicated to outside investors and stakeholders in order to create information symmetry. Previous research studying the elements and effects of corporate governance in general and specifically in emerging markets documents a number of interesting, in-depth, yet sometimes questionable studies, providing insights in effects and effectiveness of disclosure.

The McKinsey Quarterly (*Newell* and *Wilson*, 2002) published a study examining the association between good practices corporate governance and market valuation in 2002 arguing that corporate governance disclosure improves companies' financial performance and increases their market valuation, reduces risks and raises investor confidence. The study compares the level of corporate governance from India, Malaysia, Mexico, South Korea, Taiwan and Turkey and their market valuation measured by its price to book ratio. The companies' price to book ratio on the local stock exchange is compared to some key components of corporate governance like independence, shareholder equality and financial transparency.

The main outcome of this study is that corporate governance is positively associated with price to book ratios indicating investors' willingness to pay a higher premium for shares in well governed companies in emerging markets. The findings indicate a 12% increase in market valuation by moving from worst to best score in corporate governance disclosure. Moreover, their survey shows that countries like South Korea and Malaysia performed much better than India, Mexico and Turkey. The article explains this outcome by the Asian companies' effort to improve their corporate governance resulting from the 1997 Asian crisis and the country's increasing requirements regarding corporate governance disclosure.

Standards and Poor's (*Patel*, *Balic* and *Bwarkira*, 2002) published a survey studying the effects of corporate governance disclosure (ownership structure, financial transparency, board and management structure) in 19 emerging markets documenting significant differences among countries. Transparency in Asian and South African markets was much better in comparison to Latin America, Eastern Europe and the Middle East. However, no differences among business sectors are found. Furthermore, the survey indicates that the correlation between transparent disclosure and cross-holdings is negative. This means that less information disclosed to minority shareholders if large investors own a large proportion of the company. The correlation to price to book ratio is positive, suggesting a higher premium paid by the market for better disclosure - in line with *Newell* and *Wilson's* findings.

In 2004, the World Bank (*Klapper* and *Love*, 2004) initiated a survey about corporate governance, investor protection, and performance in emerging markets. The overall result of that survey was that good governance positively correlates with market valuation, measured in price to book ratio, and operating performance, measured in return on assets, whereas those correlations are even stronger in countries with weak legal systems. One possible explanation for this might be the assumption that firms in countries with weak legal structures would want to adopt better firm level governance in order to counterbalance the weakness in their country's laws and signal their intention to offer greater investor rights. The survey moreover indicates that in general, firms in countries with weak legal systems disclose less information, which might be due to the assumption that weak legal systems decrease effectiveness of disclosure practices.

A study by *Chen* (2004) examines the effects of corporate governance using the data of a survey on corporate governance by Credit Lyonnais Securities Asia. They find that a high level of disclosure can significantly lower the cost of equity, whereas this relationship is only significant in countries with weak investor protection. Comparing their findings to a country's governance environment they conclude that firm-level protection and country level protection are substitutes to each other when assessing the cost of equity. Chen concludes by stressing the importance of legal systems regulating and controlling disclosure in order to make corporate governance disclosure effective.

Reviewing literature regarding corporate governance disclosure in emerging markets it becomes clear that the associations between levels of corporate governance disclosure, profitability and performance, the country level of legal protection of investors, ratings as well as the proportion of required and regulatory disclosure are not only highly relevant but also to a certain extent ambiguous matters to discuss and analyze. Most of the studies reviewed provide information on disclosure practices concentrating on specific markets and areas of disclosure, however, are relatively; moreover the benchmark is often not clearly defined. Recognizing this deficit in the literature, this paper provides a transparent up-to-date review of the disclosure practices of the top ten companies in the five biggest emerging markets (BRIC countries and Korea) in 2005 to 2010 and their compliance with UNCTAD good practices in corporate governance disclosure, especially during the financial crisis. Furthermore, the companies' disclosure practices are compared with certain indicators like return on equity, price to book ratio, voluntary disclosure as well as the countries' governance environment.

METHODOLOGY

The purpose of this paper is to analyze practices in corporate governance disclosure in five emerging markets.

First we review the data found in the *UNCTAD* 2008 report on corporate governance disclosure, which considers a sample of 50 companies of the top five emerging markets according to the MSCI Emerging Markets Index is considered: the ten biggest companies (ranked in terms of market capitalization) in Brazil, China, India, Russia and Korea. These 50 companies represent 38% of the whole index's market capitalization in 2009 (938 companies). The benchmark used is the UNCTAD publication "Guidance on Good Practices in Corporate

Governance Disclosure" in 2006, which organizes a total of 53 individual disclosure items into five broad categories: ownership structure and the exercise of control rights, financial transparency and information disclosure, auditing, corporate responsibility and compliance, board and management structure and process.

We then compare the companies' disclosure practices to the two financial indicators price to book ratio and return on equity as well as the countries' governance environment.

Ownership Structure and Exercise of Control Rights

The control and ownership structure of an enterprise is a fundamental concern from a governance perspective in order to facilitate investment decisions with regard to the treatment of shareholders and thus should be disclosed according to UNCTAD (2006) and many other guidelines around the world. A good understanding of the company's ownership and control is particularly important to help understand corporate governance risks. On the most basic level, information on the ownership structure tells us whether the company is widely or closely held. The governance risks associated with a widely held company are quite different from those associated with a closely held company. In a closely held company, minority shareholders may run governance risks associated with the actions of a dominant shareholder. On the other hand, in a widely held company, governance risks tend to be associated with strong managers and dispersed owners.

On average 42 of the 50 companies surveyed disclosing their ownership structure. This outcome was expected as it is of major importance for shareholders or potential investors to be informed about the major shareholders and one of the basic disclosure items. In India, every single one of the 10 companies surveyed concretely made these disclosures. Important changes in large shareholdings, particularly when they reach, exceed, or fall below certain thresholds, should also be disclosed. However, only 35 of the 50 companies surveyed disclosed changes in shareholding that occurred over the past years.

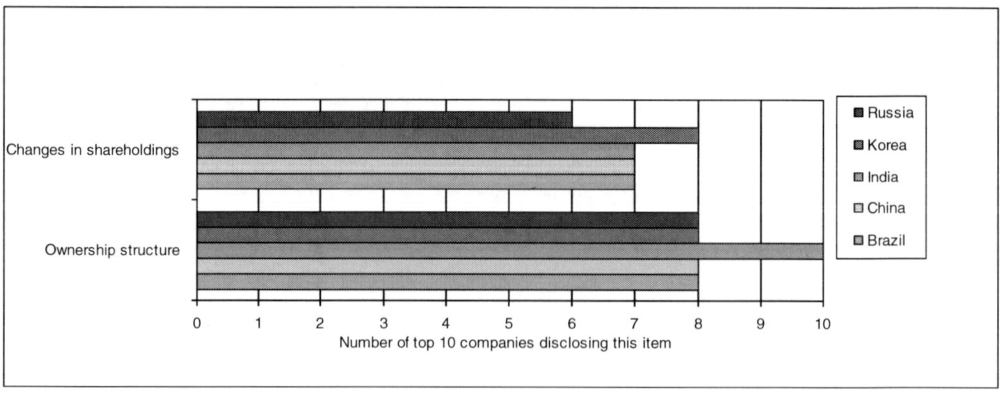

Figure 1. Ownership Structure and Changes in Shareholdings.
Source: UNCTAD (2008)

Different ownership structures may bestow different rights and obligations upon owners. Especially minority shareholders would be interested in any differences between voting rights and ownership that may occur because of, for example, different classes of shares owned by shareholders or arrangements under which certain shareholders have a degree of control disproportionate to their equity ownership. The International Corporate Governance Network strongly supports the "one share one vote" approach due to the fact that it leads to a transparent decision making process among shareholder and decreases investment risk, however, the OECD does not count among advocates of this approach. There are many examples of mechanisms that provide disproportionate control. Common examples are golden shares with special rights, or different share classes with different rights, or as a result of voting caps or special shareholder agreements.

It may, for example, not be possible for a minority shareholder to fully vote his stake in the company due to voting limits, or it may be that voting is irrelevant because the ownership structure puts control fully in the hands of a dominant shareholder. It is in the interest of shareholders to be aware of the ownership structure of the company and the rights of different owners, since they will have a direct impact on their ability to assert their own claims.

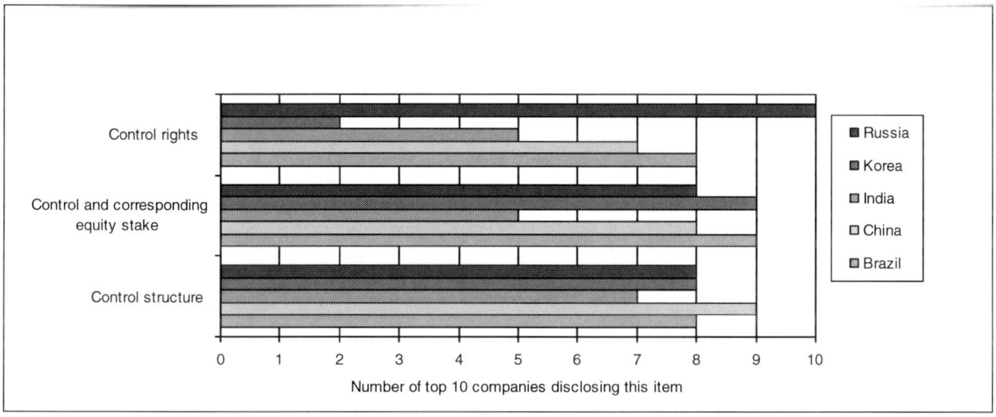

Figure 2. Control Structure, Rights and Equity Stake.
Source: UNCTAD (2008)

Sixty-four percent of the companies surveyed published in-depth information about their shareholders' rights. Every single Russian company we surveyed disclosed this kind of information, but only two of the 10 Korean companies did so – even though the disclosure of this item is mandatory according Korean regulations. Four of the 10 Korean companies surveyed are listed on the NYSE which also requires this item.

General meetings are the principal opportunity for shareholders to involve themselves in the decisions of the enterprise and should - according to the OECD principles – make shareholder participation as simple and effective as possible in order to reach consensus and for shareholders to exercise monitoring and control. Central to the organization of the meeting and shareholder participation is the meeting notice and the agenda. Both must be easily available to shareholders in order for them to participate effectively.

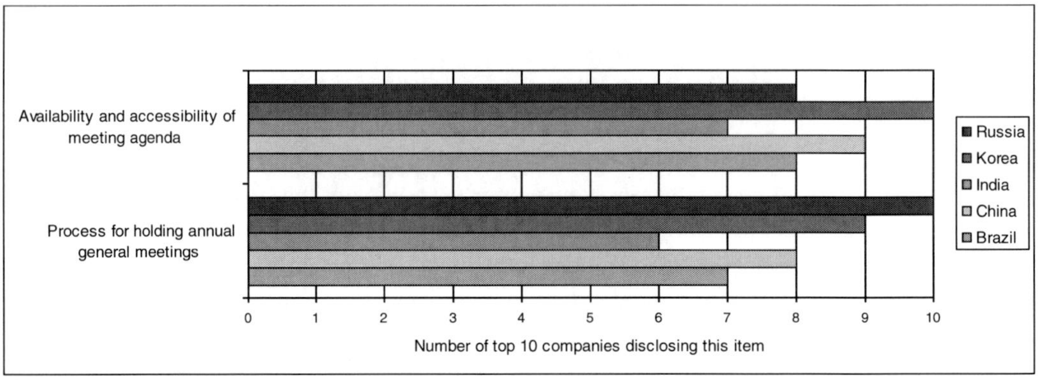

Figure 3. Annual General Meetings.
Source: UNCTAD (2008)

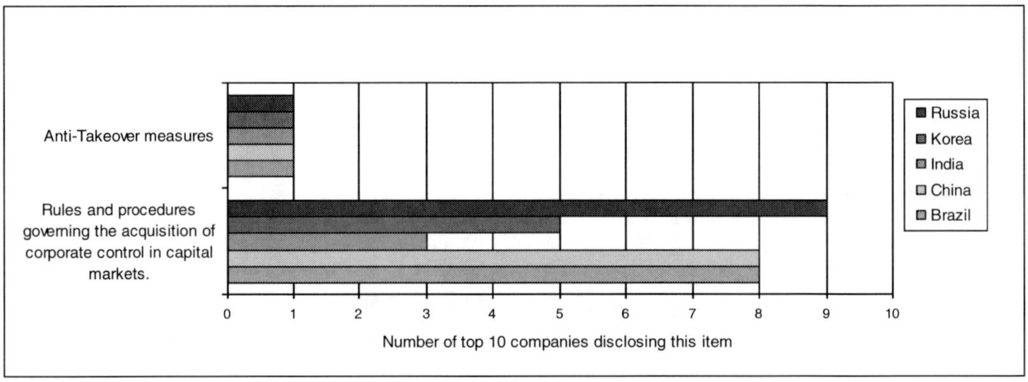

Figure 4. Anti Takeover Measures and Corporate Control.
Source: UNCTAD (2008)

The process by which the enterprise organizes an annual general meeting or extraordinary general meeting is typically found in the company's articles. Almost all of the companies surveyed publish information about the process of holding their annual general meeting and its agenda. Russia, Korea and China showed the best results in this category.

For shareholders it is important to know the rules and procedures for assuming control of an enterprise on the open market so that they understand their rights should such an event occur. The applicable laws of the country in which the enterprise is based usually determine these rules and procedures. But, any rules and procedures that are specific to the enterprise and the particular transaction should also be publicly known. Only 33 of the 50 companies surveyed published this kind information. However, important differences among countries can be noticed with respect to this item. Whereas only three of the 10 Indian companies disclosed this item, 9 out of the 10 Russian companies did so. There is no logical explanation for the weak Indian disclosure concerning this matter, especially the fact that this item is required both by Indian regulations and by the NYSE where two of the surveyed Indian companies are listed.

One of the two least disclosed items are Anti-takeover measures. These are actions that an enterprise can take to prevent a controlling interest in the enterprise from being acquired. Anti-takeover measures can be used legitimately in shareholders' interest to maximize the value of takeover bids. However, they can also be used to entrench management to the detriment of shareholders, and to destroy shareholder value. Anti-takeover measures come in many different forms and often carry evocative names like poison pills (the right to purchase discounted stock for everyone but the acquirer). Only 5 of the 50 companies disclosed information about any anti takeover measures, even though this item is required in four of the five countries examined (all except India). Paradoxically one of the few companies that disclosed this item is from India (Infosys Technologies) and not listed on the NYSE, thus voluntarily disclosing this rare information.

When examining the overall results regarding the disclosure of ownership structure and control rights we find that the 50 companies surveyed disclosed seven out of nine items of this group on average. When not considering the disclosure of anti takeover measures 80% of this group of items is properly disclosed by the 50 companies, which is a meaningful result. This could be due to the fact that nearly all the items (except anti takeover measures in India and equity stake in Russia) are required by both national regulations and the NYSE (UNCTAD, 2007).

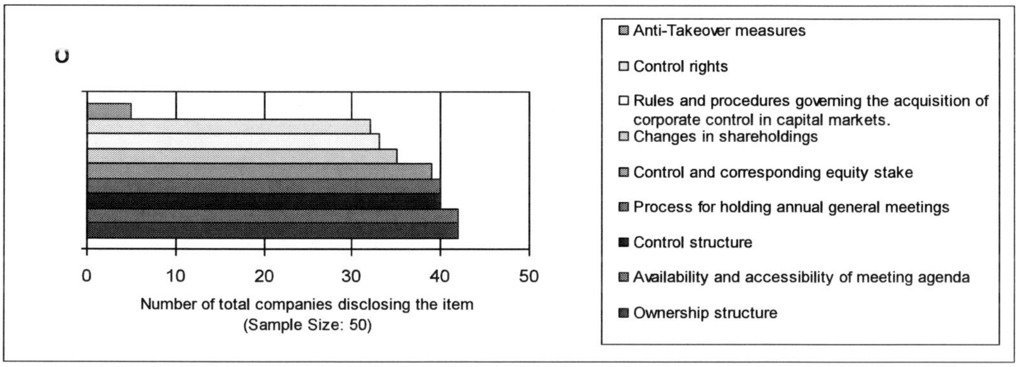

Figure 5. Group of Items: Ownership Structure and Exercise of Control Rights.
Source: UNCTAD (2008)

Financial Transparency

One of principle underpinnings of good corporate governance is to ensure that share- and stakeholders are provided with disclosure on financial and operating results in order to understand the current state of affairs. Those can be found both in annual reports and filings, should include financial statements including a balance sheet, a profit and loss statement, a cash flow statement and notes, director's reports, management's discussion and analysis. This information is requested by almost all corporate governance codes such as the OECD Guidelines or the International Corporate Governance Network Principles. The quality of financial disclosure, however, highly depends on the reporting standards and accounting principles of the country. The International Financial Reporting Standards (IFRSs) provide a widely recognized benchmark concerning the quality of this disclosure item.

Moreover, critical accounting estimates should be disclosed in order to increase the usefulness of the disclosure of operating results. Those are estimates and assumptions that are essential to understanding the financial statements, and which involve significant judgments and uncertainties. Critical accounting estimates disclosures may, for example, include a discussion of the accounting treatment of revenue recognition on long-term contracts, accounts receivable, inventory; investments, goodwill, pension and post-retirement benefit accounting, accruals and other factors that may materially affect the financial statements.

In addition, companies should disclose the impact of alternative accounting policies and decisions in their financial statements. The disclosure may include a discussion of the effects of critical accounting policies, the judgments made in their application, and the likelihood of materially different results if different assumptions were to be used. Moreover, board's responsibilities regarding financial communications, i.e. duties in the oversight of the process of producing, reviewing, approving, and submitting the financial statements to the shareholders should be disclosed in order to give investors a better understanding of the risks they are taking in relying on the management (i.e. audit committee formed by directors) and the accurateness of the presentation of financial results.

49 of the 50 companies surveyed perfectly disclosed their financial and operating results. This result was expected as financial information should be found in any annual report and is essential for shareholders to evaluate a company's performance.

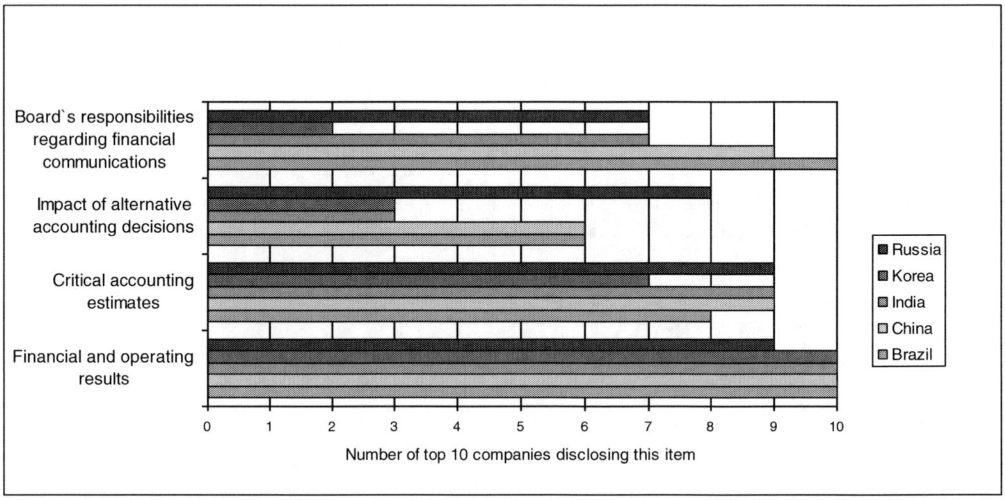

Figure 6. Financial Disclosure.
Source: UNCTAD (2008)

Critical accounting estimates were disclosed by 42 of the 50 companies, whereas the impact of alternative accounting decisions only by 26. One might think that this is due to the fact that the latter item is required by neither Brazilian nor Russian regulations, but the countries in which companies disclosed the least information concerning this item are actually India and Korea. Again, results among the five countries differ. Especially the ten Korean companies disclose very little financial information.

Given the significant potential for conflict of interest, there is a special obligation to ensure that related party transactions occur transparently and are subject to public examination (required by most national reporting standards and IFRS). Companies typically have procedures to ensure that related party transactions occur at "arm's length". Arms length transactions between two related or affiliated parties are conducted as if they were unrelated, so that there is no question of a conflict of interest, any prejudice or harm of the enterprise. A related party can be a division or subsidiary of an enterprise, a joint venture, any enterprise or person related to a major shareholder or member of management, or any enterprise in which the reporting enterprise has control or a significant financial stake.

Companies usually have procedures in place for approving related party transactions. The aim of this type of disclosure is to assure that the company is acting upon the best interest of all share- and stakeholders in the oversight of the quality of all related party transactions. Moreover the board of directors has to make sure that all affiliated entities and subsidiaries have been properly consolidated and presented.

Furthermore the occurrence of extraordinary transactions, and also the rules and procedures for approving extraordinary business transactions, such as mergers, a sale of a substantial portion of the company, or the liquidation or dissolution of the enterprise should be disclosed. Extraordinary transactions typically require approval by a vote of the shareholders and may even require a supermajority to approve them. 47 of the 50 companies disclosed information about related party transactions, but only 19 actually described the decision making process of approving those transactions. Procedures governing extraordinary transactions, however, were explained much more often. In this section we also notice country specific differences.

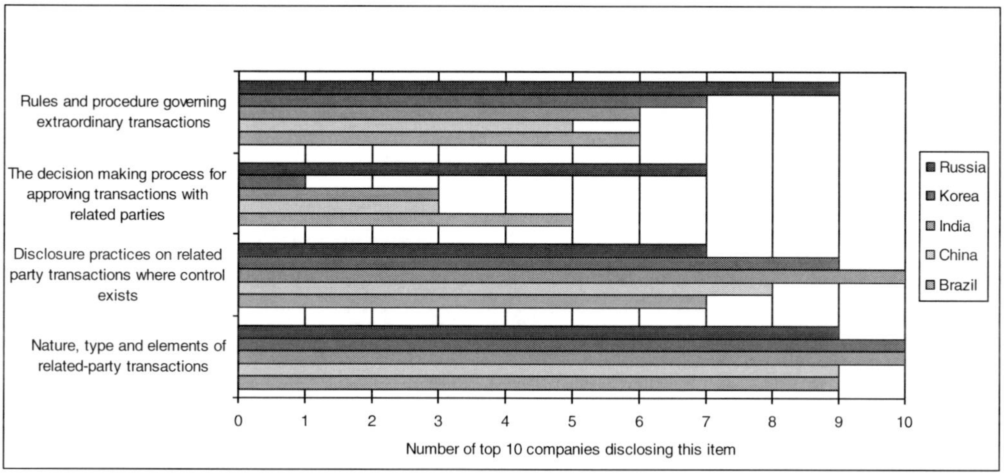

Figure 7. Disclosure of Related Party/Extraordinary Transactions.
Source: UNCTAD (2008)

Korean companies showed very weak disclosure regarding the approval of related party transactions even though regulations concerning this matter are very strict in Korea (the Corporations Code of Korea for example requires a special resolution for transactions that possibly result in a sale of a substantial part of the enterprise). Russia on the other hand showed very good results, especially when considering the fact that the disclosure of related party transaction is not required by Russian regulations (however disclosed by nine out of ten companies).

Auditing

Another fundamental pillar of good governance is the independent external audit. Shareholders rely fundamentally upon the auditor's assurances that the financial statements of the enterprise truly reflect the company's state of affairs. In the absence of the external independent auditor, the statements of an enterprise would be of questionable value. Typically, the independent auditor is paid by the company and works closely with its management and personnel in the audit of the company's financial statements. At the same time, the auditor owes its ultimate allegiance to the corporation's stockholders and creditors, as well as to the investing public. Ensuring that the auditor is objective and independent of the company and its management, and capable of providing reliable assurances on the veracity of a company's financial statements is of great importance given the potential consequences of a false presentation of the company's affairs. Thus, much attention is paid to the procedures employed to ensure the auditor's independence and the rendering of an unbiased opinion on the financial statements.

An important complement to the work of the independent external auditor is that of the internal auditor. The internal audit brings a systematic, disciplined approach to evaluate and improve the effectiveness of risk management and control within the company. The internal audit differs from the external audit in that it is an internal consulting activity designed to improve a company's operations through an independent, impartial evaluation and assurance process. Most companies report on the procedures for appointing both internal and external auditors and the procedures they have to ensure that the external auditor remains independent. Disclosures including the identity of the external auditor, how they are selected and appointed, and the processes of interaction with both internal and external auditor are often combined.

In addition to appointment and responsibilities of auditor, the duration of auditor's contracts, the rotation of audit partners (it is important to note the difference between audit partner rotation and audit firm rotation. Audit partner rotation only requires the audit partner to change, while audit firm rotation requires the company to regularly change the audit provider), the auditors' involvement in non-audit work (like advisory services or technical support functions) and fees paid to auditors should be disclosed in order to help ascertain the extent to which a threat to the auditor's independence exists. Furthermore, most companies have internal control systems that help ensure the smooth flow of operations, and provide assurances regarding the reliability of financial reporting and management information systems. Often, the internal auditor reviews the internal control systems and reports on what they find to the board.

We note large differences among countries as well as many shortfalls with respect to the disclosure of external audit services. Even though the appointment and interaction with external auditors was disclosed by 43 and 34 companies, only 19 of the 50 companies disclosed statements expressing their confidence in the auditor's independence and integrity and only 22 mentioned the duration of the current auditors.

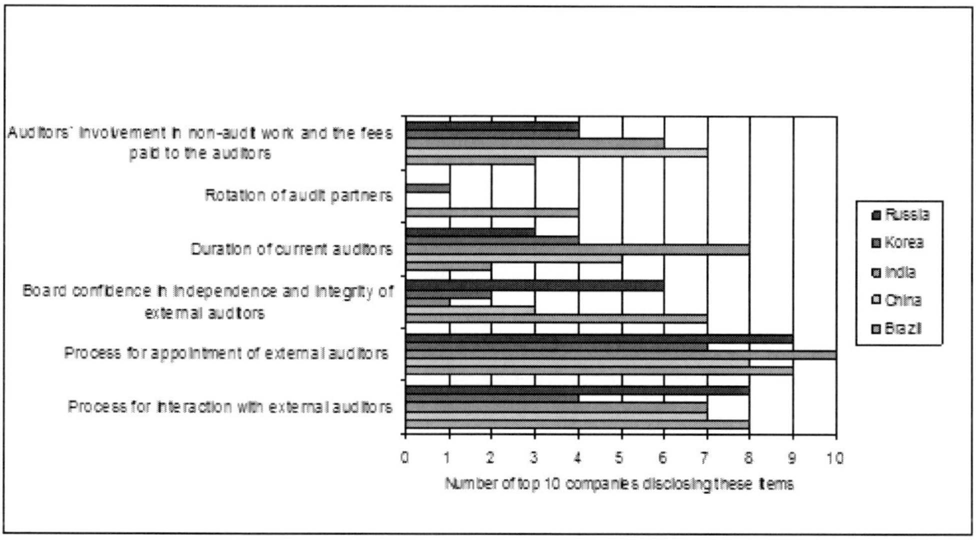

Figure 8. External Audit.
Source: UNCTAD (2008)

The best performing country concerning the disclosure of the auditors' duration is Brazil; eight out of ten companies surveyed disclosed this information. This might be because of the fact that nine out of ten Brazilian companies surveyed are listed on the NYSE and thus required to disclose this item. Many governance codes require regular rotations of the audit partners; only five of the surveyed companies (four Brazilian and one Korean Company) disclosed whether they had these kinds of processes. The fees paid to auditors as well as their involvement in non audit services were very poorly disclosed, even though required by Brazilian, Indian and Korean regulations.

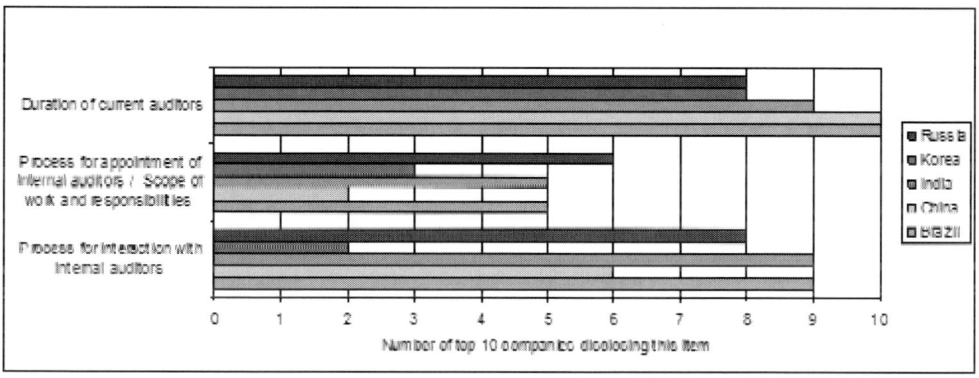

Figure 9. Internal Audit and Control.
Source: UNCTAD (2008)

The disclosure of internal audit and control systems shows better results, however, only on average. 45 of the companies surveyed disclose their internal control systems, only 21 informed about the appointment and the responsibilities of their internal audit. Again, China and Korea performed very poorly. Only three of the Korean companies disclosed information concerning their internal audit, even though required by the Korean Code of corporate governance.

Corporate Responsibility and Compliance

A company uses different resources in the production of goods and services. These include capital, human resources, other goods and services, and property. Companies generally seek to optimize the use of each production input in order to make the best product or service at the best price. However, unlike a commodity, the optimal use of some production factors such as, for example, human resources, depends to a large extent on their fair and responsible treatment. Human resources when managed properly have the capacity to bestow significant competitive advantage to companies; unlike any other factor input, well-managed human resources have the capacity to think, innovate and solve problems. Alternatively, poorly managed human resources are unlikely to contribute fully to the corporation. Their unfair treatment may even carry risks: the creation of an underproductive or alienated workforce.

Similarly, corporate relations with other stakeholders such as creditors, suppliers and the communities in which the company operates can either pose opportunities to achieve superior performance, or may pose potential risks if mismanaged. While the obligation of a company to act responsibly has been disputed at times, it is increasingly agreed that responsible corporate behaviour can enhance the performance of the enterprise and attenuate potential risks. As a consequence, it is important that boards consider not only the quality of the company's relations with shareholders, but also its relations with other contributors of resources to the company (such as employees, creditors and suppliers) in their assessment of the company's strategy, individual projects and risks.

Standards for what is responsible or appropriate corporate behaviour are often embodied in law. Thus, the front line in ensuring responsible corporate behaviour is compliance with the law. For this reason, the board has the important duty of overseeing the corporate compliance function. In other cases, what is responsible behaviour is embodied in internal and external guidelines and standards. The extent to which a company has ethics codes (along with any waivers to members of the board), and environmental and social policies, or adheres to external codes is important to understanding its commitment to responsible behaviour.

Companies increasingly disclose their environmental and social policies, and performance. These disclosures range from brief philosophical statements to in-depth disclosures of policies, goals and performance, particularly common in companies with large environmental and social impacts such as energy extraction or mining, but relevant to virtually any company.

Socially responsible investing as well as corporate social responsibility attract major attention of not only investors but also stakeholders nowadays; can be both challenging, risky but also rewarding when regarding Social Indexes like the FTSE4GOOD or the Dow Jones Sustainability Worlds Indexes.

UNCTAD (2006) also stresses that "an enterprise's environmental performance could affect it financial health and hence its sustainability. Thus, the impact of environmental and social policies on the sustainability of the enterprise is an increasingly important criterion for evaluating companies. Impact disclosures try to link corporate responsibility to the achievement of social goals, business objectives and financial outcomes. Mechanisms protecting the rights of other stakeholders like suppliers; dealers; customers; creditors; joint venture partners; banks; and employees become more and more important in times of advanced corporate social responsibility (OECD Principle IV). Stakeholders can be protected by a variety of means including the law, individual contracts, and codes or best practices.

45 of the 50 companies surveyed publish their policies and performances in connection with environmental and social responsibility; in both Brazil and Russia all of the companies did so. Not only the increasing trend of corporate social responsibility but also the high percentage of companies operating in the oil and gas industry might be a reason for that outcome.

Nine out of ten Korean companies disclosed information concerning this issue even though it is not yet required by the Korean corporate governance code. 31 out of 50 companies also stressed the impact of those activities on their firm's sustainability even though this is only required in Brazil and India. We note important differences regarding the companies' statements about the protection of other stakeholders.

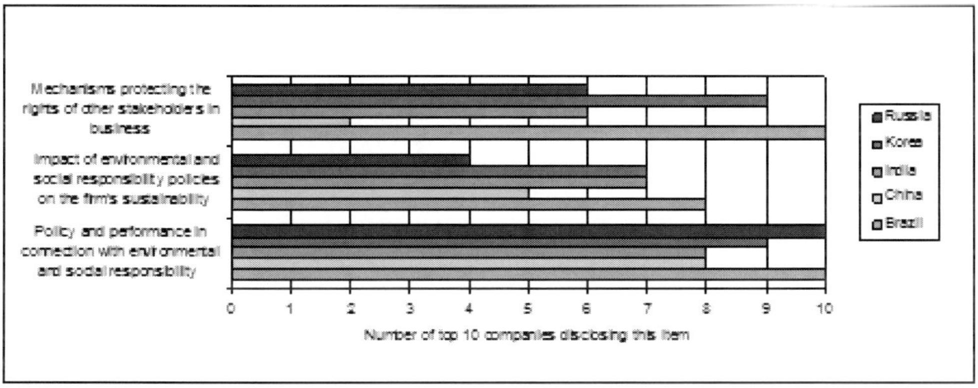

Figure 10. Corporate Social Responsibility.
Source: UNCTAD (2008)

All of the Brazilian companies surveyed had such mechanisms but only two out of ten Chinese companies even though Chinese regulations require this.

The role of employees in corporate governance is also suggested to be disclosed. It includes any formal interaction between employees and the governance structures of the company such as, for example, employee representatives on the board or employees electing some of the supervisory directors. Those structures should be disclosed to the company's shareholders. Under some circumstances, employees may become aware of cases of corporate misconduct. Misconduct can be criminal acts, infringements of an enterprise code of conduct, or a threat to the public interest as in fraud, corruption, or health and safety violations. Most cases of whistle blowing remain internal to the enterprise. External whistle blowing is when the employee reports misconduct to someone outside of the enterprise, often the media, watchdog groups, or law enforcement. Internal whistle blowing allows the enterprise to take appropriate corrective actions before the misconduct becomes a public issue. It should therefore be assisted by putting in place confidential reporting mechanisms that protect employees against any potential retribution.

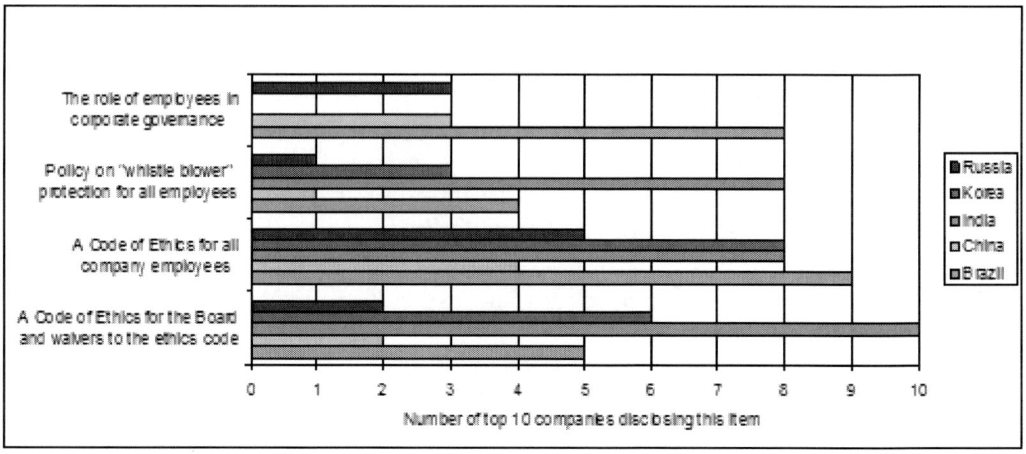

Figure 11. Ethics and the Role of Employees.
Source: UNCTAD (2008)

The role of employees in corporate governance is very poorly disclosed by Russia, China and especially Korea and India. 34 of the companies sampled outline a code of ethics for all of their employees, only 25 specifically waive to the board members. Especially Russia and China performed very weakly regarding these items. Unlike Brazil, neither Korean nor Indian companies outlined any mechanisms for employees to take a role in corporate governance.

Board and Management Structure and Process

The purpose of the board is to monitor the company and its management on behalf of the shareholders. The board is where all corporate governance issues come to a head. Without a good board, shareholders and other stakeholders may run undue risks - as will the company itself. It is because of its central role in the governance of the corporation that investors and the markets pay very close attention to the structures and procedures that determine its operation. An effective board reduces risks by monitoring the company and its management, and through the rigorous examination of fundamental business decisions. Board structures and processes, in turn, contribute to how well the board fulfils its expected functions. Board structures (i.e. committees and checks on the power of management) and processes (i.e. for selecting and interacting with an external auditor, or the approval of related party transactions) are of fundamental importance to the effectiveness of the board. If good structures and procedures are in place, investors may have a heightened sense that their interests are being protected and that fairness will prevail. In the absence of such structures, investors may perceive a higher degree of risk.

Policies to prevent or manage conflicts of interest are generally reflected in the governance structures of companies. The most common mechanisms to manage potential conflicts of interest are committees. The areas in which there is the most potential for conflict of interest are in the audit function, remuneration, nominations and the evaluation of management's performance. Committees are often established in these sensitive areas. Committees should be built in order to facilitate the board's fulfilment of its functions and are, under ideal circumstances, staffed fully by independent directors. Virtually all enterprises disclose the composition of their board of directors. Most companies accompany information on board members with an explanation of the role and function of the board of directors. Furthermore, 47 of the 50 companies surveyed published their committee structures including their functions.

In a general sense, all governance structures have to provide checks and balances. However, there are special mechanisms that a company may put in place to ensure that decisions taken by some are reviewed and approved by others. Systems of checks and balances are designed to make sure that power is not too centralized and that the decision making process is structured so as to prevent unjust benefit to any one person or group. When one talks of checks and balances, one is often referring to checks on the chief executive's powers and on management in general. Two examples of ways of providing checks on corporate leaders are two tier board structures (supervisory and management boards) or a clear division of roles and responsibilities of chairman and chief executive officer in a single tier board (especially required by the Cadburry Report as well as the Indian code). However, only six out of the ten Indian companies surveyed showed checks and balances mechanisms, whereas all of the Brazilian companies did.

Companies may disclose information on the positions that members of the board have on the boards and in the management of other companies. They may also disclose their policy with respect to the roles that executive board members can play outside of the enterprise. In order to determine whether board members are able to devote sufficient time to their duties and whether they are capable of independent judgment, it is useful to know how many other board memberships they have and whether they have any material interests. Many codes outline specific requirements and limitations concerning positions held by the directors. The FEE Report for example suggests the disclosure and differentiation of positions held in both public (also non profit) organizations and private sectors. More than 80% of the companies in India, Brazil and China published this kind of information, whereas both Indian and Korean companies did not divulge this kind of information in 60% of the cases.

Companies should disclose the terms of directors' contracts. This type of disclosure may indicate when a director started with the board, the length of the contract, when the director was re-elected, and when the director will be up for re-election (or step down if it is already known). This type of information is useful when assessing the possibilities of electing new directors, and the likelihood of being able to influence the company through director elections. It is vital that companies manage the succession of key executives as well as key board members in order to ensure operational continuity (OECD principle IV.D.2). It is important to know the process by which top executives and board members would be replaced should they retire or pass away. This item was disclosed by 46 out of the 50 companies.

Companies should also disclose the process by which a director's remuneration is calculated, or they may disclose individual compensation levels, possibly with a breakdown of the various elements that contribute to a director's total remuneration (i.e. salary, share options, pension schemes, etc.). Payments to executives who stand to lose their jobs as a result of a merger or acquisition (colloquially referred to as "golden parachutes") should be disclosed as well. All the Indian and Chinese companies sampled published their directors' remuneration, whereas four out of ten Brazilian and Korean companies did.

Reporting on director development and training activities is not as common as other types of disclosure. The availability of director training is, nevertheless, an important bit of information, since it helps assess and improve the quality and skills of the directors. The most common type of training tends to be induction training that helps orientate new directors in their new roles. Another common type of training is topical. Topical training helps directors understand specific issues that confront the company, or aids them in completing specific tasks such as the management of an audit committee. The Indian Code passed the Companies Amendment Bill in 2003 which made director training mandatory. However, only four out of ten Indian companies disclosed information regarding training mechanisms.

Some boards of directors are able to call upon independent external advisors (e.g. lawyers, accountants, etc.) to assist them in their work, in particular, in areas where there is the potential for conflict of interest or where special technical skills are required (such as developing remuneration plans, or conducting board performance evaluations). The disclosure of the ability of the board to make use of such experts may indicate to shareholders that the directors are informed and supported to the fullest extent possible. Korea is the only country among the countries surveyed where this is mandatory, thus 80% of the Korean companies disclosed these processes.

Few companies have performance evaluation processes for their directors. Assessments of director performance may compare directors' performance against a set of agreed responsibilities, general goals, and/or specific objectives. The specifics of an evaluation process are rarely disclosed. However, the existence of an evaluation process may be reported (for example directors' attendance at board and committee meetings). China is the only country whose national regulations require performance evaluation processes. In fact, eight out of ten Chinese companies surveyed disclose this information.

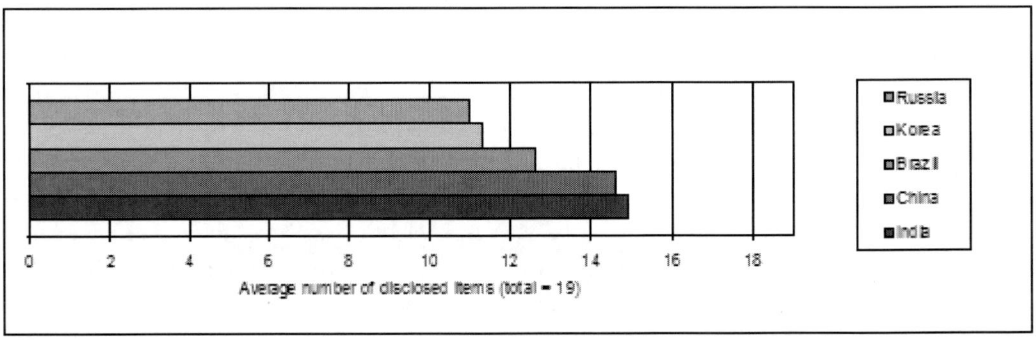

Figure 12. Group of Items – Board and Management Structures and Process.
Source: UNCTAD (2008)

In the end, one of the most common disclosures made by enterprises relates to risk management, the recognition of operating risk, the activities and strategies involved in risk management, and the systems that the enterprise has adopted to minimize risks. All of the Brazilian and Chinese companies and most of the Indian, Korean and Russian companies disclosed their risk management activities (eight, five and eight out of ten companies).When comparing the five countries, we find that India, China and Brazil disclosed the most items in this section. The fact that both Russian and Korean regulations and corporate governance codes do not require most of the items evaluated in this group of items (six and seven out of 19) explains this finding.

When examining the differences between the five surveyed countries over all, we note that Korean companies disclosed the least (30 out of 53 items on average) and Brazilian and Indian companies evenly disclosed the most information regarding their corporate governance. When comparing this ranking to the countries' performances by the five groups of disclosure items, we note that the Brazilian companies' results always ranked either first or second, whereas Korean companies were always among the three least disclosing ones. In order to compare the five emerging markets results to an international benchmark, we surveyed the top ten SandP 500 companies additionally: as expected, the finding shows that the average rate of disclosure is far better in the United States in comparison to the five emerging markets surveyed. An explanation for the great rate of disclosure of Brazilian and Chinese firms might the fact that both countries introduced new codes in 2004, whereas the Korean code of 1999 is rather outdated.

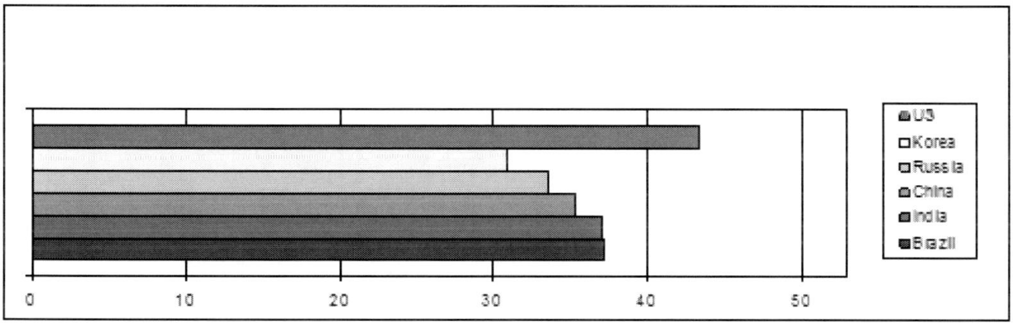

Figure 13. Average Rate of Disclosure in Emerging Markets compared to US Companies. Source: UNCTAD (2008)

When comparing the disclosure practices of the different sectors, we find differences among sectors. On average companies operating in financials disclose more information about their corporate governance in comparison to companies operating in materials - especially in the group of items board and management structure and process. Although some disclosure items have similar results, others differ tremendously. This result disproves Patel's (2002) findings which indicated no differences among sectors. When regarding the fact that the UNCTAD report (2007 and 2008) surveyed annual reports and publications of the financial year 2007, the strong disclosure practices of banks shows effects of the subprime crisis on corporate governance disclosure in this sector.

Corporate Governance Disclosure and Its Association with Profitability, Regulatory Frameworks and Governance Environment

Effects on Market Valuation and Profitability

As discussed earlier, *Klapper* and *Love* (2004) argue that good governance is positively correlated with market valuation. The McKinsey study "A premium for good governance" also finds a positive association between market valuation and good practices in corporate governance in emerging markets, measuring the market valuation by the price to book ratio (*Newell* and *Wilson*, 2002). The price to book ratio is calculated by a company's stock's capitalization (stock price times number of issued stocks) divided by the book value indicated on the company's balance sheet (in this chapter we calculated the average values of the time period 2005-2010). This indicator accounts for the premium investors are willing to pay above the company's assets.

We compared each company's price to book ratio to the number of disclosed items As figure 14 shows, there is no significant correlation between corporate governance disclosure and price to book ratio. This disproves *Klapper* and *Love's* as well as *Newell* and *Wilson's* findings. According to *La Porta* et al. (2000) investors tend not to rely on disclosed information if legal protection is weak. The fact that investors are protected very poorly in emerging markets and the risk of high information asymmetry might explain the non existing association between the two figures.

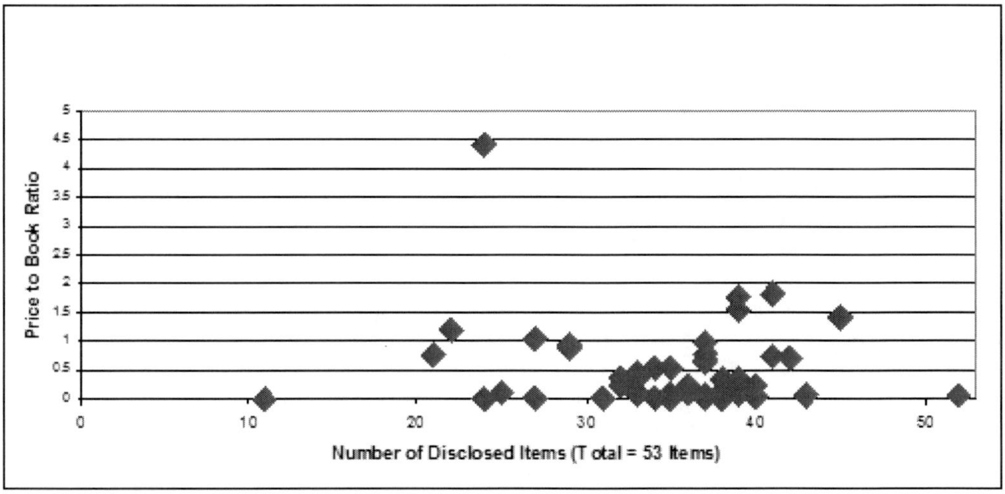

Figure 14. No Correlation between Corporate Governance Disclosure and Price to Book Ratio.

As discussed previously, some economists suggest that good disclosure practices should improve performance and profitability. We compared the companies' rate of disclosure to return on equity, i.e. the company's yearly after tax income divided by its book value, indicating how efficient and profitable a company uses the equity provided by its stockholders.

Figure 15 clearly shows that a company's return on equity and the rate of disclosure correlate positively, and thus proves economic theory reviewed and *Klapper* and *Love's* hypothesis that a firm's corporate governance disclosure is positively associated with its performance. This indicates that companies can not only reduce information asymmetry by disclosing information relevant to their stakeholders but also increase their profitability.

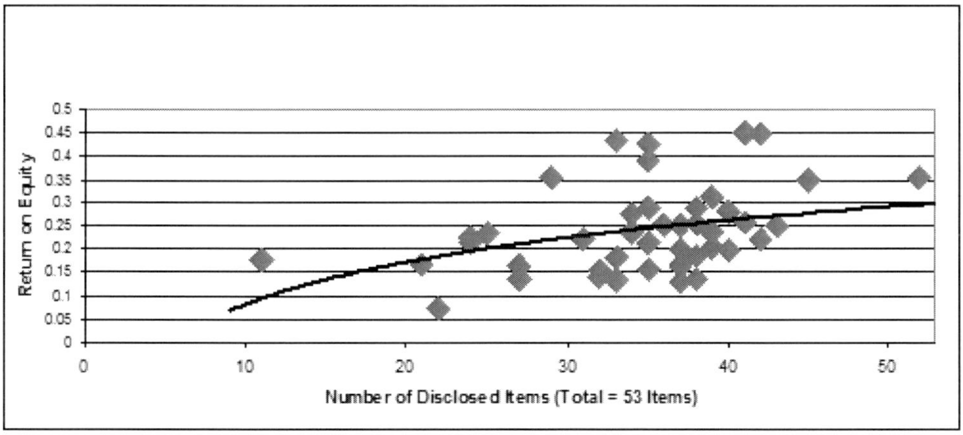

Figure 15. Correlation between Corporate Governance Disclosure and Return on Equity.

When comparing the companies' return on equity to the rates of disclosure distinguishing between the different groups of items we find very interesting results: we find *positive correlations* with the rate of disclosure of the company's ownership structure and audit. This indicates that the transparent disclosure of ownership and control structure, shareholder rights, anti takeover measures and especially audit services increases a company's return on equity.

Voluntary Disclosure and Regulatory Frameworks

As reviewed earlier in this paper, disclosure is often determined by national regulations, international standards and guidance. The regulatory framework - depending on the company's listings - provides sometimes complex, sometimes merely vague recommendations and requirements what and how to disclose. However, even where no legislation exists, it is considered good practice for companies to disclose additional information, so that stakeholders are provided with all relevant information in order to assess a company's performance according to their interests.

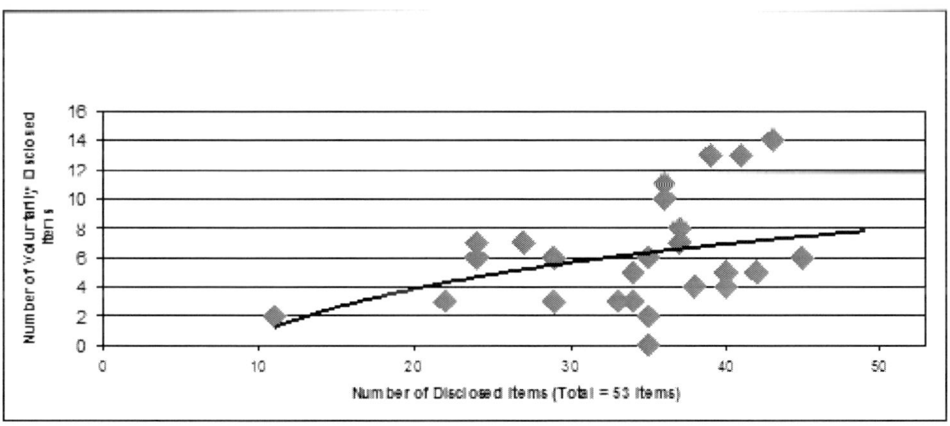

Figure 16. Correlation between Corporate Governance Disclosure and Voluntary Disclosure.

The following evaluates the disclosure practices of companies that are only locally listed (24 out of 50 companies surveyed are listed on the NYSE are thus obliged to disclose all of the 53 disclosure items). Indeed, companies that disclose items they are not required to by their national regulations voluntarily, disclose more required information as well. So we conclude that a company that makes a commitment to disclose voluntarily also meets disclosure requirements in a better way.

Chen (2004) as well as *Eng* and *Mak* (2003) argue that the existence of independent directors positively correlates with both mandatory and voluntary disclosure. They stress the assumption that independent directors tend to encourage firms to disclose more information to investors (than requested) and thus suggest more voluntary disclosure. Our testing, however, indicates only a slightly positive relationship between the independence of directors and voluntary disclosure. Companies surveyed that had no independent directors disclosed 31.5 items on average, whereas companies that have independent board members disclosed 35.4 items on average. However, this conclusion is somewhat constrained. A suggestion for further research would be to test the proportion of outside directors (not only the existence) and its correlation to the proportion of voluntary disclosure.

A Company's Governance Environment

Klapper and *Love* argue that firms in countries with weak overall legal systems have on average lower rates of disclosure; *Morck*, *Yeung* and *Yu's* findings show synchronous stock price movements in emerging markets explained by the assumption that investors do not rely on information disclosed by companies in countries with weak legal systems; *La Porta* et al. also note that poor legal protection of investors in emerging markets weakens the effectiveness of disclosure and stresses the need for legal protection of both companies and investors. Inspired by those findings this survey tried to establish linkages between corporate governance disclosure and a company's governance environment.

A report published by Standard and Poor's (*Dallas* and *Chavee* 2005) studies the correlation between a country's long term foreign currency credit rating and its governance environment, which is determines by four indicators: legal environment, market environment, regulatory environment and informational infrastructure. The "Composite Governance Index" rates 21 countries, including the ones we look at, accordingly. The results were compared to SandP's index in order to find out whether and how a company's practices in corporate governance disclosure are associated with its governance environment.

We find a positive correlation between a company's disclosure and its legal environment; i.e. "indicators of rule of law, judicial independence, efficiency of the legal framework, property rights, effectiveness of law making bodies and protection of minority shareholders". This goes in line with *Klapper* and *Love's* as well as *La Porta* et al.'s hypotheses. Companies in Russia, where the legal environment is the weakest (ranked 1) among the 21 markets ranked in the SandP index, disclose less information than companies in India, where legal environment is ranked 10. It might be argued that companies in countries with strong legal systems are urged to disclose required information when facing strong legislation. This finding again stresses the need for stronger investor protection and legal frameworks and institutions monitoring companies' disclosure. Furthermore, our findings show a slightly positive correlation between a company's rate of disclosure and its market environment, i.e.

"indicators of corruption, foreign ownership restrictions, efficacy of corporate boards, importance of corporate social responsibility and financial sophistication".

This result was expected and is also reflected in the ranking of most and least disclosing countries earlier in this paper (with reference to Russia). If companies' boards face less market barriers or corruption, they can operate in a more effective way, thus its corporate governance disclosure should also provide more transparency in comparison to a company surrounded by a corrupt market environment.

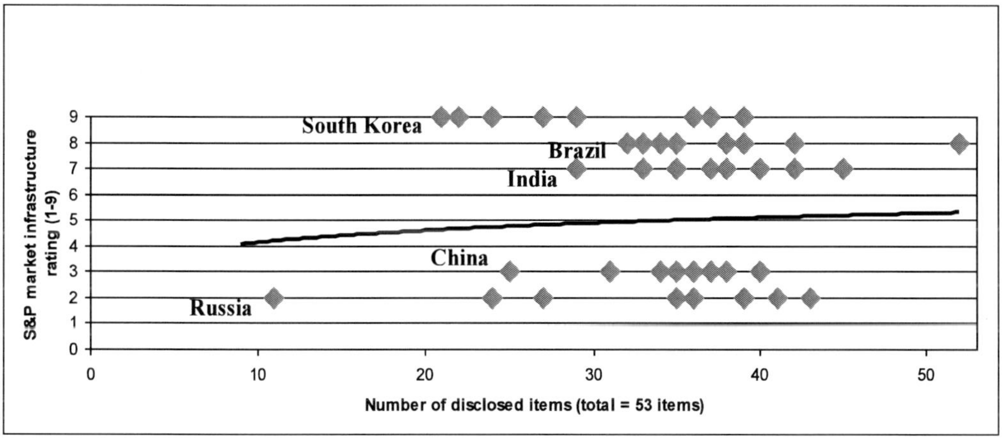

Figure 17. Correlation between a Country's Market Infrastructure and Companies' Rate of Disclosure.

However, when distinguishing between the five groups of disclosure items we find, indeed, a positive relationship between a country's regulatory framework and its disclosure of ownership structure and corporate responsibility. So as expected, companies that face greater disclosure requirements also disclose more information to their shareholders. The growing importance of policies concerning corporate responsibility and transparent ownership disclosure and adequate shareholder rights are reflected in this outcome.

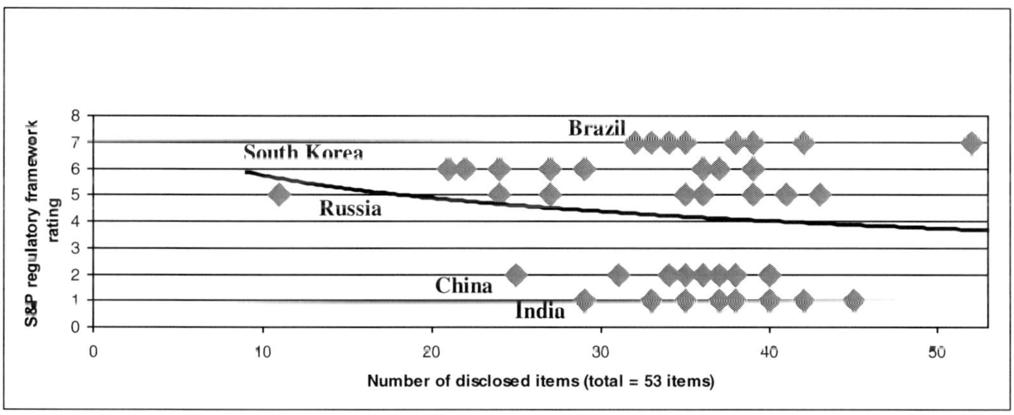

Figure 18. Correlation between a Country's Regulatory Framework and Companies' Rate of Disclosure.

Surprisingly there is a negative correlation between the companies' rate of disclosure and their regulatory environment, i.e. "indicators of regulatory effectiveness and regulatory burdens" (*Dallas* and *Chavee* 2005). A possible reason for this outcome is the fact that a large percentage of companies we look at are not only locally but internationally listed, thus their rate of disclosure is not only related to the country's regulations but for examples regulations like NYSE rules (for 24 out of the 50 companies).

CONCLUSION

This paper reviewed and analyzed the disclosure practices of a range of the most important companies in various sectors across five emerging markets in the time period 2007-2008.

The outcomes provide many interesting up to date insights in the five emerging markets. Not only main differences among the five countries but also among sectors were found. Companies in Russia and Korea clearly have to improve their governance disclosure practices, especially when comparing their results to previous studies. Not only national guidelines and regulations but also international standards have to be respected in a better way. Contrarily, all of the Brazilian companies and most of the Indian ones performed very well, complying with most of the UNCTAD guidelines as well as their national requirements.

We found that items pertaining to easily accessible information and items that are required by national regulations are more often disclosed than rather specific items, which are not commonly requested. The two groups of items auditing and corporate responsibility/compliance were the least disclosed and need further disclosure. Concerning many auditing issues, companies lack disclosure, especially rotation and duration of external audits and appointment of internal auditors. Also disclosure of corporate responsibility shows room for improvement, for example in information on the role of employees in corporate governance. The increasing trend in corporate social responsibility - especially in the energy sector - should have further effects on the companies' disclosure practices and improve results.

The testing of certain hypothesis in the last section of this paper clearly showed that corporate governance disclosure is positively associated with return on equity and therefore profitability - proving one of *Klapper* and *Love's* main outcomes. This paper, however, does not find the relationships,*Newell* and *Wilson* as well as *Klapper* and *Love* outline regarding the association between corporate governance disclosure and market valuation as well as findings by *Chen* as well as *Eng* and *Mak* concerning voluntary disclosure .

This papers findings on the relationship between corporate governance disclosure and the companies' legal environment and market infrastructure are strikingly interesting. The weaker the legal environment, the lower is the rate of disclosure. Companies disclose less if only weak legislation is imposed upon them, we assume that investors do not rely on disclosed information as their rights are less protected; thus disclosure is rendered ineffective. The better the market infrastructure, the higher is the rate of disclosure. Companies in markets with less corruption and less restrictions can operate more efficient and disclose relevant information to their stakeholders.

However, there are certain problems concerning governance disclosure in general that require further research. The question how reliable disclosed information is and whether the lack of certain disclosure items indicates that the company did not govern them the right way remain open. In the end, we have to stress the urgent need for a reorganisation of the many different guidelines, standards and regulations with regards to corporate governance disclosure worldwide. Internationally recognized standards for corporate governance disclosure – as they exist for accounting, namely IFRS - should be established in order to give companies in emerging markets the possibility to converge, to adapt their disclosure to international standards and thereby improve their profitability and grow.

ACKNOWLEDGMENTS

Thanking Mr. Anthony Miller, Ph.D. (Economic Affairs Officer, Investment and Enterprise Division, United Nations Conference on Trade and Development) for his continous support.

REFERENCES

Bhojraj, S. and Sengupta, P. (2003): Effect of Corporate Governance on Bond Ratings and Yields: The Role of Institutional Investors and Outside Directors, in: *Journal of Business*, 76, No.3, 2003, pp. 455-473.

Chen, C. and Jaggi, B. (2000): Association between independent non-executive directors, family control and financial disclosures in Hong Kong, in: *Journal of Accounting and Public Policy*, 19, 2000, pp. 285-310.

Chen, K. (2004): Disclosure, Corporate Governance and the Cost of Equity Capital in Emerging Markets, http://www.bm.ust.hk/~acct/acsymp2004/Papers/Chen_n.pdf.

Dallas, G. and Chavee, X. (2005): The Role of Country Risk In Assessing Corporate Governance Disclosure, http://www2.standardandpoors.com/spf/pdf/products/The%20Role%20of%20Country%20Risk%20In%20Assessing%20Corporate%20Governance.pdf

Diamond, D. and Verrecchia, R. (1991): Disclosure, Liquidity and the Cost of Capital, in: *The Journal of Finance*, 46, 1991, pp. 1325-1369.

Eng, L. and Mak Y. (2003): Corporate Governance Disclosure and Voluntary Disclosure, in: *Journal of Accounting and Public Policy*, 22, 2003, pp. 325-345.

Klapper, L. and Love, I. (2004): Corporate Governance, Investor Protection, and Performance in Emerging Markets, in: *Journal of Corporate Finance*, 10, 2004, pp. 703-728.

La Porta, R., Lopez-de-Silanes, F., Shleifer, A. and Vishny, R. (2000): Investor Protection and Corporate Governance, in: *Journal of Financial Economics*, 58, 2000, pp. 3-27.

Morck, R., Yeung, B. and Yu, W. (2006): The information content of stock markets: Why do emerging markets have synchronous stock price movements?, in: *Journal of Financial Economics*, 59, 2000, pp. 215-269.

Newell, R. and Wilson, G. (2002): A premium for good governance, in: *The McKinsey Quarterly*, pp. 20-23.

Patel, S., Balic, A. and Bwarkira, L. (2002): Measuring transparency and disclosure at firm-level in emerging markets, in: *Emerging Markets Review*, 3, 2002, pp. 325-337.

UNCTAD (ed.) (2006): Guidance on Good Practices in Corporate Governance Disclosure, United Nations Publication, New York and Geneva, pp.1-55, http://www.unctad.org/Templates/webflyer.asp?docid=7084andintItemID=3914andlang=1andmode=downloads

UNCTAD (ed.) (2007): Review of the Implementation Status of Corporate Governance Disclosures: An Inventory of Disclosure Requirements in 25 Emerging Markets, United Nations Publication, Geneva.

UNCTAD (ed.) (2008): Review of the implementation status of corporate governance disclosures: an examination of reporting practices among large enterprises in 10 emerging markets, United Nations Publication, Geneva.

In: Understanding Risk
Editor: Matthias Beck

ISBN: 978-1-62618-686-6

Chapter 6

IMPLEMENTING RISK MANAGEMENT: A STUDY OF MAJOR MALAYSIAN CORPORATIONS

Ahmad Shukri Yazid[1], Mohd Rasid Hussin[2] and Matthias Beck[3]

[1]Business Management and Accountancy (FBMA), Universiti Sultan ZainalAbidin (UniSZA), Terengganu DarulIman, Malaysia
[2]Risk Management at the College of Business (COB), Universiti Utara Malaysia (UUM), Sintok, Kedah DarulAman, Malaysia
[3]Public Sector Management at Queen's University Management School, Queen's University Belfast, UK

ABSTRACT

This study presents findings from a series of interviews with Risk Managers and/or Chief Risk Officers from major Malaysian companies about the prerequisites for the effective implementation of Risk Management programmes. The interviews highlight the importance of a number of factors, including: a strong commitment from the Board of Directors and Management in general, a desire for an appropriate risk culture, the development of formal Risk Management frameworks and policies, a recognition of the importance of risk communication, the appointment of a Chief Risk Officer (CRO) and the development of a complementary system of internal audit.

---

[1] Associate Professor Dr AHMAD SHUKRI YAZID is Dean at the Faculty of Business Management and Accountancy (FBMA), Universiti Sultan ZainalAbidin (UniSZA) formerly known as UniversitiDarulIman Malaysia (UDM) at Terengganu DarulIman, Malaysia.

[2] Dr MOHD RASID HUSSIN is Professor in Risk Management at the College of Business (COB), Universiti Utara Malaysia (UUM), Sintok, Kedah DarulAman, Malaysia.

[3] Dr MATTHIAS BECK, is Chair in Public Sector Management at Queen's University Management School, Queen's University Belfast, UK.

Background

In the early 1980s an increasing number of major corporations from developing countries in Asia, such as Taiwan, Singapore, Thailand, Malaysia, and Indonesia had become involved in global market operations. In so doing, these corporations exposed themselves to various forms of risks, which could crucially affect their business operations and financial status. For these companies it therefore became important to adopt a structured response to Risks Management which could help them mitigate the effects of these exposures (e.g., Crockford, 2005; Merna, 2005).

It is interesting to note that Risk Management as a management discipline became popular in the Asian region predominantly on account of the Asian Financial Crisis of 1997 (Yazid, 2001). As part of this sea change, several Malaysian companies adopted a new management paradigm which focused on the replacement of Traditional Risk Management (TRM) with the increasingly popular concepts of Enterprise Risk Management (ERM). This move toward proactive ERM was in line with the expectation that Risk Management, as a structured response to risks, could actually increase the firm's value (Smithson and Simkins, 2005).

To date, much of the literature on Risk Management has focused much on developed countries only, while very little attention has examined corporations in emerging markets such as Malaysia. This is somewhat surprising given the large number of major corporations in the region and even more so the receptiveness of companies in countries such as Malaysia to Risk Management in general. Thus it can be said that, although not many Asian companies have adopted fully integrated Risk Management systems, there has been a broad acceptance of concepts of Risk Management among large Malaysian companies for a period of more than three decades.

The main objective of this paper is to examine the factors which can be seen as contributing to the implementation of effective Risk Management strategies and techniques in major Malaysian companies. While this examination is largely descriptive in nature, it is expected that there is also a normative element in that this analysis provides insights as to how Risk Management can be embraced within a broader corporate context.

The following sections provide an overview of Risk Management processes which are relevant to major corporations in Malaysia. The next section discusses the methodology adopted in this study. Then the findings of the paper are discussed. The paper concludes by summarizing the factors that can be seen as contributing to the implementation of an effective Risk Management model in the Malaysian context.

Development of Risk Management

Risk management has been practiced as early as 3000 B.C. (Vaughan, 1997). For example, Chinese merchants used risk sharing techniques when shipping cargo by boat. In today's modern business environment companies have to manage a vast range of risks which arise from different sources and impact on company operations in different ways. These risks include the ability to penetrate into, and sustain profitable operations within, the global market; the protection of a company's image and reputation; the day to day management of strategic and operational risks; compliance with corporate and governance standards; the ability to handle potential business crises; a capacity for business recovery; and, lastly, the ongoing protection of the shareholders' interest.

Companies tend to manage risk on a portfolio basis in line with their desire to create value for shareholders. Risk management, accordingly, has been recognized as a critical success factor, with Belmont (2004) identifying benefits of risk management in terms of price earning ratios and cost of capital.

Although the literature differs in terms of terminology and definitions, there is a broad agreement that the risk management process is composed of five basic steps (e.g D'Arcy, 2001; Rejda, 2001; Theiland Ferguson, 2003 and Treischmann et al., 2005). These include: risk identification, risk measurement, examination of alternative risk management techniques, the selection of appropriate risk management techniques and finally implementation of a risk management programme.

Traditional Risk Management (TRM) typically focuses on the management of those risk exposures which present the most immediate threat to a company. This approach is now being perceived as rather limited in terms of scope and application, for a number of reasons. Firstly, by focusing on key risks, TRM lacks an integrated framework for the management of risks which can lead to a silo mentality which militates against a holistic management of risks (Lam, 2000; Davenport and Bradley, 2001; Ernst and Young, 2001; Barton, Shenkirand Walker; 2002). Secondly, unlike integrated risk management approaches which provide explicit links to organizational vision, mission, and strategies (Whitfield, 2003), it is often difficult to embed TRM measures within a broader strategic framework. Lastly, and perhaps most importantly, requirements for compliance with Corporate Governance Codes frequently mandate a broad approach to risk as vital component of corporate responsibility and accountability.

It is therefore not surprising that the concept of Enterprise-Wide Risk Management (EWRM) has gained increasing popularity. Underlying ERWM is the idea that risks should be managed on an enterprise-wide basis. Despite its popularity as a state-of-the-art technique, there is however, EWRM can still face a cloud of skepticism especially in those companies which have worked with a TRM for some time approach and thus, have become familiar and comfortable with TRM as a structured response to risks.

Risk Management Practices

EWRM as a new concept for the management of risks appears to be more attractive to larger companies than smaller ones (Miccolis et al. 2001). This is probably due to the fact that larger companies have the required resources in order to adopt EWRM. It is interesting to note that companies that adopt EWRM normally do so after having established a systematic framework for managing risks, which may include the appointment of a Chief Risk Officer and a EWRM committee (Tillinghast-Towers Perrin, 2002).

According to Scordis (2003), the Casualty Actuary Society found that vendors which included brokers, agents, consultants, and similar parties were more familiar with the concept of EWRM as compared to professionals working in other industry sectors (including insurance). As regards different professional groupings the same study found accountants, brokers, financial analysts, risk managers and underwriters to be the most likely to be involved in EWRM. Meanwhile, there was evidence that EWRM approaches were more advanced within the financial services industry as compared to the insurance industry.

It is rather obvious that companies will differ in terms of the approaches they adopt to managing their risk exposures. Much of the literature uses the word 'best practice' in order to identify 'effective' techniques which provide an appropriate means for managing the risk exposures of specific companies. In this context, Hillson (2004) has suggested that the term 'best practice' can relate to the following: a) "routine activities that lead to excellence", b) not "what everyone does"...but "what everyone should do", c) something that is accepted by leading professionals, d) something that is implemented by leading practitioners, e) a widely accessible technique, and/or f) one that is scalable, easily tailored or modified.

A study by Zecher and Putnam (2001) stated that 'best practice' was about creating a corporate culture that manages for risk-adjusted performance and argued that corporate culture itself could not be mandated as it evolved from the leadership at the top. A joint definition from PMN-KPMG (1999) put forward the idea that a 'best practice' would be a strategy, approach, method, tool or technique that was particularly effective in helping a company or organization achieve its objectives (e.g., with regard to the management of risks) and could be expected to be of value to other companies and organizations.

Based on these views it can be argued that 'best practice' in Risk Management can be defined as an approach that is appropriate to the management and mitigation of a wide spectrum of risks faced by companies. Additionally a 'best practice' approach should rest on a framework that would be acceptable, easy to understand, flexible, practical and effective, as well as offering potential future gains in terms of value to the stakeholders and companies/organizations on the whole.

METHODOLOGY

This study based on interviews with senior executives from twenty major Malaysian corporations. All of the corporations were listed on the Malaysian Bourse and all interviews were conducted with either senior Risk Managers or the Chief Risk Officer (CRO).

The main criteria set for selecting interviewees were as follows:- a) the companies selected had to meet the requirements of Main Board companies of the Malaysia Bourse; b) the companies had to fall within the criteria of 'major corporations' as defined by Yazid (2001) which meant that they had to have at least one branch or subsidiary overseas or had to be engaged in a joint venture with overseas partners; and c) these companies had to be exposed to several risks, including strategic risks, operational risks, credit risks and market risks.

RESULTS AND DISCUSSION

As mentioned above, the main objective of this study is to examine the implementation of Risk Management measures among major corporations in Malaysia. Risk management as a structured response to risks is expected to be widely established among these companies as a consequence of the requirements of the Malaysian Code of Corporate Governance (MCCG).

Risk Management Strategies

This section reports on informants' views about levels of implementation and effectiveness of Risk Management strategies.

Top Management's Commitment and Risk Management Culture

Risk Management implementation is obviously costly because it requires significant resources. In addition, a strong commitment from the Board of Directors and Management itself are crucial to ensure the successful implementation of the overall Risk Management program.

In this context, the Board of Directors must have some understanding in Risk Management. Furthermore, they must have a strong belief that Risk Management will aid them in the accomplishment of company objectives. Moreover, it has been argued that for Risk Management to be effective a 'Risk-Conscious Culture' must be developed among all staff member. This implies that top management as well as staff members are fully committed to the implementation of risk management measures.

During the interviews a number of informants suggested establishing the appropriate culture was perhaps more important than developing formal policies and framework. Moreover, the same interviewees argued that such a culture could be achieved through training which prepared staff members to manage uncertainties associated with the various risk exposures faced by their companies.

Overall, the informant highlighted five key prerequisites for the effective implementation of Risk Management programs, which included the following:

- The Board of Directors are willing to allocate a budgetary and human resources to the effective implementation of Risk Management measures;
- Specialist committees were set-up at various levels within the companies to manage the potential risk exposures;
- The majority of staff members are aware of the key risk exposures in relation to the companies' daily operation;
- There is a risk-conscious culture among staff members;
- The Top Management is willing to spend time and money on training staff members to ensure programme implementation.

Roles and Responsibility for Managing Risks

The role and responsibility for managing risks within a company normally rest upon several parties, namely, the Board of Directors, the Risk Management Committee, the Chief Executive Officer or Managing Director, the Head of Units and Risk Managers.

The Malaysian Code of Corporate Governance (2000) explicitly states that the Board of Directors have a responsibility to identify the principal risks and implement the appropriate systems to manage risks. This was reflected in the views of informants who suggested that the

Board is expected to introduce appropriate strategies including the Risk Management policies as well being responsible for setting the company's risk appetite and tolerance levels.

Regarding the role of the Risk Management Committee, informants noted that the committee has to play a key role of overseeing risks which affect the company. This includes the setting up of procedures to identify and evaluate the potential risk exposures as well as the introduction of appropriate techniques for mitigating. Lastly, the committee also has key responsibilities for the monitoring of risk management measures and specifically for ascertaining that the techniques chosen in this context are effective. Regular reporting to the Board of Directors is also considered as part of the committee's responsibility.

According to our informants the Chief Executive Officer (CEO) or Managing Director (MD) was the person responsible for ensuring the smooth running of the company. The CEO (or MD) oversee the task of managing potential risk exposures in relation to all the company activities. The CEO (or MD) also report to the Risk Management Committee on a regular basis. These reports should include the status of all risk mitigation measures that are being carried out. Furthermore, the CEO (or MD) should monitor levels of awareness and overall compliance among management and staff members in the company.

Similarly the respondents noted that Heads of Units or Sections also had an important role to play in the implementation of risk management measures. Specifically it was felt Heads of Units were responsible for identifying, evaluating and mitigating all potential risk exposures at the unit level. Moreover it was noted that whenever there were potential high risk exposures, Unit Heads had to quickly communicate these to Senior Management. Another important responsibility of Unit Heads was to make sure that everyone was clear about their responsibilities in mitigating risks within the company or organization.

Finally, informants commented on the role and responsibility of Risk Managers. Most informants considered Risk Managers to be the risk coordinators of the company. Accordingly, it was their responsibility to coordinate actions with other managers in order to establish an effective Risk Management programme. At the same time, they had to monitor the progress of risk mitigation measures within the company and assist other managers in reporting relevant risk information to the Senior Management concerned.

Risk Management Process

According to (Vaughan, 1997), the Risk Management process comprises the following aspects: (a) determining objectives (b) identifying risks (c) evaluating risks (d) considering alternatives and selecting the most appropriate risk treatment techniques (e) implementing the chosen techniques, and (f) evaluating and reviewing the overall Risk Management programme. There is evidence that historically most companies managed risks in the absence of a structured Risk Management programme. The rise of more structured approaches meanwhile has been associated with the AS/NZ framework and/or the Committee of Sponsoring Organisations (COSO) framework. Lastly, some companies draw on both approaches and/or develop their own hybrid approach.

According to the informants who participated in this study, a Risk Management framework (such as COSO) was important because it served as a guide or standard for companies who had decided to adopt a structured approach. Such a framework typically included general policies, risk identification and assessment methodologies, strategies for mitigating risks, evaluating and monitoring procedures, and statement regarding risk communication structures. The interviewees felt that having such a framework would make the implementation of Risk Management more effective, especially when it had been approved by the Board of Directors.

Following on from this line of argument a number of informants suggested that Risk Management initiatives needed leadership or so called the 'risk champions' who set the tone and called the shots.Several informants suggested that it was best for the Chief Executive Officer (CEO) or Managing Director (MD) to act as leader in Risk Management initiatives. Other interviewees suggested that the Risk Management Committee should lead the Risk Management program.

As regards the initiation of a Risk Management program, it was felt that this could come from various sources such as Top Management, a Head of Unit, a Risk Manager or a Chief Risk Officer (CRO). In this context it was also noted that there was an increasing trend for companies to appoint the CRO to lead the Risk Management initiatives and activities. Lastly there was a consensus that the person who acted as the 'risk champion' should come from within the company so that risks could be dealt with effectively.

Risk Communication

Almost all informants felt strongly about the need for good risk communication and stressed the importance of all staff members receiving the right messages. In this context it was suggested that the CRO played an essential role of cascading down Risk Management imperatives throughout the company/organization. Moreover it was felt that CRO had to ensure that all the risk managers concerned conveyed the same message to staff members. This was based on the assumption that if staff members understood that Risk Management initiatives could add value to the company, then the implementation of such a programme would be easier and more effective.

It was interesting to note that some interviewees saw the implementation of Risk Management measures as a Key Performance Indicators (KPIs) for individual executive. Even though this is not a common practice yet, this approach appears to have become more widespread among Malaysian companies.

Examples of good practice in terms of risk communication included the following: (a) some companies organize monthly meetings to monitor progress of their Risk Management program and to discuss different approaches for ensuring that all staff members understand what Risk Management is all about, and (b) some companies specifically task Unit Head with the responsibility of conveying information about risk related issues to staff.

Role of Internal Audit

This study also indicated that many informants viewed internal audit and control as an integral part of Risk Management. Lam (2003) argued that the roles of internal auditors and risk managers should be complementing each other, whereby the Risk Management unit typically provides reports on risk profiling to the internal auditor.

As far as the informants of this study were concerned many internal auditors already relied on Risk Management frameworks and guidelines to audit the Risk Management initiatives. Where this was the case, the activities of auditors were key to ensuring that staff members followed Risk Management frameworks and guidelines. Furthermore it was felt that the internal audit report provided independent assurance that the company followed the Risk Management activities it had decided earlier to implement (Ernst and Young, 2003).

Views on the role of Internal Auditor thus can be summarised as follows: (a) auditors provide assurance on Risk Management activities, (b) they complement Risk Management functions, (c) they audit actions taken in relation to significant risks as well as the Risk Management process, and (d) they co-ordinate risk reporting to the Audit Committee and the Board of Directors.

CONCLUSION

This study provides an insight into what senior risk managers and CRO consider to be an 'effective' Risk Management model. These views are of some interest to Malaysian companies in general, in that they provide a useful guideline which is based on current 'best' or 'good' practice.

Risk Management frameworks and policies are a key starting point for the implementation of Risk Management initiatives. These frameworks provide a standard for Management to follow and facilitate the gradual expansion of specific Risk Management initiatives.

Commitment and support from the Top Management is another critical factor for an 'effective' Risk Management model. Thus many informants suggested that senior Management must demonstrate their willingness to support Risk Management initiatives and in so doing actively contribute to the creation of a risk-conscious culture within the company. In this context it was noted that this could not be achieved if Risk Management activities solely related to compliance purposes.

Risk Communication was seen as another key feature for the successful implementation of a Risk Management programme. Accordingly, it was noted that companies needed to be able to cascade down risk relevant messages and initiatives to all staff members.

The appointment of Chief Risk Officer (CRO) or the Risk Manager was also seen as a critical success factor. In addition, many respondents argued that individuals who were responsible for the setting-up of Risk Management programmes needed both relevant insider information about the company and relevant Risk Management qualifications.

Finally, the interviewees suggested that internal audit had an important role to play in complementing the risk managers' function and was another factor that contributed to an 'effective' Risk Management model. Specifically, auditors were able to provide assurance on Risk Management initiatives, with a special focus on significant risks that might affect a company's ability to achieve its objectives.

REFERENCES

Belmont, D.P. 2004. *Value Added Risk Management in Financial Institutions*. Singapore, John Wiley and Sons.

Barton, T.L., Shenkir, W.G., and Walker, P.L. 2002. *Making Enterprise Risk Management Pay Off: How Leading Companies Implement Risk Management.* New Jersey: Financial Times/Prentice Hall PTR, Pearson Education, Inc.

Crockford, G.N. 2005. The Changing Face of Risk Management. *The Geneva Papers,* 30, 5-10.

D'Arcy, S.P. 2001. Enterprise Risk Management. *Journal of Risk Management of Korea.* 12(1). 207-228.

Davenport, E.W., and Bradley, L.M. 2001. Enterprise Risk Management: A Consultative Perspective. Retrieved August 28, 2005, http://www.casact.com.

Deloach, J.W. 2000. *Enterprise-Wide Risk Management: Strategies for Linking Risk and Opportunity.* London: Financial Times, Prentice Hall.

Ernst and Young. 2001. *2001 Risk Management Guide from Theory to Practice: Evolving Your Organization's Risk Management.* Insurance and Actuarial Advisory Services.

Ernst and Young. 2003. *Brave New World: Risk Measurement and Capital Management in the Insurance Industry*: Insurance and Actuarial Advisory Services.

Hillson, D. 2006. Surveying the Risk Management Universe – Where are We Now? In Hillson, D (Ed), *The Risk Management Universe: A Guide Tour p. 1-9.* London, British Standards Institution.

KPMG 1999. Best Practices in Risk Management: Private and Public Sectors Internationally. Retrieved September 17, 2005, http//:www.tbs-sct.gc.ca/rm-gr/site/altformatnotice.aspx?Language=ENandid=959andfid=17

Lam, J. 2000. Enterprise-Wide Risk Management and the Role of Chief Risk Officer. *eRisk.* March, 1-5.

Lam, J. 2003. Enterprise Risk Management. New Jersey: John Wiley and Sons, Inc.

Merna, T., and Al-Thani, F.F. 2005. *Corporate Risk management: AnOrganisational Perspective,* London, John Wiley and Son.

Miccolis, J. A., Hively, K., and Merkly, B. W. 2001. *Enterprise Risk Management: Trends and Emerging Practices.* Florida, The Institute of Internal Auditor Research.

Miller, K.D. 1992. A Framework for Integrated Risk Management in International Business. *Journal of International Business Studies.* 23(2), 311-331.

Panning, W.H. 2006. Making ERM Happen. *Best's Review,* 106, 88.

Rejda, G.E. 2001. *Principles of Risk Management and Insurance, (7th ed.).* New York: Addison Wesley Longman.

Scordis, N. 2003. Emerging Trends in Risk Management: From the Insurer's Perpective. *Review of Business*, 24(3), 5-8.

Smithson, Charles and Betty J. Simkins. 2005. Does Risk Management Add Value? A Survey of the Evidence. *Journal of Applied Finance*Vol 17, No. 3.

Stroh, P.J. 2005. Enterprise Risk Management: At Unitedhealth Group. *Strategic Finance,* July: 27-35.

Theil, M., and Ferguson, W.L. 2003. Risk Management as a Process: An International Perspective. *Review of Business,* 24, 30-35.

Treischmann, J.S., Hoyt, R.E., and Sommer, D.W. 2005. *Risk management and Insurance, (12th ed.).* Ohio: Thomson Learning.

Vaughan, Emmett, J. 1997. *Risk Management.* Canada, John Wiley and Sons.

Whitfield, R.N. 2003. *Managing Institutional Risks: A Framework.* PhD Dissertation, University of Pennsylvania. Retrieved April 14, 2006.

Yazid, A. S. 2001. "*Perceptions and Practices of Financial Risk Management in Malaysia*." Glasgow Caledonian University, Scotland. Ph.D Thesis.

Zecher, R. and Putnam, B. 2001. "*Best Practice Begins with CEO*". Global Investor. London: Jun 2001., Iss. 143; pg.46.

Section B:

International Relations

In: Understanding Risk
Editor: Matthias Beck

ISBN: 978-1-62618-686-6

Chapter 7

FOREIGN DIRECT INVESTMENT AND COUNTRY RISK: IS THERE EVIDENCE OF 'MALIGN' INVESTMENT IN FORMER SOVIET STATES?

Matthias Beck[1,*] and Nataliya Acc-Nikmehr[2]
[1]Queen's University Management School, Queen's University Belfast,
Belfast, Northern Ireland, UK,
[2]formerly, Cullen Centre for Risk and Governance
at Glasgow Caledonian University, Scotland, UK

ABSTRACT

The policy of key international organisation continues to be informed by the assumption that Foreign Direct Investment (FDI) has an unambiguously positive effect on recipient nations. However, there is increasing evidence that, on a global scale, increased trade and investment flows from rich to poorer nations have not contributed to a convergence of levels of income and well-being. This is particularly apparent in the context of former Soviet states, many of which continue to experience a decline, in both relative and absolute terms, in per capita GDP alongside a diminution in the life expectancy of their populations. Examining data on FDI received by former Soviet States from 1997 to 2005, this paper notes, firstly, that these investments have been concentrated on a few, typical natural-resource-rich states. Secondly, it observes that even these resource-rich countries experienced massive fluctuations in terms of the amounts of FDI they received over this time period. Lastly, the paper examines the impact of FDI on a number of country risk indicators via a pooled regression model which includes data for twelve former Soviet countries, namely the Central and Eastern European States of Belarus, Moldova, Russia, and Ukraine, and the Central Asian Republics of Armenia, Azerbaijan, Georgia, Kazakhstan, Kyrgyzstan, Tajikistan, Turkmenistan and Uzbekistan. This analysis indicates that FDI has either a marginally negative effect on individual country risk measures such as in the case of 'Overall Country Risk', or significantly negative effects as in the case of 'Economic Risk' and 'Legal Risk'. The paper concludes that there is a strong case for questioning the existing orthodoxy which argues that problems of

* E-mail: m.beck@qub.ac.uk.

transition can be overcome via increased FDI and which continues to advise former Soviet states to pursue foreign capital at all cost.

INTRODUCTION

The goal of this paper is to question the dominant orthodoxy of FDI which suggests that increased foreign investment will, in virtually all instances, benefit the recipient nation. This orthodox has an extensive academic pedigree (Balasubramanyam, Salisu, and Sapsford, 1996; Borensztein, De Gregorio and Lee, 1998; De Melo, 1999; Dyker, 1999) which loosely underpins a well established policy discourse which emphasises 'the creation of a positive investment climates' and the need to 'create institutions which are complementary to investment' (Guisinger, 1985; Mudambi and Navarra, 2002). Implied in this orthodoxy is the assumption that, firstly, the failure by certain regions to exhibit sustained growth can be attributed to a lack of?ability to attract foreign investment, and, secondly, that the inability to attract lasting foreign investment, itself, can be attributed to institutional deficiencies of the potential recipient country. Applied to former Soviet states, other than the Baltics, this narrative typically identifies corruption, lack of legal and institutional reforms and insufficient liberalisation as the root cause for the insufficiency of economic and social development in these countries (Estrin, Hughes and Todd, 1997; Fabry and Zeghni, 2002; Bevan, Estrin and Meyer, 2004).

One of the obvious weaknesses of this narrative is that it oversimplifies the experiences of different countries within larger regions. Thus, there is significant evidence that, contrary to the assumption that the entire region has been an FDI laggard, FDI in former Soviet states has been highly concentrated in a number of countries which rank, by international standards, amongst the top FDI recipients (Meyer and Pind, 1999). Moreover, there is no consistent evidence that the top FDI recipients amongst former Soviet states also rank at the top in terms of social and institutional development and/or political stability (Abbott, 2002; Abbott and Beck, 2003). Lastly, there are some, largely qualitative analyses, which suggest that some countries which have been targeted by FDI have in fact experienced a deterioration in their institutional capacities (Marriott and Muttitt, 2005).

As an alternative to these conventional views on FDI, this paper examines the possibility that foreign investment in former Soviet states has not only failed to produce the expected effects, but also may have had a discernibly negative impact on certain regions. The paper is structured as follows. The first section briefly reviews conventional arguments on the benefits of trade and investment and contrasts these with recent developments in the region. The second section presents a more recent neo-institutionalist model of economic development together with some alternative interpretations of the impact of investment and trade on domestic economies. These alternative views form the basis for the empirical analysis of section three, which focuses on the link between investment flows in former Soviet states from the late 1990s to mid 2000 and levels of stability amongst these states, and highlights the potentially negative effect foreign investment may have had on the region. This paper concludes with a discussion of the policy implications of these findings.

CONVENTIONAL VIEWS ON TRADE AND INVESTMENT

Since the 1970s, much of the literature on economic growth has focused on the question as to why the 'West' has been able to accumulate significant amounts of wealth while other regions of the world suffer from comparable poverty (Lucas, 1988). Up until the mid 1990s this issue was widely disputed, not least on account of the different disciplinary approaches which contributed to this debate. However, partly due to the influence of the World Bank, International Monetary Fund and World Trade Organisation, a new consensus formed in the 1990s which emphasised trade as a principal source of wealth, and argued that the economies of wealthy nations could be distinguished from poorer ones primarily on account of their greater participation in world trade. Implicit in this new orthodox was a barely hidden policy agenda which advocated, for various reasons, the lifting of trade barriers and the expansion of global trade. Academically the new orthodoxy was underpinned most eloquently by the works of Jeffrey Sachs and Andrew Warners, whose 1995 Brookings Paper Economic Reform and the Process of Global Integration, stated categorically that ".. Countries that are open to trade ... experience unconditional convergence to the income levels of rich countries". Apart from underpinning Sachs' unquestionably disastrous role in advising the collapsing Soviet Union on matters of economic restructuring, this view formed the groundwork for a host of policy initiatives which advocated the integration of transition and developed countries in the world economy as a means of combating poverty.

While political support for this orthodoxy has been strong, it has never been fully accepted amongst mainstream economists. Thus Rodrik's (2003) review of the literature on gains from foreign trade concluded that the evidence was clear that "trade yields relatively small income gains which do not translate into persistently higher growth". In as far as evidence for the positive effects of participation in trade and foreign investment was concerned, economists found that those directly employed by foreign companies experienced some, albeit fairly limited, welfare benefits. For instance, Aitkin, Harrison and Lipsey (1996) noted that foreign firms operating in developing countries tended to pay higher wages than indigenous firms; which they attributed to the possible application of superior technology. Similarly, Budd, Konings and Slaughter's (2004) investigation of multinational firms, led them to conclude that these firms engaged in patterns of rent sharing where the greater profitability of the parent company gave rise to higher wages. However, another study by Konings (2004) concluded that the employment effects of FDI itself were generally limited, primarily because employment relocation was mainly taking place between trans-national company parents which were located in similar, high-wage, countries. A study by Pavlinek (2002) on acquisitions and joint venture agreement in Central Europe was even more pessimistic in that it concluded that these activities did not result in improvements in employment conditions, but rather in the introduction of more effective managerial control and measures to enhance labour discipline (see also Woolfson and Beck; 2004).

While many of employment and wage effects of FDI suggest caution with regard to Sachs' proposition, it is on the level of aggregate data that the pro-trade/foreign investment hypothesis appears to suffer its greatest weaknesses. Although there is evidence of a long term, albeit inconsistent, growth in trade volumes over at least the last three decades, most historical studies of growth across regions find no evidence of an 'unconditional narrowing' of global income differentials. As one of the most comprehensive and thorough studies of long-term world income distribution, Maddisons's (2001) book The World Economy: A Millenial Perspective, instead strikingly observes an increase in inequality, in which the positions of 'Eastern Europe and the former USSR' and 'Africa' have markedly deteriorated (see Table 1).

Table 1. Interregional spread of per capita GDP (in USD, PPP, source Maddison, 2001, p. 126)

		1950	1973	1998
Western Europe		4,594	11,534	17,921
US, Canada, Australia, NZ	(1)	9,288	16,172	26,146
Japan		1,926	11,439	20,413
Asia (excl Japan)	(2)	635	1,231	2,936
Latin America		2,554	4,531	5,795
Eastern Europe and former USSR	(3)	2,601	5,729	4,354
Africa	(4)	852	1,365	1,368
World wide average		2,114	4,104	5,709
Ratio (1) to (2) Asia		14.5:1	13.1:1	8.9:1
Ratio (1) to (3) EE and USSR		3.6:1	2.8:1	6.0:1
Ratio (1) to (4) Africa		10.9:1	11.8:1	19.1:1

Although Maddison's classification of 'US, Canada, Australia and New Zealand' into one group is perhaps somewhat counter-intuitive, his aggregate data permit some useful comparisons (see also Berger, 2006 who discusses this data in some detail). Particularly interesting, in the light of the claim of 'unconditional convergence' are comparisons between the richest group (1) including the of 'US, Canada, Australia and New Zealand' with the three non-Western groups 'Asia' (2), 'Eastern Europe and former USSR' (2) and 'Africa' (3). Of these three groups only 'Asia' (2) experienced a significant reduction in income inequality from 14.5 to 1, to a still sizable 8.9 to 1 as compared to the richest group from the period from 1950 to 1998. 'Eastern Europe and the former USSR' (2), by contrast experienced an initial narrowing of its income differential to group (1) from 3.6 to 1, to 2.8 to 1 during the period from 1950 to 1973. From 1973 to 1998, however, the income differential of the 'Eastern Europe and former USSR' (2) group relative to the richest group more than doubled from 2.8 to 1 in 1973 to 6.0 to 1 in 1998. Although it can be reliably argued that 'Asia' experienced a massive expansion of trade during this period, the pro-trade argument breaks down when we consider that the 'Eastern Europe and former USSR' and 'Africa' groups also experienced increased trade and integration in the world economy. On the basis of aggregate data, then, there is not only evidence of a recent increase global polarisation, but also of trade having a polarising effect on at least two regions.

That this widening of income differential is not merely a matter of academic debate and economic data is perhaps best illustrated by linking this analysis to the, by now, well known phenomenon of the Russian mortality crisis. This data is reproduced in Table 2, not so much to illustrate the shocking decline of life expectancy among Russian males and the still quite pronounced decline among female which had occurred by 1994, but to point to the lesser known fact that the situation had not improved significantly by 2000.

Table 2. Life expectancy in Russia and other countries (from Gavrilova, Semyonova & Evudkushkina, 2002, p. 20)

Country	Year	Life expectancy at birth	
		Males	Females
Russia	1991	63.5	74.3
	1992	62.0	73.8
	1993	58.9	71.9
	1994	57.6	71.2
	1995	58.3	71.7
	1996	59.8	72.5
	1997	60.8	72.9
	1998	61.3	72.6
	1999	59.9	72.4
	2000	58.8	71.7
India	1994-1997	62.4	63.4
China	1994-1997	69.0	73.0
US	1994-1997	73.6	79.4

Source Goskomstat, WHO.

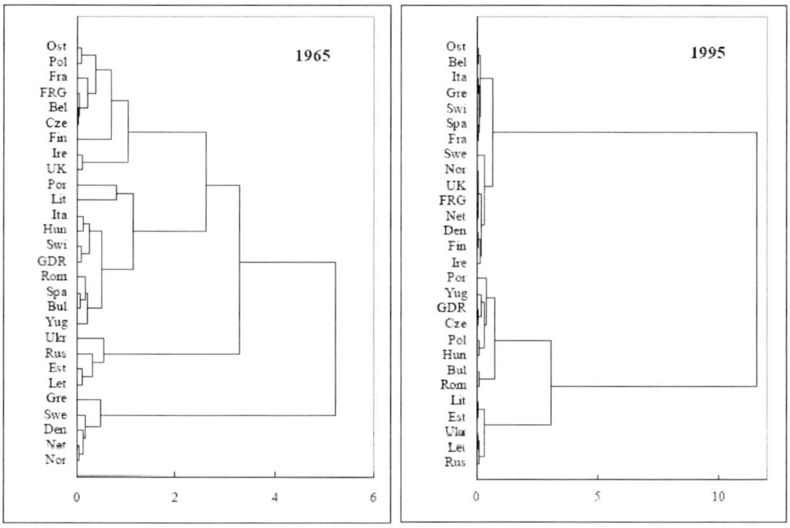

Source: Mesle and Vallin, 2002.

Figure 1. Dendrograms resulting from the hierarchial analysis of male age-specific death probabilities in 28 European countries, in 1965 and 1995.

While the simultaneous occurrence of increased income inequality of the 'Eastern Europe and the former USSR' with the Russian mortality crisis is at least suggestive of a link, it would, of course, be difficult to draw direct causal connections. What is worth pointing out, however, is that there are several analyses which illustrate a close connection between the worsening economic position of the region post 1990 and indicators of well–being. One particularly striking study, conducted by Mesle and Vallin (2002), for instance, illustrates that, whereas in 1965 a ranking of male life expectancy included a mix of western and eastern nations, by 1995 a clear dichotomy had occurred in which the top portion of the table was occupied exclusively by western nations, while the bottom was occupied by eastern ones (see Figure 1).

Taking into account these and other sources of evidence, it is perhaps no overstatement to argue that the recent two decades of trade liberalisation have brought few tangible benefits to Eastern Europe and Russia as a region. What is more difficult to answer is the question as to whether trade liberalisation itself has damaged the region. To contextualise this question into a broader debate, the next section will review more recent neo-institutionalist theories of trade together with some of their more radical alternatives.

Neo-Institutional and Alternative Models of Trade and Development

Contemporary theoretical approaches to the impact of trade on development no longer take an unambiguously positive role of trade and investment for granted. In particular there is now a broader acknowledgement of the fact that institutional structures mediate the impact of trade and investment. However, within this literature a number of micro-narratives continue to suggest that trade and investment are linked to increased growth and prosperity, even to the extent of having a 'unambiguously' positive impact on existing institutional structures. Specifically, the literature continues to recognise three mechanisms which allegedly create benefits from trade and investment. These include, firstly, strategic modernisation which describes a process where the recipient country gains access to the know-how and finance necessary to update equipment and bring about strategic restructuring together with an imposition of efficient corporate governance (Blanchard, 1997). Secondly, trade and investment are expected to create positive externalities which extend to a process where the introduction of new products and processes by foreign firms creates spillovers for the domestic economy (Teece, 1977). Lastly, and perhaps most controversially, increased trade and investment are expected to result in hardening budget constraints, where foreign participation in firms reduces financial links of local firms with government organisations, allowing central government to impose harder budget constraints and improve performance (Dewartipont and Maskin, 1995; Roland 2000).

At their core, neo-institutionalist narratives on trade and economic growth suggest that the integration of an economy into the work market cannot alone explain growth. Rather, growth is, apart from obvious factor endowments, dependent on the interaction of three factors, namely; i) participation in trade, ii) institutional development and iii) existing productive capacity (Rodrik, 2003). According to Rodrik, the income level of a country is dependent on its factor endowments which, in turn, are determined by the availability of physical and human capital. However, the effect of these factor endowments is mediated by economies' levels of productivity. In other words, economies with similar levels of physical and human capital can differ significantly in terms of their wealth and growth potential on account of different levels of productivity. In Rodrik's model (see Figure 2) factor endowments and productivity are 'endogenous.' The elements which establish these endogenous levels of factor endowments and productivity include trade and institutions, which Rodrik describes as being 'partly endogenous.' In other words, the positive effect which trade is likely to have on an economy depends in part on the absorptive capacity of institutions, with institutions having a more pronounced influence on income levels than trade (see also Rodrik, Subramian and Trebbi, 2001).

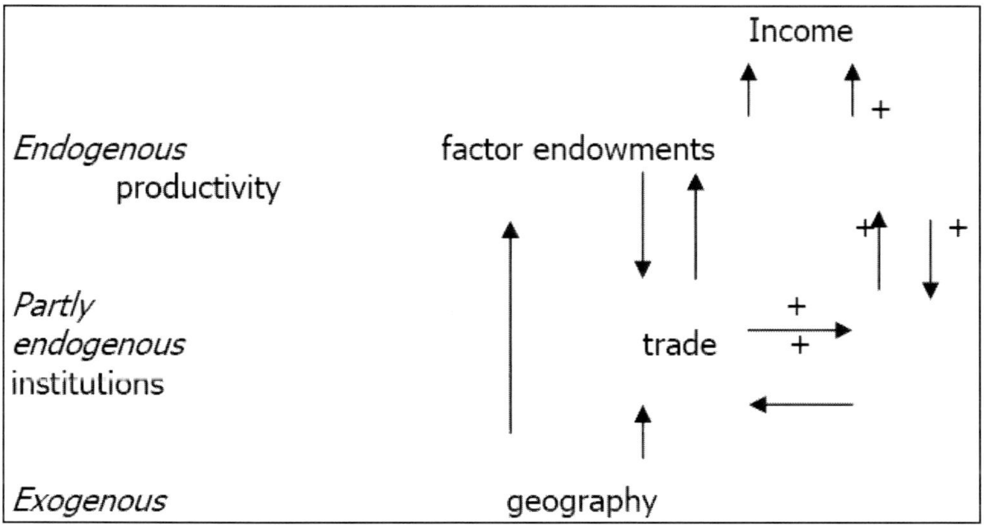

Figure 2. Rodrik's model of income generation.

Ultimately, therefore, the principal source of wealth for an economy is its productivity, albeit that improvements in a country's trade position can lead to improvements in its institutional make-up, which, in turn, positively affect the crucial parameter of productivity. Lastly, both trade and factor endowments are affected by a country's geography which, as exogenous factor, can play a key role in shaping a national economy's competitive position.

In terms of its policy implications Rodrik's model represents a limited, but not insignificant, deviation from Sachs' orthodoxy on at least two counts. Firstly, it suggests that trade is not sufficient to initiate growth through productivity enhancement, if institutional structures are deficient. Secondly, it makes an implicit assumption that trade and foreign investment are likely to have a impact on both institutional developments and only indirectly on productive capacity (see plus signs in Figure 2).

While Rodrik's model and similar neo-institutionalist narratives on income and growth have their appeal, particularly when compared with earlier uncritical assumptions with regard to the benefits of international trade, they have struggled to find convincing empirical support. Rodrik's own (2003) work entitled *The Search for Prosperity*, purports to include case studies in support of the model's core assumptions. Accordingly, the book includes fourteen country studies which are meant to illustrate how the interaction of institutions and trade either created, or failed to create, prosperity. Interestingly, none of these country examples include a post-Soviet country. Examples of a successful translation of trade into wealth include Australia, India, Botswana, Vietnam, Mauritius, Venezuela, Poland, China and Mexico. Examples of largely unsuccessful absorption of trade include the Philippines, Indonesia, Romania and Bolivia, with Pakistan representing an 'undecided'. While it is futile to unpick these arguments at any length, it is probably worth mentioning that Botswana's economy recently faced a near complete collapse, triggered partly by its close economic ties with Zimbabwe. Similarly, Venezuela, despite its oil wealth underwent a major economic crisis in mid 2000 which brought a socialist government to power. The Philippines, Indonesia and Romania, rather than being condemned to hopeless underperformance, meanwhile, appear to experience moderate economic growth.

The fact that applications of neo-institutionalist models of growth do not perform unambiguously well when applied to concrete case studies, needless to say, does not necessarily discredit this intellectual enterprise. What is perhaps more troubling are other issues which include the fact that, as a theory, Rodrik's model is potentially overdetermined. In other words, it offers an opportunity to explain the absence or presence of trade-induced growth on the basis of institutional weaknesses, while institutional stagnation or development, in turn, can be linked to the presence of absence of trade. This offers the very real possibility that virtually any event or development with regard to a country's economic fate can be explained on the basis of at least some of the elements of the model. Perhaps even more troublesome, is the fact that the model ignores a significant intellectual tradition which views, and has viewed, trade as a potentially detrimental force in as far as the institutional, social and political development of developing and transition nations are concerned.

While it is beyond the scope of this paper to examine this alternative literature at any level of detail, it is perhaps worth briefly mentioning some of its key milestones. Economists first voiced concerns over the impact of trade and investment on lesser developed economies in connection with the, largely continental, imperialism debate of the early 20th century. At the time an intense debate took place among leftist intellectuals who examined the instability of contemporary advanced capitalist systems and highlighted the economic role of colonialism and imperial expansionism as practised by the main European powers and the US (see e.g., Luxemburg's *The Accumulation of Capital*, originally published in 1913 and Bukharin's, *Imperialism and the World Economy*, originally published in 1916). Bukharin's work in particular hypothesised that export of capital by heavily industrialised nations would lead to the subjugation of the economic interests of the recipient country. In chapter seven of his *Imperialism and the World Economy,* Bukharin stated:

> Looked upon from the point of view of the spreading of the organisational forms of modern capital, capital export is nothing but a seizure and a monopolisation of new spheres of capital investment by the monopoly enterprises of a great nation or - taking the process as a whole - by the organised "national" industry, by "national" finance capital. Capital export is the most convenient method for the economic policy of finance groups; it subjugates new territories with the greatest ease.

In the 1970s a number of researchers attempted to re-examine earlier notions of imperialism within a structuralist context, with a view toward explaining the persistence of underdevelopment within certain regions. In his, at the time, widely read paper *A Structural Theory of Imperialism,* Galtung (1971) proposed a concept of 'core and periphery' in which Core, or industrialised, nations established core areas within the Periphery, or developing nations, in order to facilitate trade. According to Galtung, this core and periphery system superficially benefited both Core and Periphery nations, while, at a deeper level, sustaining a type of unequal trade and exchange which Galtung described as imperialism or structural violence. Specifically Galtung (1971, p.81) noted that:

> Imperialism will be conceived as a dominance relation between collectives—particularly between nations. It is a? sophisticated type of dominance relation which cuts across nations, basing itself on a bridgehead which the center of the Center [sic] nation establishes in the center of the Periphery [sic] nation, for the benefit of both. ... Briefly stated, imperialism is a system that splits up collectives and relates some of the parts to each in relations of harmony of interests, and other parts in relations of disharmony of interest, or conflict of interest.

While Galtung's analysis was primarily concerned with the role Western economic activity played in fermenting conflict within periphery nations, he attributed a crucial role to trade and foreign investment in supporting institutional structures which cemented existing relationships of exploitation and contributed to political instability.

Galtung's core and periphery theory was further developed by Wallerstein's (1979) who introduced the concept of the 'semi-peripheral state'. According to Wallerstein, semi-peripheral states played a key role in the capitalist system, on account of their ability to absorb products of richer nations. However, Wallerstein argued that there was no guarantee for the future prosperity of the nations and no evidence that these nations would benefit from a future expansion of trade. In his chapter *Dependence within and Interdependent World* (1979, p.71), Wallerstein specifically argued:

> In a system of unequal exchange, the semiperipheral country stands between in terms of the kinds of products it exports and in terms of the wage levels and profit margins it knows. Furthermore, it trades or seeks trade in both directions, in one mode with the periphery and in the opposite with the core. Whereas at any given moment, the more *balanced* trade a core country or a peripheral country can engage in, the better off it is in absolute terms, it is often in the interest of the semiperipheral country to *reduce* external trade, even if balanced, since one of the major ways in which the aggregate profit margin can be increased is to capture an increasingly large portion of the *home* market for its *home* products. (emphasis in the original)

Wallerstein was not only reluctant to accept the assumption that foreign investment and trade will have a positive effects on the recipient economy, but went as far as to argue that foreign investment which was led primarily by the needs of the developed country was destined to be detrimental to the recipient economy.

While the structuralist analysis of inequality has ceased to attract the attention of mainstream scholarship on development, a series of more recent papers have borrowed heavily from some of the core notions of this literature. A striking example of this is the work of Moran whose notion of benign and malign foreign investment relies heavily on earlier ideas about the potentially undesirable effect on unconstrained trade. In his book *FDI and Development: A New Policy Agenda for Developing Countries and Economies in Transition*, Moran (1998, p. 20) argues that:

> Instead of filling the gap between savings and investment, Multinational Enterprises (MNEs) may lower domestic savings and investment by extracting rents and siphoning off the capital through preferred access to local capital markets and local supplies of foreign exchange. Instead of closing the gap between investment and foreign exchange, they might drive domestic producers out of business and substitute imported inputs. The MNE may reinvest in the same or related industries in the host country and extend its market power. The repatriation of profits might drain capital from the host country.

> MNEs' use of "inappropriate" capital intensive technologies may produce small labour elites while consigning many workers to the ranks of the unemployed. Their tight control over technology, higher management functions and export channels may prevent the beneficial spillovers and externalities hoped for in more optimistic scenarios.

Implicit in Moran's analysis is the assumption that, rather than contributing to institutional development and productivity, certain types of FDI have the potential to undermine existing institutional growth trajectories and, in so doing, forestall future economic growth and development.

Although analyses of the type presented by Moran still represents a minority view amongst development economists, it is interesting to note that even some researchers involved in contemporary international policy making have started to adopt a critical perspective on the institutional impact of foreign investment. One example of this are the economists Hausmann and Fernandez-Arias (2000) who presented a paper to the Annual Meeting of the Board of Governors, Inter-American Development Bank and Inter-American Investment Corporation which noted that "the view that capital inflows tend to take the form of FDI – share of FDI in total liabilities tends to be higher – in countries that are safer, more promising and with better institutions and policies was misleading". Specifically Hausmann and Fernandez-Arias found that, while some capital flows tended to target countries that were safer, more developed, more open, more stable and had better and advanced institutions and financial markets, the share of FDI in total capital flows to these countries tended to be lower than that to less stable regions. This analysis not only suggested that FDI often targeted countries that were riskier, poorer, more volatile and more closed, but also that foreign investment quite possibly contributed to regional instability.

Collectively these alternative approaches to foreign investment suggest a model of trade and development which differs radically in its outcomes from the neo-institutionalist paradigm. Applying the notion of malign investment to Rodrik's framework, it can be argued that certain types of investment (here denoted as mFDI for malign FDI) can weaken existing institutions, while being themselves attracted to institutionally weaker environments. This potentially vicious cycle of institutional erosion and malign FDI inflows, in turn, is likely to adversely affect the domestic productive capacity of the recipient country productivity and, ultimately, its wealth (see Figure 3).

While there is no conclusive empirical study which documents the institution-eroding effects of malign investment, there is ample anecdotal evidence on how developing and transition countries suffered from institutional disintegration and political instability as a consequence of FDI (see, e.g., Marriott and Muttitt, 2005). This pattern appears to be particularly pronounced where these investments centre on primary and/or extractive industries at the costs of the recipient country's secondary and tertiary sectors.

The remaining sections of this paper will examine firstly, some of the key characteristics of FDI in former Soviet states. Secondly, it will seek to analyse the potential link between FDI and political instability in some post-Soviet states.

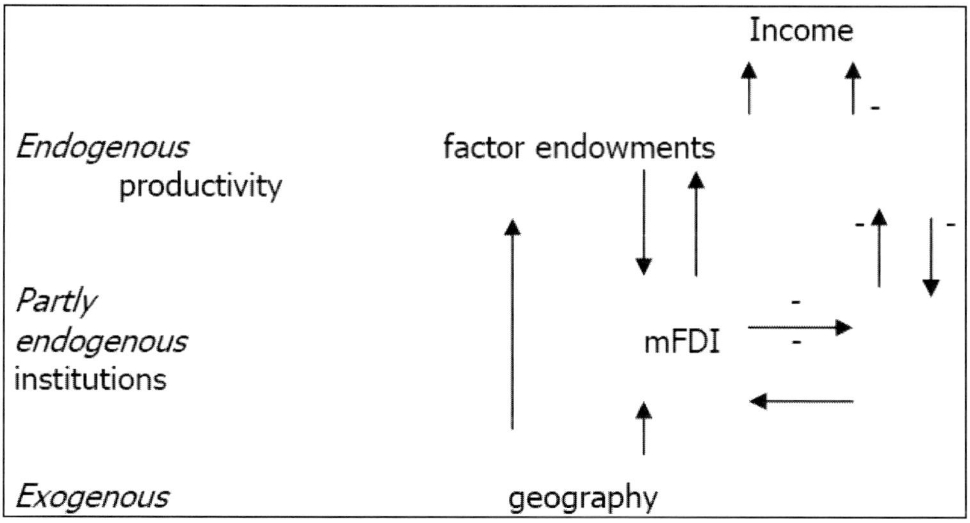

Figure 3. Malign investment and the erosion of domestic capacities.

FOREIGN DIRECT INVESTMENT IN FORMER SOVIET STATES

Since the collapse of the Soviet Union the FDI performance of its former constituents has been patchy. Table 3 lists absolute figures for FDI inflows into former USSR countries from 1997 to 2005. Perhaps unsurprisingly, this data indicates a massive acceleration of FDI inflows into the Baltic countries in the run-up to their EU accession. By contrast, a number of former Soviet states with significant levels of industrial development, such as Belarus, Moldova and the Ukraine, either have experienced no significant increases in FDI inflows, or have received FDI inflows which are disproportionately low given their level of industrial development and population size; particularly in comparison with the Baltic states.

The two oil producing Central Asian countries, Azerbaijan and Kazakhstan, stand out in terms of FDI inflows and FDI growth with FDI figures for recent years exceeding all other former Soviet states, including the Baltics (with the sole of exception of Russia). This contrasts dramatically with the other Central Asian countries of Armenia, Georgia, Kyryzstan, Tajikistan, Turkmenistan and Uzbekistan, which have experienced negligible FDI inflows.

While it is obvious that in absolute figures, as well as in per capita terms, Azerbaijan and Kazakhstan, vastly outperformed other former Soviet states, it is important to note that even these countries have experienced dramatic fluctuations in terms of the amounts of FDI they have received during this period. This pronounced instability of year by year FDI inflows is depicted in Figure 4, in which recent figures for Russia and Ukraine have been excluded in order to provide a more readable scaling of the trend lines. Apparently, in as far as there has been substantial investment in former Soviet states, this has centred on a very limited number of countries, who themselves could not rely on stable and regular inflows of foreign capital.

Although there is a long history of complaints among potential foreign investors about the vagueness of government attitudes to foreign investment, the existing differences in FDI inflows can only be insufficiently explained by the attitudes and actions of these post-Soviet states. Rather, the unequal regional distribution of FDI in the post-soviet territories appears to be primarily determined by the presence, or absence, of natural resources.

Table 3. FDI inflows in million US dollar

Foreign Direct Investment Inflows, $m

Country	Years								
	1997	1998	1999	2000	2001	2002	2003	2004	2005
1. Former USSR Countries									
1. 1. *Central & Eastern Europe:*									
1. Belarus	352	203	444	119	96	247	172	164	305
2. Moldova	79	76	38	129	156	132	78	154	225
3. Russia	4865	2761	3309	2714	2469	3461	7958	15444	14600
4. Ukraine	623	743	496	595	792	693	1424	1715	7808e
1.2. *Central Asia:*									
5. Armenia	52	221	122	104	70	144	157	217	220
6. Azerbaijan	1115	1023	510	129	227	1392	3285	3556	1680
7. Georgia	243	265	82	131	110	165	340	499	450
8. Kazakhstan	1321	1152	1472	1283	2823	2590	2092	4113	1738
9. Kyrgyzstan	84	109	44	-2	5	5	46	175	47
10. Tajikistan	18	25	21	22	9	36	14	272	54
11.Turkmenistn	108	62	89	131	150	100	100e	-15e	62e
12. Uzbekistan	167	140	121	73	570	65	70e	1e	45e
1.3. *Baltic Countries/ New EU Countries:*									
13. Estonia	267	581	305	387	542	284	919	1049	2853
14. Latvia	521	357	347	410	164	254	292	699	632
15. Lithuania	355	926	486	379	446	732	179	773	1009

Hitherto, natural resource and food industries have been the most attractive targets for foreign investment. In Russia, the fuel and food sectors lead in terms of share of total FDI inflows with 23% and 28%, respectively. They are followed by trade, transport and telecommunication. The machinery, timber and other sectors, meanwhile, have hardly received any investment at all.

Large scale investments in the oil and gas sectors have included about 50 joint ventures and involved American, British, French, German, Canadian, Japanese and other companies. The scale of projects in the food sector is significant as well with foreign companies showing an interest in pastries and meat industries as well as the production of non-alcohol drinks, beer and tobacco (Yacheistova, 2001).

As an example of an industrialised state which has attracted only limited amounts of FDI, Ukraine had attracted less than 6 billion dollars in FDI by 2004, which comprised only about a seventh of the officially estimated 40 billion dollars required for restructuring its economy. A detailed analysis of FDI flows indicates that these were quite small and often used inefficiently. For example, foreign investment inflows in Ukraine during the first half of the year 2001 were 12.4% less then the amount of FDI inflows during the corresponding period of the year 2000. As in Russia, foreign investors targeted the Ukrainian food and agricultural processing industry. The FDI share into this sector comprised 19.8% of the total investment inflows. Wholesale and sale mediation attracted 13.9% of investment. Investment into machine-building industry, finance sectors and transport were equal to 8.2%, 7.9% and 6.8% of total investment inflows, respectively (State Statistics Committee of Ukraine, 2002).

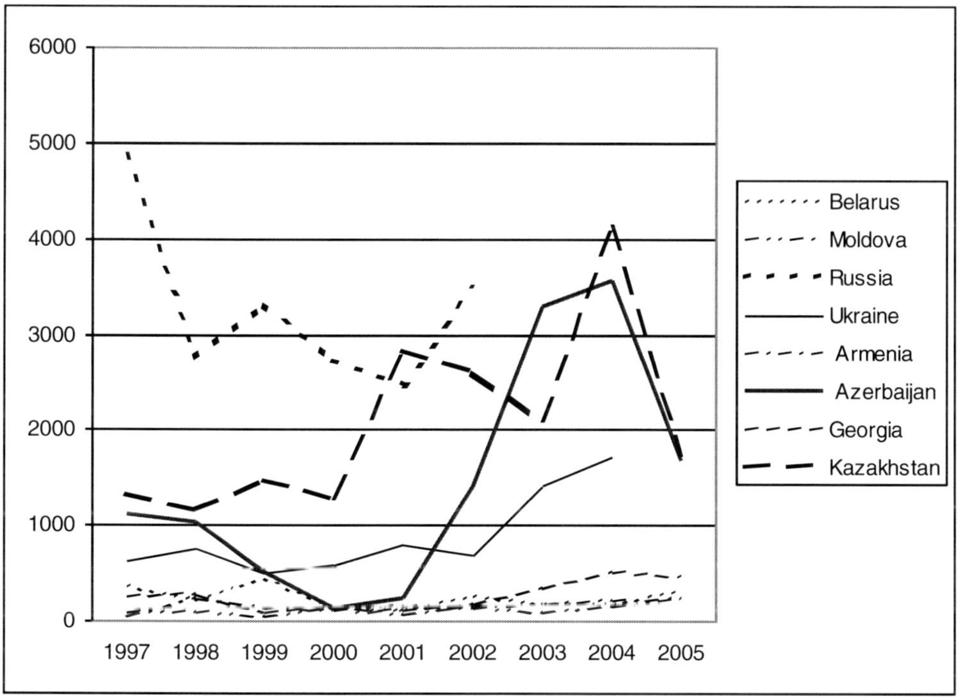

Figure 4. FDI inflows in million US dollar.

In Azerbaijan the largest share of FDI was received by the country's main industry – oil. The high level of investment in this area, however, has hardly benefited other sectors. For instance, amidst complaints about corruption and unfair practices by officials, as well as declining traffic volumes, several international airlines have abandoned their operations in the country. Specifically, during the period of 1999-2000, six different companies, Austrian airlines, Pakistan Air, British Airways, KLM, Lufthansa and Emirates have ceased operations in Baku's Bina International Airport (WMRC, 2004a).

In Kazakhstan, which, by 2004 had received seventeen billion dollars in FDI since independence, there is evidence that foreign investment had a de-stabilising effect on the local economy, which has led to increased frictions between the states and foreign investors. Thus, a number of high profile international investors, such as TengizChevroil, Canada's Hurricane Hydrocarbons Ltd and the Carachaganak Petroleum Operating Company, have faced Environment Ministry accusations of opaque sales and environmental breaches. Moreover, a newly enacted Investment Law, approved in 2003, stipulates that new contracts negotiated with foreign companies will no longer contain a "grandfather clause" that shield the company from regulatory and tax changes. The law also prevents companies from resorting to international arbitration if the Kazakh government forbids this. Furthermore, the law eliminates preferences for foreign investors with a view towards "creating a level playing field between domestic and foreign companies" (WMRC, 2004b).

Both Kazakhstan and Azerbaijan, meanwhile, appear to suffer from a rise of governmental authoritarianism and are even showing 'dynastic' tendencies. In October, 2003, for instance, for the first time, the rule of a post-Soviet state was passed from father to son as a result of Azerbaijan's presidential elections. In Kazakhstan, President Nursultan

Nazarbayev's eldest daughter, the country's biggest media baron, is creating a new political party and is believed to be groomed for the succession of her father. These and many other events are indicative of the potentially adverse effects of the newly found foreign-sponsored wealth.

FOREIGN INVESTMENT, CORRUPTION AND POLITICAL INSTABILITY: AN EMPRICAL ANALYSIS

Today, any evidence regarding the link between foreign investment and increases in corruption and political instability remains largely anecdotal. Nevertheless, as far as former Soviet states other than the Baltics are concerned it is difficult to find instances in which foreign investment appears to have had a positive impact on the recipient countries political institutions. Put simply, FDI inflows have increased in a number of former Soviet states, and where this has been the case, so typically has corruption.

Figures 5 to 7 depict scatterplots of the *Corruption Perception Index* rank and FDI inflows for the period from 1999 to 2005 (Transparency International, 2006). The *Corruption Perception Index* is collected by the international voluntary association *Transparency International* and ranks countries according to a number of criteria, including bond ratings, as those which are internationally perceived as most or least corrupt.

As concerns the scatterplot for Russia, it can be noted that the country experienced a small decline in its corruption ranking alongside a decline in FDI. This situation, however, changed from 2002, when a massive increase in FDI inflows was accompanied by a modest increase in the country's corruption rank. Between 2004 and 2005 a small decline in FDI inflows occurred which was accompanied by a pronounced increase in the country's corruption perception ranking.

This pattern is closely mirrored by the scatterplot for Azerbaijan. Here too an initial decrease in FDI was accompanied by a decline in the country's corruption ranking. From 2001 onwards, however, Azerbaijan experienced both a massive increase in FDI inflows and in its corruption ranking. This situation changed only between 2004 and 2005, when the annual FDI more than halved and the country's corruption perception ranking declined from 140th to 137th.

The scatterplot for Kazakhstan deviates from the previous two patterns in several minor respects. Initially, Kazakhstan's corruption ranking decreased alongside a decline in FDI. From 2000 to 2001, both FDI inflows and the country's corruption rank increased. This was followed by a period from 2001 to 2003, when FDI inflows decrease while the corruption rank continues to increase. Between 2003 and 2004 a massive increase in FDI inflows took place which was again accompanied by an increase in the country's corruption perception rank, this time from 100th to 103rd . The period from 2004 to 2005, lastly, saw a decrease in FDI alongside a continuing increase in the corruption index, this time to 107th.

Taken together these analyses lend limited support to the hypothesis that increased inflows in FDI are likely to be linked to increases in corruption and possibly political instability in the recipient country. Needless to say, the simultaneous occurrence of increased FDI inflows together with increased corruption, if this is indeed measured by this index, does not in itself imply a causality. What it does suggest, however, is that FDI has not had, as previously often assumed, a corruption-reducing effect on post-Soviet recipient states.

The remaining sections test the relationship between country risk indicators as reported by World Market Research Centre (WMRC) country reports and various economic variables (including FDI) for the above listed countries. This analysis deliberately excludes the three Baltic states, whose economic development was affected relatively early on by their eventual succession to the European Union (Hunya, 2004).

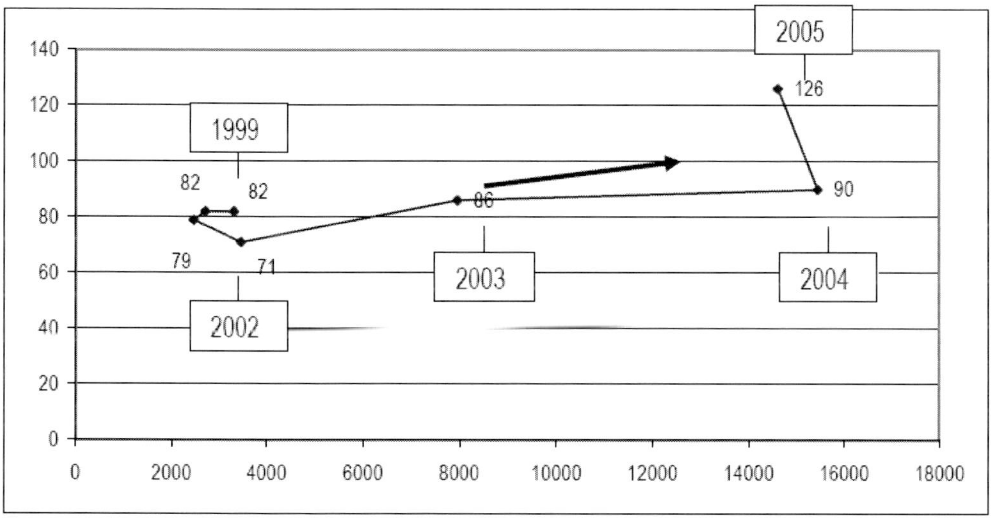

Figure 5. Russia: Scatterplot of *Corruption Perception Index* rank and FDI inflows, 1999-2005.

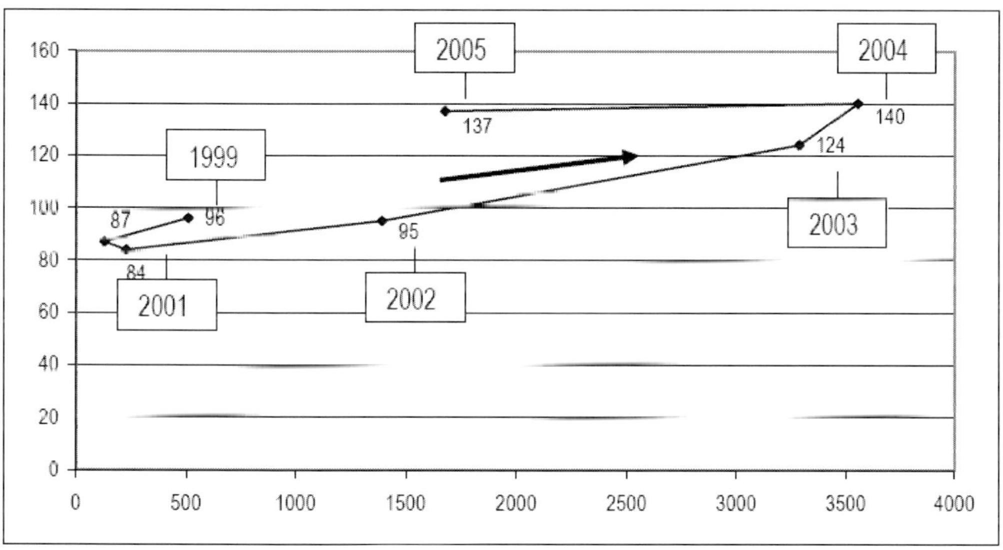

Figure 6. Azerbaijan: Scatterplot of *Corruption Perception Index* rank and FDI inflows, 1999-2005.

This analysis is conducted via a pooled regression analysis where data for twelve countries (namely the Central and Eastern European States of Belarus, Moldova, Russia, and Ukraine, and the Central Asian Republics of Armenia, Azerbaijan, Georgia, Kazakhstan, Kyrgyzstan, Tajikistan, Turkmenistan and Uzbekistan) and nine years (1997-2005) are investigated in terms of three models. These include Ordinary Least Squares (OLS), Least Squares Dummy Variables (LSDV) and the General Least Squares Error (GLSE) Model. Of these models, the LSDV model can be considered the most reliable since the OLS model is likely to produce over-inflated t values on account of serial correlation, and the GLSE is likely to underestimate the significance of coefficient (Stimson, 1985).

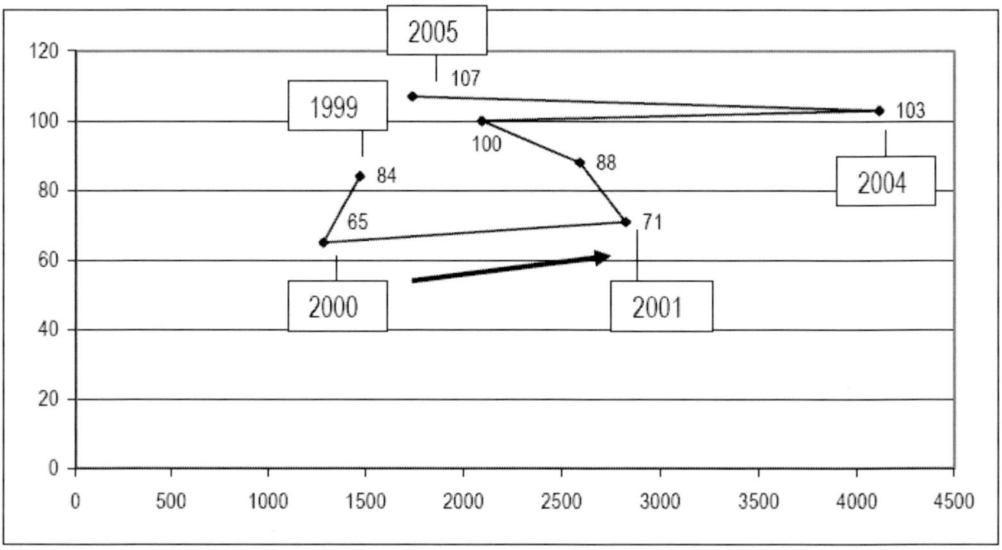

Figure 7. Kazakhstan: Scatterplot of *Corruption Perception Index* rank and FDI inflows, 1999-2005.

In the following analysis, tests are conducted for the WMRC variables, Overall Country Risk (OCR), Economic Risk (ER) and Legal Risk (LR).[1] World Market Research Centre (WMRC) defines:

- Economic Risk (ER): as degree of market orientation, policy consistency and forward planning, diversity and resilience of the economy, macroeconomic fundamentals;
- Legal Risk (LR): as a measure of a country's legislation, transparency, independence, and experience; and
- Overall Country (OCR): as a composite indicator of these risks plus Tax Risk, Operational Risk and Security Risk.

[1] It should be noted that this analysis has excluded a fourth WMRC variable, namely political risk. The reason for this is that this variable shows a strong path dependency in the sense that the stability of democratic governance systems has strong historical determinants and appears to change only marginally over time. For the purpose of our argument regarding the potentially malign effects of FDI, both economic and legal risk appear to be the more suitable variables.

Despite the lack of more detailed data and the fact that these risk variables are based on a number of assumptions, the relationship between these variables and FDI is remarkably stable; with FDI having a significant positive (risk increasing) coefficient for most of the relevant LSDV model outputs.

The first part of the analysis utilizes WMRC's score for 'Overall Country Risk' (OCR) as dependent variable (Table 4). Overall this analysis performs well for both the LSDV and the GLSE variant. For the more reliable LSDV variant, 53.1% of the total variation is explained by the five independent variables, 'FDI as % of GDP', 'Government Debt as % of GDP', 'GDP per capita', 'Unemployment rate' and 'Trade Balance as % GDP'. Of the independent variables both 'Government debt' and the 'Unemployment rate' have a significant, risk increasing, effect on overall country risk at the .05 level of significance or above. 'FDI as % of GDP' also has a risk increasing effect, but here the significance is more marginal (.12 level of significance).

Table 4. Overall Country Risk (OCR)

Model	OLS	LSDV	GLSE
Indep Variables			
FDI as % of GDP .	0295	.0249	.0065
	(1.915)	(1.544)	(.858)
Gov Debt as % GDP .	0106	.0197	.0048
	(4.160)	(5.281)	(2.885)
GDP per capita .	0003	.0002	.0001
	(3.275)	(1.119)	(0.644)
Unemployment rate .	0185	.0665	.0387
	(1.279)	(2.058)	(3.249)
Trade Balance/% GDP -.	0065	-.0019	-.0021
	(-.965)	(-.0168)	(-.512)
R square adjusted 28.9	28.9	53.1	21.5

t values in parenthesis

Table 5. Economic Risk (ER)

Model	OLS	LSDV	GLSE
Indep Variables			
FDI as % of GDP	.0169	.0314	.0068
	(1.060)	(1.744)	(.915)
Gov Debt as % GDP	.0109	.0191	.0027
	(4.150)	(4.597)	(1.592)
GDP per capita	.0003	.0001	-.0001
	(2.717)	(1.080)	(-1.729)
Unemployment rate	.0300	.0768	.0530
	(1.999)	(2.1297)	(4.175)
Trade Balance/% GDP -	. 0112	-.0037	-.0023
	(-1.596)	(-.301)	(-.558)
R square adjusted	30.0	46.4	21.6

While it is probably not surprising that government debt and unemployment would increase the overall riskiness of a country or decrease its overall stability, it is interesting to note that, contrary to the assumptions of the benign model of FDI, the variable 'FDI as % of GDP' also exerts a negative influence on 'Overall Country Risk'.

This pattern of a risk increasing role of FDI is confirmed for the dependent variable 'Economic Risk' which is examined in the next set of models (Table 5). Again this analysis performs well for the LSDV model which yields an adjusted R Square value of 46.4%. In this model, 'Government debt' and the 'Unemployment rate' have again a significant, risk increasing, effect 'Economic Risk' at the .05 level of significance or above. 'FDI as % of GDP', meanwhile also has a significant risk increasing effects, however, at the lower .01 level of significance.

Perhaps the most interesting results are gained by re-examining this model with the third dependent variable of 'Legal Risk' (Table 6).

Table 6. Legal Risk (LR)

Model	OLS	LSDV	GLSE
Indep Variables			
FDI as % of GDP	.0263	.0337	.0126
	(1.494)	(1.916)	(1.552)
Gov Debt as % of GDP .	0070	.0197	.0031
	(2.408)	(4.7064)	(1.540)
GDP per capita	.0004	.0012	.0001
	(3.587)	(1.494)	(1.316)
Unemployment rate	.0070	.0363	.0250
	(.419)	(1.003)	(1.822)
Trade Balance/% GDP-	.0054	-.0047	.0002
	(-.694)	(-.037)	(0.033)
R square adjusted	*32.0*	*48.9*	*30.1*

This variable, which assesses a country's system of legal and commercial governance, probably most closely mirrors the assumptions of the previously discussed opposing models of benign versus malign foreign investment, as it focuses on country-specific governance competencies. Again the result of these models closely mirrors those of the previous analysis, with the LSDV model performing well and yielding an adjusted R square value of 48.9%. However, in case of the dependent variable 'Legal Risk', the independent variables 'Government debt' , the 'Unemployment rate' and 'FDI as % of GDP' have a significant, risk increasing, effect at the .05 level of significance. The significance of the 'FDI as % GDP' in this model in particular, lends strong support to the previously discussed hypothesis of a malign effect FDI in terms of political stability in the context of post-Soviet states.

Although the previous regression analyses are inevitably affected by any weaknesses in the underlying data, they strongly point to the possibility that, at least for the period during which these countries were examined, FDI was having an overall destabilising effect on domestic institutional competencies. While this analysis does not necessarily confirm the hypothesis of a malign effect of foreign investment, it certainly contests the conventional assumption that FDI will positively impact on the institutional structures and the stability of recipient countries.

CONCLUSION

The paper has sought to examine the conventional assumption of a benign role of foreign investment, together with its opposing hypothesis of malign FDI in the context of post-Soviet states. Although our results point to the possibility that, on the whole, foreign investment may have had negative effects on the region, this analysis must necessarily be interpreted with caution. Specifically some of the factors which limit the generalisability of these findings include the fact that the regression analysis covers a limited time frame during which some parts of the region, such as Georgia and Azerbaijan were, *ab initio*, characterised by involvement in conflict and instability. Secondly, during the period examined here a very large amount of foreign investment was concentrated on a small number of natural resource-endowed states, which could have a distorting effect on the overall data analysis.

Despite these caveats it is probably valid to note that this analysis throws doubt on the, often politically motivated, advocacy of FDI which presupposes that the interests of multinational investors are identical with those of recipient states. Without more concrete evidence in its support, the assumption of a benign effect of foreign investment is no more than speculation, irrespective of how many international organisations pay lip service to this; and what is more, it is an assumption that needs to be very carefully and critically examined.

REFERENCES

Abbott, P. 2002. *Living Conditions, Lifestyles and Health in Armenia, Belarus, Georgia, Kazakhstan, Kyrgyzstan, Moldova, Russia and Ukraine*. Vienna, Institute for Advanced Studies.

Abbott, P. and Beck, M. 2003. The Post-Soviet Health Crisis: A Sociological Explanation, in Haerpfer, C., Rotman, D., Turmov, S. (eds) Living Conditions, *Lifestyles and Health in Post Soviet Societies*. Minsk, Minsk University Press.

Aitkin, B., Harrison, A., Lipsey, R.E. 1996. Wages and Foreign Ownership: A Comparative Study of Mexico, Venezuela and the United States. *Journal of International Economics*, 40(3/4): 345-371.

Balasubramanyam, V., Salisu, M. and Sapsford, D. 1996 Foreign Direct Investment and Growth in EP and IS Countries. *The Economic Journal*, 106: 92-105.

Berger, J. 2006. Warum sind einige Laender so viel reicher as andere? Zur insitutionellen Erklaerung von Entwicklungsunderschieden. Max-Planck-Insitut fuer Gesellschaftforschung, Discussion Paper 06/6.

Bevan, A., Estrin, S. and Meyer, K. 2004 Foreign Investment Location and Institutional Development in Transition Economies. *International Business Review*, 13: 43-64.

Blanchard, O. 1997 The Economics of Post-Communist Transition. *Gloucestershire*, Clarendon Press.

Borensztein, E., De Gregorio, J. and Lee, J. 1998. How Does FDI Affect Economic Growth? *Journal of International Economics*, 45: 115-135.

Budd, J.W., Konings, J., and Slaughter, M.J. 2004 International Rent Sharing in Multinational Firms, *Review of Economics and Statistics*, _____

Bukharin, N. (originally published in German). 1916. Imperialism and the World Economy, online English translation available at www.marxists.org.

De Melo, J. 1999. Foreign Direct Investment-Led Growth: Evidence from Time Series and Panel Data. *Oxford Economic Papers*, 51(1): 133-151.

Dewatripont, M. and E. Maskin. 1995. Credit And Efficiency in Centralized and Decentralized Economies. *Review of Economic Studies*, **62:** 541–556.

Dyker, D.A. 1999. *Foreign Direct Investment and Technology Transfer in the FormerSoviet Union*. Cheltenham, Edward Elgar.

Estrin, S., Hughes, K. and Todd, S. 1997. Foreign Direct Investment in Central and Eastern Europe. London, Cassel.

Fabry, N. and Zeghni, S. 2002. Foreign Direct Investment in Russia: How The Investment Climate Matters. *Communist and Post-Communist Studies*, 35: 289-303.

Galtung, J. 1971. A Structural Theory of Imperialism. *Journal of Peace Research*, 3: 81-113.

Gavrilova, N., Semyonova, V. and Evudkushina, G. 2002. Mortality Crisis in Russia: New Health Threats. Chicago, Center on Aging, University of Chicago.

Guisinger, S. 1985. Investment Incentives and Performance Requirements; Patterns of International Trade, *Production and Investment*. New York, Praeger.

Hausmann, R., Fernandez-Arias, E. 2000. Foreign Direct Investment: Good Cholesterol? Washington: Seminar Paper for the Annual Meeting of the Board of Governors, Inter-American Development Bank and Inter-American Investment Corporation.

Hunya, G. 2004. FDI in Small Accession Countries: The Baltic States. *European Investment Bank Papers,* 9(2): 92-115.

Konings, J. 2004. The Employment Effects of Foreign Direct Investment. *European Investment Bank Papers*, 9(1): 87-108.

Lucas, R.E. 1988. On the Mechanics of Economic Development. *Journal of Monetary Economics,* 222: 3-42.

Luxemburg, R. (originally published in German in 1916). 1956, *The Accumulation of Capita.*, New Haven, Yale University Press.

Maddison, A. 2001. *The Wold Economy: A Millenial Perspective*. Paris: OECD.

Marriott, J., Muttitt, G. 2005. BP's Baku-Tbilisi-Ceyhan Pipeline: The New Corporate Colonialism, in Woolfson C., Beck, M. (eds) *Corporate Social Responsibility Failures in the Oil Industry*. Amityville, Baywood.

Mesle, F., Vallin, J. 2002. Mortality In Europe: The Divergence Between East and West. *Population-E*, 57(1):157-198.

Meyer, K., Pind, C. 1999. The Slow Growth Of Foreign Direct Investment in The Soviet Union Successor States. *Economics of Transition*, 7(1): 201-214.

Moran, T. 1998. FDI and Development: The New Policy Agenda for Developing Countries and Economics in Transition. Washington, Institute for International Economics.

Mudambi, R., Navarra, R. 2002. Institutions and International Business: A Theoretical Overview. *International Business Review*, 11(6): 635-646.

Pavlinek, P. 2004. The Role of Foreign Direct Investment in the Privatisation and Restructuring of the Czech Motor Industry. *Post Communist Studies*, 14(3): 359-379.

Rodrik, D., Subramian, A., Trebbi, F. 2001. Insitutions Rule: The Primacy of Institutions Over Geography and Integration, in Economic Development. *Washinton, National Bureau of Economic Research Working Paper 9305.*

Rodrik, D. 2003. *In Search of Prosperity: Analytical Narratives on Economic Growth.* Princeton, Princeton University Press.

Roland, G. 2000, On the Speed and Sequencing of Privatisation and Restructuring, *The Economic Journal*, 104(426): 1158-1168.

Sachs, J., Warners, A. 1995. *Economic Reform and the Process of Global Integration.* Washington, Brookings Institution.

State Statistics Committee of Ukraine (2002) *Statystychnyi Shorichnyk Ukrainy: 1995-2001* (Statistical Yearbook of Ukraine for 1995-2001). Kyiv, Texnika.

Stimson, J. 1985. Regression in Time and Space. *American Journal of Political Science*, 29(4): 914-947.

Teece, D. 1977. The Multinational Corporation and the Resource Cost of International Technology Transfer. Cambridge, Ballinger.

Transparency International. 2006. Corruption Perception Index, available at http://www.transparency.org,

UNCTAD .2003. World Investment Report – 2003: FDO Policies for Development, National and International Perspectives. New York, United Nations.

Wallerstein, I. 1979. The Capitalist World Economy. Cambridge, Cambridge University Press.

WMRC--World Market Research Centre. 2004a. Country Report: Azerbaijan (Country Analysis and Forecast), available at http://www.worldmarketanalysis.com,

WMRC--World Market Research Centre. 2004b. Country Report: Kazakhstan 2004 b (Country Analysis and Forecast), available at http://www.worldmarketanalysis.com,

Woolfson, C., Beck, M. 2004. The End Of Labour Quiesence? Industrial Unrest in Contemporary Lithuania. *International Journal of Comparative Labour Law and Industrial Relations*, 20(1): 227-252.

Yacheistova, N. 2001. Russian Experience Regarding the Competition Policy on FDI Flows, *Paper for the OECD Global Forum on International Investment*, 11-12.

In: Understanding Risk
Editor: Matthias Beck

ISBN: 978-1-62618-686-6

Chapter 8

OIL AND DEPENDENCY: THE CASE OF KAZAKHSTAN

Aigerim Amirzhanova** *and Matthias Beck
The York Management School, University of York, York, UK

ABSTRACT

Following the collapse of the Soviet Union in 1991, the newly independent oil-rich country of Kazakhstan has become a major recipient of foreign direct investment (FDI). Although international organisations such as the IMF and UNCTAD have claimed that FDI can be considered as an engine in the transition from state socialism and as a powerful force for integration of this region into the global economy, this investment also poses significant risks to Kazakhstan. These risk fall into two broad categories. The first category can be broadly described as issues associated with the "resource curse" or the "Dutch disease". The term Dutch disease describes a situation where booming demand in oil exporting countries due to high oil revenues leads to shift of an economy's productive resources from the tradeable sector to the non-tradeable sector. The second category is associated with the over-dependency of oil exporting countries on a relatively small number of large multinational corporations (MNCs). This over-dependency can lead to a situation where licenses and concessions are granted at less favourable conditions than if they were auctioned in an efficient market. Examining the licensing policy of the Kazakhstani Energy and Mineral Resource Ministry, this paper notes that the latter issue of over-dependency has become less of a risk due to deliberate efforts to diversify investment relationships. Notwithstanding this situation there is some evidence that it remains difficult for oil exporting nations such as Kazakhstan to ensure that oil revenues are channeled into sustainable economic development.

COUNTRY BACKGROUND

Kazakhstan possesses one of the largest shares of proven oil and gas reserves in the Commonwealth of Independent States (CIS) countries, which makes it an important player in

* Currently completing her MSc in Management under the supervision of Matthias Beck at The York Management School, Sally Baldwin Buildings, Block A, University of York, York, YO10 5DD, UK, Aigerimkz@gmail.com.

the world energy market. Independent since 16 December 1991, Kazakhstan has a brief history of 17 years. This follows 70 years of being part of the Soviet Union, during which the region has endured massive transformations from nomadic life styles to collectivization. After recovering from World War II, the 'virgin lands' campaigns in 1950s, and political conflicts with Moscow (including a tragic demonstration in Almaty in December 1986, when a great number of Kazakh people died while protesting against Moscow's government), Kazakhstan was been through massive cultural and educational changes. Since independence Kazakhstan has become one of the largest net recipients of Foreign Direct Investment (FDI), surpassing by far the cumulative FDI receipts of other CIS countries. The reason for this disproportional accumulation of foreign investment is Kazakhstan's ownership of one of the largest shares of currently identified resources of gas and oil in the region.

By contrast to some countries in this regions, Kazakhstan has experienced a relatively high level of political stability. In 1989 Nursultan Nazarbayev became the first secretary of the Kazakh Soviet Socialist Republic. As a result of the Belavezha Accords (8th December, 1991), which declared the Soviet Union effectively dissolved, Nursultan Nazarbayev became the first president of Kazakhstan. Nazarbayev led the country onto the world stage as an independent state (Terterov, 2004) and was elected again as a president for a period of seven years in the 2005 presidential elections. The executive branch of the Kazakh government is headed by Prime Minister Karim Massimov (incumbent since 10 of January 2007) who is responsible for reporting daily activities of the Government [1]. The Parliament consists of two chambers: the Majilis (lower house of Parliament) and the Senate (upper house), whose members are elected for five-year and six-year terms respectively [2]. Although the parliament is the supreme legislative body, its powers are relatively weak in comparison to those of the executive. In 2007 the Parliament underwent fundamental changes by adding members to both the Senate and Majilis, with the latter body elected exclusively through a system of proportional representation (Bowyer, 2008). The Constitutional Council of the Republic of Kazakhstan which consists of seven members has a special position in the political system of Kazakhstan. The ex-Presidents are the life time members of the Constitutional Council.

The role of political parties in Kazakhstan is governed by the 2002 Law "On political parties". Today eleven political parties are officially registered, including the dominant ruling Nur-Otan party [3]. This party, which dominates parliament and most public debates, was established in February 1999 under the original name of Otan [4]. In the second half of 2006 the four pro-presidential parties, including ASAR, Civil Party, Otan, and Agrarian Party) were merged into Nur-Otan (Light of the Fatherland). Nur Utan exists principally as a vehicle to support and promote the president, similar to its Russian counterpart the United Russia party (Denison and James, 2008).

However, there are several other political parties in Kazakhstan's political scene. Apart from Nur-Otan, the present-day political parties in Kazakhstan can be grouped into three categories. These include Pro-presidential parties such as Rukhaniyat (which addresses social issue and seeks to develop spirituality of society); "soft" opposition parties such as Adilet (which fights against corruption) and Ak-Jol (which advocates an independent, democratic and free Kazakhstan; opposition parties such as the Kazakh Social Democratic Party Auyl (which focuses on the development of agriculture and the protection of the interests of agricultural workers) and the Communist Party of Kazakhstan (which is the successor to the Communist Party of the Kazakhstan SSR); and "hard" opposition parties such as Azat (opposition to the ruling elite), the National Social Democratic Party (which emphasizes the establishment of democracy, rule of law, and a socially-oriented state) and the Alga People's Party (which maintains two newspapers, conducts its own public opinion surveys, and monitors the work of parliamentary deputies). The political opposition in Kazakhstan has weakened following the August 2007 elections to the Majilis (Bowyer, 2008). This is primarily due to the fact that according to the Law "On Political Parties" parties must poll at least 7% of the vote to obtain seats in parliament. As a results of the 2007 election "Nur-Otan" won by a wide margin (88,41%) and none of other political parties reached the 7% requirement.

The level of Kazakhstan's human development as measured by the United Nations Development Program (based on a combination of life expectancy, basic level conditions, education level, and GDP) is similar in position to that of Mexico and Poland (Olcott, 2002). Because of its large territory Kazakhstan is one of the least densely populated countries in the world, with a population density of 5.7 persons per square kilometer. Approximately 15 million inhabitants live in Kazakhstan which includes 53.4% Kazakhs, 30% Russians 30%, 3.7% Ukrainians, 2.5% Uzbeks, 2.4% Germans, 1.7% Tatars, 1.4% Uygurs and 4.9% others [5]. Currently Kazakhstan continues to experience migration from poor rural areas into to urban areas, which has led to a situation where almost 56% of the population now live in urban areas. This has been coupled by a decline of the birth rate to around 1.8 – 1.9 children per couple, which, although higher than that of Russia will not sustain the current population level. This situation is aggravated by the fact that a significant share of the of the ethnic non-Kazakh population left to their countries of ethnic origin, including 63.2% of Germans, 28.6% of Russians, 38.9% of Ukrainians, 24.1% of Tatars, 38.7% of Belarusian's, 3.5% of Koreans, 13.1% of Azeri 13,1 %, and 21.1% of Poles [6]. In order to combat this decline in population, the Kazakhstani government is actively encouraging the return of ethnic Kazakhs living abroad, officially called 'oralmans', to the country. In 2004 and estimated 44,300 Kazakhs registered as returnees, and it is assumed that the inflow of this skilled immigrants helped boost the country's economy (Bilalov, 2005).

ECONOMIC DEVELOPMENT

Kazakhstan is rich in mineral resources including oil and gas, gold, copper, magnesium, and uranium. Like most newly independent CIS countries Kazakhstan's development agenda has focused on accelerating economic growth and creating an infrastructure capable of sustaining that growth.

During the Soviet period Kazakhstan was considered an agrarian state and a supplier of raw materials. Additionally, military production played a major role in the economy. Following its independence, Kazakhstan therefore faced numerous economic, social and environmental challenges. The first few years of Kazakhstan's independence were characterized by economic decline, mostly due to the destabilizing influence of the collapse of the Soviet Union. Nonetheless, in 1993 the National Bank of Kazakhstan introduced its own currency, the tenge. This currency was subsequently devalued by almost 85 % in the course of a year (KPMG Audit LLC, 2008).

Since 1992 Kazakhstan has actively pursued a program of economic reform. During the period from 1995 to 1997 this government program of economic reform and privatization was accelerated, resulting in a substantial shift of assets from the government sector into the private sector. In 1998 Kazakhstan's economy experienced a 2.5% decline in GDP due to slumping oil prices which were partially due to reduced demand for Kazakhstan's oil in Asia. A devaluation of the national currency in early 1999 and a bumper harvest in fall, however, revived the economy. In 2000 soaring oil prices led to a massive growth in the Kazakh GDP of almost 10%. When the oil prices stabilized in 2001, Kazakhstan achieved a GDP growth of 13.2%, its best economic performance since 1991. Thereafter cumulative foreign investments, high oil prices and conservative fiscal policies allowed Kazakhstan to maintain economic stability together with relatively high growth levels. This growth has stimulated the construction industry leading to the rapid expansion of the former capital Almaty as well as the construction of the new capital Astana.

Overall Kazakhstan's GDP has grown by 8% or more per year between 2000 and 2006 and now is approximately US$ 5,241 per capita. The country's international reserves have risen to about US$ 20 billion. Driven by high inflows of foreign currency into the country, the national currency, the tenge, has appreciated 20% against the US Dollar since 2002, despite persistent National Bank interventions to slow down this increase [7]. A sudden increase in real estate prices in 2007 together with the international liquidity crisis hit the country's financial and construction industries hard and left many construction companies and banks struggling with bankruptcy. In 2007 inflation also reached double digits for the first time. This caused international credit ratings agencies to lower Kazakhstan's sovereign credit ratings. Despite these turbulences, Kazakhstan's unemployment rate has continued to decrease, following a slight increase from 1996 to 1999 and a sudden drop in 2000 and 2001 [7]. Today imports are mostly dominated by investment goods (plant, machinery and production equipments) and intermediate industrial use goods. Food and non-food consumer items are imported in very small amounts, but this has been increasing year by year (Salimov, 2008). At this stage it is unclear how the current credit crunch will affect the future expansion of the Kazakhstani economy. Although Kazakhstan maintains strong trade ties with Russia which is already showing the effects of this crisis, there is a possibility that high oil price will leave Kazakhstan largely unaffected by ongoing problems.

KAZAKHSTAN AND THE "RESOURCE-CURSE"

Although there is evidence that Kazakhstan's economy has been suffering from turbulences in the world oil market, it is difficult to describe the country as a victim of the so-called "resource-curse". In particular, this is evidenced by the fact that Kazakhstan's growth has been continuous over a period of nearly ten years and. Perhaps more importantly is the fact that this growth has been accompanied by a growth in employment.

In its most basic form, the so-called "resource curse", refers to the empirical observation that the economies of resource-rich countries grow on average more slowly than those of resource-poor countries (see, e.g., Auty, 1990, 1993; Volchkova and Suslova, 2006). The idea that natural resource endowments could have an adverse effect on development among development economists such as Raul Prebisch, Hans Singer, and Alfred Hirschman in the

1950's and 1960's (Stevens, 2003). Underlying these analyses was the assumption that positive linkages from primary product exports would be limited compared to manufacturing, leaving these economies uniquely exposed to shocks as a result of the sharp increase or decreases in raw material prices (Neary, 1986). Further evidence of this problem was found in connection with research on the so-called "Dutch" disease (Corden and Neary, 1982; Rosenberg and Saavalainen, 1998). This research emerged in connection with the supposed observation that Dutch natural oil and gas discoveries in the 1960s lead to a slowdown in Dutch manufacturing. According to Corden and Neary (1982) the notion of a Dutch disease can be applied to any three sector economy which includes (1) a booming sector, such as oil or other primary product exporting industry, (2) a sector of other tradeable, which would include both manufacturing and agriculture, and (3) non-tradeable. In a simple static model, a boom in the primary sector affects the rest of the economy in two main ways; namely though a spending effect and long term resource movements. This is accompanied by an appreciation of the exchange rate whereby an increased inflow of foreign exchange will initially raise the nominal exchange rate value of the domestic currency. However, if there is a sharp increase in domestic demand accompanied by inflation, the increased demand for foreign exchange may be offset the initial nominal exchange rate appreciation, causing the nominal exchange rate not to appreciate or even to depreciate. If there is a real exchange rate appreciation this may be reflected in an increase in the prices of non-tradeables relative to those for tradeables (Kuralbayeva, 2001). This process in turn has the effect of increasing the domestic costs of producing tradeable goods and reducing country's international competitiveness. Corden (1984) has argued that this analysis is applicable to a number of similar phenomena such as gold discoveries in Australia, capital inflows to Switzerland, and the inflow of American gold to Spain in the sixteenth century, among other cases.

Egert and Leonard (2007) have examined the evidence for Dutch disease symptoms in Kazakhstan. This analysis led to the following findings:

(1) During the period from 1999 to 2005 the price of crude oil had risen continuously from below USD 10 a barrel to above USD 50 a barrel, with Kazakhstan benefiting from world oil price increases.
(2) During the same time period the share of investment in the Kazakh oil sector as a share of total investment has been declining. FDI flows to the oil sector recorded an upsurge from 1999 to 2001, but then the relative share of FDI in this sector declined. Meanwhile, the share of investment in the manufacturing sector remained relatively stable from 1996 to 2004, and FDI slightly picked up after 2000, which coincided with the drop in FDI in the oil sector.
(3) Regarding productivity, real and nominal wages and relative prices, there is no clear evidence of Dutch disease symptoms. The same applies to the potential appreciation of the real exchange rate.
(4) Perhaps most importantly there is no evidence of declining output, employment and exports in non-oil manufacturing.

Overall this analysis lends only very limited evidence to the presence of Dutch disease symptoms in the Kazakh economy. Thus, although the price of oil increased from 1998 to 2005, this did not lead to dis-proportionate growth in investment in the oil sector. Also there was little, if any, effect on the relative prices of non-tradeables and non-oil tradeables through the wage channel. However there appears to be an increasing nominal appreciation of the exchange rate which could have further effects on macroeconomic parameters.

Thus, if oil prices remained high in the future, there is every possibility that nominal and real exchange rates will continue to appreciate. This would be very likely to put pressure on non-oil industries and adversely affects their position.

DEPENDENCY ON MULTINATIONALS

Organizations like the IMF and UNCTAD have maintained fairly consistently that FDI was a an engine in the transition from state socialism and a powerful force for the integration of these countries into the global economy (Bandelj, 2002). Similarly, the economist Schmidt has argued that "... without vast inflows of foreign capital, successful transition was unlikely" (Schmidt, 1995).

Empirical studies of FDI in transition economies have suggested that these investments are driven by a number of factors such as domestic and potential export market size, natural resources endowments, levels of bureaucracy, economic and political stability, labour skills and cost and level of progress in transition reforms (Bevan and Estrin, 2000; Kinoshita and Campos, 2003). This observations closely match the earlier work of Dunning (1993) who suggested that the investment behaviour of multinational enterprises was driven by three most common motivations; namely, market-seeking FDI, resource-seeking and effciency-seeking FDI.

It is fairly obvious that FDI in Kazakhstan is primarily resource- seeking and as such driven by the abundance of available oil and gas reserves. However, there are also a number of institutional factors which make Kazakhstan a preferable target for foreign investment as compared to other oil provinces. These include, apart from the country's political stability, its relatively favourable treatment of foreign investors. Thus, there is no evidence that, since independence. Kazakhstan has conducted any form of expropriation of foreign investors or that the country has restricted in any significant way the outflow of oil revenues. This position has been strengthened with Kazakhstan's law "On Investments" (January 2003) that superseded and consolidated past legislation governing foreign investment, establishes a single investment regime for domestic and foreign investors and provides guarantees of non-discrimination against foreign investors.

One major concern associated with resource-seeking FDI is the possibility of over-dependency on a relatively small number of multinationals (Moran, 1998). These concerns are aggravated where there is evidence of close collaboration among these multinationals which is potentially more likely to occur if these multinationals originate from the same country and maintain close links to home-country national elites. Regarding the potentially over-powering nature of such coalitions, Stallings (1990 has argued that

> In its extreme version, the issue at stake is whether the state's choice of development strategy determines the role of foreign capital or whether foreign capital determines development strategy. (p80)

Up until the late 1990s, there is evidence that Kazakhstan did indeed develop a strong dependency on a relatively small number of US oil companies, including Exxon Mobil,

Chevron, Texaco and ConocoPhilips. This was paralleled by other major US investments including an agreement signed by Philip Morris with Almaty Tobacco Company in 1993, stipulating a US$ 350 million investment over the first five years. Philip Morris started producing cigarettes for domestic consumption in 1994, and in early 2000 opened a US$ 200 million cigarette manufacturing plant, employing 3,000 on the outskirts of Almaty with production capacity of 25 billion cigarettes annually (Terterov, 2004).

More importantly there was a notable dominance of US companies in major Kazakh oil developments. Thus the largest of the three major oil extraction consortia in Kazakhstan, TengizChevrOil (TCO), is dominated by Chevron Texaco. Chevron Texaco is a 50% participant in the venture and leads TCO's development of the giant Tengiz Field. ExxonMobil has 25%, KazMunaiGas has 20%, and Russian-US LUKARCO holds the remaining 5%. Tengiz, one of the largest hydrocarbon discoveries in the world over the past 30 years, holds an estimated nine billion barrels of recoverable reserves. The Tengiz project is the largest Western-run oil producer anywhere in the former Soviet Union, currently producing 286,000 barrels a day. Most of the oil is exported to the Black Sea through a US$ 2.7-billion pipeline run by the Caspian Pipeline Consortium. In order to increase production capacity, TCO is installing Second Generation Production (SGP) and Sour Gas Injection (SGI) facilities. Industry sources suggest that TCO is to invest at least US$ 2-2.5 billion in the development of these projects in Kazakhstan's major Tengiz oil and gas deposit in the coming years. The company has already invested about US$ 1.4 billion in Kazakhstan to date. TCO plans to invest US$ 550-750 million in materials and equipment required to increase oil output. The investments will be carried out under a plan for financing the second stage of the Tengiz oil field adopted by the company's partners' council.[8]

As regard the licensing policy of the Kazakhstani Ministry of Energy and Mineral Resources, there is evidence that US and Canadian oil companies did indeed establish a dominant role during the early years of oil production. Thus, US and Canadian companies obtained a total of 38 out of total of 48 licenses awarded between 1994 and 1997, as well as playing a major role in virtually all key oil developments of this period [8]. This pattern, however, changed on account of the government's 1997 announcement of a "multi-vectoral" policy as part of the "Kazakhstan 2030" programme (Saurbek, 2008). Thus, as of the late 1990s there is evidence of the involvement of a wider variety of companies as well as of efforts to reduce dependency on a small number of existing transport routes.

This is evidenced, *inter alia*, by the creation of the Offshore Kazakhstan International Operating Company (OKIOC), an international oil and gas consortium comprising nine companies including BP-Amoco, Statoil, Agip, British Gas, Mobil, Royal Dutch Shell, Inpex, Philips and Total. This consortium has invested more than US$ 600 million in oil and gas exploration in the northern Caspian Sea. In 2001, OKIOC was renamed to Agip Kazakhstan North Caspian Operating Company (Agip KCO). In 2001, BP-Amoco and Statoil sold their shares to TotalFinaElf. In June 2002, Agip KCO announced estimated extractable oil reserves at 7-9 billion barrels (Terterov, 2004).

Another production sharing agreement signed in 1997 between Kazakhstan and the consortium of British Gas, Agip, and Texaco was to develop the giant Karachaganak oil and gas field in northwestern Kazakhstan. At present the Karachaganak consortium is led by BG Group Plc and Agip, which each hold a share of 32.5%. US based ChevronTexaco holds a 20% share and Russia's LUKoil holds a 15% share. This project is expected to run through 2036 with oil and gas production capacity peaking at 12 million tons per year and 25 billion cubic meters per year, respectively. Karachaganak Petroleum Operating BV (KPO), the operator of the Karachaganak oil and gas condensate field, has signed contracts with the Greek-Italian consortium CCC Saipem for construction work at the field and with Parker Drilling Co., a US-based oil and gas drilling contractor, to conduct drilling operations. Reserves at the Karachaganak field, are estimated at 1.2 billion tons of oil and condensate and 1.35 trillion cubic meters of gas. Capital investments into the project amounted to US$ 4 billion to develop the Karachaganak gas condensate facility and increase liquid hydrocarbon production there to 51.3 million bbl per annum [8].

The third biggest oil extraction consortium, Kashagan, has been carrying out exploration drilling in the Kazakh sector of the Caspian since August 1999. According to Agip KCO, recoverable reserves at the Kashagan field are 11.2 billion bbl. The consortium will start to produce oil at this field around October 2008 and full commercial production will begin in 2009. Total development costs for the deposit are approximately US$ 29 billion. Agip KCO - is the field operator. Agip was chosen to operate the 11-block Kashagan production sharing contract area by project partners Shell Group, BG PLC, ExxonMobil Corp., ConocoPhillips, Total, Inpex and KazMunayGas in February 2001. About US$ 8 billion have been invested in the exploitation of Kashagan from 2001 to 2006. In July 2002 the contracting companies declared the commercial viability of Kashagan, in conjunction with KazMunaiGas. Agip KCO, on behalf of the consortium completed a 24- month period of geological and reservoir appraisals, as well as engineering and transportation studies and environmental and health and safety assessments. Some industry observers have suggested that recoverable reserves from the field could rise to 13 billion. With the Kashagan oilfield discovery, Kazakhstan hopes to triple its oil output in 15 years from its current level of 900,000 barrels per day to between 2 million and 3 million barrels a day. The early-oil phase of the Kashagan project is expected to produce 300,000 bpd [8].

In 1996 the Canadian Petroleum Company Hurricane Hydrocarbons bought state oil company Yuzhneftegas. Hurricane paid US$ 120 million and pledged to invest US$ 280 million. It owns a majority interest in the Shymkent refinery, with a 6.6 million tons annual oil processing capacity, and produces gasoline, diesel, boiler fuel, fuel oil, kerosene, jet fuel, and liquefied gas. The refinery provides about 50% of domestic petrochemicals. According to the company's policy by year end total investments in Kazakhstan should each US$ 1 billion (Terterov, 2004).

Kazakhstan has three main active export routes: northward, southward and westward. The Caspian Pipeline Consortium is a major westward export route. The carrying capacity of this pipe is planned to be expanded to 58 million tons by 2008, and to 67 million tons by 2011. The multinational ownership in the CPC is as follows: Russian Federation - 24%, the Republic of Kazakhstan - 19%, the Sultanate of Oman - 7%, Chevron Caspian Pipeline Consortium Company - 15%, LUKARCO B.V. - 12.5%, Rosneft/Shell Caspian Ventures Limited - 7.5%, Mobil Caspian Pipeline Company - 7.5%, Agip International (N.A.) NV - 2%, BG Overseas Holding Limited - 2%, Kazakhstan Pipeline Ventures LLC - 1.75%, and Oryx Caspian Pipeline LLC- 1.75% [8].

Today most of Kazakhstan's oil and gas continues to be transported through Russian-controlled routes. The main northward oil pipeline is Uzen - Atyrau - Samara. Given planned growth of oil production in Western Kazakhstan, there is a plan for a staged build-up of the pipeline's carrying capacity. Thus the Baltic Pipelines System is a promising route to increase Kazakhstan's oil supply to the market of East Europe and Baltic States. Other alternatives include a pipeline to China and agreeing to future shipments through the US-backed Baku-Tbilisi-Ceyhan oil pipeline. Access to the Chinese and Asian Pacific market is seen as a promising means of diversifying Kazakhstan's portfolio of buyer. There is now a master agreement between the Kazakhstan Ministry of Energy and Mineral Resources and the CNPC (Chinese National Petroleum Corporation) to construct a pipeline running from Western Kazakhstan to Western China in the form of the Atasu - Alashankou pipeline which was launched in July 2006 (Denison and James, 2008; Saurbek, 2008).

CONCLUSION

Kazakhstan has had the highest cumulative net FDI inflows during the period from 1989 to 2006 of any CIS country, which has been estimated at US$ 28 192 millions. The largest share of FDI has been in the oil and gas sectors. Estimates indicate that from 1999 to 2001 three quarters of inward FDI flows went into the oil and gas sectors. Today FDI remains concentrated in the oil and gas sector which so far has accounted for 37.2% of all investments over the period 2000-2007. As next highest category real estate and renting accounted for 35% of cumulative FDI in the period 2000-2007 [7], which can be explained by the booming building campaign in the new capital city of Kazakhstan – Astana. Although the 2002 law about the Special Economic Zone "Astana new city" can be considered a success in terms of attracting foreign investment, investments in the services sectors, agriculture, education and health continue to be low.

With a heavily oil-dependent economy Kazakhstan continues to face considerable risks in terms of potential exposure to macro-economic shocks, currency exposures and "Dutch-disease" type symptoms. While the "multi-vectorial" diversification of oil investments has helped reduce some of the most immediate problems of Kazakhstan's resource-driven economy, it remains to be seen whether Kazakhstan's oil wealth will ensure the creation of a sustainable post-oil economy.

INTERNET/GOVERNMENT SOURCES

[1] http://ru.government.kz/structure/government
[2] http://www.parlam.kz/Information.aspx?doc=1andlan=en-US
[3] http://www.parlam.kz
[4] http://www.ndp-nurotan.kz/index.en.php?type=36andft=1
[5] http://cia.gov/library/publications/the-world-factbook/goes/kz.html
[6] http://iicas.org/articles/anv_35_10_01.htm
[7] http://www.nationalbank.kz
[8] http://www.e.gov.kz and personal communications with the Mininstry of Energy and Mineral Resources

REFERENCES

Auty, R. M. 1990. *Resource-based Industrialisation: Sowing the Oil in Eight Developing Countries*. New York, Oxford University Press.

Auty, R. M. 1993. *Sustaining Development in Mineral Economies: The Resource Curse Thesis*. London, Routledge.

Bandelj, N. 2002. Embedded Economies: Social Relations as Determinants of Foreign Direct Investment in Central and Eastern Eeurope, *Social Forces,* 81(2): 81(2):411-444.

Bevan, A., and Estrin, S. 2000. The Determinants of Foreign Direct Investment in Transition Economies. *Centre for Economic Policy Research Discussion Paper* no. 2638, London.

Bilalov, A. 2005. Problems of Adaptation of Kazakh-repatriates in Kazakhstan. *Paper of the Institute of Ethnology and Anthropology named after Miklukho-Maklai,* Moscow [in Russian].

Bowyer, A. C. 2008. Parliament and Political Parties in K azakhstan. Silk Road Paper of the Central Asia-Caucasus Institute and Silk Road Studies Program, A Joint Transatlantic Research and Policy Center Johns Hopkins University, Washington, DC.

Corden, W. M. 1984. Booming Sector and Dutch Disease Economics: Survey and Consolidation, *Oxford Economic Papers*, 36(3):359-380.

Corden, W. M., and Neary, J. P. 1982. Booming Sector and Deindustrialization in a Small Open Economy, *Economic Journal*, 92(368): 825-848.

Denison, M. K., and James, O. 2008. *Kazakhstan: State Ambition and Investor Realism in the New Business Environment*. Control Risk Group, June.

Dunning, J. H. 1993. *Multinational Enterprises and the Global Economy*. Workingham, Addison-Wesley.

Egert, B., and Leonard, C. S. 2007. Dutch Disease Scare in Kazakhstan: Is it Real? William Davidson Institute Working Paper No. 866, and Bank of Finland BOFIT Discussion Paper 9.

Kinoshita, Y., and Campos, N. 2003. Why Does FDI Go Where it Goes? New Evidence from Transition Economies. *International Monetary Fund Working Paper* No. 03/228.

Kuralbayeva, K., Kutan, A.M.. and Wyzan, M.L. 2001. Is Kazakhstan Vulnerable to the Dutch Disease? *Paper of the Center for European Integration Studies*, Rheinische Friedrich-Wilhelms-Universität Bonn.

Moran, T.H. 1998. Foreign Direct Investment and Development, *The New Policy Agenda for Developing Countries and Economies in Transition*. Washington, DC, Institute for International Economics.

Neary,V.W., and van Wijnbergen, S. 1986. *Natural Resources and the Macroeconomy*. Cambridge, MA, The MIT Press.

Olcott, M. B. 2002. *Kazakhstan: Unfulfilled Promise*. Washington, Carnegie Endowment for International Peace.

Rosenberg, C. B., and Saavalainen, T.O. 1998. How to Deal with Azerbaijan's Oil Boom? Policy Strategy in a Resource-rich Transition Economy. *International Monetary Fund Working Paper*, No. 98/6.

Salimov, G. 2008. *Kazakhstan, Bridging the Funding Gap*, Renaissance Capital, March.

Saurbek, Z. 2008. Kazakh-Chinese Energy Relations: Economic Pragmatism or Political Cooperation? *China and Russi Forum Quarterly*, 6(1):79-93.

Schmidt, K.-D. 1995. Foreign Direct Investment in Eastern Europe: State-of-the- Art and Prospects, in Dobrinky R. and Landesmann, M. (eds) in *Transforming Economies and European Integration*, 268-89. Aldershot, Edward Elgar Publishing.

Stallings, B. 1990. The Role of Foreign Capital in Economic Development, in Gereffi, G. and Wyman, D.L. (eds) *Manufacturing Miracles: Paths of Industrialization in Latin America and East Asia.* Princeton, Princeton University Press.

Stevens, P. 2003. *Resource Impact - Curse or Blessing?* A Literature Survey. Paper of the Centre for Energy, Petroleum and Mineral Law and Policy University of Dundee.

Terterov, M. (ed) 2004. *Doing Business with Kazakhstan*. London, GMB Publishing.

Volchkova, N., and Suslova, E. 2006. Human Capital and the "Resource Curse". *Centre for Advanced Studies and New Economics School Working Paper* No. 13/2007/11.

In: Understanding Risk
Editor: Matthias Beck

ISBN: 978-1-62618-686-6

Chapter 9

MULTINATIONAL ENTERPRISES AND BARGAINING POWER: SOME CRITICAL REFLECTIONS

Nataliya Acc-Nikmehr*

University of Edinburgh Business School, UK

ABSTRACT

This paper examines the relationship between concepts of MNE bargaining power and broader concepts of political power. It notes that the analysis of MNE bargaining power presents a number of puzzles from the perspective of political theory. These puzzles arise, in part, from the fact that the overlap between traditional concepts of MNE bargaining power and broader concepts of political power is only a partial one. Despite these problems, it is suggested that political- theory-based approaches can add realism to our understanding of bargaining power.

STATES AND MULTINATIONALS

The role of Foreign Direct Investment (FDI) has grown dramatically in the developing countries and economies in transition over recent years (Vernon, 1971: 14). Between 1983 and 1988 FDI volumes grew at 20 per cent annually in real terms, while world trade volumes grew only at a compound annual rate of 5 per cent (Moran, 1998: 15). Over the course of the 1990's FDI volumes rose from 24 billion dollars per year in 1990 to approximately 120 billion dollars per year by the beginning of 1998. As a result, private capital flows totalled more than four fifths of all capital inflows to less developed countries and countries in transition in 1998. Among these capital inflows FDI was and stays the largest and most stable source of capital (Moran, 1998: 15).

The role of FDI and multinational enterprises (MNEs) in the world economy has continued to grow during the last decade even in spite of the dampening effect caused by

* Nataliya Acc-Nikmehr is currently a PhD student at the University of Edinburgh Business School, e-mail: N.Acc-Nikmehr@sms.ed.ac.uk .

global financial and economic crisis (UNCTAD, 2009). In 2009 the overall volume of FDI inflows and outflows was equal to $1,114 and $1,101 billion, respectively (UNCTAD, 2010). According to Stopford, Strange and Hensley (1991: 15), the raising flows of FDI are closely linked to the increasing significance of multinational enterprises in world trade. The authors emphasize that a portion of MNEs' capital transfers is much smaller than their stake in world trade and production.

> Directly or indirectly they have been estimated to control over one quarter of world economic activity outside their home countries; over half of the world trade in manufactured goods and even more of the growing trade in services; 80 per cent of the world's land cultivated for export crops and the lion's share of the world's technological innovations.

This distribution of world economic power is a significant issue, as it can be assumed to affect the power of states (host countries) to control economic events. Stopford, Strange and Hensley (1991: 14) specifically suggested that:

> States still can retain considerable negative power to disrupt, manage or distort trade by controlling entry to the territory in which the national market functions. However, they cannot easily control production which is aimed at a world market and which does not necessarily take place within their frontiers. And even when most supply is under control, the market may not be, as OPEC discovered to its cost in the 1980s. In other words, states' positive power to harness internal resources is decidedly constrained when they try to influence where and how international production takes place. They find they cannot direct; they can only bargain.

The growing role of MNEs in the world economy, and in particular the significant rise of their power and the synchronous reduction of states' power—which John Stopford, Strange and Hensley (1991) describe as a transition from directing (by the state) to bargaining (between state and MNE)—raises important issues about the nature of bargaining power. These questions include the following: Do power and bargaining power differ? and, if so: How do concepts of power and bargaining power relate to each other? What are the areas of overlap and discrepancy? Is there a credible model that fully captures the MNE – host country power relationship? What would be the key dimensions of such models?

DIMENSIONS OF BARGAINING POWER

Power is probably one of the most important universal and fundamental concepts of social, political and economic analysis, and Colin Hay's (1997) work "Divided by a Common Language: Political Theory and the Concept of Power" has rightfully highlighted that power has been and still is the subject of extended debate. In the past, a significant amount of academic research has been devoted to the problem of defining the concept of power and its various types, subtypes and aspects. In this context those researchers who consider the concept of power to be of key importance as well as those who tend to minimise its significance have participated in a struggle for definitions (Oppenheim, 1981).

The complexity of the task of finding a general definition of power and attempting to explain the nature of power relations can, among other issues, be attributed to the complexity, multiplicity, versatility of the power relationships among world actors. In this context, the simplification of models of power to a two-variable model (by means of reducing it to the consideration of power relationships between two actors, for example, host country and MNE) has become one of the key techniques for simplifying and explaining the concept of power; and much of the literature on bargaining power has followed this simplification. However, this simplification is not necessarily adequate in light of the fact that host country – MNE power relationships can also be seen within more complex frameworks such as Lukes' (1980) radical three-dimensional view of power.

How many dimensions then does bargaining power have? To answer this question it is useful to explore the three key approaches to power prevalent within the bargaining literature in relation to corresponding approaches in the philosophical and political literature. Samuel Bacharach and Edward Lawler (1981) have offered an approach to the resolution of the conceptual problem of power definition which is associated with Lukes' three-dimensional view of power and a critique of Dahl's (1957) one-dimensional as well as Bachrach and Baratz's (1970) two-dimensional views of power. Specifically Bacharach and Lawler (1981) suggest that failures to adequately conceptualise power have resulted from the assumption that the definition can and should be a precise term. They, in their turn, assume that (1981: 44):

> ... power is inherently a sensitising concept or primitive term. A sensitising concept points to a series or range of phenomenon but not in a manner that allows precise definition or measurement. Such ideas capture the complex multidimensionality of phenomena while implying more specific ideas that may be subject to more precise treatment.

Bacharach and Lawler (1981:45) argue that the conceptualisation of power as a sensitising device allows them to distinguish three types of approaches to power:

1. power as an outcome;
2. power as a potential;
3. power as tactical action.

'Power as an outcome' is a concept that is closely associated with Dahl's (1957) one-dimensional view of power. In his work Dahl conceives power, influence and control as "serviceable synonyms" and defines power as "the capacity of one actor to do something affecting another, which changes the probable pattern of specified future events" (Lukes, 1980: 13). The author suggests that the analysis of a series of decision-making situations would provide the best visualization and support for his definition of power (Lukes, 1980). Here, the necessary conditions for identification of a decision-making process as a power event is the presence of 'direct' power, which is actual and observable, conflict (Lukes, 1980). According to Dahl's view, the presence of conflict is imperative for an empirical test on authentication of existence and utilization of power. So, without conflict a decision-making situation cannot be recognized as a power event (Lukes, 1980). The conflict, in turn, arises as a result of expressing and pursuing different preferences, which can be considered similar to what pluralists would describe as interests. Therefore a conflict of interests is equivalent to a conflict of preferences (Lukes, 1980).

The 'power as an outcome' approach is almost identical to Dahl's notion of power view. However, here it is suggested that the exercise of power in a case of bargaining relationship is determined by and depends on the outcome of the negotiations, including attributes of arrangements, agreements, transactions, etc. (Bachrach and Lawler, 1981). As a result, empirically bargaining power can be only detected and established post factum based on the evaluation of the bargaining outcome (Bachrach and Lawler, 1981).

Although concepts of bargaining power assume the presence of conflict, as Dahl does, these conflict and interests are much more narrowly defined within a bargaining context. What is especially important about this it is that, according to Bachrach and Lawler (1981: 79) "bargaining implies conflict of interests over goals that no party can achieve without taking the other into account". This definition implies that dependence is the defining characteristic of bargaining power. Thus Bacharach and Lawler (1981) assume that at least some minimal degree of dependence is intrinsic to all manifestations of bargaining power. They, therefore, specifically claim that dependence, as bargaining power, is not just one of the bargainng attributes it is a principal element and an integral part of bargaining relationships (Bachrach and Lawler, 1981). Without discerning the nature of dependence, which stipulates multiple aspects of bargaining relationship, it would be impossible to capture all the diversity in bargaining relationships and analyse, examine, evaluate and interpret the impact of these variations on bargaining relationships and outcomes (Bachrach and Lawler, 1981).

None of the three other views of power suggested by Dahl (1957), Bachrach and Baratz (1962), and Lukes (1980) utilise explicit notions of dependence to underpin their studies of power; though this can be seen being implied in their respective definitions power. However, despite these complications, it can be concluded that the first two views of power distinguish only one possible type of power that is 'actual' power. By contrast the 'power as a potential' approach assumes the necessity of a differentiation between potential and an actual, or successful, use of power. Again it is worth quoting Bachrach and Lawler (1981: 45-46):

> From this standpoint, power is a resource that may or may not be used, and if used may or may not be effective. Power is a structural element of the relationship within which parties act to influence each other; consequently, one can identify empirical indicators of potential bargaining power independent of the outcome of the bargaining. This approach to power enables one to predict the outcome from the resources lodged in the social relationship. Here the outcome does not simply describe power, but power may precede and predict bargaining outcomes. That is bargaining power and bargaining outcomes become empirically distinct but related phenomena. Bargaining power can have a small, large or even no effect on bargaining outcomes.

In their critique of Dahl's view, Bachrach and Baratz (1970: 24) suggest that power has two faces. For them a power relationship exist when:

- there is a conflict over values or course of action between A and B;
- B complies with A's wishes;
- B does so because he is fearful that A will deprive him of a value or values which he regards more highly than those which would have been achieved by non-compliance.

Based on these assumptions Bachrach and Baratz (1970) develop a typology of power, which embraces coercion, influence, authority, force and manipulation as different forms of power manifestation. They also bring in the idea of mobilisation of bias (see Lukes, 1980: 17). Barach and Baratz's (1970) central point is that an amplitude of personal or group power depends on the degree to which this person or group obstruct or further the dissemination of the information about policy conflicts to general public both consciously and unconsciously. In making this claim, Barach and Baratz (1970) are able to highlight the importance of examining both decision-making and nondecision-making components of power relationships, whereby "Nondecision-making is a means by which demands for change in the existing allocation of benefits and privileges in the community can be suffocated before they are voiced, or kept covert ..." (Lukes, 1980: 18-19). Accordingly, Barach and Baratz suggest that detecting and revealing potential issues, prevented from being actual by nondecision-making, is pivotal for securing pursued disposition of power balance (Lukes, 1980).

The analysis of nondecision-making by Bachrach and Baratz (1970) at first glance can be seen as anticipating the idea of a non exercising potential power component within the 'power as a potential' approach. However, the two approaches are not identical. The 'power as a potential' approach separates bargaining power and bargaining outcomes: they exist at different stages of power relations. Bachrach and Baratz's (1980) nondecisions are a new component which is inherent to most power relationships.

The discrepancy between these two approaches is also inherent in the definition of nondecion-making itself. In nondecisions, interests can be kept covert. This means that the two-dimensional view of power now expands the notion of conflict and sees this as an empirical phenomenon, which can be overt or covert (Lukes, 1980). By contrast, the simplifying assumptions of bargaining power theory, first of all, exclude the possibility of doubting the presence of conflict in bargaining relationships by definitional fiat and secondly state that this conflict is always actual and overt. The presence of overt observable conflict is determined by the restriction of notions of conflict within the bargaining power concept to a "conflict of interests over goals that no party can achieve without taking the other into account" (Bachrach and Lawler, 1981:79). There is a possibility that intermediate goals exist, but both parties in a bargaining relationship can always identify the final goal of their opponent. For each participant this final goal can typically be expressed in terms of profit maximisation. That is why there is reason to question the two-dimensionality of 'power as a potential' approach because it ultimately leads to the conclusion that the outcome of bargaining is the only empirical indicator of power (Bachrach and Lawler, 1981: 46; and Appendix A, Table 1).

According to Bachrach and Lawler (1981: 46), the last category of power, that of 'power as a tactical action':

> ... implicitly accepts the distinction between potential and actual power, but discerns the third dimension – the use of power. This approach views potential power in terms of power tactics and attempts to predict bargaining outcomes from tactical actions. The focus is on the use and effectiveness of specific tactics, such as threats, bargaining toughness, and others....
>
> ... this tactical concept emphasises the active manipulative quality of power relationships.
>
> Power is not simply a structural or contextual condition, and it is certainly not an abstract description of the bargaining outcome. A tactical approach assumes potential

power and stresses the tactical use of the potential rather than the specific dimensions that define the potential.

Is this then the third dimension of power? The classification of the suggested use of potential power in terms of tactics supports a typology which introduces the three key types of power distinguished by Bachrach and Baratz (1970), namely coercion, force, and manipulation. These three types of power are complemented by the 'influence' type which relates to the two-dimensional 'power as a potential' approach.

So, at this stage, the three-dimensional 'power as a tactical action' approach can be viewed as a bargaining power concept based on the application of four (influence, force, coercion, and manipulation) out of the five types of power identified by Bachrach and Baratz (1970). The presence of the fifth type of power, 'authority', is not implied by any of the three approaches to bargaining power. This element is excluded by the nature of the assumed bargaining power relationships. A conceptual analysis of bargaining relationships between host country and MNE suggests that in a case where both actors' main goals are profit maximisation, the authority component is a passive host country's characteristic that is not relevant to the bargaining power relationship. Nevertheless, under any other conditions the authority element is an intrinsic component of a host country power relationship.

Finally there remains the question as to how the bargaining power concept relates to Lukes' three-dimensional view of power. In his critique of the two-dimensional view of power, Lukes (1980) argues that its recognition of actual conflict as sole form of conflict is inadequate. He identifies two reasons for this. The first is that this assumption disqualifies authority and manipulation as forms of power. Bachrach and Baratz (Lukes, 1980: 30) conceive these two types of power as an "agreement based upon reason" that does not necessarily rest on the threat of actual conflict. Lukes suggests that the existence of potential or latent conflict is a necessary condition for securing a place for authority and manipulation in a power typology (Lukes, 1980).

The existence of latent conflict, however, is not a necessary condition for the bargaining power relationships. It is excluded from the definition of conflict. Therefore Lukes' new dimension is not applicable to a bargaining power concept. Lukes identifies another problem within the one-dimensional and two-dimensional views of power which directly implies that the power concept in general would not be applicable to the bargaining idea. For him this problem stems from the fact that both Bachrach and Baratz (1970) and the pluralists assume that power materializes only where actual conflict can be detected (Lukes, 1980). Subsequently, for them actual conflict is necessary to power (Lukes, 1980). As a result, they ignore the fact that prevention of such conflict is a primary purpose and the most operative attribute of exercising power (Lukes, 1980). This point stands in clear contradiction to the bargaining powers concept as it rests on the simultaneous existence of bargaining and of conflict.

Lukes' insistence on the necessity of a distinction between subjective or perceived interests and actual or real interests cannot be supported by a simple model of the bargaining power relationships between host country and MNE either. Within this model, there is no need to perceive any subjective interests (See Appendix A, Table 2). They do not matter because it is assumed that bargaining relations between two economic actors are defined by their ultimate interests (i.e. their profit maximisation goals) which are always in conflict.

Colin Hay's (1997) critique of Lukes' three-dimensional view of power also questions the validity of his differentiation between real and perceived interests. He stresses that Lukes's perception of interests as an evaluative matter contradicts his preference-shaping context. As a result, such a differentiation cannot be sustained. He also points to another gap in Lukes' work, which he identifies as the lack of an empirical basis for identifying real interests (Hay, 1997).

On the basis of this comparison of bargaining and three-dimensional views of power (in the case of host country – MNE power relationships) it can be concluded that the concept of bargaining power relationships has no third dimension. In so far as we can identify two dimensions, even these are incompatible with Bachrach and Baratz's (1970) two-dimensional view of power, as the bargaining power model does not consider authority to be an element of the bargaining relationship. The result of this is a conversion of the complex model of power suggested by Lukes (See Appendix B, Figure 1) into a simplified model of bargaining power applicable to the simple case of host country – MNE power relationship (See Appendix B, Figure 2).

Alternative Models of MNE Power Relationships

Colin Hay's (1997) critique of Lukes three-dimensional view of power highlights the necessity to rethink Lukes approach. Specifically, Hay proposes a new definitional approach that implies a rejection of the behavioural definition of power. He also suggests that this new definition of power should not be in itself a value judgement.

Hay suggests that two dimensions components of power must be distinguished to allow for an adequate definition; namely power as represents a context-shaping (indirect) and conduct-shaping (direct) force. Specifically, Hay (1997: 51) notes that:

> ... direct power is immediate, visible and behavioural, and is manifested in such practices as decision-making, physical and psychological coercion, persuasion and blackmail. On the contrary, context-shaping constituent of power must emphasise power relations in which structures, institutions and organisations are shaped by human action in such a way as to alter the parameters of subsequent action.

How does the introduction of this new concept of power change the bargaining power relationships between host country and MNEs? First of all, the introduction of a context-shaping dimension of power implies that the simple two-variable model (host country - MNE) of bargaining power relationship is no longer an effective devise for understanding and explaining a host country and MNE power relationship.

Following Gunneman (1975) it is possible to formulate a more complex multivariable model of MNE bargaining power relationships based on a basic Burk Marshall's model of corporation (See Appendix C, Figure 1). This model consists of five constituent elements, which are assumed to be the most important and influential partners that are able to put constraints on and change the strength of MNE's bargaining power. These constituents are stockholders, host country government, host country employees, home country government, and home country employees. Stockholders are the only partner in this MNE bargaining relations by which the MNE is not only constrained in the bargaining processes but also to which the MNE is also responsible for its decisions. All other constituents have only potential and actual power to constrain MNE's bargaining abilities (Gunneman, 1975: 55-56). The MNE's responsibility to shareholders is defined by their real interests over the ultimate economic goal, i.e., the profit-maximisation goal. On the basis of economic theory the ultimate real interests of all other constituents is also profit-maximisation.

However, given the previous simplified two-variable model of bargaining power, it can be argued that this model lacks important variables. These include, firstly, the presence of a competitor. Additional elements include the home or host country's resource endowments (land, human resources, oil, gas and others). Gunneman (1975) suggests that resources are integral parts of a potential home or host country's bargaining power, which means that they are already intrinsically taken into account as this host country's power components. The inclusion of employees as a separate category, meanwhile, can be attributed to the potential power of labour unions in a specific country.

The importance of competitors arises primarily from the way conflict is modelled within the bargaining power concept, whereby the presence of competitors influences (or, better, reduces) the potential and actual bargaining power of MNEs. This model is closely associated with Nicholson's (1972: 5) definition of oligopolistic conflict in that it is assumed that "if we have a situation where, if A made one announcement rather then another, it would alter B's decision, than we shall call it a decision taken under conflict". In other words there is an assumption that the presence of credible and adversarial competitors can lead to a redistribution of power in favour of a host country.

Other important elements that constraints both MNE's and host country's bargaining power are international organisations. The growing role of international institutions cannot be ignored in a model where components are highly integrated and readily affect power distributions. The introduction of these two important elements (competitors and international organisations) into the simple corporation model can be assumed to entail a crucial redistribution of power among each constituent's potential and actual power (See Appendix C, Figure 2).

A further element of ineterminacy can be introduced into these models by assuming that host states and MNEs are further constraint by responsibility relationships vis a vis their constituents. The consideration of such responsibilities would entail the recognition of such types of power as 'authority' which otherwise would not have been viewed as a type of power exercised within MNE bargaining power relationships by definitional fiat. It can be assumed that as MNEs have responsibilities vis a vis other constituents, the MNE can be "seen as one who has options as to which of those constituencies it has to be responsive, and responsible, to in any context" (Gunneman, 1975: 56). As soon as an MNE admits that it is accountable to multiple constituencies it is moreover exposed to the problem of a priority of choice (Gunneman, 1975: 56). Once the decision about responsibility is made, MNEs, through the acknowledgement of responsibility also acknowledge their obligation to comply with the values of dominant constituents' values. These values then become the MNE's values as well, which implies a further constraint of MNE's bargaining power (See Appendix C, Figure 3).

CONCLUSION

The analysis of MNE bargaining power presents a number of puzzles from the perspective of political theory. These puzzles arise, in part, from the fact that the overlap between traditional concepts of MNE bargaining power and broader concepts of political power is only a partial one.

This is most evident in the context of notions of authority. The MNE bargaining power framework, for instance, excludes authority from the analysis of bargaining power—which limits the realism of this approach. This lack of realism can be partially overcome when additional components are included in the host country - MNE bargaining model. Two most significant constituents include competitors and international organisations, both of which can be assumed constrain and/or reduce the power of MNEs. These new participants significantly influence the process of power redistribution in the contemporary economic context.

The obvious drawback of developing richer models of host country - MNE bargaining relationships is that these models become easily overdetermined in the sense that it becomes increasingly difficult to predict specific power constellations or bargaining outcomes. Despite this, there is a strong case for integrating political theory-based concepts of bargaining power into the analysis of host country - MNE relationships.

APPENDIX A

Table 1. Three dimensions of power

3-dimentional	concept of power	(preference-shaping)
2-dimentional concept of power	(agenda-setting)	
1-dimentional concept of power (decision-making)		
• decision-making • direct observable conflict of interests = preferences	+ non-decision making (locating decision-making within the context of agenda-setting)	+ potential conflict + differentiation between real and perceived interests (distinction between subjective or perceived interests and actual or real interests)

Table 2. Bargaining power

		power as a tactical action
	power as a potential	
power as an outcome		
• actual or successful power • direct observable conflict of interests over goals (that no party can achieve without taking the other into account • dependence	+ potential power influence	= power of tactics + use of power coercion, force, manipulation

APPENDIX B

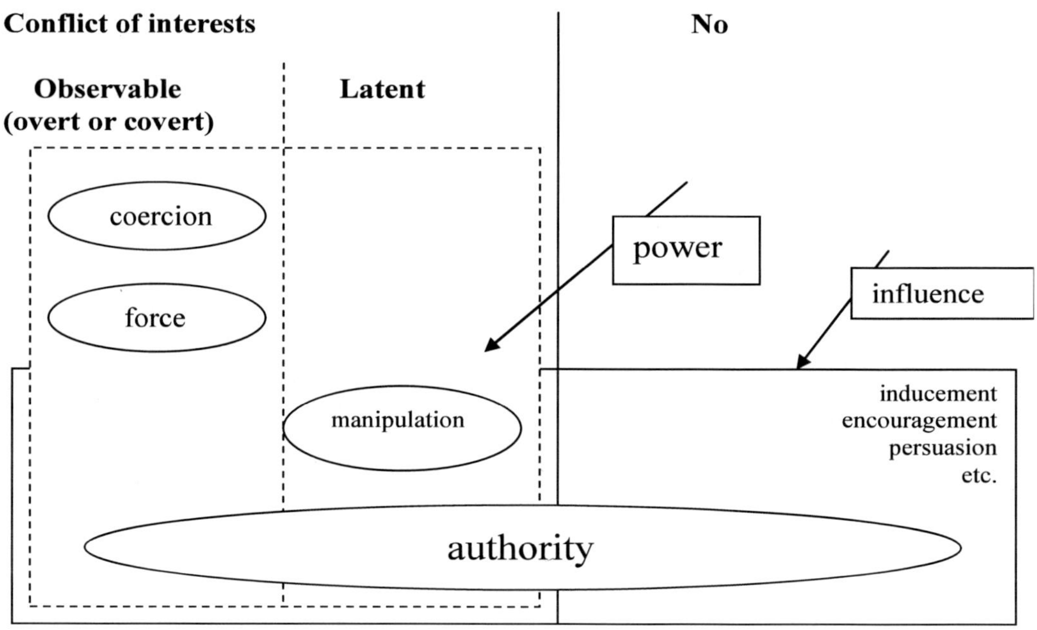

Figure 1. Three dimensions of power (Source: Lukes, 1980).

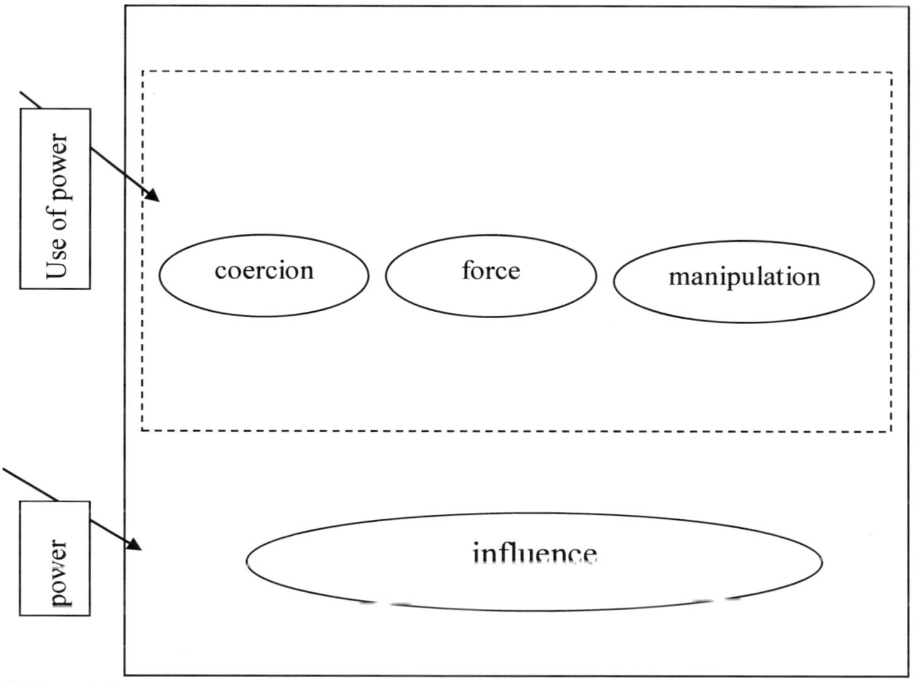

Figure 2. Bargaining power.

APPENDIX C

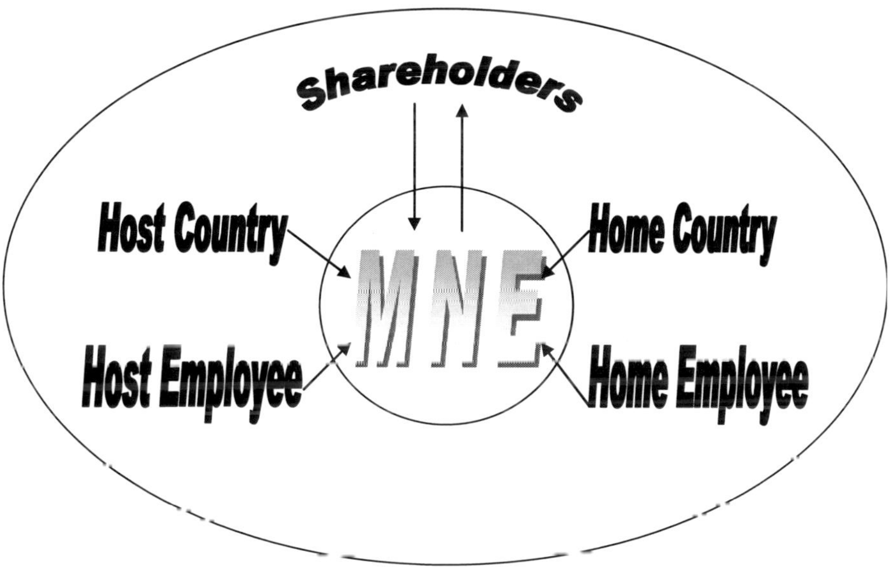

Figure 1. Marshall's basic model of the corporation (Source: Gunnemann, 1975).

Figure 2. An alternative model of MNE bargaining power relationships.

Figure 3. The responsibility model of MNE bargaining power relationships.

References

Bacharach, R., Lawler, E. J. *Bargaining: Power, Tactics, and Outcomes.* San Francisco: Jossy-Bass Inc. Publishers, 1981: 234.

Bachrach, P., Baratz, M. S. *Power and Poverty: Theory and Practice.* New-York: Oxford University Press, 1970: 220.

Gunnemann, J. P. *The Nation-State and Transnational Corporation in Conflict: With Special Reference to Latin America.* New-Yrok: Praeger Publishers, 1975, 244.

Hay, C. Divided by a Common Language: Political Theory and Concept of Power. *Politics, no. 17 (1), 1997:* 45-52.

Lukes, S. *Power: A Radical View.* London: Macmillan press Ltd, 1980: 64.

Moran, T. *FDI and Development: The New Policy Agenda for Developing Countries and Economies in Transition.* Washington DC: Institute for International Economics, 1998: 192.

Nicholson, M. *Oligopoly and Conflict: A Dynamic Approach.* Liverpool: Liverpool University Press, 1972: 228.

Oppenheim, F. *Political Concepts: A Reconstruction.* Oxford: Basil Blackwell, 1981: 227.

Stopford, J., Strange S., Hensley, J. *Rival States, Rival Firms: Competition for World Morket Shares.* UK: Cambridge University Press, 1991: 321.

UNCTAD. 2009. *World investment report 2009: Transnational corporations, agricultural production and development.* New-York and Geneva: United Nations, 314.

UNCTAD. 2010. *World investment report 2010: Investing in a low-carbon economy.* New-York and Geneva: United Nations, 221.

Vernon, R. *Sovereignty at Bay: The Multinational Spread of US Enterprises.* London: Longman, 1971: 326.

SECTION C:

PUBLIC PRIVATE PARTNERSHIP

In: Understanding Risk
Editor: Matthias Beck
ISBN: 978-1-62618-686-6

Chapter 10

RISKS IN PRIVATE FINANCE INITIATIVE PROJECTS: A PUBLIC SECTOR PERSPECTIVE

***Darinka Asenova*[1,*] *and Matthias Beck*[2,†]**
[1]Division of Accounting, Finance and Risk, Caledonian Business School, Glasgow Caledonian University, Glasgow, Scotland, UK
[2]The York Management School, University of York, York, UK

ABSTRACT

The management of public sector risk is increasingly seen as a priority area of UK government policy. This has been highlighted recently by the Prime Minister Gordon Brown who stated that "the issue of public risk is one of the most challenging areas of policy-making for any government" (Strategic Risk, 2008). In response to these challenges, the UK Prime Minister has appointed a new body - the Risk and Regulation Advisory Council (RRAC) which is tasked with improving the way risk to the public is understood and managed. One area of particular concern with regard to the governance of public sector risks involves projects procured via the Private Finance Initiative (PFI). These projects involve long-term contracts, complex multi-party interactions and thus create various risks to public sector clients. Today, most PFI actors acknowledge the potentially adverse effects of these risks and make an effort to prevent or mitigate undesirable results. As a consequence, issues of risk allocation, risk transfer and risk management have become central to the PFI procurement process. This paper provides an overview of the risk categories and risk types which are relevant to the public sector in PFI projects. It analyses risk as a feature of uncertain future project-related events and examines potential pitfalls which can be associated with PFI risk management on the basis of a case study of a high-profile PFI hospital in Scotland. The paper concludes that, despite the trend towards diminished risk profiles during the operational phase, the public sector continues to be exposed to significant risks when engaging in PFI-based procurement.

* E-mail: d.asenova@gcal.ac.uk.
† E-mail: mb541@york.ac.uk

BACKGROUND

Over the past 20 years, there has been a global trend towards the private sector financing of infrastructure projects (Merna and Njiru, 1998). This process has been particularly pronounced in the UK, where by 2004 the Private Finance Initiative (PFI) accounted for as much as 13.5% of total public investment (HM Treasury, 2003). Although PFI originated during the Conservative rule, it only became prominent during New Labour's administration which, since its election in 1997, consistently emphasised its commitment to PFI based procurement (HM Treasury, 1999; HM Treasury, 2003).

Although there is a strong emphasis within UK PFI procurement on the transfer of risks from the public to the private sector, it is clear that these projects pose considerable risks to their public sector clients. These risks arise from a number of sources which include the long-term nature of PFI contracts as well as the complex multi-party interactions involved in PFI procurement. While it is hitherto unclear how much of its effort the UK Prime Minister's newly appointed body, the Risk and Regulation Advisory Council (RRAC), will focus on PFI risks, the creation of this body itself can be seen as evidence of the increased risk exposure of the public sector, to which PFI and other forms of public-private partnership contributed significantly.

The following sections provide an overview of some of the key notions of risk and the main risk categories which are relevant to the public sector in PFI projects. Section one commences with a review of alternative concepts of risk and uncertainty which forms the basis of a discussion of the notion of risk cultures in the context of public and private sector organizations. Section three examines the risks of PFI projects and together issues of risk transfer. Section four briefly reviews some of the problems and pitfalls associated with PFI procurement with a special focus on issues of risk management, allocation and transfer. Section five presents a case study of a large high-profile PFI hospital project which, following a period of initial enthusiasm, is now increasingly as exemplifying the problems of PFI procurement. The paper concludes by arguing that the problems of associated with PFI procurement cannot be seen exclusively in terms of a culture clash between risk-averse public sector organizations and risk-taking private sector PFI partners, but rather as the outcome of an ill defined suboptimal procurement process where it is falsely assumed that different categories of risk can be managed discretely outside an institutional framework which explicitly champions the interests of the public sector client.

RISK AND UNCERTAINTY

In modern societies the notion of risk has become a key concept which bears broad relevancy in different areas including the natural and scientific world, social interactions, organisational behavior and government policy. As concerns policy initiatives, different views of key risks can give rise to definitional disagreements and political controversies. In the PFI context, for instance, the notion of risk can convey different meanings to different stakeholders as well as having diverse disciplinary connotations.

At present, there is no single universally accepted definition of risk. What most definitions of risk have in common is that they refer in one way or another to uncertainty (see, e.g., Dickson, 1991). Often the focus of specific definitions of risk is on unexpected events that have the potential to jeopardise the successful completion of a certain action, venture or project. Some authors seek to draw a clear distinction between uncertainty and risk. Reddy (1996), for instance, has argued that risk tends to have a purely technical meaning, which allows for explicit, probability based numerical assessments. Meanwhile, uncertainty is associated with random events, where no rational calculation of the likelihood for different outcomes is possible. By contrast, some theorists (Douglas, 1992; Adams, 1995; Lupton, 1999) have argued that the precise numbers necessary to assess risk are often unavailable and that the difference between the two notions is often not relevant. Irrespective of the possibility for precise quantification, or otherwise, risk can be broadly interpreted as some type of danger, in a sense, which makes the two notions of risk and uncertainty practically interchangeable. Using a parallel between the classical and the relativistic physics, Adams (1995) has therefore argued that notions of risk can be applied to any context where the classical deterministic physics no longer yield results and less certain probabilistic categories have to be introduced. Similarly, some authors have argued that risk is encountered in any activity or decision where the outcome or consequence is less than certain (McKim, 1992; Boothroyd and Emmett, 1996). Conrow and Shishido (1997) define risk as "the probability of failing to achieve particular cost, performance, and schedule objectives, and the consequence of failing to achieve those objectives". Similarly Kerzner (1995) defines risk as "a measure of the probability and consequence of not achieving a defined project goal". According to the HM Treasury's "Orange Book" (2000) "risk is the uncertainty of outcome, within a range of potential exposures, arising from a combination of the impact and probability of potential events". Despite the apparent connection between risk taking behaviour and expected rewards, notions of risk are often associated with adverse events and the threat of loss (Raftery, 1994; Lupton, 1999). Thus, risks are sometimes interpreted as the "unwanted events in the future" (Dickson, 1991), while the possibility for positive outcome is usually known as opportunity or chance.

Many authors have highlighted the inherent subjectivity associated with the understanding and treatment of risks (Adams, 1995; Holton, 2000). In line with other social scientists, researchers concerned with risks have been striving to substantiate their statements by adopting certain tools and methodologies which are derived from the positivistic science. These approaches are limited, however, by the fact that not all risks can be precisely measured and quantified. Therefore, a distinction is commonly made between two categories of risk; these are described respectively as either objective or subjective. Objective risks are those risks that have a finite number of outcomes and lent themselves to precise scientific measurement. For objective risks, independent risk evaluations via different methods should produce identical results. Objective risks can therefore be considered as being free of bias in line with physical characteristics (Hood and Jones, 1996). By contrast, subjective or perceived risks depend on the criteria and the assumptions utilised. They can have an infinite number of outcomes and their evaluation reflects individual or group opinions. For subjective risks different estimates of the same risk can yield different results.

The distinction between these two categories is essential in terms of assessing the accuracy and limitations of risk analyses in general. Notably, there are several factors that can turn an objective risk analysis into a subjective one. Hood and Jones (1996) emphasise that sometimes apparently rigid quantitative approaches, such as those related to risk modelling, can reflect external pressure and yield biased risk estimates. In many cases, when performing risk calculations, experts utilise probability estimates based on historic information. Therefore, the availability of reliable historic data has a direct effect on the accuracy of the risk estimates. Furthermore, Fischhoff, Watson and Hope (1991) have argued that public opinion is capable of carrying elements of objectivity, while, in some cases, expert opinions can include implicit biases.

Hood and Jones (1996) have further questioned the appropriateness of quantitative methodologies for risk assessment on the grounds that they were initially developed under the assumption of “closed systems”. Their application to “open systems” with unlimited and unpredictable numbers of options, such as humans or organisations, accordingly, is bound to produce unreliable results.

RISK CULTURES

Social scientists have noted a link between cultural tendencies which emphasise the value of personal freedom, individualistic attitudes and choice, and the need for higher risk responsiveness in personal decision-making (Douglas and Wildavsky, 1983). Although, many risks are assessed in conjunction with expert judgements, Lupton (1999) has argued that most individuals also have to deal with risk at a private level. At this level different individuals exhibit different basic risk orientations, attitudes and dispositions, which, in turn, moderate their decision-making (Dickson, 1991). The mechanism guiding individual attitudes towards risks are not completely understood. Overall, it is assumed that these mechanisms vary across different risk categories, as well as between the occupational and social groups. However, it is unclear how stable these relationships are either across cultures or across time.

Risk attitudes are difficult to measure because they are based on innate characteristics of individuals such as personal risk propensity and risk aversion. Personal assessment of a risky situation, nonetheless, often determines the final risk decision in terms of risk acceptance or refusal. The whole process is distinctive, individual and involves some degree of pre-established knowledge and experience for dealing with similar situations (Pidgeon et al., 1992). These problems are aggravated by the fact that decisions take pace in certain personal, societal and cultural context, which themselves influence the outlook of individuals.

It has been generally accepted that, on average, most people dislike risks and tend to exhibit risk-averse behaviour (Lupton, 1999). Douglas and Wildavsky (1983) note that, “careful to avoid disgrace and conscious of the need of support, the social being is a sensitive scanner of safety signs in a universe of critical fellow humans who share his commitments”. Similarly, Uher and Toakley (1999) claim that, in a survey of risk attitudes, only one-third of their respondents identified themselves as active risk-takers. However, Boothroyd and Emmett (1996) asserted that in some circumstances the attitudes towards risk could become more positive. Beetsma and Schotman (2001) conducted research with Dutch TV game show participants, which were overconfident about their chances for success in a risky situation. The researchers reported that while the actual chance for winning was about two-thirds, the participants perceived it to be 15% higher. In another survey based on a set of questions on lotteries, Donkers, Melenberg and Soest (2001) found a strong relationship between risk attitudes and individual characteristics such as age, gender, income and level of education. According to their findings, females and older people are more risk averse, while higher income and education groups have a higher degree of acceptability towards some risks. Douglas and Wildavsky (1983) noted that most people did not like to be seen as rushing into presumably important risk decisions. When pressed for answers many individuals, therefore, tended to rely on expert, and seemingly 'objective', opinions. Expert opinions are, of course, based on the current levels of knowledge and often cannot answer to all relevant risk-related questions. Expert judgment, moreover, contains embedded subjective elements in the form of informed assumptions, which can mirror personal bias.

Cassidy and Lynn (1989) also associate risk with individual psychological settings and personal goal achievement strategies. They suggest that only a harmony between individual and organisational goals could motivate individuals to support organisational risk taking. Similarly, Kliem and Ludin (1997) emphasise the importance of the environment and point out that risk will be viewed more positively in an environment where risk taking is rewarded and the consequences of failure are perceived as being marginal.

As concerns risk taking in the public sector, there is some evidence that public sector decision makers are relatively risk averse when compared to their private sector counterparts (Bellante and Link, 1981; Blank, 1985; Juerges, 2002). This phenomenon is relatively poorly understood as it can be attributed to a number of potentially competing factors. One of the most prevalent explanations is that more risk-averse individuals sort into the public sector employment as part of a general labour market matching mechanism (Bellante and Link, 1981). This mechanism is said to be re-inforced by the fact that risk taking is rewarded with higher wages in the private sector, but not necessarily in the public sector (Pfeifer, 2008). Alternatively there is the possibility that pubic sector organisations foster risk averse cultures and behaviours by rewarding, for example, actions which avoid risks, rather than rewarding risky and innovative actions which might pay off in the future (Dror, 1964; Cates 1979). Lastly there is the possibility that decision making mechanisms within pubic sector organisations encourage risk averse behaviour on account of the in-built emphasis on consultation and committee work (Richardson and Jordan, 1997).

Risk and Risk Transfer in PFI Projects

Although many different risks accompany particular PFI projects, it is possible to classify PFI risks into a number of categories. Thus the Private Finance Panel (PFP) (1995) distinguished between the following categories of risk:

1. Design and construction risks – refer to the possibility for design and construction faults, cost and time overruns, which are common in large-scale construction projects.
2. Commissioning and operating risk - include any problems such as maintenance and life-cycle costing, which often occur during the commissioning and operating phases.
3. Demand for the facility/ volume or usage risk – reflect the uncertainty that is economically viable and will attract sufficient number of customers/ users.
4. Residual value risk – arise from the uncertainty about the value of the asset at the end of the concessional period.

5. Technology/ obsolescence risk – arises in sectors where new or unproven technology is used.
6. Regulation and legislative risk – reflect the possibility for the introduction of new legislation, which can require different standards.

In addition to the above categories there is financial risk which is partly transferred to the private sector (Allen, 2001), on account of the assumption that this sector is better equipped to manage it. Allen (2001) distinguishes between two categories of financial risk in PFI, namely disposal risk and external financing risk. The disposal risk is associated with the possibility that the cost of some project related assets has deflated. For example, as a result of re-evaluation of the current needs, an educational authority might have surplus school buildings and attached to them surplus land. The exposure to such risks can be reduced if the assets are transferred to the private sector but they cannot be entirely eliminated. The external financing of risk, on the other hand, can be associated with the inability of the project company to raise capital, or other financial risks such as interest rate risks. In this context, public sector departments have to pay special attention to the financial backing of the project company, as well as its ability to overcome any shortcomings. Interest rate risks before reaching the contract award arise from increases in interest rates occurring during long negotiation periods, which can reduce the appeal of a venture to the private sector. This financing risk is normally also transferred to the private sector (Allen, 2001).

In the UK a substantial transfer of risk to the private sector is seen as a key prerequisite for the implementation of a PFI project. What is less well understood is how an extensive transfer of risks to the private sector affects the pricing of PFI projects. Most guidelines suggest that transferred risks should be well understood in order to be properly assessed and priced in the contract, with, e.g., Whitfield (2001: 25) arguing that "risk transfer involves identifying the different types of risk, allocating legal responsibility and pricing each element so that it can be recharged to the public sector". However, the pricing of different element of risks is likely to involve elements of subjective judgement and as such can easily become a source of controversy.

In technical terms, the transfer of risk in PFI projects involves two elements. Firstly, the payment mechanism is subject to availability and performance of the facility. Secondly, the contractual terms identify the party responsible for each particular risk. One major tool for achieving value for money in PFIs lies in the mechanism for efficient transfer, allocation and management of project risks, whereby the implicit presumption is that the private sector is better equipped to manage the main project risks, or at least those over which it has a high degree of control.

In some early PFIs, risk allocation issues were often misinterpreted, in terms of the public sector client seeking to transfer of all risks to the private sector partners. This approach was costly and contradicted one of the key principles of PFI, according to which project risks have to be allocated to the party best placed to manage them (HM Treasury, 1995). In each project there are certain categories of risk, over which the private sector has no control, and which therefore are better shared or handled by the public sector. Examples for such risks include volume or usage risk in prisons, court or road projects. Inevitably, the public sector also retrains the risk of improper specifications, as well as any reputational risks associated with project failure (HM Treasury 1995). In educational projects, the local authority cannot transfer the ultimate responsibility for the provision of education to the school children. In some cases, private sector companies are willing to take particular risks, but this inevitably increases the project's risk premium and affects its costs. Therefore, as a general rule, there is now an understanding that private partners should only be allocated such risks that they are capable of handling. In this context it is increasingly assumed that big and well established private sector companies which have been involved in a number of PFI projects and have developed the resources and expertise required to manage PFI risks effectively. Over the recent decade most public sector departments have placed significant emphasis on a careful allocation of PFI risks which is preceded by a detailed analysis of key project risks allocation (in contrast with total risk transfer). However, while the public sector has arguably acquired certain experience and understanding in relation to contract negotiation, many PFI projects have now entered the operational phase, which has presented the public sector with new risks; for example, risks associated refinancing (NAO, 2006), or contract modifications (NAO, 2008).

OTHER RISK CATEGORIES

Other risk categories include reputation risk, political risk, environmental risk, and force majeure risk.

Reputation risk is any threat to the organisational image, which can result in mistrust from stakeholders, and can affect the value of the organisation (Brotzen, 2002). Over recent years, several UK government departments have suffered substantial reputational damage, in events which included the loss of 25 million child records. Reputational risk can be associated with a malfunction of internal controls, monitoring procedures or failure to respond adequately to other risks. Thus the withdrawal of a consortium from the PFI bidding process or service failures can have potential reputational implications for the public sector. The same is true for contractual renegotiations of PFI contract which allowed for refinancing deals which channelled huge profits to private sector PFI parties, without these benefits being shared by the public sector.

Political risk is primarily related to the actions of governmental and non-governmental actors (Zonis and Wilkin, 2002). It is prominent in countries with social and political instability, but can also be encountered in some domestic projects. As a general rule, the proper assessment of the political risk requires a good understanding of the socio-economic and historical context (Deep, 2002). Following a period of stabilisation, the current post cold war political environment is again characterized by high volatility which requires diligent risk assessment (Skinner, 2008). An extreme example of political risk is the expropriation of project assets (Sapte, 1997), political violence and contract frustration. Domestic political risks in the UK include changes of political power, which can impose different views, priorities, and regulations. For example, when in 2007 the Scottish National Party came to power in Scotland, it declared its commitment to alternative non-PFI forms of financing public facilities and services. Different forms of intervention can create complications at different transaction stages. For example, at the beginning of a project, risk can arise from the activities of a cumbersome and bureaucratic local and central administration or changes in political power, while at the later stages obstacles of legislative and regulatory nature can prevail.

Despite the fact that environmental liability is usually incurred by PFI project members, the public sector also can encounter a share of the environmental risk. If the project has environmental impact and breaches environmental laws this can have significant reputational effects. In developed countries, the environmental laws and regulations have changed substantially over recent years, as new restrictions have been imposed to protect the environment (Finnerty, 1996). At the same time business ventures in other countries, especially in the developing world have been a subject of close observation and scrutiny by the media. Thus, projects, which contribute to the destruction of the natural environment in terms of noise, pollution, etc., may have damaging effect on all project participants in terms of generating bad publicity.

Force majeure risks arise from sudden catastrophic events that are beyond the reasonable control of the affected party. Examples for such events include war, flood, earthquakes, fire, etc. Some of these events can be insured, but a part of them will usually be uninsurable (Finnerty, 1996). In project finance, lenders usually insist on a clear contractual definition of force majeure. Wherever possible, they also require a complete insurance cover or government guarantees including provisions in the contract that, if the force majeure events are specific to the project rather than general, the public sector bears the risks.

All of the above risk categories can affect the public sector in PFIs to various degrees, as these risks form a part of the overall project risk portfolio. Even risks that are contractually transferred to the private sector, such as design, construction, or technology related risks in reality cannot be completely transferred, because the public sector has the ultimate responsibility for the provision of public services.

Notwithstanding the complex nature of PFI risks, a project risk profile is not fixed, and changes occur over the life span of the project. At any point of time, and especially in the early project stages when most of the risk evaluation takes place, precise risk quantification is difficult. This can necessitate a degree of subjective judgment, based on specific project features and commercial expertise which is not always readily available in some public sector bodies (Asenova and Beck, 2003; Hood and McGarvey, 2002). Unlike traditional procurement, PFI projects are characterized by a heightened risk profile at the beginning and during the construction phase. Once they enter the operational phase, these projects provide a continuous cash flow to the private sector while the associated risks tend to decrease. This creates the possibility for refinancing the original PFI transaction, which, in turn, can lead to excessive profits for the private companies while additional risks are being transferred back to the public sector (NAO, 2006; HM Treasury, 2003).

Despite the trend for diminished risk profile during the operational phase, the public sector therefore needs to continue to show commercial awareness. This issue has been highlighted in a recent report by the UK government's financial watchdog, the National Accounting Office (NAO) (2008), which noted that post-financial-close contractual changes instigated by the private sector can give rise to overpayment at the costs of the pubic sector. Edward Leigh, chairman of the Commons Public Accounts Committee, which oversees the NAO, noted that in some cases the commercial expertise demonstrated by the public sector managers is still insufficient (Hencke, 2008):

The public sector has allowed itself to be taken for a ride ... changes during a 25- to 30-year PFI contract are inevitable, but they should not be costing the taxpayer an arm and a leg, as they often are. Public sector contract managers for PFI deals have insufficient commercial experience to negotiate with and develop effective relationships with their private sector counterparts.

According to the report the introduction and the implementation of some of these changes, which were largely forced on the public sector, resulted in typical increases of the management fees in the range of 10-15 per cent (NAO, 2008). These increases are likely to undermine gains which were initially assumed to arise when the project was procured as a public-private partnership.

FAILURES AFFECTING THE PUBLIC SECTOR

Since the introduction of PFIs in 1992 public sector departments have faced many difficulties. Early PFIs, as well as some more recent projects exploring new sectors, have faced unanticipated problems and risks. An example for an early project which encountered major problems is the Royal Armouries museum, where the volume risk was underestimated. In 1993, the contract was signed for transferring the museum from London to Leeds. The relocation caused a substantial decrease in the customer demand. The private sector consortia known as RAI had undertaken the obligation to build the new building in Leeds and run the museum for sixty years. RAI intended to service their debt through the income generated by the visitors. The project was completed on time and without exceeding the fixed budget. However, due to insufficient customer demand, by 1999 the RAI had made a loss of £21 million including the outstanding loans and operating losses (NAO, 2001). At that time the financiers (Bank of Scotland) decided to withdraw support and the consortia became insolvent. The closure of the museum was not an acceptable option for the public sector, which chose to step in and to provide financial support for the project. Consequently, the project agreement was revised as a non-PFI service contract where the client took over the running of the museum, while the RAI provided all related services. The IT sector also has proved to be a very risky sector for PFI procurement, in which failures have been particularly frequent under the regime of compulsory testing. This was illustrated by one of the first IT PFI projects, the Benefit Payments Card Project, which had to be abandoned. In 1996 the project agreement was signed between the Benefit Agency and Post Office Counters Ltd., which joined as a public sector client, and Pathway, a subsidiary of the computer service group ICL as a project company. This was a large-scale project, which intended to modernise the operation of 40,000 offices from the national post office network by May 1999. It involved replacing outdated paper based methods for paying social security benefits to 17 million benefit recipients, with a single swipe card. The projected advantages were twofold: first, the project was thought to bring efficient and convenient service, and second it was expected to save an estimated £100 million on account of preventing benefit fraud (NAO, 2000).

In 1999, when according to the schedule the project was supposed to be completed, it was only at the stage of early, limited scale tests. The clients decided to prevent further losses by cancelling a part of the project. The project was simplified to include only partial automation of the post offices, which allowed the claimants to receive the payments in their bank accounts. The estimated losses from the cancellation of the swipe card component amounted to about £1 billion including fraud savings, nugatory expenditure and write-down assets (Jason, 2001).

An investigation conducted by the NAO into this project found that, despite the huge complexity of the project, some avoidable mistakes had been made. Both the public and the private sector sides had not fully recognised the deliverability risk arising from the scale of the project, and its technical complexity. The NAO report (2000) noted that other important risks were also underestimated in this project. Firstly, while the clients had conducted a comprehensive risk identification exercise, subsequent risk evaluations in terms of probability and impact were incomplete. Secondly, due to the tight time scale, this project would have required a far more focussed and proactive management. Thirdly, the two client organisations had inconsistent objectives and could not co-ordinate their efforts when risks materialised. Lastly, at the stage of signing the contract and financial close, the client was not ready to present detailed specifications, which further increased the uncertainty and allowed ambiguity.

Other unsuccessful IT PFI projects include the new system for the passport agency, which made a loss of £12.6 million, and the National Insurance computer, which led to losses of £25 million (NAO, 1998). In order to prevent similar mistakes and to help with future IT projects the Treasury Taskforce (TTF) and Cabinet Office issued separate guidance documents.

Management failures have also accompanied otherwise successful projects, such as the early road schemes. In 1996, the Highways Agency acting as an arm of the Department of Transport signed four road contracts which were used to test the market interest and the potential of PFI in this sector. These included the M1-A1 link road near Leeds, the widening of A1 between Alconbury and Peterborough, the A419/A417 between Swindon and Gloucester, and A69 between Carlisle and Newcastle-upon-Tyne. Payments were agreed on the basis of 'shadow tolls', which involved estimates of the road usage in terms of vehicle kilometres. The shadow tolls were subject to a pre-determined ceiling. The agreed concession period for all roads was 30 years.

The projects were successful in creating sufficient market interest and the public sector client managed to maintain sufficient competitive tension between the bidding companies up to the point of the financial close. According to the estimates by the client (the Highways Agency), the total savings from these projects were about £167 million. An investigation conducted by the NAO (1999), however, revised this figure to around £100 million or 13% of the total price. The client was criticised for overstating the benefits and for the usage of shadow tolls, which is not necessarily the best payment mechanism in terms of the potential efficiency savings. The contracts also included an inappropriate transfer of the volume risk to the private sector, which affected the pricing, because the private companies had no control over these risks.

The application of PFI to the healthcare sector has also been accompanied by series of problems (Asenova et al., 2004). The first 'flagship' hospital built from scratch under PFI was the £87 million Cumberland Infirmary in Carlisle, whose contract was signed in 1997. The hospital, which was designed as an impressive modern construction and being completed ahead of schedule, was officially opened by the Prime Minister in 2000. However, subsequently the private sector has come under criticism for cutting corners. Thus, the new hospital accommodates 90 beds less than the older one (Anon, 2001), which means that, at times, accommodation capacity is insufficient. Further to this, the small size of the wards has required new smaller resuscitation trolleys at the cost of £180,000. Due to the shortage of storage space, the patients' records and X-ray images had to be gathered in the old premises which, in effect, has increased the waiting time for radiologists. There have been different instances of poor quality materials used by the builders which have led to accidents. For example, in the absence of air-conditioning or ventilation, the glass roof construction has led to very high temperatures during the hot season, and noise during rainfalls. Further to this, there have been broken pipes and floods in the operating theatre, falling ceilings, sewage system problems, and damage to some expensive equipment (Prentis, 2001). On one occasion, the emergency power generator stopped working for 20 minutes, with the life-supporting equipment being shut down without warning. Washing machines were few and of poor quality and because the engineer servicing the autoclave ovens for sterilisation was made redundant, there was no qualified staff to repair equipment (Unison, 1999).

In the case of the Guy's hospital in London, the PFI project involved the refurbishment of the existing facilities. It also gained bad publicity due to disputes between the consortia members, which delayed the completion period by three years. In addition, the review conducted by NAO found that the works went £68.7 million over the initial budget (Anon 2002). In most cases, problems with PFI based NHS hospitals seem to relate to a reduction in the number of beds in the new built facilities. A survey conducted by *The Times* claims that more that 2,000 beds have already been cut, while research conducted by University College London estimates that the first wave of PFI hospitals will cut the existing capacity by nearly 30% (Wright, 2000).

MANAGEMENT OF RISK IN PFI CONTRACTS

There is a substantial body of literature relating to the management of risk in PPP/PFI. PFI contracts have generally been characterised by features such as substantial running costs, complex contractual arrangements and extended contractual periods, all of which contribute to a heightened risk profile. In addition to the risk categories already identified, PFI projects are exposed to financial risk which can arise from the inability of the project company to raise capital or other financial factors such as changes of interest rates (HM Treasury, 1997a). In a typical PPP/PFI contract, each of these risk categories is broken down into a number of individual risks in order to create a detailed risk map. For example, design and construction risk can also relate to site risk and industrial relations risk, as well as problems related to design and construction features (Hodge, 2004).

The contractual framework of individual PFI projects usually goes beyond the risk identification to prescribe different treatment for different risk categories. Thus, most of the risks associated with design, construction, operation as well as project finance are typically transferred to the private sector. The demand risk and the technology risk are treated on a project-by-project basis (PFP, 1996), while the regulation/legislative risk are either partially shared or retained by the public sector. The fact that PFI contracts concern the provision of services over a long period of time means that the residual value risk is generally not a major issue. However, rather than utilising in-house teams and systems, local authorities and other public sector clients often rely extensively on external consultants to provide expertise on technical, financial and operational issues as well as assurance that all project risks have been identified and evaluated for the entire duration of the contract.

Guidance documents by the UK Treasury (HM Treasury, 1997b) suggest that risks affecting particular projects should be treated as variations in the profits or losses which have to be allocated to the appropriate contractual partners. Notwithstanding the detailed guidance and attention to risk, the experience with PPP/PFI projects has highlighted a number of difficulties associated with the practical implementation of this risk management process. These failures have been attributed to several causes. According to Lonsdale (2005), some contracts have failed to account for key characteristics and relations associated with the main parties which can have a decisive impact on the treatment of risk. These issues include an asymmetry of balance of power between the partners, superior commercial capabilities of the private sector and the political nature of public sector decision making. These imbalances can explain the minimum level of risk transferred in some projects to the private sector in contracts which favoured the interests of private sector shareholders.

Some technical issues and methodologies have also been a source of concern. For example, a report by Pollock et al. (2005) questioned the evaluation of PPP/PFIs and specifically the methodological approach used in five government commissioned studies which compare the performance of PPP/PFI against traditional capital finance projects. The authors argued that, while PPP/PFI projects are designed to include up to 24% 'optimism bias' risk adjustment, they fail to present any sound data-based proof for the achievement of the key targets in terms of time and cost overruns. Specifically Pollock et al. note (2005: 3):

Although 677 projects have been approved or completed since 1992, the Treasury has not fulfilled its objective of "sound evidence base" for rigorous investigation" of PFI. There is no evidence to support the Treasury's chief justification for the policy, namely that PFI generates value for money savings by improving the efficiency of construction procurement.

At a more conceptual level, Hodge (2004) notes that the utilisation of PPP/PFI as a purchasing device can potentially jeopardise the public interest. Hodge notes that, while the risks in the commercial domain are given a lot of attention and are investigated in detail, the risks in the governance domain are often neglected. One direct result of this neglect is a questionable analysis of the value for money associated with PFI projects. More importantly there is a loss of control and "shrinking stewardship responsibilities in governance" (Hodge, 2004:46).

Investigating the impact of long term contractual commitments typical of PFI contracts on the ability of the public sector to deliver services, Froud (2003) has questioned the compatibility of PFI with traditional assumptions about the appropriate role of the public sector. Froud's analysis centres on the question as to how the contractual management of risks in PFI projects impacts on the ability of the state to respond flexibly to the needs of the public. According to Froud (2003: 587):

> The argument here is not that the private sector cannot provide a range of lower cost services…but that the tasks of planning and monitoring public services, of modifying policy, or working towards goals of equality and balanced interests are those which require the authority and mentality of well motivated state.

While the PPP/PFI capital finance option has been rigorously pursued by the government, these criticisms of PFI suggest that the underlying risk allocation and transfer model has not been an unambiguous success. However, the existence of comprehensive risk allocation model is a basic prerequisite for a more or less systematic approach to project risk and risk management. What is more, it corresponds to the current endorsement of risk management and the increased level of regulation and governance in local authorities.

Case Study

The following case study focuses on the problems, risks and risk management issues in a high-profile PFI hospital in Scotland, which is a major provider of acute medical services and teaching facilities officially opened in 2003 by the Prime Minister.

Project Background

The project was commissioned by the local NHS Trust and represents one of the most significant PFI hospitals in the country. In line with the strategy review conducted by the Hospital Trust in 1993 (Scottish Executive, 2003) the new hospital was intended to modernise four smaller local hospitals units at different locations and to promote a new integrated approach to service delivery. The Hospital Trust decided to achieve these objectives and to realise additional efficiency gains through the involvement of the private sector companies. The combination of contemporary medical resources and teaching facilities was also expected to contribute to the advancement of healthcare provision in the local area. The decision of the Hospital Trust to utilise the PFI option was underpinned by four main objectives, including (Scottish Executive, 2003):

- The achievement of improved standard of care in a cost efficient way,
- The reinvestment of surplus resources in other areas such as primary and community care,
- The promotion of excellence in teaching and healthcare,
- The provision of attractive environment for the clinical staff and the users.

Under the contractual arrangements the private sector consortium was required to build and maintain the facilities for a period of thirty years and to provide a number of ancillary services such as cleaning, laundry, catering, security, and portering. All core medical services were retained by the public sector. The PFI contract also included the sale of some hospital owned sites to the private companies while the new hospital was built on a greenfield site.

Due to the novelty of this project and the lack of experience with PFI contracts, the public sector client and indeed the private sector companies have experienced a range of problems. The following section investigates the main difficulties encountered by the public sector client in this project, and specifically problems and risks associated with the interaction between the public and the private sector partners. It is based on two extensive interviews conducted with the public sector project manager and the general manager of the private sector consortia. It also includes information in the public domain as well some project documentation.

THE PUBLIC SECTOR PERSPECTIVE

In the interview with the authors, the public sector manager noted that the provision of the hospital within the relatively limited time scale of four and a half years had had a decisive positive impact on the health services in the local area. In his opinion the new facilities are of reasonable quality and generally fit for the purpose. Despite the overall positive assessment of the interviewee, it became clear that during the operational phase of the project there have been a number of problems between the private and the public sector partners, some of which are still to be resolved.

One contentious issue in the PFI procurement, which often determines the financial viability of this procurement option, relates to the contractual treatment of project risks. It has major implications for the achievement of the value for money requirement and for the off-balance-sheet treatment of the project[1]. According to the interviewee, in order to assess the value of the risks transferred to the private sector, the public sector client undertook three exercises including identification of the risks within the contract, separation of the risks peculiar to the PFI option and quantification of those risks. Table 1 summarises the main risks transferred to the private sector in this project which include environmental factors, risks associated with ground conditions, life-cycle costs, legislation, financial, insurance and constructions risks. In theory, the contract should ensure optimum risk distribution between the parties, whereby each party knows and accepts its contractual responsibilities. However, due to discrepancies and vague contractual terms, the practical enforcement of the initial risk allocation scheme has created tensions. Thus, according to the contractual risk distribution, the private sector is responsible for the operational risks including hard and soft facilities management services. On the other hand, increases of utility costs, which are associated with gas and electricity consumption, and arguably represent operational costs, remained with the public sector. According to the public sector manager:

> The output specifications say that the public toilets have to be cleaned four times a day. We suggested the introduction of an electronic sign that monitors the number of times the toilets have been cleaned. They say that if we want this modification we have to pay for it, while we say that it should have been provided for it in the first place. Another example. Instead the hand towels the contractor decides to introduce wall hand dryers, but the increased electricity costs come to us. We are now debating if this is the right thing to do and what the implications are. The issue is: has the risk been transferred or not? So, we are now in a debate.

Drawing a line between the operational costs and utility costs is problematic and subsequently this issue became a source of disputes. Similarly, increases in insurance provisions driven by the insurance market remained the client's responsibility and also lead to additional costs. In this context, the public sector manager noted that there was a difficulty in translating some apparently overly general contractual terms into practice:

---

[1] On the public sector side, most of the PFI transactions are designed to occur off balance sheet, which reflects that fact that at the time when a PFI contract is signed the transaction does not involve any payment and therefore it does not appear on the current government accounting statements. When the project's construction phase is completed and the facility becomes operational, the public sector provides regular payments to the private sector companies, and these payments are reflected in the future government balance sheets.

> Risk transfer is a very difficult issue. More so in theory than in practice. Within the contract there are a number of provisions such as demand re-basing that allow the private sector companies to adjust the benchmarking process for the soft and hard maintenance services on the basis of the actual number of patients, so that they can maintain their cost recovery. So, we transferred that risk but there is still a facility which allows some of the commercial risks to be transferred back to us.

To a large extent the difficulties experienced in this project in relation to risk transfer are the result of a lack of sufficient expertise and understanding among the public sector project team. With some action the interviewee noted that:

> Sometimes the risk transfer issues do not become apparent until you get into a dispute. So you think you have transferred risk, then you enter a debate and you discover that you have not transferred this risk.

In May 2005, on the grounds of the increased number of patients and the benchmarking exercise, the private sector contractors demanded an annual increase of service charges of £1.1m, which is in addition to the initially agreed payment of £7.5m. If the contract allows fee adjustments on the basis of benchmarking exercises, this undermines the whole idea of operational risk transfer and allows both parties to pursue their own interpretations, which of course questions the authenticity of the entire process of risk transfer. The public sector client maintains that additional payments will arise only if the private companies are presented with new demands such as requirements for new premises. The dispute was taken to the Court of Session, but at the moment of writing, it has been put on hold in an attempt to achieve mutually acceptable solution through negotiations. Meanwhile both parties have reiterated their commitment to working together and the client representative even characterised the problem as a "technical issue". While this dispute is not necessarily indicative of the standard communication practices in this project it still illustrates that the loose language of the contract makes different interpretations tenable.

Table 1. The main risks transferred to the private sector under the PFI procurement

Risk Category	Description
Environmental factors	Different social pressures associated with environmental pollution, emission charges, transport policy implications, etc.
Ground conditions	Includes all additional expenses which may be related to the ground works.
All facilities management costs	Includes all operational costs as well as latent defects in the building.
Legislative changes	In terms of non-discriminatory changes which affect all market participants.
Financial risks	These include inflation and interest rates fluctuations.
Insurance risks	The private sector is responsible for all insurable events.
Construction risks	Including time and costs overruns, as well as insolvency of contractor.

Additional problems were encountered by the public sector on account of the open specifications and the imprecise wording of some contractual clauses which failed to specify the precise characteristics of the services required. Due to the considerable cost implications associated with such vagueness, such cases have also resulted in prolonged disputes. For example, according to the public sector respondent, some of the criteria for the payment deductions, which are, in theory, the main tool for correcting unsatisfactory services are ineffective when it comes to the measurement of the actual performance:

In order to introduce payment deductions, the providers have to fail against a number of criteria or key performance indicators (KPI). These criteria were introduced when the contract was signed and in many cases are useless. For example, if the contract says that they need to turn the boiler on in the morning by pressing the switch, they tick the box. The contract does not ask whether the boiler is working or not. We are now in a process of discussing a revision to the KPIs in order to be able to measure against them.

Moreover, the interviewee emphasised the lack of flexibility in the contractual arrangements, which explicitly prohibited the public sector from making any changes during the construction period. Considering that the project was initiated in 1992 and the contract was signed six years later, some preliminary solutions required alterations. Particular difficulties have been caused by the complicated solution used in relation to the maintenance of the hospital equipment. Thus, under the project agreement each piece of equipment is assigned into one of five categories A, B, C, D, E and F, whereby both parties have different responsibilities for the maintenance of each category. This arrangement which is clearly inconvenient was intended in the first place to resolve affordability issues for the client, but in effect it has created numerous cases of confusion over the division of responsibilities and operational delays. In addition to these contractual issues, there have been other operational problems related to the quality of the services provided by the private sector subcontractors. For example, there has been criticism about the standard of catering provisions, ventilation problems during the summer, power cuts, etc. Some of the hospital design solutions have also been considered inconvenient for the patients, for instance, the long walking distance from the point of arrival to the hospital and to the treatment rooms are problematic.

According to the initial plan, the new hospital was intended as a key component of an integrated quick treatment scheme for healthcare provision, where the treatment of the patients starts from the emergency room or from the doctor's referral and should be delivered in the most effective way:

> The whole philosophy of moving from the old site to here wasn't just to get a new hospital. The idea was also to modernise the way services are delivered. So we are supposed to have moved forward in terms of how we deliver services. The hospital here is supposed to be part of a bigger plan in terms of service delivery....The whole plan was that services can now be delivered efficiently, this will result in short stay in the acute location and then patients can move on either back home or to somewhere else to rehabilitate. Great plan.

The interviewee noted that in some cases, particularly for elderly patients, the expediency of the hospital services and the expected efficiency gains are obscured by the lack of post-hospital healthcare which should be provided by other parties in the community. In theory, the expedient treatment should result in shorter bed occupancy and faster movement of patients. Thus, patients who no longer need specialised hospital care should be able to return to the community for community care, or according to their needs should be allocated to rehabilitation centres or care homes. However, when the hospital became fully operational in

2003 it transpired that the post-hospital healthcare including rehabilitation and/or other support services were largely unavailable. For this reason, despite the innovative ideas and some state-of-the-art equipment, the hospital by itself has been unable to fulfil entirely its planned potential.

According to this interviewee, in addition to the technical and operational issues during the first years of operation of the hospital, the public sector management team has also encountered problems relating to different values, standards and priorities of the parties. In his opinion, so far the private sector companies have not entirely appreciated their real role in the healthcare provision:

> The biggest thing for the contractor is to understand that what drives the hospital is the provision of healthcare to patients. It is not about providing rooms and offices for people, it is not a hotel. It will take some time to understand that.

Thus in one occasion power failure resulted in a long battle over actual causes and responsibilities, while the key priority for the public sector is to have confidence that the problems are timely resolved and will not be repeated. As concerns the actual process of dispute resolution between the partners, the fact that the construction company and the operational company are subsidiaries of the same parent company was considered by the public sector manager a problem which makes it more difficult to draw a line between individual responsibilities. Apparently, similar problems can be anticipated in the process of inspection and approval of local authority care homes due to the possibility for conflict of interest.

The Private Sector Perspective

In order to gauge the views of the private sector companies we conducted an interview with the General Manager of the project company. From the beginning of the operational phase the General Manager and a small team of employees have been based on the hospital site. The respondent emphasised his understanding that the key intermediate role of the on-site team is to act as a focal point of all activities.

The main focus is to look after the facilities and to act as a pivot or a broker between the public sector and private sector partners, which will allow the project company to fulfil its obligations while looking after the shareholders interests.

The project members are not directly involved in the actual service provision and in order to provide the services required they rely on two main subcontractors including a company responsible for the car parking facilities and a building management company which is in charge of the facilities management side. In this project the facilities management company is a subsidiary of the main construction company which according to this interviewee facilitated close working relations and therefore was advantageous to the project. As noted earlier, this view was not shared by the public sector respondent as it was seen more as an obstacle.

As concerns the overall communication with the public sector the General Manager described it as "very good, regular and at a variety of different levels" while at the same time it has been a steep learning curve in terms of learning how to interact. Meanwhile, the communication has not always been smooth and in fact there have been many differences of opinion, but importantly both parties have been trying to understand each other and to maintain the communication process. The interviewee emphasised the scale and the complexity of the operational side, which requires regular communication on issues such as health and safety, security, clinical governance as well as the supporting services. As a part of the communication process he participates in different committees and meetings at grassroots level as well as at strategic level and is able to require from the subcontractors some adjustments of the services delivered to the client within the framework of the project agreement.

According to the General Manager cleaning and catering are most problematic of all services due to a couple of reasons. Firstly, they require constant interaction with the users and the members of the public, and secondly there are some difficulties associated with their precise definition and measurement. At present, the food is produced non-locally, frozen and transported to the hospital where it is regenerated and served to the users. The management was looking for better ways of resolving the catering, for example by using local produce and local preparation. Also, at the time when the contract was signed there were other details that were not envisaged such as different catering requirements for differing wards. For example, the hospital might be serving the same food but the way in which it is delivered could vary. With cleaning there are also different requirements for different wards. According to the interviewee, there have been remarkable differences to the previously existing hospital and nursing provisions. On the other hand, as a part of the contract the General Manager is responsible for auditing and monitoring the quality of the services provided by the subcontractors. In cases when these services are not corresponding to the service specifications deficiency points are allocated which result in penalty deductions. Therefore, the project team has a dual role and acts as a service provider for the hospital but also as a client for the subcontractors.

Similarly to the view expressed by the public sector manager, the private sector representative noted that the main problems encountered so far relate to the interpretation of some contractual clauses. Due to the fact that the project was signed in 1998 virtually all individuals that are currently involved with the project are new and did not have any involvement in the contract negotiations. This leads to a lot of uncertainty in relation to some practical issues related to the quality of the services. One of the most problematic areas relates to the interpretation of the four hundred and twenty key performance indicators (KPI) which are monitored on a monthly basis. According to the interviewee:

> There can sometimes be a misinterpretation of what the KPI means and people form different opinions. We try to resolve the problem and non-escalate the differences amongst everyone. The KPI monitoring system for the quality of the services was meant to be more transparent to the public. However, the interpretation of the contract sometimes differs between the groups (NHS and private sector) and the NHS often has difficulty monitoring the service.

The respondent noted that the issue of quality of services is linked to the issue of risk transfer. In the first instance he uses common sense approach and seeks resolution with the service providers, which is feasible if the problem does not entail serious financial implications. In some cases tension has arisen where the private sector believes there are requirements in excess of the original contract which amount to changes of quality of the service, while the public sector view is that the requirements are built into the contract. So far, both parties have made efforts to resolve the problems first of all through negotiations and a large number of such issues have been resolved this way. However, there are still outstanding problems, where the private sector companies have tried to seek legal definitions:

> Where necessary we have had to discuss with our legal advisors 'what did you actually mean when you drew this up, we know what it says but what does it actually mean, where do we stand as a result of changes that have happened in the interim period?'.

As concerns the main risks that have been allocated to the private sector, the respondent noted that designing and building the facilities within the tight time scale and without exceeding the budget was associated with various risks, which have been successfully managed. According to the contract during the operational phase any problems and risks related to the availability of the facilities as well as cost increases are allocated to the private sector. However, as noted earlier the contract allows the private sector some recourse in terms of bench marking, market testing and indexation which reduce the financial consequences for the private sector. According to the private sector manager these mechanisms allow certain adjustments which correspond to the market conditions at a certain period of time. Meanwhile, the fact that the principle for full operational risk transfer is not entirely enforceable can potentially affect the risk profile of the project and jeopardise the operational risk transfer. The interviewee noted that so far there have been cases when the project company has accepted penalties as a result of non-compliant performance and/or service failures and a proportion of these penalties have been further passed on to the actual service provider. For example in order to ensure to compliance with the environmental regulations the private sector had to install additional ventilation equipment. Other occasions when the costs were born by the private sector include power failures as well as the amendment of some construction solutions in line with the operational requirements. According to the interviewee, there have been also changes in the usage of some areas/facilities, or even new specifications have been produced; however, in such circumstances the public sector bears the costs. According to the respondent the smoking areas have not been given proper consideration in the contract, the hospital was intended as non-smoking grounds which has not worked in reality. The allocation of smoking areas and primarily their maintenance has resulted in additional costs which had to be allocated between the partners.

As concerns the availability of PFI expertise among the NHS staff, the interviewee noted that while there was sufficient expertise in relation to design and construction, as concerns the operational issues, he would like to see some improvement. In his opinion, due to the fact that this was one of the first PFI contracts in the NHS, the level of risk transferred to the private sector was lower compared to more recent contracts. The respondent also noted that future projects could benefit from more transparent risk transfer analysis especially on technical/operational issues. Moreover, it is important that the parties have very clear understanding of their contractual responsibilities, i.e. who is responsible for what should be apparent from the documentation, which will prevent different contractual interpretations. In hindsight, the interviewee believes that the open specifications allowing different interpretation should be avoided. Another obstacle to the communication process with the public sector was attributed to the frequent personnel changes amongst the public sector management, while the private sector representatives have not changed a great deal.

When considering the balance between risks and responsibilities the interviewee noted other positive aspects of the private sector involvement, particularly the access to best industry practice and added value to NHS services. In that respect, the facility management provider has a key role due to the possibility to utilise technology built into the facility. In his opinion there are already some services which provide better value compared to the NHS standard. For example in security services the private sector has been using dedicated security systems, while the previous standard was mainly based on porter staff.

Overall the General Managers believe that the facilities and the services that were initially envisaged in the project agreement have been delivered and so far the project has worked. Meanwhile, it is important to maintain the sense of partnership and to remain responsive to a host of operational, political, financial and other changes which have not been considered in the initial project agreement but have occured on a day-to-day bases.

This case study illustrates that while a risk allocation and management framework was consciously built into this PFI project contract, the vague contractual terms failed to guarantee its practical implementation. During the operational phase there were some disputes, one of which led to a court case. Despite the existence of many risk issues, only some were considered explicitly in the original PFI contract as part of a structured approach to risk assessment, and a number of anticipated operational risks remained unresolved. All these areas of tension and risk have substantial implications for the final service users or patients and potentially important implications for healthcare quality. Obstacles to the resolution of these problems were exacerbated by the different values, standards and priorities possessed by the private sector partners.

CONCLUSION

Past analyses of PFI procurement have frequently attributed problems with this procurement approach to differences in the culture of public sector and private sector decision makers. According to these narratives, private sector PFI participants value speedy and professional decision making and, as a consequence, have difficulties in coping with the allegedly slow and consultative approaches of public sector clients. These problems are said to be aggravated by the risk-averse attitude of public sector clients, their frequent lack of experience in public-private procurement and their lack of precise criteria for the evaluation of bidding documents and design alternatives (Ahadzi and Bowles, 2004). Public sector PFI participants, by contrast, have been reported as criticizing the private sector's lack of sensitivity to the involvement of users and stakeholders (Ruane, 1997; Asenova et al., 2002). This perception of a culture clash has been reinforced by a series of early government reports (Bates, 1907, 1999; Gershon, 1999) which highlighted the need for private sector clients to acquire commercial skills.

While there is some support for the notion that different attitudes towards risk and risk management among public and private sector protagonists may indeed hamper closer collaboration, there is increasing evidence that some of the problems regarding PFI risk management in particular stem from some sub-optimal approaches which characterize contemporary PFI procurement. Thus the previously discussed case study indicates that problems arose not so much due to differences in attitudes toward risk, but rather due to the way the PFI procurement process approaches the management of these risks. This is apparent on several levels. Firstly, the PFI process forces public and private sector partners to come to an early arrangement with regard to which party bears which risks. While the contractual division of responsibilities for different risks may have some advantages in accounting terms, it also has serious drawbacks. By assigning the responsibility for different risk to different parties early on in the procurement process, a level of inflexibility is introduced which has the potential of forestalling potentially fruitful avenues for future collaboration. This inflexibility can have a number of consequences. For instance, where, as in the case of the Royal Armory in Leeds, the private sector has taken on a risk it cannot adequately cover, the cost of remedying this mistake usually falls to the public sector; if only because it is in the interest of the public sector to ensure that the service is provided. Alternatively, there is, as in the previously discussed hospital case study, the possibility that the private sector will seek to re-negotiate the level of payments in order to cover unforeseen costs. In either case, the public sector is likely to become the ultimate bearer of risk, irrespective of prior contractual arrangements.

Secondly, and related to this issue of inflexibility in risk assignment is the issue of front-loaded contractual specifications. As part of an overall incentive and performance monitoring system, PFI contracts have to specify relatively detailed criteria or performance indicators for specific services. However, the upfront specification of these services and standards can be highly problematic; as has been exemplified in the previously discussed hospital case study. As a consequence, PFI projects during the operational phase are often plagued by disputes over performance criteria. These disputes are often difficult to settle, since disagreements over performance criteria directly affect the profitability of the PFI project to the private sectors, and the level of service quality delivery to the public sector. Needless to say, this situation is aggravated where there are genuine changes in the type of service demanded or where different approaches for the delivery of these services become feasible. Like the possibility of payment re-negotiation in the operational phase, these disputes heighten the risk exposure of the public sector; both because of the costs associated with these disputes and their potential adverse effects on the quality of service delivery.

Although some of these problems could, at least theoretically, be reduced through the introduction of flexibility and arbitration clauses to PFI contracts, it is obvious that the degree to which PFI procurement can be reformed is ultimately limited. For instance, if PFI contracts were to allow for a re-examination of risk transfer arrangements after a certain time period, this would increase the already costly negotiations. Similarly, if service disputes were to be minimised, this could be achieved through the creation of co-management forums which continuously and jointly monitor service levels. However, not only would the creation of such forums be costly, but they would also make the revenue streams a PFI project creates for its public sector partners less predictable (as some of these revenues would depend on the outcome of *ad hoc* negotiations).

In summary, therefore, it can be argued that PFI procurement in its current form entails several elements of suboptimality, which significantly exacerbate the risk exposure of the public sector in these projects.

References

Adams, J. 1995. *Risk* (3rd edition). London, University College London Press.

Ahadzi, M., Bowles, G. 2004. Public-private Partnership and Contract Negotiations: An Empricial Study. *Construction Mangement and Eocnomics*, 22(9): 967-978.

Allen, G. 2001. The Private Finance Initiative (PFI). *Research Paper 01/117, Economics Policy and Statistics Section*, House of Commons Library, London.

Anon. 2001. Comment: A Dogma that Fails the People: Labour's Very Public Private Disgrace. *The Observer*, July 8.

Anon. 2002. Business and Media: Special Report: Public Private Partnerships: 1992 to 2002: A Decade of Reform and Wreckage. *The Observer*, April.

Asenova, D. and Beck, M. 2003. Scottish Local Authorities and the Procurement of Private Finance Initiative Projects. *Public Works, Management and Policy*, 8(1): 11-27.

Asenova, D., Beck, M., Akintoye, A., Hardcastle, C., Chinyio, E. 2003. Partnership, Value for Money and Best Value in PFI Projects: Obstacles and Opportunities. *Public Policy and Administration*, 17(4): 5-20.

Asenova, D., Beck, M., Akintoye, A., Hardcastle, C., Chinyio, E. 2004. Obstacles to Best Value in NHS PFI Projects: Evidence from two Hospital Projects. *Journal of Finance and Management in the Public Sector*, 4(1): 33-50.

Bates. M. 1997. *First Review of the Private Finance Initiative by Sir Malcolm Bates.* London, HMSO.

Bates. M. 1999. *Second Review of the Private Finance Initiative by Sir Malcolm Bates.* London, HMSO.

Beetsma, R., Schotman, P. 2001. Data from the Television Game Show Lingo, *Economics Journal*, 111(474): 821-848.

Bellante, D., Link, A.N. 1981. Are Public Sector Workers more Risk Averse than Private Sector Workers? *Industrial and Labor Relations Review*, 34(3): 408-412.

Blank, R.M. 1985. An Analysis of Worker' Choice between Employment and Unemployment. *Industrial and Labor Relations Review*, 38(2): 211-224.

Boothroyd, C., Emmett, J. 1996. *Risk Management – A Practical Guide for Construction Professionals.* London, Witherby.

Brotzen, D. 2002. Wise Words and Firm Resolve when Times get Tough, in Pickford J. (ed) *Financial Times: Mastering Risk, Volume1: Concepts.* London, Prentice Hall.

Cassidy T., Lynn R. 1989. A Multifactorial Approach to Achievement Motivation: The Development of a Comprehensive Measure *Journal of Occupational Psychology*, 62: 301-312.

Cates, C. 1979. Beyond Muddling: Creativity. *Public Administration Review*, 39(6): 527-532.

Conrow, E.H., Shishido, P.S. 1997. Implementing Risk Management on Software Intensive Projects. *IEEE Software*, 14(3): 83-89.

Deep, A. 2002. A Firm Foundation for Project Finance, in Pickford J. (ed) *Financial Times: Mastering Risk, Volume1: Concepts.* London, Prentice Hall.

Dickson, G.C.A. (1991) *Risk Management.* Cambridge, The Chartered Insurance Institute.

Donkers, B., Melenberg, B., van Soest, A. 2001. Estimating Risk Attitudes Using Lotteries. *Journal of Risk and Uncertainty*, 22(2): 165-195.

Douglas, M. 1992. *Risk and Blame: Essays in Cultural Theory.* London, Routledge.

Douglas, M., Wildavsky, A. 1983. *Risk and Culture, An Essay on the Selection of Technological and Environmental Dangers*, London, University of California Press.

Dror, Y. 1964. Muddling Through-'Science' or Inertia. *Public Administration Review*, 64: 154.

Finnerty, J.D. 1996. *Project Financing, Asset-Based Financial Engineering*. Boston, John Wiley.

Fischoff, B., Watson, S., Hope, C. 1991. Defining Risk, in Glickman, T., Gough M. (eds) *Reading in Risk* (2nd edition). Washington, Resources for the Future.

Froud J. 2003. The Private Finance Initiative: Risk, Uncertainty and the State. *Accounting Organisations and Society*, 28: 567 – 589.

Gershon, P. (1999). *Review of Civil Procurement in Central Government*. London, Office of Government Commerce.

Hencke, D. 2008. Private Contractors Take Taxpayers for a Multimillion-Pound Ride. *The Guardian*, 17 January, Available at: http://www.guardian.co.uk/guardianpolitics/story/0,,2241990,00.html, Accessed on 18 January 2008.

HM Treasury. 1995. *Private Opportunity, Public Benefit: Progress the Private Finance Initiative*. London, HM Treasury.

HM Treasury. 1997a. *Partnership for Prosperity: The Private Finance Initiative*. London, The Stationary Office.

HM Treasury. 1999. *Modern Government Modern Procurement. London*, HM Treasury.

HM Treasury "Orange Book". 2000. *Management of Risks – A Strategic Overview*. London, HM Treasury.

HM Treasury. 1997b. *Technical Note No 1 (Revised) How to Account for PFI Transactions*. London, The Stationary Office.

HM Treasury. 2003. *House of Commons, Committee of Public Accounts, PFI Refinancing Update, Twenty-second Report of Session 2002-3*. London, HM Treasury.

HM Treasury. 2007. *House of Commons, Committee of Public Accounts, Update on PFI Debt Refinancing, Twenty-fifth Report of Session 2006-7*. London, HM Treasury.

Hodge, G. 2004. The Risky Business of Public-Private Partnerships, *Australian Journal of Public Administration*, 63(4): 7-49.

Holton, G. 1998. The New Climate of Risk. *Treasury Management International*, 69: 24-28.

Hood, C., Jones, D. 1996, Accident and Design, Contemporary Debate in Risk Management. London, University College London Press.

Hood, J., McGarvey, N. 2002. Managing Risk of Public-Private Partnerships in Scottish Local Government. *Policy Studies*, 23(1): 21-35.

Jason, B. 2001. Benefits Card a 1bn Pound Failure. *The Scotsman*, December 7: 9.

Juerges, H. 2002. The Distribution of the German Public-Private Sector Wage-Gap. *Labour*, 16(2): 347-381.

Kerzner, H. 1995. *Project Management – A Systems Approach to Planning, Scheduling and Controlling* (5th edition). Boston, Van Nostrand.

Kliem, R.L., Ludin, I. S. 1997. *Reducing Project Risk.*, Aldershot, Gower.

Lonsdale, C. 2005. Risk Transfer and the UK Private Finance Initiative. *Policy and Politics*, 33(2): 231-249.

Lupton, D. 1999. *Risk*. London, Routledge.

McKim, R.A. 1992. Systematic Risk Management Approach for Construction Projects: Discussion. *Journal of Construction Engineering and Management*, 117(1): 414-415.

NAO. 1998. *The Contract to Develop and Upgrade the Replacement National Insurance Recording System.* Ordered by the House of Commons, Prepared by the Controller and the Auditor General, National Audit Office. London, Stationary Office.

NAO. 1999. *Examining the Value for Money of Deals Under the Private Finance Initiative.* Ordered by the House of Commons, Prepared by the Controller and the Auditor General. London, Stationary Office.

NAO. 2000. *The Cancellation of the Benefits Payment Card Project.* Ordered by the House of Commons, Prepared by the Controller and the Auditor General. London, Stationary Office.

NAO. 2001. *The RE-Negotiation of the PFI-type Deal for the Royal Armouries Museum in Leeds.* Ordered by the House of Commons, Prepared by the Controller and the Auditor General. London, Stationary Office.

NAO. 2006. *Update on PFI Debt Refinancing and the PFI Equity Market.* Ordered by the House of Commons, Prepared by the Controller and the Auditor General. London, Stationary Office

NAO. 2008. *Making Changes in Operational PFI Projects.* London, The Stationary Office.

Pfeifer, C. 2008. Risk Aversion and Sorting into Public Sector Employment. *Discussion Paper No. 3503, Forschungsinstitut zur Zukunft der Arbeit*, Bonn.

Pidgeon, N.F., Hood, C., Jones, D., Turner, B.A., Gibson, R. 1992. Risk Perception, in Pidgeon, N.F., Hood, C., Jones, D., Turner, B.A., Gibson, R. (eds) *Analysis, Perception and Management.* London, The Royal Society.

Pollock, A., Price, D., Player, S. 2005. *The Private Finance Initiative: A Policy on Sand, An Examination of the Treasury's Evidence Base for Cost and Time Overrun Data in Value for Money Policy and Appraisal. London*, UNISON.

Prentis, D. 2001. We Won't Put up with Privatisation: Public Sector Unions Want to Modernise, Not Compromise Quality. *The Guardian*, July 19.

Private Finance Panel. 1995. *Private Opportunity, Public Benefit: Progressing the Private Finance Initiative*. HMSO, London.

Private Finance Panel. 1996. *Risk and Reward in PFI Contracts: Practical Guidance on the Sharing of Risk and Structuring of PFI contracts*. London, London.

Raftery, J. 1994. *Risk Analysis in Project Management*. London, E and FN Spon.

Reddy, S.G. 1996. Claims to Expert Knowledge and the Subversion of Democracy: the Triumph of Risk over Uncertainty. *Economy and Society*, 25(2): 222 – 254.

Richardson, J.J., Jordan, A.G. 1979. *Governing Under Pressure*. London, Martin Robertson.

Ruane, S. 1997. Public-private Boundaries and the Transformation of the NHS. *Critical Social Policy*, 17(51): 53-78.

Sapte, W. 1997, *Project Finance, The Guide to Financing BOT Projects*, Euromoney Publications PLC, Hong Kong.

Scottish Executive. 2003. *PFI Data Sheets:* Internet Article. Available at www.scotland.gov.uk/pfi, Accessed on 30 October 2004.

Skinner, N. 2008. The Spread of Political Risk, Available at: www.strategicrisk.co.uk/story.asp?source=srbreakingnewsandstorycode=368839, Accessed on 19 January 2008.

Strategic Risk. 2008. Brown Calls for Better Management of Public Risk, Internet publication, Available at: www.strategicrisk.co.uk/story.asp?source=srweekthursandstorycode=368808, Accessed on 16 January 2008.

Uher, T.E., Toakley, A.R. 1999. Risk Management in the Conceptual Phase of a Project. *International Journal of Project Management*, 17(3): 161-169.

UNISON. 1999. *'The Only Game in Town', A Report on the Cumberland Infirmary Carlise PFI by UNISON Northern Region,* London, UNISON.

Whitfield, D. 2001. *Public Services or Corporate Welfare.* London, Pluto Press.

Wright, O. 2000. NHS Plans May Lead to 2,000-Bed Shortfall. *The Times*, August 14.

Zonis, M., Wilkin, S. 2002 Driving Defensively Trough Minefield of Political Risk, in Pickford J. (ed) *Financial Times: Mastering Risk, Volume1: Concepts.* London, Prentice Hall.

In: Understanding Risk
Editor: Matthias Beck

ISBN: 978-1-62618-686-6

Chapter 11

DOES THE UK LOCAL FINANCE IMPROVEMENT TRUST (LIFT) INITIATIVE IMPROVE RISK MANAGEMENT IN PUBLIC-PRIVATE PROCUREMENT?

Deborah Fitzsimmons*[*]*, Sally Brown and Matthias Beck
The York Management School, University of York, York, UK

ABSTRACT

The UK government introduced the Private Finance Initiative (PFI) and, latterly, the Local Improvement Finance Trust (LIFT) in an attempt to improve public service provision. As a variant of PFI, LIFT seeks to create a framework for the effective provision of primary care facilities. Like conventional PFI procurement, LIFT projects involve long-term contracts, complex multi-party interactions and thus create various risks to public sector clients. This paper investigates the advantages and disadvantages of LIFT with a focus on how this approach facilitates or impedes risk management from the public sector client perspective. Our paper concludes that LIFT has a potential for creating additional problems, including the further reduction of public sector control, conflicts of interest, the inappropriate use of enabling funds, and higher than market rental costs affecting the uptake of space in the buildings by local health care providers. However, there is also evidence that LIFT has facilitated new investment and that Primary Care Trusts (PCTs) have themselves started addressing some of the weaknesses of this procurement format through the bundling of projects and other forms of regional co-operation.

INTRODUCTION

In the early 1990's, the UK government sought to address inefficiencies it believed existed in the National Health Service (NHS). This involved the introduction of hospital trusts and the quasi-market for hospital-based health care to increase the cost-effectiveness of

[*] E-mail: df537@york.ac.uk.

tertiary health care delivery and the introduction of GP Fund-Holders (GPFHs), making them the gatekeepers of funding for their patients and ensuring that funding followed service provision. Additionally there was a belief infrastructure procurement within the NHS procurement would benefit from attracting private sector funding and expertise previously unavailable to the sector. Since the government struggled to find adequate funding for basic maintenance, "let alone large scale investment without infringing Treasury limits on the PSBR and financial markets' expectations regarding the long term sustainability of government expenditures" (Clark and Root, 1999), PFI was seen as a way of providing desperately needed upgrades (Clark and Root, 1999; Spackman, 2002). Following the introduction of the Public Finance Initiative (PFI) in 1992, by November 1994 it had become mandatory that all capital projects in the public sector requiring Treasury approval should explore the use of private finance options (Private Finance Panel, 1995) unless it was absurd or unrealistic to do so (Private Finance Panel, 1996; Akintoye et al., 2003). Whilst strongly criticised by the opposition at the time, PFI in various guises eventually became the lynchpin for capital estates reform for the subsequent labour governments and facilitated an increased commitment to the "buy now, pay later" approach which characterises much of the development and management of NHS estates (Clark and Root, 1999).

Among PFI supporters there was an expectation that new approach would attract private sector funds, resources, management skills, expertise and innovation to the provision of public sector infrastructure (Mustafa, 1999). It was also hoped that PFI would prevent many of the issues prevalent in public sector managed capital projects, including over-spend, delays, poor design, high operational and maintenance costs and low residual values (Forshaw, 1999) while introducing more commercial discipline and encouraging value for money (Birnie, 1999).

Whilst the government hoped that PFI would see private sector investment in the public sector increase significantly, in reality this failed to be the case (Clark and Root, 1999). Up until the mid 1990s, PFI failed to produce the levels of investment expected when it was announced, with targets for PFI investment being on average 50 per cent less than planned (Daily Telegraph, 1995). This was in part due to a feeling among public sector clients that they would be overwhelmed by this process, as well as due to reluctance by major private sector players to engage in the process (Asenova and Beck, 2003).

From a risk-management perspective, the implementation of the PFI process brought to light a number of issues which affected the uptake and effectiveness of PFI in the provision of public-sector services. Each of these is reviewed below.

Poor Risk Management (PFI)

Whilst PFI was "not originally devised as policy for managing risk", as Froud (2003) identifies, "risk has emerged as the key feature that legitimates the shift in public services management". Initial guidance on PFI procurement suggested that that not all risks associated with a PFI project should automatically be transferred to the private sector. Rather, appropriate risks should be transferred to the private sector (Lonsdale, 2005) if they were better placed to handle them (Treasury Taskforce, 1997) to ensure "optimal allocation which is assumed to maximise value for money" (Froud, 2003). Since proposed PFI projects often failed to meet Value for Money criteria as embodied in the Public Sector Comparator, the quantification of risks transferred to the private sector often tipped the balance in favour of public-private finance over traditional delivery methods (Pollock, 2002). This, in turn, has led to widespread criticism of the PFI process on the grounds of inappropriate risk transfer (Clark and Root, 1999). Froud (2003), for instance, argued that, because of its size, the State is better placed to manage risk, while Gaffney (1999) suggested that risk transfer was unlikely to occur in reality as private contractors would seek to protect their income from uncertainty whenever possible.

Whilst it was apparent early on that it was not always possible to specify the precise nature and distribution of risk (Clark and Root, 1999), it would seem that the public sector had particular difficulty understanding risk assessment and management. This was particularly true with regard to risks associated specifically with PFIs, with the public sector even struggling to find consultants who could help them with this process (Private Finance Panel, 1995; Akintoye et al., 2003). In a Treasury commissioned report it was found that "in over two thirds of the business cases for hospital PFI schemes the risk could not be identified. In other cases risk transfer was largely attributed to construction cost risks, which would be dealt with by penalty clauses under traditional procurement contracts" (Pollock et al., 2002).

In 1997, the Treasury Task Force identified seven groups of risk: "design and construction; commissioning and operating; demand (or volume/usage); residual value; technology and obsolescence; regulation (including taxation and planning permission); and project financing". The Audit Commission (1998) later provided examples of generic risk categories associated with a serviced building, including such factors as "delays in planning permission, changes in interest and tax rates, higher than expected maintenance and costs of meeting new statutory requirements" and the risk that "essential public services cease to be available". Given the breadth of these potential risks, it is easy to understand the scale of the learning curve faced by the public sector which had limited, if any, experience in these areas.

Lonsdale (2005) notes that uncertainty is "likely to be a considerable problem in complex contractual situations, especially when supply involves an innovation or constitutes a new venture". This would certainly seem to describe the context of PFI which, for most public sector, was a novel approach for funding and procuring public services (Froud, 2003). Whilst public sector organisation struggled to understand the risks associated with PFI, they were further hampered by a lack of central guidance (Pollock et al., 2002). This resulted in public sector organisations trying to develop their own evaluation criteria. This has been both time consuming and costly, incurring high levels of professional fees (Akintoye et al., 2003). Retrospective reviews of specific projects therefore often noted that some risks had been transferred to the private sector that the public sector was better placed to take. Some of this could have been avoided through an improved knowledge of PFI risks within client teams and a more standardised approach to project and risk management (Akintoye et al., 2003; Asenova et al., 2002).

Lack of Required Skills in the Public Sector (PFI)

Over time it has become evident that local authorities and other public sector bodies continue to struggle to become equal partners in PFI projects (Clark and Root, 1999). This appears to stem from a number of factors. Firstly, the PFI process inherently suffers from asymmetry of information (Asenova et al., 2002). The private sector partners already have all the technical skills required to complete the design, negotiations, construction and management of a new building as they are required to do this on a frequent basis. For the public sector partners, involvement in PFI is often a unique experience that challenges their commercial capabilities. In theory, public sector clients must lead the entire process if they do not wish to be at the mercy of the contractors; but in reality many clients feel as though they are "walking in the dark" (Akintoye et al., 2003). Asenova et al. quote one NHS Manager as saying that "building a hospital is a once in a lifetime experience" (Asenova et al., 2002). Similarly, HM Treasury publications note that skill shortages occurred in the healthcare sector, particularly in areas such as contract negotiation and project risk management (HM Treasury, 1999).

PFI contracts are legal arrangements that contain clauses designed to apportion risk equally between the two parties, the idea being that risks are managed by creating a balanced relationship through mutual dependence. It has been suggested that this dependence creates "incentives to make the relationship efficient and disincentives to behave opportunistically" (Lonsdale, 2005). The government advised public sector bodies entering into PFI contractual arrangements that this should be done on the basis of genuine partnerships aimed at optimising the sharing of risks. According to the Treasury (2003) "where this sharing of risks is done appropriately and effectively, it is the key to ensuring that the value for money benefits in PFI projects are realised". In reality, it has become evident that the public sector does not always have the capabilities or resources required, to ensure that this balance is achieved (Lonsdale, 2005). Considering that the budget of some PFI projects has exceeded £100 million (Spackman, 2002), it is somewhat disturbing that these skill shortages continue to be apparent many years after PFI has been introduced.

Lengthy Negotiations and Complex Contracts (PFI)

One specific criticism of PFI concerns the length and complexity of negotiations. Where projects have involved multiple partners and funding streams, PFI negotiations were renowned for being exceedingly long (Asenova et al., 2002; Akintoye et al., 2003), slow (Asenova et al., 2002) and complex (Akintoye et al., 2003). This has been attributed to a lack of experience on the part of public sector staff who appear to have required lengthy discussions with consultants in order to gain the required degree of understanding of the PFI process (Asenova et al., 2002; Akintoye et al., 2003) and/or lengthy time periods for arriving at decisions among multiple stakeholders (Asenova et al., 2002). Notwithstanding these problems, some research suggests that consultants may have exacerbated this by providing excessive levels of technical detail (Asenova et al., 2002; Akintoye et al., 2003), while some private sector partners were less forthcoming with detail, preferring a 'black box' approach (Akintoye et al., 2003).

Once the bidding process has identified a preferred bidder, as stated above, the negotiations may proceed for many months. Whilst there may have been a number of competitive companies seeking the PFI contract at the bidding stage, later this may not be the case, and the public sector bodies may not have the option of going back to original bidders. Consequently, a breakdown in negotiations would mean not just a repetition of the final bidding stage, but possibly another complete tendering exercise which could delay the project by months (NAO, 1999).

Lonsdale (2005) suggests that the difference between PFI contracts and more traditional government contracting is the general tendency for PFI contracts to contain greater levels of asset specificity and uncertainty compared with traditional contracting. Lonsdale believes this to be attributable to the bundling of services (discussed in more detail in the next section) and the duration of the PFI contract which increases the asset specificity and degree of uncertainty respectively. Once a buyer has made significant transaction-specific investments they are in a weakened position unless they are able to write off those investments. Even though a buyer may have the legal right to walk away from a contract, the sunk costs of the investments and the cost of switching to an alternative provider may prove to be an insurmountable barrier. Consequently, the buyer may find themselves 'locked in' to the contract and struggling to proceed with the supplier in difficult circumstances (Lonsdale, 2005; Froud, 2003). This may also be true where the supplier threatens an increase to the agreed prices (Lonsdale, 2005). Whilst PFI contracts do contain termination clauses, it has been noted that they may be somewhat academic where there are practical barriers to existing the relationship (PAC, 2003; Lonsdale, 2005; Froud, 2003; Pollock et al., 2002). Gaffney, D. et al. (1999) provide an example of this:

> The recent crisis over private finance schemes for the new national insurance and passport agency computer systems (with private sector partners Siemens and Andersen Consulting) illustrate the problems. The Public Accounts Committee notes that the government's refusal to fine the contractors "would result in the risk purportedly transferred to Andersen Consulting under the PFI contract being transferred back to the public sector" (Committee of Public Accounts, 1999). This negates the key justification for the higher costs of the private finance initiative – the transfer of risk and the "efficiency" of the private sector.

Froud (2003) believes that the provision of public services through this type of medium-term contract increases the inflexibility of the public service, as managers are no longer able to make changes and redeploy their staff within and between units, thereby making the State less able to act. Froud claims that this inflexibility, and potentially increased cost, may also be passed on to "other parts of the public sector beyond the contracting organisation". If there is significant change in a product or service originally specified in the contract it will be necessary to change the statement of work provided under the terms of the contract. This argument is closely linked to Lonsdale's (2005) observation that that the supplier may see this as an opportunity to increase their revenue and, if the buyer has become 'locked in', they will be unable to threaten to return to the market (Lonsdale, 2005).

In essence both Froud (2003) and Londsdale's (2005) would suggest that some of the risk management problems associated with PFI are systemic rather than being attributable to temporary skill shortages among public sector clients. This however, does not contradict the observation of other researchers who continue to attribute the slow pace of the negotiations typical of PFI projects to the public sector's bureaucratic attitudes" (Asenova et al., 2002; Akintoye et al., 2003; Stewart and Butler, 1996), prolific regulations (Stewart and Butler, 1996) as well as a (lack of) efficiency and validity of procedures (Clark and Root, 1999).

Structure (PFI)

To "obtain the benefits of (allegedly) superior private sector management skills" (Lonsdale, 2005), many contracts bundle a variety of products and services that will be managed and coordinated by the primary contractor. This 'bundling' typically facilitates off-balance sheet treatment (Froud, 2003) but it also increases the asset specificity and uncertainty as it brings together a number of different client requirements within one contract (Lonsdale, 2005). The PFI process often requires private sector partners to price their facilities management services in a vacuum during the bidding process (Akintoye et al., 2003). It also means that the supplier is involved with many aspects of the client's business and, consequently, it becomes more difficult to remove them even if the buyer has legitimate grounds under the terms of the contract. The purchase of full-service contracts poses further problems, as it requires clients to define the quality of service they expected. Without the required skills and experience to do this effectively, this can give rise to lengthy post-contract disputes (Akintoye et al., 2003).

The financial structure of PFI is very attractive to the government as they obtain the new infrastructure with minimal initial financial cost (Clark and Root, 1999; Spackman, 2002). However, this places a financial burden on the supplier who must then enter into lengthy contracts with the public sector bodies to recoup their investment (and increase their returns). Given the duration of the contract, it is necessary for the terms of the contract to be relatively vague and there is an expectation that the terms will be renegotiated at some point (Lonsdale, 2005). However, as already stated, during these renegotiations, the supplier is likely to have the upper hand knowing that the public sector body is unable to go back to the marketplace. With regard to risk management, this means that the public sector client faces undue burdens during both the procurement and the post-contract-completion phase.

Cost (PFI)

When compared to projects purchased via traditional procurement methods many PFI projects involved higher purchase costs (Akintoye et al., 2003; Akintoye et al., 2003). This applies to the health sector in particular, where, in a 1996 survey of 202 NHS Trust Chief Executives, only 17 per cent believed that PFI would be cost-effective in the long term (UNISON, 1996). The same survey noted that even where a PFI project was shown to provide Value for Money, there was still a question of affordability as the hospital trust had to pay rent for the new facilities for the entire tenure of the contract which gave rise to a long-term affordability gap (UNISON, 2002).

Interestingly, private sector PFI participants have also noted that PFI, as a procurement process, imposes significant costs and risks on them. A series of interviews with private sector partners identified concerns over the high bidding costs they faced when competing for PFI contracts which were largely attributable to the cost of consultancy and legal services (Akintoye et al., 2003; Asenova et al., 2002). Moreover they noted that establishing and maintaining a consortium came at added cost and required time and effort (Akintoye et al., 2003). For the private sector PFI projects, moreover, often come with a high opportunity cost, since bidding for these contracts required greater efforts and resources to improve the chance of success, which could have been utilised for smaller and more numerous projects (Akintoye et al., 2003). When queried about the cost of PFI, private sector partners therefore noted that PFI bids placed a significant financial burden on them, which had to be recouped on consecutive projects (Asenova et al., 2002).

Notwithstanding the concerns of the private sector, there is evidence that the bidding process has placed significant demands on the resources of the NHS Trusts. Thus, the aforementioned 1996 UNISON survey notes that 76 per cent of NHS Trust Chief Executives believed that the costs of preparing PFI bids were excessive (UNISON, 1996). There are also concerns that where a company becomes the preferred bidder, they may be in a situation where the public sector is 'locked in' and they can use this leverage to raise their prices (PAC, 2003).

Further concerns about the cost of traditional PFI projects have arisen in connection with the issue of project refinancing. After a project has been commissioned, banks may be willing to refinance for a longer term at a lower rate. Refinancing increases the expected dividends which will accrue to the shareholders. This has raised concerns about fairness to the taxpayer and in particular the need for refinancing gains to be shared fairly with the public sector client (Asenova et al., 2007; Spackman, 2002).

Building Quality (PFI)

One of the expectations associated with the involvement of private sector partners in PFI projects was an improvement in both the design and quality of buildings in the NHS estate. The Commission for Architecture and the Built Environment, the Government's architectural watchdog, however, has raised concerns about the quality of design in PFI schemes (UNISON, 2002). Sunand Prasad, Commissioner at the Commission for Architecture and the Built Environment) claimed that "There is a legacy of sub-standard buildings in primary care and we are still, tragically, constructing buildings in PFI that are not buildings to be proud of in the future" (Davis, 2002).

Whilst some of the issues stem from the designs put forward by the architects, some blame has been laid with the public sector who, the private sector partners claim, have put forward either unclear or unreasonable demands which subsequently lead to delays and mistakes (Asenova et al., 2002; Akintoye et al., 2003). Notwithstanding this debate, there is also a strong possibility that risk averse attitudes among private sector investors in PFI projects have militated against the adoption of innovative design solution.

Local Improvement Finance Trusts (LIFT)

PFI in the health service was initially conceived as a means for procuring new hospital infrastructure for the health service. More recently, there has been a growing recognition that similar improvements were required in the primary care sector. However, since GP-owned premises are usually relatively small, their procurement or refurbishment does not typically represents the type of project that would appeal to private sector PFI investors. In response to this issue, in 2001 the Department of Health (DoH) introduced its new Local Improvement Finance Trust (LIFT). A key component of LIFT is an exclusivity clause giving the successful LIFTCo the right to build all primary care premises for a Primary Care Trust (Aldred, 2007). As a consequence, the LIFT process removes the need to go out to tender for construction projects in the future as all facilities can be delivered by the same local LIFTCo (Ballantyne, 2005; Little, 2006). It is assumed that this ensures good quality bids for relatively small capital schemes and can save on bid costs (Ballantyne, 2005). However, the House of Commons Committee of Public Accounts identified that

> For the LIFT model to work efficiently there needs to be a continuous flow of developments. The LIFTCo is intended to operate as a local property development business with overhead costs spread over a number of projects. Given the cost to the local health economy of developing LIFT buildings, and the long term funding requirements, there is a risk that a continuous flow of projects may not be taken forward. If so, the model may not achieve the expected benefits(House of Commons, 2006).

But ignoring this possibility, is there evidence that LIFT can address the risk-management related shortcomings of PFI? The following sections address each of these issues in turn.

Poor Risk Management (LIFT)

In interviews with members of public sector bodies undertaking LIFT projects, Aldred (2008) noted that they believed that private sector companies, "in particular banks", were highly risk averse and suggested that "the public sector may not get good value for money when attempting to transfer risk to the public sector". The Public Accounts Committee (PAC) recognised that the returns for LIFT were perceived to be very high in relation to the level of risk assumed by the private sector partners, a fact confirmed by Holmes et al. (2006) who felt that "contractors involved in the LIFT process are making a greater return on their investment than the much-criticised PFI schemes". However the PAC argues that this may have been the case in the early schemes "because of perceived greater risk associated with the newness of the schemes, and uncertainty over the pace of future developments" (HoC, 2006). This view has been confirmed by the NAO (2005) who noted that the returns should reduce over time as learning curves are overcome.

Notwithstanding this expectation, criticisms are still being voiced with regard to the risk premium achieved by LIFT companies, with UNISON (2006) claiming that "the projected LIFT rate of return of 15.1% on average compares with 8-9% for traditional third party development – a lot of extra profit given that a PCT may pay around £1 million per year or more to lease each LIFT health centre". Others, like Dawson (2001) would argue that a 15% return should be considered standard for a low-risk, privately financed project. Overall, there appears to be little agreement as to how private sector companies involved in LIFT projects should be rewarded for the risk of their investment. As of now, the going rates of return for LIFT projects appear to have ensured adequate market interest from the private sector, but there is every possibility that this has been achieved at the cost of excessive risk premia.

Lack of Required Skills in the Public Sector (LIFT)

Whilst the Primary Care Trusts have little, if any, experience of property (re)development and management, the consultants required to assist them with those critical skill sets (Hines, 2003) have little, if any, experience of health care and special requirements in terms of design and specifications. In their study, the NAO (2005) found that PCTs found the development of plans understandably "complex and time consuming". According to Holmes et al. (2006) this "inequality in the size and expertise of the negotiating parties has given the upper hand to the contractors when discussing technical specifications and operational arrangements". To try to overcome this, the PCT requires a project team that is adequately resourced with the appropriate skills and management/leadership support (Hines, 2003). Although this may seem a basic requirement, according to the NAO (2005), 56 per cent of PCTs felt that they did not have sufficient resources to complete their project efficiently. Whilst some authorities provided centralised resources to assist with this process where they had several concurrent LIFT projects, other authorities were slower in providing this support (Ballantyne, 2005). Like the public sector bodies procuring facilities under the PFI, it would seem that the PCTs struggle with developing the capabilities necessary to enter into the required bilateral contracts and partnerships with the private sector.

Lengthy Negotiations and Complex Contracts (LIFT)

There is evidence that the bidding process creates particular difficulties to all parties involved in LIFT procurement. Andalo (2003) noted that LIFT requires the submission of detailed plans very early in the process which significantly increases costs for potential bidders. Gaining sign-off is also perceived to be a "pretty painful process" (Sansom, 2007). Little (2006) notes that for one super surgery "the planning took several years" and for one LIFT project Parker (2006) claimed that the process lasted for two years:

> Three consortia were picked to bid, one dropped out halfway through. It took six months for the LIFT to get a preferred bidder, then a year until financial close.

Consequently, some individuals involved in the process have queried whether the process could be streamlined and whether the front-end planning costs could be reduced as they current act as a deterrent (Meara, 2001).

LIFT "represents a shift in the way governments contract with private firms: from short-term, discrete contracts, to long-term, complex and open-ended contracts" (Aldred, 2007). Such contracts are inherently complex, and perhaps unsurprisingly, a UNISON report (2006) has suggested that "The extra layers of bureaucracy diminish the ability of NHS directors and managers to control the services provided and make it still harder for patients and staff to make their voices heard".

Negotiations with local health care providers seems to have taken longer than expected with varying degrees of success in gaining buy-in to the process (NAO, 2005). Even when the buildings are occupied, health care professionals working within LIFT buildings have noted that the terms of the contracts make it difficult and expensive to undertake minor alterations to the property once it has been completed (HoC, 2006) as "the lease agreement states that tenants can only do so with prior consent of the LIFTCo, but the time delay and bureaucracy involved in getting LIFTCo approval often causes frustration".

The scale of some combined LIFT projects means that companies bidding for the work must go through a detailed procurement process governed by European legislation. This means that a bidding company must have the requisite skills and adequate resources not only to complete the job, but also to develop and fund expensive, and potentially unsuccessful, bids (Hudson et al., 2003; Holmes et al., 2006). Holmes et al. (2006) suggest that submitting a bid may cost an organisation between "£500,000 and £1 million, with only a one-in-three chance of success". Consequently, some smaller developers are unable to compete and are squeezed out by the large development companies (Hudson et al., 2003). However, these larger, often national, companies often have higher overheads which can be a significant factor in the overall construction costs of the schemes (Hudson et al., 2003; Holmes et al., 2006).

Some private partners consider the pressure of the bidding process as "too onerous"; with one company Managing Director stating that "I think that the selection process is asking too much. Originally we had been asked to develop 11 schemes over two months. We managed to compromise and agreed on six, but this is still a huge amount of work bearing in mind that one scheme alone was worth £12m" (HD, 2003). This Managing Director believes that the selection process should be refined so that the preferred bidder is chosen on the design approach and track record rather than the actual design (HD, 2003). Another developer is quoted as saying "the process is very lengthy and it puts pressure on medium-sized organisations. You can't go forward to the next bid" (HD, 2003).

Given the duration of the LIFT negotiation process, and the cost involved, it would seem likely that the public sector bodies would be reluctant to withdraw from the process and return to the marketplace. Consequently, like PFI, LIFT may well place the PCTs at risk of becoming locked-in to the process and committed to the preferred bidder irrespective of any decline in their relationship.

Structure (LIFT)

By grouping a number of projects together and including the long-term operation and management of these facilities, the scale of each initiative is increased considerably, making them viable and attractive to private investors (Hudson et al., 2003; Holmes et al., 2006; NAO, 2005). One example of this is a project where a company is providing design services on a range of schemes forming part of a £125 million programme to deliver over 40 health care centres (HD, 2006a). Another project will provide nine new healthcare centres, a 72-bed care home for the elderly, a new HQ for the lead primary care trust as well as additional facilities in the first 18 months (HD, 2006a). Other examples include an integrated health and leisure scheme in Burnley where an eleven storey building of 12,600 sq. m. housing a health centre shares a common entrance and reception with a three storey, 5,000 sq.m. leisure centre. In Knowsley, a new LIFT centre will accommodate three GP Practices, council services, a library, a treatment centre offering extended hours and will facilitate local access to a range of new health services including a cardiac clinic. Similarly, the new Halewood Health and Social Care Centre is contributing to complete town centre regeration and, in addition to extended clinical services, will offer a café, access to housing trust and town council offices, a library, post office, Citizens Advice Bureau and community meeting rooms.However, as stated earlier, bundling can also increase the risks associated with asset specificity and uncertainty. In health care, a PFI contract is typically with a single Trust for one building and the services contained within it. However, under LIFT - as the examples above demonstrate - the contract is often for multiple buildings with many tenants who may have competing demands.

As would be expected, the financial structure of LIFT is very similar to that of PFI. As already stated, by bundling various smaller projects into one contract, LIFT increases the value of the contract to make it attractive to investors. This then replicates PFI by placing a heavy financial burden on the suppliers who must enter similar long-term contracts with the public sector to recoup their investment. Although, like PFI, the private sector has the benefit of knowing that it would be very difficult for the public sector to withdraw from the contract once they are committed.

Cost (LIFT)

The funding mechanism behind LIFT has been described as "very complicated" (Tyndale- Biscoe, 2003). With the current lack of any form of evaluation, it is understandable that costs associated with the LIFT process are being questioned, from initial set-up (Tyndale-Biscoe, 2003), fees payable to Partnerships for Health (NAO, 2005), and operating costs (Comerford, 2004) to the rents being charged to tenants (Holmes et al., 2006). The House of Commons (HoC) Public Accounts Committee has stated that "Primary Care Trust accommodation spending on patients registered with GPs in a LIFT development is up to eight times higher than total primary care spending on accommodation. The difference mainly reflects the cost of providing new, high quality and purpose built buildings" (HoC, 2006). Given this analysis, it is understandable that the Chairman of this committee argued that

> What we really need to know is whether the expected benefits to patients justify the cost of using LIFT to provide the new facilities. Providing new, purpose-built buildings for GPs and other primary care services is obviously going to be more expensive than carrying on with older premises. (Guillochon, 2006)

In an interview with a mental health trust director, it was revealed that one financial institution had imposed insurance charges of more than double the usual rate, and these costs had been passed on to the NHS organisations involved (Aldred, 2008). Others perceive LIFT as being effective but costly and drawn out (HD, 2006b), suggesting that these two characteristics will prevent the public sector from walking away from a contract if they run into difficulties.

In the past the NHS, and individual GPs, could choose to reduce immediate expenditure by deciding to postpone building maintenance, or the replacement of equipment. With the advent of LIFT this no longer remains an option as all maintenance now falls under the remit of the LIFTCo contract and the PCT will automatically have a share of these charges routinely included in their fees (Dawson, 2001). Similarly, whilst PCTs and GPs may have chosen to expand or refurbish premises on a piecemeal basis, with LIFT new buildings are delivered in entirety committing the PCT, and their tenants, to their maximum rent immediately with no potential for any phasing (Dawson, 2001). Both factors are likely to raise overall costs but there is also a possibility that they will contribute to higher levels of maintenance and higher residual values.

Building Quality (LIFT)

The implementation of LIFT has kick-started the regeneration of primary care premises on a major scale. For example, in Merseyside alone it is envisaged that there will be 30 schemes with a total value of £100 million (Burton, 2004). Given that many GP practices were housed in poor accommodation with only 40% of premises purpose built, and almost 50% in either converted shops or former residential buildings (Montague, 2004), the government has high hopes for LIFT-built premises. However, in the main, there is no evidence that this has been the case. One author goes so far as to state that "LIFT as a vehicle, is not necessarily producing very much better buildings. Generally speaking, they are mediocre at best" (Simpson, 2007). Peter Wearmouth, chief executive of NHS Estates, identified a lack of innovation in design and said

> We are still designing buildings that look the same as they did 30-40 years ago. We still have waiting rooms and consulting rooms, but society has changed. Patients are no longer submissive yet we build architecture that is submissive.(Davis, 2002)

Mathieson (2003) confirms this view by describing one proposed centre with five stand-alone GP surgeries, each with their own waiting room. Even Lord Hunt, Ministerial Design Champion is quoted as saying "It is striking how unambitious the health service has been in the quality of the design of what it produces" (Davis, 20028). Prasad supported the aims of the NHS Achieving Excellence in Design evaluation Toolkit, intended by NHS Estates to raise the general standards of design in the NHS building programme, but conceded that it would not 'produce genius designs' (Davis, 2002). Whilst this lack of "flair" was perhaps understandable during the first wave where the impetus was to get the first projects completed (Parker, 2006), it is less acceptable for these issues to characterise later projects.

Designing for a health care market was something new for most architects and design companies (Holmes et al., 2006) and seems to have posed some challenges. These challenges included the need to take into account the "unique aspects of each centre such as the acoustic features for those which had audiology departments, the need to develop bespoke characteristic entrances to each site" (HD, 2006) as well as the security concerns of staff (Holmes et al., 2006). Whilst it was recognised that the health service did not "want to make the same mistakes as we did in the 1950s and 1960s" when "we built health centres, which are now unloved buildings surrounded by security fences and covered in graffiti" (Andalo, 2003), some initial designs were likened to 'car show-rooms' or 'prisons' by lay stakeholders (Holmes et al., 2006).

Whilst the multi-disciplinary, open-layout approach to working in some new LIFT buildings has created a "sense of community spirit" that has been well received by some (Gilbert, 2005), it has also created problems. For example, in one location the creation of a centralised reception area for four physician practices has reduced patient privacy as any discussion with the medical secretaries can be easily overheard (Gilbert, 2005). There have also been basic oversights, such as the lack of a patient call system so doctors must leave their rooms to call in their next patient, insufficient car parking spaces and a common alarm system that prevents GPs from calling in to their practice to work out of hours (Gilbert, 2005).

The LIFT process is credited with attracting national construction and design teams (Holmes et al., 2006.) and for facilitating attention to detail, such as the creation of a design with features to maximise light and ventilation (Montague, 2004). However, bringing this "sophisticated design expertise" into the procurement process also brought negotiation teams into the bidding process who "used this experience to drive a hard bargain with the PCT teams for whom each negotiation was a first" (Holmes et al., 2006). Today private sector partners claim that they are "on the hook" to deliver "decent buildings" that are "affordable", "efficient" and "good-quality" whilst being "architecturally-striking civic landmarks" (Sansom, 2007). At the same time there are economic incentives for the private partner to design and build in a way that will minimise costs (Dawson, 2001). This is related to worries that LIFT will inadvertently lock the health service may into inflexible contracts for poorly constructed building with high operating costs for the next 25 years (Paxton and Lissauer, 2000).

NEW ISSUES CREATED BY LIFT

According to the literature, the LIFT scheme seems to replicate many of the problems associated with the PFI procurement process. In addition there is some evidence that, as a significant modification of PFI, LIFT suffers from specific new difficulties.

Control

Whilst with PFI the public sector retains responsibility for deciding on the public sector services to be provided, the quality and performance standards of these services, and taking corrective action if performance falls below expectation" (Akintoye et al., 2003) the same is not true for all LIFT projects. New language in LIFT contracts authorises some LIFT companies to "privatise clinical services in LIFT and non-LIFT buildings" by getting them to "engage private medical companies to provide GP services, or agencies to provide district nursing services" (UNISON, 2006). Assuming that LIFT companies do engage others to provide these services, there are fears that such deals would be "shrouded in 'commercial confidentiality'" and embedded in highly complex, long-term contracts making it impossible for others to intercede, even if public safety was at stake (Aldred, 2005). There are also concerns that the planning function of the NHS will be further eroded and allowing the LIFTCos to determine how, and by whom, service will be delivered (Aldred, 2005). Hellowell (2004) quotes Brian Johns, chief executive for Partnerships for Health, as saying:

> The department is not yet clear on the best way to take this forward. It could be that a new-wave LIFT company would be expected to build clinical services into its delivery model – perhaps even taking financial risk on clinical outcomes as in the elective care programme. More likely, LIFT companies would be expected to procure clinical services

> such as diagnostics and out-of-hours services as part of the supply chain. Interestingly, this is not an innovation that existing private sector players in LIFT are keen on.

Similarly David Toplas, Chief Executive of Mill Group, a prominent investor in the LIFT programme, believes this would "make many people think again about their involvement in LIFT" (Hellowell, 2004).

Under current contractual arrangements, LIFT companies can determine which private businesses are able to move into their buildings. This is of some concern to the GPs. As one GP noted in an interview with Dix (2001), they did not want to see a "McDonald's next to the waiting room" as had already appeared in some NHS hospitals (UNISON, 2006). Some LIFT project managers have negotiated the right of veto to ensure that the public sector partner can determine who is allocated a tenancy agreement. In one such project the co-ordinator explained that other complementary shops and services could rent spaces on the site, such as social housing related activities, opticians, dentists and pharmacies. They may also allow third party revenue generation from private businesses such as "a veterinary practice, but not a tobacconist. We wouldn't have betting shops, but retail outlets complementary to health might be accepted such as health food outlets" (Mathieson, 2002).

It is recognised that the public sector will be forced to consider how the profitability of new premises can be maximised whilst enhancing the services available to the local population (Aldred, 2007). However, it may be hard to ignore the fact that "The more professionals you cram into a one-stop shop, the more profitable the site" (Andalo, 2003).

Conflicts of Interest

In an NAO study, two thirds of Primary Care Trust Chief Executives or Finance Directors had been appointed to act as public sector directors on their LIFTCo (NAO, 2005). In their employment contracts these individuals have a duty to protect the interests of the PCT, such as minimising the costs of purchasing services from the LIFTCo. However, their new roles with the LIFTCo would require them to act in the interest of the LIFTCo board, including maximising profits for the shareholders. This could create a potential for conflict of interest (Unison, 2006; NAO, 2005). There are similar concerns over potential conflict of interest for GPs who become members of a local LIFT Company and who are required to act in the best interest of their patients (Mathieson, 2002). The King's Fund (2001) notes that whilst the private sector will be "seeking to develop sites with profitable complementary uses… the public shareholders will be seeking to ensure good locations and a good mix of (non-profit making) users".

Similarly, the recruitment of independent non-executives to Chair the PCT and strategic Partnering Boards has proved difficult for many LIFT areas (NAO, 2005). Whilst it is recognised that there is a need for the board to have the requisite skills to protect public interests, in practice this has resulted in the recruitment of individuals with conflicting interests. In one third of the NAO case studies the Chair of the Strategic Partnering Board was a local stakeholder in LIFT (NAO, 2005) who could clearly have an influence on the bidding process (Tyndale- Biscoe, 2003).

Use of Enabling Funds

To facilitate the start of LIFT projects, the Government made 'enabling funds' available to the projects to "remove obstacles to a project going ahead by, for example, purchasing sites or releasing GP practices from negative equity" (Hines, 2003). These funds could also be used to reconvert primary care premises back into residential premises in order to make them more attractive to the market and easier to sell if the GPs were prepared to relocate into LIFT premises (DoH, 2000). These funds are "not automatically refundable". However, in the limited guidance provided by the Government, it was stated that "there may be circumstances in which the Department would be keen to reclaim funding to enable it to be recycled into further LIFT developments" (NAO, 2005). The NAO go on to state that one third of project managers were uncertain as to how to use the enabling funds, leading to "variation" in usage (NAO, 2005). The NAO also notes that as of January 2005, "no funds have been paid back to the Department. This has prompted a review of the efficiency of how funds are used and recycled".

Whilst the LIFT process was supposed to reduce the involvement of the PCTs in the construction and day-to-day management of the buildings, it would seem that they are still required to take on the initiation and management of revenue contracts, including undertaking "all the leg work, paying solicitors' costs, accountants and consultants when they set them up" (Comerford, 2004); costs which Comerford claims are higher than those under the previous system of fixed cost or notional rent. Whilst this may be done using the enabling funds, it is still an additional cost in the process.

Revenue

Rental income has, understandably, been a consideration of developers given the significant opportunities for revenue raising (Paxton and Lissauer, 2000). Some have designed and built more traditional GP surgeries, preferring GP stability and steady rental income over multi-use facilities with "more risky tenants" (Mathieson, 2002). It is interesting to note that at one LIFT project, the LIFT coordinator has chosen not to discuss rents with its GPs as:

> It does not want them to become alarmed over figures that are still being discussed: the bidders have put indicative rental figures in their bids and we are in negotiation with them over those figures (Dudman, 2003)

This suggests that the rent could be considerably higher than the GPs would anticipate. Holmes et al. (2006) describe the major concern over rents to be paid by tenants of LIFT buildings by stating that "there is a perception that the higher costs of LIFT, compared to current rent payments, outweighs the benefits of new, purpose-built premises".

UNISON (2003) notes that LIFT companies have to pay back the capital borrowed to fund the development, pay to maintain the buildings and must still make a profit for investors; and that all of these costs must be reflected in the rents charged to the PCT and other tenants. Holmes et al. (2006) note that there are hidden costs associated with unsuccessful bidders which need to be "built into other rounds". It is not surprising that the PCTs are being charged a higher rent than their previous market-rate cost-rents which, according to Comerford (2004), amounts to an eight to ten per cent increase.

Obtaining tenants for all LIFT spaces has not been as straightforward as it may be perceived. Some GPs, including those approaching retirement age, are not in a position to sign a 25 year tenancy agreement. PCTs can take over a head lease with the developer and then sub-let to GPs or other tenants on a shorter-term basis; an option which may be more attractive to practitioners (Paxton and Lissauer, 2000; Unison, 2003; Aldred, 2007) including those who wish to work in an inner city location or to obtain new skills before relocating elsewhere (Sansom, 2007). However, this leaves the NHS at risk of GPs either leaving or defaulting (Aldred, 2007; Aldred 2008) or coming to the end of their lease and the PCT being unable to find a replacement tenant (Unison, 2003).

These concerns have been examined by Aldred (2007) who interviewed a number of dentists, pharmacists and local authority representatives. Holmes (2006) goes on to say that "In the case study area the rent charged for the new LIFT premises is in the order of £210/m2. Similar, if not superior accommodation provided by the third party procurement is in the region of £160/m2. When a comparable facility management package is added, the rent from a third party developer will be approximately 175-190/m2. In real terms, the facilities provided are expensive when compared to market rents in the locality". For this reason it is suggested that local authorities and allied health practices, including pharmacies and dentists, have chosen not to rent spaces in the LIFT buildings, preferring in some cases to rent retail premises adjacent to the doctor's practice at a "considerably" lower rent (Holmes et al., 2006). The reason pharmacies in particular may not wish to relocate into a LIFT building was identified by the NAO (2005) who stated that, whilst primary care providers such as dentists and doctors receive some automatic reimbursement for the rent paid for primary care premises, the PCT determines whether a pharmacy is similarly classified. In the main pharmacies tend to be considered a business and as such will be expected to pay full rent for their space. As the NAO (2005) identifies that pharmacies are "likely to be the most significant source of third party income" which can be used to "plug funding gaps and reduce the rent levels paid by other tenants", pricing them out of the market would seem to be a short-sighted approach. This may be why alternatives such as cafes, vending machines, internet training facilities and complementary therapists are now being encouraged to locate within the space. There is evidence that in order to encourage healthcare professionals to relocate into LIFT premises, some PCTs have now even agreed to subsidise rents (NAO, 2005).

CONCLUSION

Whilst it is evident that the PFI process had inherent risk-management issues, there are strong suggestions that the LIFT process has not fully addressed these. It would seem that the public sector is still struggling to identify the risks associated with a PPP project. They still do not appear to have the resources required to be on an equal footing with their private sector partners and to enable them to undertake their part in the procurement process efficiently and effectively. There are also ongoing concerns over whether using some form of risk-transfer mechanism through a contract can truly protect the public interest, especially given the difficulties encountered within the public sector when trying to identify risks in the first place.

If the literature is correct, LIFT would seem to have created additional problems including the further reduction of public sector control, conflicts of interest, the inappropriate use of enabling funds, and higher than market rental costs affecting the uptake of space in the buildings by local health care providers. Furthermore, there are ongoing concerns about the high costs of the bidding and procurement process and the complexity of the contractual negotiations and arrangements. Some of these problems have been addressed by individual PCTs who have engaged in a bundling of projects and/or partnerships with other PCTs in the procurement of LIFT projects and the creation of LIFT companies. While these measures are likely to reduce transaction and bidding costs as well as having a potentially positive impact on the Value for Money, they also increase the possible exposure of PCTs to lock-ins and their vulnerability to private sector financial failure. Overall there is therefore an urgent need for PCTs to gain awareness and skill in the management of the unique risks this form of public-private partnership poses.

Acknowledgment

The authors would like to thank the NHS Service Delivery and Organisation (SDO) programme for its support of this research. Thanks also go to the other project participants, J. Steven Toms, Ian Greener, Russell Mannion and Neil Lunt.

References

Akintoye, A., Hardcastle, C., Beck, M., Chinyio, E. and Asenova, D. 2003 Achieving Best Value in Private Finance Initiative Project Procurement, *Construction Management and Economics*, 21: 461-470.

Aldred, R. 2005. Challenges of Private Provision in the NHS: Real Story is Beginning to Emerge, *British Medical Journal*, 331: 1338.

Aldred, R. 2008. Managing Risk and Regulation Within new Local 'Health Economies: The Case of NHS LIFT, *Health, Risk and Society*, 10(1): 23-36.

Aldred, R. 2007. Closed Policy Networks, Broken Chains of Communication and the Stories Behind an 'Entrepreneurial Policy': The Case Of NHS Local Improvement Finance Trust (NHS LIFT), *Critical Social Policy*, 27(1): 139-151.

Andalo, D. 2003. 'One Stop to Cure All Ills, *Medeconomics*, 24(1): 16-18, 20.

Asenova, D., and Beck, M. 2003. The UK Financial Sector and Risk Management in PFI Projects: A Survey, *Public Money and Management*, 23(3): 195-203.

Asenova, D., Beck, M., Akintoye, A., Hardcastle, C. and Chinyio, E. 2002. Partnership, Value for Money and Best Value in PFI Projects: Obstacles and Opportunities, *Public Policy and Administration*, 17(4): 5 – 19.

Asenova, D.; Beck, M and Toms, S. 2007. The Limits of Market-Based Governance and Accountability – PFI Refinancing and the Resurgence of The Regulatory State, paper presented at the 7th European Critical Accounting Studies conference, University of Glasgow.

Audit Commission. 1998. Taking The Initiative: A Framework for Purchasing Under the Private Finance Initiative. London, Audit Commission.

Ballantyne, N. 2005. Getting Lift off the Ground, retrieved October 23 2007 from www.cipfa.org.uk/publicfinance/news_details.cfm?News_id=25327.

Beck, M. and Hunter-Beck, C. 2003. PFI Uptake in UK Local Authorities, in A. Akintoye, M. Beck and C. Hardcastle (eds.) *Private Partnerships: Managing Risks and Opportunities*. Oxford, Blackwell Science.

Bunce, C. 1997. Laying the Foundations for a GP-led study, *General Practitioner*, Feb 24: 32-33.

Burton, R. 2004. Regeneration Game, *Hospital Development*, 35(6) pp 11-13.

Clark, G.L. and Root, A. 1999. Infrastructure Shortfall in the United Kingdom: the Private Finance Initiative and Government Policy, *Political Geography*, 18: 341-365.

Comerford, C. 2004. Is .108m of Premises Funding Just Papering Over the Cracks?' *Doctor*, Aug 20: 10.

Committee of Public Accounts (1999) *Twenty-third Report: Getting Better Value for Money from the Private Finance Initiative*. London, House of Commons Committee Office.

Daily Telegraph. 1996. Whitehall PFI Taken Into its Next Phase, April 4: 19.

Davis, K. 2002. *Primary Concerns*, Hospital Development, 33(6): 8-9.

Dawson, D. 2001. The Private Finance Initiative: a Public Finance Illusion? *Health Economics*, 10(6): 479-486.

Dix, A. 2001. Delayed LIFT-off... (Local Improvement Finance Trust), the Replacement or Refurbishment of 3,000 GP Premises and 500 'one-stop health centres', *Health Service Journal* , 111(5752): 1-3.

Department of Health. 2000. *New Initiatives to Modernise GP Premises*. London, Department of Health.

Department of Health. 2001. *NHS Local Improvement Finance Trust (NHS LIFT) Prospectus*. London, Department of Health.

Dudman, J. 2003. Ready for Lift-off, *Public Finance*, Feb 7: 24-25.

Froud, J. 2003. The Private Finance Initiative: Risk, Uncertainty and the State, *Accounting, Organizations and Society*, 28: 567-589.

Gaffney, D., Pollock, A.M., Price, D. and Shaoul, J. 1999. The Private Finance Initiative: The Politics of the Private Finance Initiative and the New NHS, *British Medical Journal*, 319: 249-253.

Gilbert, H. 2005. Super Size Me, *Care and Health Magazine*, 104: 20-22.

Guillochon, R. 2006. MPs say Government Scheme forr GPs' Premises Threatens Other Primary Care Needs, *British Medical Journal*, 333: 64.

Hospital Development . 2003. East London LIFT Raises Questions, http://www.hdmagazine.co.uk/story.asp?storyCode=2018286.

Hospital Development . 2006a. WYG Supports £124m LIFT Project, http://www.hdmagazine.co.uk/story.asp?storyCode=2035925.

Hospital Development . 2006b. Design Improved under PFI, http://www.hdmagazine.co.uk/story.asp?storyCode=2036179.

Hellowell, M. 2004. PPPs in Perspective - Uplifting Experience, *Public Finance*, 24: 23.

Hines, C. 2003. How LIFT is Helping Cornwall Experience a Taste of Eden, *Primary Care Report*, 5(3): 22-23.

HM Treasury. 1999. *Modern Government, Modern Procurement.* London, HM Treasury.

HM Treasury. 2003. *PFI: Meeting the Investment Challenge*. Norwich, HMSO.

HoC. 2006. *NHS Local Improvement Finance Trusts: Forty Seventh Report of Session 2005-06*. London, HMSO.

Holmes, J., Capper, G. and Hudson, G. 2006. Public Private Partnerships in the Provision of Health Care Premises in the UK, *International Journal of Project Management*, 24(7): 566-572.

Hudson, G., Capper, G. and Holmes, J. 2003. The Implications of PFI on Health Care Premises, Engineering_Design, Durability, and Maintenance, London, Institution of Mechanical Engineers Conference.

Little, W. 2006. Primary care. Settle for Super, *Health Service Journal*, 116(6000): 26-8.

Lonsdale, C. 2005. Risk Transfer and the UK Private Finance Initiative: a Theoretical Analysis, *Policy and Politics*, 33(2): 231-249.

Mathieson, S. 2003. LIFT-long Learning, *Health Service Journal*, 113(5850): 33-35.

Meara, R. 2001. Do we Have Lift-off, *Private Finance Initiative*, 6(2): 76-78.

Montague, A. 2004. A LIFT for local communities, *Hospital Development*, 35(9): 19-20.

National Audit Office. 1999. *The PFI Contract for the New Dartford and Gravesham Hospital*. London, NAO.

National Audit Office. 2005. *Innovation in the NHS: Local Improvement Finance Trusts*. London, The Stationery Office.

Parker, J. 2006. Street Life, *Hospital Development*, 37(1): 18-19.

Pollock, A.; Shaoul, J. and Vickers, N. 2002. Private Finance and "Value for Money" in NHS Hospitals: a Policy in Search of a Rationale? *British Medical Journal*, 324(7347): 1205-1209.

Private Finance Panel. 1995. *Private Opportunity, Public Benefit: Progressing the Private Finance Initiative.* London, HMSO.

Private Finance Panel. 1996. *Private Finance Initiative: Guidelines for Smoothing the Procurement Process*. London, HMSO.

Public Advisory Committee. 2003. *Delivering Better Value for Money from the Private Finance Initiative*. London, Public Accounts Committee.

Sansom, A. 2007. London LIFT Projects. Meeting of Minds, *Hospital Development*, http://www.hdmagazine.co.uk/story.asp?storyCode=2041823.

Simpson, V. 2007. Primary and Community Care: Changing Faces, *Hospital Development*, http://www.hdmagazine.co.uk/story.asp?storyCode=2041695.

Spackman, M. 2002. 'Public-Private Partnerships: Lessons from the British Approach, Economic Systems, 26: 283-301.

Stewart, A. and Butler, E. 1996. *Seize the Initiative*. London, Adam Smith Institute.

The King's Fund. 2000. *Health Care UK*. London, The King's Fund.

Treasury Taskforce. 1997. *Partnerships for Prosperity: The Private Finance Initiative*. London, HM Treasury.

Treasury Taskforce. 1999. *Standardisation of Contracts*. London, HM Treasury.

Tyndale Biscoe, J. 2003. Why LIFT isn't Hitting the Mark, *Medeconomics*, 24(5): 26,29-31.

UNISON. 1996. *NHS Trust Chief Executives Give Thumbs Down to PFI. London,* UNISON.

UNISON. 2002. *PFI: Failing Our Future - A UNISON Audit of the Private Finance Initiative.* London, UNISON.

UNISON and R. Aldred 2006. *In the Interests of Profit at the Expense of Patients: An Examination of the NHS Local Improvement Finance Trust (LIFT) Model, Analysing Six Key Disadvantages.* London, UNISON.

In: Understanding Risk
Editor: Matthias Beck

ISBN: 978-1-62618-686-6

Chapter 12

UK PUBLIC-PRIVATE PARTNERSHIPS AND THE CREDIT CRUNCH: A CASE OF RISK CONTAGION?

Stephen Bailey[1*], Darinka Asenova[2,†] and Matthias Beck[3,‡]
[1]Department of Law, Economics, Accounting and Risk, Glasgow School for Business and Society, Glasgow Caledonian University, Glasgow, UK
[2]Department of Law, Economics, Accounting and Risk, Glasgow School for Business and Society, Glasgow Caledonian University, Glasgow, UK
[3] Queen's University Management School, Queen's University Belfast, Belfast, UK

ABSTRACT

During the past twenty years, the UK has relied heavily on Public-private Partnerships (PPP) and especially the Private Finance Initiative in the procurement of infrastructure and services. Discussing the causes of the credit crunch and its effects on PPP, this paper notes that the provision of new public sector infrastructure and related services has been adversely affected by the impact of the credit crunch on Private Finance Initiatives (PFIs). These problems have arisen primarily from the unwillingness of commercial banks to replace collapsed PFI bond financingunless new PFI contracts reduce financial risks; which, in turn, is likely to increase the cost of these projects to the public sector. Additional financial strains have arisen for the UK government from the need to bail out collapsed PFI projects. Overall we find evidence that the UK commitment to PFI has not only increased immediate fiscal pressures on the UK when these have become least palatable, but has also created fiscal vulnerabilities at local and national levels which are likely to hamper the country's ability to launch counter-cyclical responses to the ongoing crisis.

* S.J.Bailey@gcu.ac.uk
† D.Asenova@gcu.ac.uk
‡ m.beck@qub.ac.uk

THE MAKING OF THE CREDIT CRUNCH

The term 'credit crunch' describes the collapse in bank lending as the cost of (both retail and wholesale inter-bank) credit became prohibitively expensive or simply unavailable during 2007-09. The origins of the credit crunch can be traced to lax regulatory regimes for banks, weak central bank safety nets for banks facing liquidity problems, growth of the much less heavily regulated shadow banking system, rapid innovation in financial products as banks competed aggressively for business, and the increasingly substantial international movements of capital. In the period leading up to this crisis, financial innovation was encouraged by banks and other financial institutions that paid substantial annual bonuses to their directors and other employees to reward increased short-term sales of new financial products. Enjoying increased annual dividend payments financed by the resulting rapid growth of bank turnovers and profits, shareholders generally did not question the long-term sustainability of this expansion. In combination, these developments resulted in the systemic failure of the financial services industry to abide by fiscal rectitude and prudential lending and borrowing.

While bank failures, recessions and credit crunches are not new (see, e.g., Klein and Shabbir, 2006), the 2007-09 credit crunch differed from previous crisis on account of the increasing use of 'securitisation', whereby banks and other financial institutions packaged together mortgage debts and sold them on to other financial institutions both in their home countries and abroad. This included the 'sub-prime mortgages' later subject to high default rates in the USA, UK and elsewhere.

As part of this pattern, mortgages became increasingly large multiples of house-buyers' incomes and, with ever-lower cash deposits being required from borrowers, it became common for banks and building societies to supply 100+% mortgages. This expansion of mortgage debt was further accelerated by the fact that banks allowed borrowers to self-certify their ability to repay debt, without carrying out the customary checks. Additionally, more mortgages were being used for speculative buy-to let properties and homes were increasingly being re-mortgaged for non-residential purchases such as cars and foreign holidays. This lack of diligence by lenders was largely based on the assumption that mortgage default did not matter because rising house prices meant that these borrowers could always either refinance their mortgages or pay them off by selling their houses at inflated prices. Meanwhile, loan originators quickly sold sub-prime loans to other financial institutions which, in turn, repackaged and sold them to investors as innovative financial products (e.g. collateralised debt obligations) paying higher rates of interest than offered by banks. Such financial innovation went hand-in-hand with the growth of non-bank financial institutions, these being less regulated than banks.

With hindsight, there is now evidence that, in pursuit of high profits, banking regulators, directors of banks and shareholders allowed banks to expand too rapidly and to buy and sell exotic investments (including mortgage-backed bonds) that they themselves poorly understood. This was paralleled by a lack of financial transparency and a poor appreciation of the increasingly risky nature of banking operations; which, in turn, encouraged banks to move rapidly from traditional (relatively safe) retail banking into (higher risk) investment banking (see, e.g., Crotty, 2007 for a detailed analysis of the developments, which led this author to predict the current crisis in April).

As part of this highly competitive scramble for higher turnovers and increased market shares, many banks became reckless in their operations and largely abandoned past practices of ensuring due diligence. Potential fears about these developments, meanwhile, were countered by assurances within financial academia that sophisticated modern risk management techniques—such as widespread agreement on the use of VAR (value at risk) models— had made practices safe which had formerly been considered too risky (Davis, 2003). These views were shared by senior financial regulators who, like Alan Greenspan (2004, cited from Crotty, 2007) attributed the paradox of high financial firm profits notwithstanding intense financial market competition, not to dangerous risk taking, but rather "to the development of a far more flexible, efficient, and hence resilient financial system than existed just a quarter-century ago."

In reality, however, the risks associated with the extensive securitisation were unclear and most banks had no clear overview of their total risk exposure because of the failings of the ratings agencies. Investors who thought they were holding high-grade debt (rated AAA by the credit-ratings agencies) became exposed to rising rates of default in the USA sub-prime mortgage market. For some time this process was masked by financial globalization which created a new type of 'toxic liquidity' by allowing investors in other countries to buy 'toxic debt'. In this process, banks, pension funds, insurance companies and other financial institutions across the globe that had bought debt to diversify their financial portfolios and so supposedly reduce risk (being less exposed to a recession in their own countries) were inadvertently acting as a 'transmission mechanism' for recessions to spread like a virus from one country to another (the collapse of Icelandic banks in late 2008 being a case in point).

Government Responses

The burden of resolving or ameliorating the global crisis has now fallen predominantly to national governments who have been forced to return to their traditional roles as risk takers of last resort. The activities have put significant strain on public finances which has led critics to accuse some governments of being reckless with future tax-payers' money as they borrow increasingly large proportions of GDP in order to 'bail out' those heavily indebted banks and other private sector organisations.

The International Monetary Fund (IMF) calculated the ratios of fiscal stimulus relative to GDP based on the initial measures announced by national governments in 2008 as: UK 1.5%, USA 4.9%, Japan 9.1%, Germany 3% and France 1.15%. Subsequently, in early 2009, the UK government began to exchange mortgage bonds (i.e. the toxic debt) for government bonds, take majority shareholdings in banks and insure bank loans against default. The IMF calculated that these additional measures increased the UK's ratio to 19.8%, as of February 2009; by far the highest ratio in the G20 countries (the USA's rose to 'only' 6.8%).

The accelerating cost to the public purse of these measures, meanwhile has raised questions about fiscal prudence, especially in the UK. If the hoped-for higher levels of economic growth are not forthcoming in the UK, a deepening and prolonged recession/depression will make what had already been a long-term 'structural gap' between (higher) government expenditures and (lower) revenues much greater (Bailey 2004). This will exacerbate any losses the government (and, ultimately, the taxpayer) incurs on its ongoing purchases of increasingly large proportions of bank shares, swaps of government bonds for toxic mortgage-backed bonds, guarantees of bank loans on both wholesale and retail money markets, etc., (Goodhart 2009).

As a consequence of these measures, the UK central government had to abandon its own fiscal rules, namely the 'golden rule' (borrow only for capital, not current, expenditure) and the 'sustainable investment rule' (net public debt no greater than 40% of GDP). Its own figures show that net public debt exceeded 50% of GDP in January 2009 and forecast it to peak at almost 60% by 2012/13. Nevertheless, this still seems low compared with those EU eurozone countries rapidly approaching breaches of the Stability and Growth Pact. In January 2009 the EC forecast 15 of them to be in breach of the Pact in 2009. It also forecast budget deficits to average 4.4% in 2010 and government debt to average 76% of GDP, both well above the Pact's ceilings of 3% and 60% respectively (Fingland and Bailey 2008).

In buying up very large proportions of shares in several UK banks and introducing special liquidity schemes, the UK government has effectively allowed banks to nationalise their rapidly increasing losses whilst privatising their profits. At the same time, largely incalculable financial risks have been transferred from the private to the public sector. This hardly seems prudential on the part of national governments as it creates moral hazard by setting a precedent for future taxpayer bailouts of highly irresponsible bank lending. Justifying the current high-risk fiscal largesse by arguing that doing nothing would be more costly for the future health of the economy is an act of faith in the success of the ever-increasing bank bailouts and fails to address how the huge increases in government debt will be repaid.

From the perspective of public sector organizations such as the UK's local authorities and its National Health Service (NHS) the problem associated with these policies is more than a purely technical question about the likelihood of recovery of the country's financial sector. UK public sector organizations and their employees will bear the costs of future budget cuts which have arisen from a crisis which these organizations have not caused and from whose past excesses they did not benefit. In this context it is notable that, whilst the UK central government is now guaranteeing bank bonds, it does not guarantee bonds issued by local governments (Bailey et al., 2009). It also does not guarantee the safety of local authorities' bank deposits outside the UK, many having deposited large sums of money in Icelandic and other off-shore banks because of the higher rates of interest they offered on deposits compared with UK banks. In this sense the commitment of the current UK government to the well-being of the country's financial sector seems to vastly outstrip its concerns with the financial sustainability of its public service providers.

PFI and the Credit Crunch

Over the past two decades the UK has pioneered the provision of public infrastructure and services via PFI (McQuaid and Scherrer, 2008). Academic research has tried to explain the use of private finance for public purposes in a number of ways. For example, Cohn (2004) has argued that PFI could be seen as an attempt by governments who had been starved of revenue by neo-liberal reforms, to tap into global surplus capital. By contrast, Asenova and Beck (2009) have suggested that, especially following the Asian and Russian financial crises, the desire of finance capital to access low risk investment opportunities has been a driver for the creation of PFI with the state acting as facilitator and broker. Notwithstanding these factors, it can be argued that the growth of PFI has at least been facilitated by the availability of easy money from banks and capital markets during the sustained economic growth of the mid-to-late 1990s and early 2000s.

While up until 2009 the UK was able to procure 860 signed PFI projects with capital value exceeding £68 billion, most of which (650) are now in the operational phase (Timmins, 2009a), there is evidence that this type of procurement has now become difficult to implement. In a typical PFI contract banks were initially providing 80 per cent and later on, with increased market confidence, up to 90 - 95 per cent of total capital requirement. During the 2007-09 credit crunch, global economic downturn and unprecedented multi-billion pound state bailouts of banks etc., the finance system moved from highly speculative lending to a drastic reduction of the availability of finance. As a consequence, cheap corporate bond financing practically disappeared due to lower credit ratings of the insurers that had previously guaranteed returns to investors (Stiff, 2008). The availability of cheaper bond financing is not likely to return until recovery of the capital markets so, until then, bank finance remains virtually the only alternative. As banks have become more risk averse in their lending, it has also become much more difficult and expensive to secure finance and this affected the number of planned projects reaching financial close of contracts. Thus, during 2008 only 34 projects' financing agreements were finalised, which is about half of the annual rate for the previous years (Timmins, 2009a).

As an example of these changes, HSBC, a commercial bank heavily engaged in lending to PFIs before the credit crunch began restricting its lending for PFIs to short-term funding and now only lends to clients it knows and trusts to repay those loans. RBS and HBOS, two other commercial banks, had also both been large PFI lenders prior to the credit crunch. RBS (now 70% state-owned) subsequently scaled down its involvement and the takeover of HBOS (also majority state-owned) by Lloyds TSB further reduced its willingness to lend to PFIs.

In addition to the drastic reduction of funding available from banks, large-scale projects have experienced even more severe problems because banks' appetite for buying syndicated debt, which is a part of the total PFI debt, has been substantially reduced. This in turn increased the overall financing costs (O'Connor, 2008), which have contributed to an increase of PFI costs by as much as 30 base points.

In so far as PFI deals are still progressing, the financial arrangements now tend to involve multiple investors, instead of only one or two banks, and the duration of contracts has typically been reduced from 25-30 to 7-10 years. Moreover, banks are generally unwilling to finance more than £30 to £50 million on a single transaction and so are looking for other participants to provide the rest of the capital requirement (Timmins, 2009a). This means that the process of arranging PFI finance has become slower, costlier and more uncertain. Additionally, banks require credit risk to be passed to service providers and, where possible, they have been looking for government guarantees in case of financial difficulties.

Additional problems for the PFI market are likely to arise from financial difficulties faced by public service providers such as the UK local authorities and the NHS. UK local government, being responsible for providing most public services in the UK, were already having to deal with demographic changes, an ageing population, centrally-required efficiency savings and other financial cuts prior to the credit crunch (Anon, 2008a). Their future buying power is now further circumscribed by a number of factors including, government announcements of further funding cuts in the April 2009 Budget; reduced demand for some chargeable services and falling asset sales.

It had been feared that local authorities would lose the £840 million that they had deposited in the collapsed Icelandic banking system because of the lack of UK government protection (Anon, 2008b). However, the UK government covered those deposits as an interim emergency measure, controversially freezing Icelandic deposits held in the UK. In August 2009, the Icelandic Parliament agreed to reimburse the UK (and Netherlands) governments. Starting in 2016, those payments (plus interest) will be spread over 15 years (Tran 2009).

These developments are likely to impact significantly on the provision of future roads, recycling plants, schools and hospitals, which will further reduce the UK's ability to push ahead with future plans for PFI-based procurement. A report by the NAO revealed that the Building Schools for the Future (BSF) programme, a version of PFI in England and Wales, was two years behind schedule and £10 billion over budget (McAlpine, 2009). The program effectively stalled, with only two projects being signed during the previous six months (Hayman, 2009).

Similarly, notwithstanding the future implementation of drastic budget cuts, the credit crunch has already severely affected the capital investment plans of the NHS. This is due to the fact that the NHS hospital rebuilding program depended entirely on PFI and there was no 'plan B' for meeting the financial requirement (Curtis, 2009). In 2008, twelve major PFI hospital projects were abandoned due to lack of finance. In March 2008, it was announced that the plans for financing a PFI hospital for Maidstone and Tunbridge NHS Trust in Kent through corporate bonds issue had to be abandoned and the client had to revert to more expensive bank finance (O'Connor, 2008). Similarly, it has been announced that major hospital projects such as the £711 million project for University Hospitals Leicester and the £600 million scheme for Leeds Teaching Hospitals will not be taken forward though PFI (Kirkup, 2009). Altogether, current estimates indicate that hospital PFIs worth £2.532 billion have been either abandoned or shifted to alternative forms of finance (Kirkup, 2009).

These problems are likely to be compounded by other forms of disruption which are increasingly faced by local service providers on account of the UK's heavy commitment to sub-contracting and contracting out. Thus it is foreseeable that the reduced availability and increased cost of credit will increase costs to, and reduce the working capital of, suppliers. This is likely to result in the default of some suppliers, which in turn could increase long-term costs to clients on account of a shrinking supplier market.

One exception to these developments is the NHS Local Improvement Finance Trust (LIFT) scheme, which has recently been modified under the name of Express LIFT. Recent reports in the media indicate that the types of PFI procured by the Department of Health in England and Wales under Express Lift may be better suited to the current financial environment (Timmins, 2009b). These are typically smaller projects, in the range of £3 million to £7 million, which means that the arrangement of the capital requirement is not as problematic as for large-scale PFIs. The Express Lift model involves a joint venture between the primary care trusts (and sometimes local authorities) which own 40 per cent of the equity stake, and the private companies for the purpose of financing, building and running GP (i.e. family doctor) surgeries and other health facilities over 20 years. Under Express Lift there is a framework contract with seven selected private sector consortiums which have quasi-monopoly power over the entire market. NHS primary care trusts are no longer required to prepare and conduct a full EU-wide tendering process as they can choose any one of these seven consortia. This means a considerable speeding up of the procurement and negotiation time scale from a typical two years to several months, which is also likely to reduce the excessive bidding costs typical of PFI projects.

While Express LIFT appears to offer significant advantages to procurers in the current climate, its future is by no means secure. Thus, a recent study (Beck et al., 2009) has indicated that many public sector LIFT participants viewed this type of procurement as being expensive and were concerned about its long-term affordability implications. Given that local NHS Trusts will face drastic budget cuts in the future (together with the pressures associated with a declining supplier market already mentioned), there is therefore every possibility that they will rethink plans to become heavily involved in these schemes.

PFI and the Illusion of Risk Transfer

With the UK PFI programme being severely affected by the funding crisis, the UK government announced in March 2009 that taxpayers' money would be used to rescue PFI projects in the form of bridging loans of between £1 billion and £2 billion in 2009-10 (Hayman, 2009; Hencke, 2009, Milmo et al. 2009). This policy appears to have evolved from two objectives. Firstly, as was evidenced by announcements that PFI projects which had been 'in the pipeline'would now be accelerated, the UK government initially viewed PFI procurement as one of its principal tools for stimulating the economy as well as a means for protecting vulnerable sectors such as the construction industry (Hellowell, 2009). Secondly, the UK has recently reiterated its commitment to PFI as a means of coping with the expected 'cash freeze' in public sector capital expenditure from 2011 (Gribben, 2009).

Irrespective of these objectives, the UK's planned recovery via PFI has largely stalled. This has led critics such as the Liberal Democrat Shadow Chancellor Vince Cable to call for a move to a simpler, more honest, system of public investment for public projects, while encouraging the government to dedicate greater resources to the rescue of PFI. As a consequence of these measures the UK government's Infrastructure Finance Unit (dubbed 'the Treasury bank') now lends directly to PFI projects and also indirectly to them via government-owned banks. Although initially restricting its support to bridging loans, the Treasury bank can also provide the full amount of senior debt required by a PFI project. It is also considering other ways of helping finance stalled PFI projects by, for example, underwriting bank debt and by providing equity bridging loans.

According to the UK Treasury, 110 major PFI infrastructure projects worth an estimated £13 billion then in the pipeline would be saved from collapse by this support. In this context the Treasury has announced that it plans to provide co-funding, as well as provide the full financial requirement for some projects if necessary. Priority will be given to waste recycling schemes with a view of helping the UK avoid the heavy EU fines it will incur if it misses the mandatory targets to halve landfill use by 2013 (Hencke, 2009). Additionally, promises have been made of financial help for ten PFI hospital projects delayed due to lack of finance.

Notwithstanding questions about the economic efficacy of these measures in light of the severe problems faced by the UK PFI market, these proposals face severe conceptual and political objections. Perhaps most significantly, the high cost of PFI has traditionally been justified on account of the significant, and often disputed, transfer of risk from the public to the private sector (see, e.g., Broadbent, Gill and Laughlin, 2005). Under current plans, the notion of risk transfer, which is assumed to create important incentives for a prudent structuring of deals by the private sector partners, would be largely undermined (because these financiers could rely on government guarantees or subsidies in case of project default). Moreover, given that a number of studies have highlighted the high cost of PFI projects (see, e.g., Froud and Shaoul, 2001; Shaoul, 2009) such guarantees and subsidies would have the potential of pushing the cost of these deals beyond what is politically defensible.

Perhaps unsurprisingly, the proposed support by the government for PFI has faced criticism from several political quarters. Accordingly, the Treasury spokesman of the Conservative party, Phillip Hammond, noted that "if you take the private finance out of PFI, you haven't got much left…and if you transfer the financial risk back to the public sector, then that has to be reflected in the structure of the contract" (Timmins, 2009a, p. 11). Similar criticisms have been made by the general secretary of the Trades Union Congress (TUC) who noted that such an arrangement will allow the privatisation of the profits and the nationalisation of the losses (Leftly, 2009). His main concern is that many PFIs have been, and are being, financed by HBOS and RBS which would mean that government is subsidising PFI contracts in order to guarantee returns to the banks rescued with tax payers' money.

THE GERMAN EXPERIENCE

While the discussion about appropriate approaches to the rescue or reform of the UK PFI market is ongoing, news about the gradual recovery of the French and German economies are likely to add a new angle to this debate. Although Germany was initially criticised for the relative modesty of its stimulus package of ca $50 billion (Dougherty and Dempsey, 2009), it has now become obvious that the country has in fact invested heavily in a recovery package which is already paying off. Thus, it has been reported that Germany's public spending ratio will rise to about 49% of gross domestic product this year and to over 50% in 2010, which would represent the highest ratio since the 1960s (Reuters, 2009). Specifically, an IMF survey reports that Germany is engaging in a wide range of stimulus measures including cuts in personal income tax, increased spending on infrastructure and especially transportation, special measures to protect liquidity-constrained or vulnerable groups via measures such as increased child support and support for vulnerable sectors such as the construction industry (IMF, 2009). Additional measures include a loan guarantee programme to support small and medium sized enterprises and a simplification of public procurement.

What is less well known is that some of these measures have been possible, in part, because Germany does not have a strong tradition of relying extensively on private finance, PFI and other forms of PPP in infrastructure procurement. This avoidance of complex deals with private financiers, not only enabled the country to procure infrastructure at competitive prices in the past (see, e.g., Proverbs and Holt, 2000 for analysis of productivity and costs in the German construction industry), but also made it possible for policy makers to respond quickly to the challenges of the current crisis.

While it would be premature to compare recovery rates across European countries (especially on account of the more pronounced downturn experienced in Germany and France), and even more so to argue that the recovery in the UK is hampered by the government's ongoing commitment to PFI, these observations nonetheless raise serious questions about the sustainability of the UK PPP model in times of crisis.

CONCLUSION

At the macro-level, PFI by its very nature increases the reliance of the state on private capital and creates strong dependencies on a well functioning and liquid system of private credit and finance. When this system breaks down, the state faces strong imperatives to provide financial support to financial services providers, not only because it is essential to ensure the continued functioning of this system, but also because now public finance provides essential public services by proxy. However, the provision of such financial support can be very costly as has been illustrated by the fact that measures to rescue banks undertaken by the UK government increased the UK's ratio of fiscal stimulus relative to GDP to 19.8% (by far the highest ratio in the G20 countries); even though other stimulus measure accounted for only 1.5%. Meanwhile, the fact that a large proportion of procurement is conducted with the involvement of private finance is likely to reduce the ability of the state to launch counter-measures speedily and effectively.

This increase in vulnerability of the state sector is paralleled by problems at the local level. For local public sector procurers, for whom involvement in PFI is challenging at the best of times, participation in such projects may well be prohibitive in light of future budget cuts and uncertainties about the liquidity of potential private sector partners. As a consequence, there is a possibility that, unless alternative financing mechanisms such as municipal bonds are available, these procurers will be unable to benefit from competitive tension which a future market for construction and services is likely to offer. At the very worst the combination of these factors could result in a vicious cycle where increasingly costly investment in failing models of PPP-based procurement deprive the public sector of the means to contribute to a recovery via public sector investment.

PFI at its core is based on the assumption that the private sector, and especially private financial services providers are well placed to take on some of the risks involved in public sector procurement. One the fundamental problems with this idea is that the actions of financial services providers create downside risks on their own. These downside risks, in turn, appear to be more contagious where the public sector relies on close collaboration with private capital.

The experience of the 2007-09 credit crunch is that the new and innovative financial instruments did not so much transfer risk to those more able to manage it efficiently as hide or obscure risk such that it could hardly be managed at all.

Perhaps not surprisingly, there are now proposals by the Policy Exchange think-tank for establishment of a publicly-funded UK infrastructure bank to provide the necessary finance not only for state schools and hospitals, but also for energy, transport, communication and utility projects (Helm et al., 2009; Timmins, 2009c).

Drawing lessons from Germany, Ireland and Australia, the proposed infrastructure bank would combine the roles of the Public Works Loan Board (the central government conduit for borrowing by local governments and health authorities etc.), the HM Treasury Infrastructure Finance Unit (which provides public finance for PFI projects) and Parnerships UK (which advises government departments, local authorities and others about PPPs). The bank would set investment priorities and guarantee an element of senior debt so as to reduce the cost of the remaining private sector borrowing.

By such means, the UK government would move as much infrastructure investment as possible off the public sector balance sheet by creating a new low-risk framework to encourage private investment and so significantly reduce the cost of capital for infrastructure projects. This proposal would seem to retain the advantages of PFIs and PPPs whilst avoiding (or at least minimizing) a repeat of the unsustainable costs imposed on the public sector in the event of any future financial meltdown.

REFERENCES

Anon. 2008a. How the Financial Crisis will affect Local Government. *The Guardian*, 8 October.

Anon. 2008b. Council not 'reckless' with Cash. *BBC News*, http://news.bbc.uk/1/hi/uk politics, Accessed on 10 October.

Bailey, S. J., Asenova, D. and Hood, J. 2009. Making Widespread Use of Local Government Bonds in Scotland? *Public Money and Management*, 29(1):11-18.

Bailey, S.J. 1999. *Local Government Economics: Principles and Practice.* London: Palgrave Macmillan.

Bailey, S.J. 2004. *Strategic Public Finance.* London: Palgrave Macmillan.

Beck, M., Toms, S., Greener, I., Mannion, R., Brown, S., Fitzsimmons, D. and Lunt, N. 2009. *The Role and Effectiveness of Public – Private Partnerships (NHS LIFT) in the Development of Enhanced Primary Care Premises and Services*" (Report for the National Co-ordinating Centre for NHS Service Delivery and Organisation RandD (NCCSDO) (pp.330).

Broadbent, J., Gill, J. and Laughlin, R. 2005. *Risk, Uncertainty and Accounting: The Case of the Private Finance Initiative in the UK's National Health Service*. Critical Perspectives on Accounting Conference, New York, April.

Cohn, D. 2004. The Public-private Partnership 'Fetish': Moving Beyond the Rhetoric. *Revue Governance*, 1(2), December.

Crotty, J. 2007. *If Financial Market Competition is so Intense, Why are Financial Firm Profits so High? Reflections on the Current 'Golden Age' of Finance*. Political Economy Research Institute, Working Paper Series, Number 134, University of Massachusetts Amherst.

Curtis, P. 2009. Government may have to take on Risk of PFI Deals. *The Guardian*, 27 January.

Davis, S. 2003. *Investment Banking: Addressing the Management Issue.*, New York: Palgrave.

Dieter Helm, D., Wardlaw, J., and Caldeco, B. 2009. *Delivering a 21st Century Infrastructure for Britain.* London: Policy Exchange.

Dougherty, C. and Dempsey, J. 2009. Germany at Odds with U.S. Over Crisis. *New York Times*, 10 March.

Fegan, C. 2008. Scots Councils' £40m Invested in Icelandic Banks at Risk. *The Herald*, 11 October.

Fingland, L. and Bailey, S.J. 2008. The Stability and Growth Pact: Its Credibility and Sustainability. *Public Money and Management,* 28(4): 223-30.

Froud, J. and Shaoul, J. 2001. Appraising and Evaluating PFI for NHS Hospitals. *Financial Accountability and Management*, 17(3): 247-70.

Goodhart, C.A.E. 2009. *The Regulatory Response to the Financial Crisis.* Cheltenham: Edward Elgar Publishing.

Greenspan, A. 2004. Economic Flexibility. Speech to HM Treasury Enterprise Conference, London.

Gribben, R. 2009. Government Plans for New PFI 'Bank' Criticised. *The Daily Telegraph*, 2 March.

Hayman, A. 2009. £13 Billion Rescue Plan for PFI Projects. *Regeneration and Renewal*, 9 March, 5.

Hellowell, M. 2009. Loss of Initiative. *The Guardian*, 4 February.

Help, D., Wardlaw, J. and Caldecott, B. 2009. *Delivering 21st Century Infrastructure in Britain*, Internet publication available from *www.sussex.ac.uk/.*

Hencke, D. 2009. Treasury Rescues Big Building Projects with £2 billion Injection. *The Guardian*, 3 March, 12.

IMF. 2009. Stimulus Measures Bolstering Demand Amid Crisis. IMF Says, IMF Online Survey, 6 February.

Kirkup, J. 2009. Hospital Projects Scrapped as Credit Crunch hits PFI Schemes. *The Telegraph*, 3 March.

Klein, L.R. and Shabbir, T. 2006. *Recent Financial Crises.* Cheltenham: Edward Elgar Publishing.

Leftly, M. 2009. Treasury's New Man to Review the Future of 'Broke' PFI Schemes. *The Independent on Sunday*, 22 March, 78.

McAlpine, J. 2009. Schools Suffer Over PFI Mess. *The Sunday Times*, 22 February.

McQuaid, R.W., and Scherrer, W. 2008. Public-private Partnerships in the European Union: Experiences in the UK, Germany and Austria. *Uprava*, 6(2): 7-34.

Milmo, D., Inman, P., and Durrani, A. 2009. A Bridge too far for PFI Schemes. *The Guardian*, 18 April.

O'Connor, S. 2008. Hospital Project Hit by US Bond Insurers Crisis. *Financial Times*, 3 March.

Proverbs, D. and Holt, G. 2000. Reducing Construction Costs: European Best Practice Supply Chain Implications. *European Journal of Purchasing and Supply Management*, 6(3-4): 149-58.

Reuters. 2009. German Public Spending up 50%. Reuters Report in *Strait Times*, 7 June.

Shaoul, J. 2009. *Financial Black Holes: Accounting for Privately Financed Roads in the UK*, Report to ICAS, Edinburgh.

Stiff, P. 2008. Hospital and Road financing Squeezed by Credit Crunch. *The Times*, 10 March.

Timmins, N. 2009a. Projects Seek Partners. *Financial Times*, 24 February, 11.

Timmins, N. 2009b. Seven Groups set to win NHS Building Deals. *Financial Times*, 13 March, 2.

Timmins, N. 2009c. Think-tank Pushes for Rreform to Infrastructure Finance. *Financial Times*, 31 August, 2.

Tran, M. 2009. Iceland Votes to Repay Britain's Lost Bank Savings. *The Guardian*, 29 August.

Section D:

Health, Safety and the Environment

In: Understanding Risk
Editor: Matthias Beck
ISBN: 978-1-62618-686-6

Chapter 13

RISK AND HEALTH POLICY: THE CASE OF THE UK NATIONAL HEALTH SERVICE

Ian Greener*

School of Applied Social Sciences, Durham University, Durham, UK

ABSTRACT

A central tenet of the risk society thesis is that, in today's world, individuals are required by the State to take on far greater responsibility for their own welfare provision. The present wave of NHS reforms have systematically moved risk away from the State and towards not only individuals (Beck, 1992; Giddens, 1994), but also to the public, private and not-for-profit organisations that now provide healthcare in the UK, and to the managers and doctors within them. This paper examines the process by which this has happened, particularly since 1997, exploring the ways that risk has passed away from the state. It is argued that the State has created national bodies such as the Healthcare Commission and National Institute for Clinical Excellence (NICE) which have little independence from government in practice, but which allow the current Labour government to argue that they are not making contentious decisions concerned with treatment regulation and inspection. As well as this, the health service can be conceptualised as inverting the settlement upon which the NHS was created in 1948, moving from a system of central accountability but local paternalism, to central paternalism but local accountability (Greener and Powell, 2008). Organisational risk has therefore passed from the State to local organisations, especially in relation to NHS budgeting, and at the same time the State has managed to achieve unprecedented operational control over the NHS through its use of performance management. This process is exemplified by the Public Finance Initiative (PFI), which should be regarded as transferring risk between the public and private sectors, and needs to be assessed in terms of the relative capacities of each of those sectors to manage that risk (Asenova and Beck, 2003).

* E-mail: ian.greener@durham.ac.uk.

Introduction

This paper is concerned with the transfers in risk that have resulted as a consequence of health reforms from the UK Labour government, especially since 2000. It suggests that, considering reform as a process of reallocating risk, shows that these reforms are unsustainable as they have misaligned risk and accountability, largely as a result of the individualisation of individual health risk and by blaming organisations such as Hospital Trusts and Primary Care Trusts when things go wrong. This paper suggests that it is possible to construct an alternative programme of reform that aligns risk and accountability, and which can also serve to reinvigorate local debates around the delivery of health services.

Health and Risk

An excellent starting point for considering the role of risk in health, especially with regard to health reform, is work by Peter Taylor-Gooby (2006). This author argues that the present wave of reforms in the UK, because of their over-concern with business plans and rationality, are in danger of undermining public trust in health services. Taylor-Gooby suggests that the main reason for this is that the relationship most people have with healthcare in primarily emotional and affective, a relationship based on their trust in health institutions, whereas the present reforms ignore these factors and assume a rational model of the patient-actor that does not allow reference to such ties. The result is a decline in public trust in the health system, in this case, specifically the NHS. The picture Taylor-Gooby presents is not a promising one, but rather one in which reform undermines public trust in the NHS.

It is possible to take Taylor-Gooby's insights further. This paper will argue that the present wave of health reforms undermine trust relationships not just between the state and the public, but also across the health system more generally. To illustrate this, it is first necessary to explore how risk has been used in social analysis. After working through a range of risk areas where the paper will make its case, it will then conclude by suggesting an alternative framework upon which health services might be organised.

Risk

Work examining risk can appear a little bewildering in terms of the multiple ways the word is defined. Beck's analyses (most widely read in Beck, 1992), which include examinations of health more generally, tend to cast risk as a general 'bad'; a range of problems from which the public are trying to escape. As individuals are risk-averse (which is hardly surprising given that risks in Beck's work are usually conceptualised as being bad things), they seek to avoid these risks, but are asked by the state to take more and more on board. Specifically in healthcare, individuals are asked to become more and more aware of lifestyle factors such as smoking and drinking, around which extensive television advertising takes place, but also increasingly for their weight (in the face of huge media concerns about obesity), their cholesterol level (with products abounding that promise to lower it) and their diet (in which we are encouraged to eat more fruit and vegetables, although national guidelines as to how much seem to differ considerably). As the public become more and more aware of the risks that seem to surround them, and the dangers of not conforming to them, they are required to modify their behaviour and take responsibility not only for their health, but also for their day-to-day lifestyle.

However, in terms of day-to-day health, there is something of a problem with this analysis. Even though individuals might be aware that they are eating unhealthily, the effects of doing so often don't appear for several years. Smoking might make us a little short of breath today, but is unlikely to cause a serious disease until well into the future. Being obese today may only cause heart disease or diabetes well into the future. There is a substantial time lag between much unhealthy behaviour and its consequences.

The importance of the link between risk and time does not just appear with regard to the public and their lifestyle. It is also important across a range of other relationships within the health system. This has become particularly important in recent health reforms because of the UK government's obsession with trying to drive improvements that occur extremely quickly. Time has become an obsession for Labour with clearly specified performance targets (Secretary of State for Health, 2000) that have clear milestones and are often themselves concerned with time, particular with respect to how long patients might have to wait for their care. Overall, labour have invested considerable additional sums in the NHS (Wanless, 2002) and are to be congratulated for it after decades of comparative under-funding, but have demanded significant, rapid reform in return.

It is therefore extremely important to understand the link between risk and time in health care systems, and to do so the paper will introduce an additional mediating concept; namely that of accountability. The application of this concept highlights show the importance of time when considering health and risk.

Accountability

Because of the importance of time to individuals in need of care, to the Labour government, and, as a result of Labour's health reforms, to health organisations more generally, there is a need to conceptualise how these relationships have changed, and to assess what they might have in common.

In the context of exploring health and risk, accountability can be considered as the means by which the two become linked. In the sense of being brought to account, accountability links risk to health through time. Behaviour, by both health organisations and the general public, can be regarded as having to engage frequently with risks of various kinds. At an individual level, every time we eat or drink we have choices between healthy and unhealthy options. However, these choices do not really matter at the individual, one-off level; but they do come to matter cumulatively, and over what are often substantial periods of time. If the individual is unfortunate in terms of the combination between food choices (or choices about drink, drugs or tobacco) and their biological ability to withstand such substances, then their body will literally bring them to account at a later date through illness or injury. Some of us are just unlucky, and may lead relatively blameless lives and still become extremely ill due to factors entirely outside of their control. Others may put their material bodies through years of abuse and apparently escape blameless. However, death comes to us all, and there is some link between how we choose to live and the quality of life we might expect to have. We are all brought to account for our lifestyle risks to some extent.

Equally, at the organisational level, the raft of performance measures introduced by Labour have imposed a new locus of calculation upon those working in healthcare. If the NHS, for its first forty years at least, was primarily organised around trust relationships (Klein, 1993), it has increasingly become organised around contracts, service frameworks and performance management systems that specify exactly what is required of them. In order to measure whether these are being satisfied, some system of measurement is necessary. However, as soon as systemic measurement begins to occur, it has the potential to undermine and replace trust. Doctors, required to work specific hours rather than being expected merely to do their job, might actually work less, and become begrudging of the additional time they formerly gave the NHS through goodwill. Managers, having to conform to national standards rather than being given discretion on how best to run their services, might game performance management systems rather than doing what they regard as the best thing for their local public (Greener, 2005; Mannion et al., 2001). In each case, the problem is that, by being brought to account for their behaviour through a performance management system, there is a danger that the performance management system becomes, not a guide to behaviour, but a rulebook instead. It comes to specify not the minimum standard expected, but the only standard. As Le Grand (1997) has suggested, by treating all those working within health services as 'knaves', professionals no longer wish to behave as 'knights'.

Accountability links risk with time in that it introduces both a system for measuring risk, and also a temporal element that decides what the consequences of not dealing with risk might be. In the case of individual behaviour, our material bodies may bring us to account for not taking care over lifestyle risks. We cannot really control when this might happen, and we may be brought to account for relatively minor examples of careless behaviour if we are unfortunate.

Organisationally, the systems by which risk is measured are designed not naturalistically through an independent measure over which we have no control (although policymakers or managers may wish them to appear as such), but instead through the creation of systems of measurement that bring organisational risks to light, and then create discretion in how policymakers deal with such risks. Risks often create spaces in which policymakers, far from taking objective, scientific behaviours, may engage in highly opportunistic behaviour where it suits them politically (Beck et al., 2005). As Munro (1999) illustrates, systems of performance management are not automatic, but instead give those who control them discretion in how they deal with those who seem to be failing to deal with them, in whether or not they are used to bring risk violators to account. This creates windows for time to enter the analysis – there may be a considerable gap between a violation of a measure and being brought to account (as in unhealthy behaviour), or it may occur far more quickly, with a swift penalty being introduced.

In the context of a modern health system such as the NHS, at least four dimensions of risk can be demonstrated using this analysis; health risk (as in the example of health lifestyle risk discussed above); political risk–the risk of being held to account in a political system when things go wrong; clinical risk–the risk of being held to account for a particular clinical intervention; and organisational risk–the risk of being held to account for the way a particular health organisation is run. These four elements will now be analysed in turn.

Health Risk

Health risks are the risks to the individual, or group of individuals, which are incurred as a result of their lifestyles. This is not to say that lifestyle, even broadly defined, is the only factor relevant to health. Both our environment and our genetics are also hugely important, with the former being regarded as particularly important in public health movements examining improvement in sanitation and public disease risks (McKeown, 1976) and the latter in much modern research attempting to establish the link between hereditable conditions and illness. Both environment and lifestyle bring their own risks, but because of the increase in focus, especially in health policy in the UK, upon lifestyle (Secretary of State for Health, 1996, 2006), it is worth considering this factor in greater depth here.

The increase in concern with lifestyle factors in healthcare is most associated with the movement known as the 'new public health' (Peterson and Lupton, 1996) which brings together risk and accountability in an explicit way. The new public health analysis suggest that, as the state requires us to take greater responsibility for our lifestyles, advertising to us on television (the UK government is now the largest single advertiser on British television) and trying to get us to see our GPs for health check-ups as well as when we are ill, that it is attempting a kind of Foucaultian move in getting us to police our own healthcare. As we become more and more aware of the health risks that surround us, and how dangerous they might be to us (or how they can bring us to account through illness, disease and injury in the language of this paper), we are meant to try and change our behaviours and mitigate these risks as a result.

A process of learning and time is involved in the movement towards us becoming fully-fledged risk adjustors for our own health, however. Even though children are encouraged to eat healthily in schools, it does not seem to diminish their demands for chocolate. In order to understand that they are being subject to lifestyle risk, the public must first be given a means to understand that risk, and of knowing they are subjecting themselves to it. If smoking is not regarded as unhealthy behaviour in a community, individuals that smoke may not regard themselves as subjecting themselves to risk.

Once a health risk has been established in a community's mind, it must then be persuaded to take some responsibility for it. The straightforward way to try and achieve this is to show how they will be held to account if they do not. Cigarette packets are stamped with bold words such as 'Smoking kills' to try and achieve this; but time creates a problem for such campaigns in that smoking a packet of cigarettes is unlikely to kill any individual immediately. In health lifestyles, what economists call the 'tyranny of discounting' reigns, in that the consequences of an individual unhealthy act are likely to be years away. Although individuals may understand the risk they are subjecting themselves to, it is made an abstract, theoretical risk because the consequences are so far off. Cause and effect are broken through the considerable time gap between the two. Therefore we may come to believe that unhealthy behaviour is not bringing us to account, and this belief may be exacerbated by us all knowing individuals who (at least anecdotally) have been fortunate enough to engage in unhealthy behaviours and still live long lives.

What has made this problem worse in the UK is that the National Health Service has been more concerned with illness than with health (Baggott, 2006). The funding of acute care ahead of primary care or public health has been a long-standing feature of the health service, and is entirely understandable from a political standpoint. It takes a brave policymaker to be able to make a stand on delivering less care today for those suffering from illness and injury in order to spend more on preventative care; as future illnesses, by definition, have not yet occurred. People have not yet been brought to account. However, those that need treatment now will be prepared to campaign and will be supported by the media in demanding that new drugs are made available, and that their care is funded today. Today's ill people provoke an emotional response of needing care, and potentially bad publicity for even the most altruistic politician. Tomorrow's sick do not. Moving resources from acute care to primary care may mean that less of today's sick are treated; and they are unlikely to let this pass without campaigning.

Equally, moving resources away from acute care may lead the public to believe that the state is not longer taking responsibility for their care. The NHS was set up at the time of the founding of the modern welfare state in the UK as a means of tackling what Beveridge described as the 'giant' of disease, metaphorically presented as an obstacle blocking the path to a civilised society (Beveridge, 1942). The public regard access to the NHS as a right, but only tend to make use of it when ill. Attempts to persuade the public that they must take a more general notion of health will take a great deal of time and energy, and even then may not succeed.

The most visible means by which the state is attempting to form a close link between health risk and treatment is through its suggestion that those who have led more blameless lifestyles will have better access to health services in some treatment areas than those who have not. This has only occurred across a limited range of areas so far, but has the potential to be expanded, particularly in the future in relation to genetic risk. So at present, smokers may be required to give up before receiving cancer treatment (or at least non-smokers be treated first), the obese required to give up weight before being given NHS resources, and those that have drug problems and are HIV-positive be required to give up drugs before they are treated. An extension of this mentality would mean that, in the future, those with genetic predispositions to breast cancer, for example, may have to fund their own cancer treatment if they did not have a voluntary mastectomy through publicly funded care first.

What this indicates is that the state, although it has largely failed in the UK to move resources significantly from acute care into public health and primary care settings, is requiring us to take greater responsibility for our own lifestyles, and suggesting that if we do not, that it will make us take responsibility for the consequences, should our bodies later hold us to account.

POLITICAL RISK

Political risk is clearly linked to health risk in healthcare, and is the risk of who is held to account when things go wrong in the healthcare system. At the time of the NHS's founding, a system of central accountability and local paternalism was in place (Greener and Powell, 2008). The state was held to be politically accountable for the activities of the NHS through Parliament, whereas most healthcare decisions were actually in the hands of doctors employed in local healthcare organisations. To paraphrase Bevan, the corridors of Whitehall rang to the sound of every dropped bedpan. When things went wrong in the early years of the

NHS, especially with regard to funding, it was the job of the opposition to try and hold the government to account. The public, still largely grateful for receiving the NHS's care free, were rather more compliant in waiting and in receiving care in (by today's standards) poor facilities and surroundings, and so there was little pressure locally to try and drive improvements in care.

This system of accountability, however, has undergone something of a transformation over the sixty years of the NHS, and particularly in more recent times. The Labour government has created a number of notionally arms-length NHS organisations such as the National Institute for Clinical Excellence (NICE) and the Healthcare Commission, that are responsible for decisions about which treatments will be funded through the NHS and for the inspection of healthcare, respectively. Alongside the creation of these organisations, it has delegated NHS funds to Primary Care Trusts (PCTs) so that they now control over 85% of the total healthcare budget. Politicians have argued that, as result of these changes, they are no longer responsible for particular problems in the NHS; they have tried to pass accountability elsewhere, typically to local healthcare organisations. At the same time as this, the state has found increasingly sophisticated ways of calculating what poor performance entails, and of trying to hold local managers to account through threats that managers of low performing organisations will be sacked. The state, however, is able to get involved where situations judged to be locally unfair emerge–where local PCTs refuse to prescribe new drugs, the Secretary of State for Health has got involved and over-ruled them. The NHS is now a system of national paternalism, but local accountability – an inversion of the organisational form of sixty years ago. The risk for political problems resulting from NHS organisation have been passed squarely to the local level.

A singular example of this change is the Private Finance Initiative (PFI). PFI attempts to address the long-standing problem of how to pay for infrastructural improvements to the NHS. In this, the problem of time and its link to accountability have again been at the fore (Greener, 2008a). Because capital projects take an often substantial period of time to complete, and NHS budgets have been under considerable pressure for much of the service' history, capital expenditure has usually been regarded as a low priority. The Hospital Plan of the 1960s attempted to address the problem of crumbling NHS infrastructure, but was substantially undermined by the financial crises of the late 1960s (Klein, 2006). This situation was not helped by publicly-funded projects often running well behind schedule and over cost (Mohan, 2002). Politicians, having to choose between public investment made today that might subject them to risk if it comes in behind time or over-budget, and health expenditure on today's ill or injured, understandably perhaps, in times of financial stringency, chose the latter. Equally, engaging in capital building requires politicians to effectively bequeath new facilities to their successors. They may be reluctant to do this, since doing so would mean taking responsibility for the risk of such projects today, whereas the rewards would fall to their successors.

PFI attempts to get around these problems in a number of ways. First, it involves a transfer of risk from the public to the private sector (Asenova and Beck, 2003) in which the private sector takes on the capital building project and provides maintenance to the project. In return, the public sector pays for the project over a period of between typically twenty-five and thirty-five years. Capital building projects are approved and delivered quickly, the state is able to claim that any problems with regard to the problems are outside of its control, as it is the result of local decisions, and the NHS gets new facilities it desperately needs. It would seem that everyone is happy as a result.

However, there are substantial questions as to whether the private sector is being paid an unreasonably large premium for taking on the risk of new capital builds, and questions as to the quality of the new builds have also been raised. More generally, the question as to whether the private sector is effectively un-accountable for its involvement in PFI projects also remains open at present (Monbiot, 2001). Political risk, in sum, appears to be passing from the state to local health organisations, who in the case of PFI, were often left to negotiate contracts with private providers without much guidance or help from the state, despite the policy originating there and it being effectively the only way to raise finance (Public Finance, 2007).

As the state has passed control away from itself and to local health organisations, the assessment of both medical risk and organisational risk have become more acute. These will be dealt with in turn.

Clinical Risk

Clinical risk is defined as the risk taken, usually by front-line staff such as doctors and nurses, when engaging in clinical interventions. As noted above, at the creation of the NHS doctors took little clinical risk in practice, even though most healthcare decisions were largely made by them in their local NHS organisations, as accountability was taken by central policymakers through the Parliamentary system. Doctors took risks in respect of the medicine they practiced, but this was in an age before national medical ethics bodies existed, where patients were unlikely to challenge a diagnosis, and where medical negligence cases were virtually unheard of. Doctors seemed to hold all the decision-making power, but, as a result, had relatively little say in terms of how they were remunerated or as to the total budget allocated to healthcare, which was decided by the government of the day (Klein, 1990). However, in line with the changes in political accountability outlined above, the way that medical risk was assessed have changed significantly.

A number of factors fed into changes in the way that clinical risk and accountability were reformulated. In the 1960s particularly, disability rights campaigners questioned the way that doctors were attempting to 'normalise' people with limbs missing through the use of prosthetics, for example, with less regard for whether these improved people's lives than whether they made the public generally more accepting (Welshman and Walmsley, 2006). The feminist movement in the same period questioned the medical treatment of childbirth particularly, and whether confinement and the use of techniques such as episiotomy were being done to make doctors' lives easier rather than to achieve patient benefit (Lewis, 1990). Increasing clamours for greater medical regulation came about after high profile cases. This was due in part to the fact that the UK body responsible for the self-regulation of medicine, the General Medical Council, had come under question from the media and government for appearing to be more interested in protecting the reputation of individual doctors rather than protecting the public (Salter, 2004).

Successive governments, especially during the 1980s, appeared to regard the medical profession more as a barrier to managerial change than a partner in running healthcare; and what measurements were possible seemed to indicate large variations in medical practice (Carter et al., 1992). Within the medical profession, the movement towards 'Evidence-based medicine' offered a more scientific way of giving care, and was latched onto by the state as a means of standardising treatment while allowing deviations from those standards to be measured (Maynard, 2006). The state made these changes in the name of patients of the NHS, who had become more and more likely to blame doctors where they failed to save the lives of their friends and family, and where medical insurance became an increasing necessity to protect clinicians from any mistakes they might make in their practice.

Evidence-based medicine, medical insurance, performance measures of clinical practice and the increased focus on clinical governance, which attempts to assess cases where clinical problems have occurred and to rigorously investigate them, have meant that notions of medical risk has become increasingly more fine-grained and pervasive. Medical cases where a case for negligence can be made are widely reported in the media, which seems unable to differentiate between poor clinical practice and cases where patients demands have become unreasonable (Tallis, 2005). Patients are encouraged to consider themselves consumers, and legal practices specialising in medical negligence claims are able to try and claim compensation for them where they believe they have been harmed as a result of NHS treatment. Clinicians can be forgiven for believing that they are sometimes under siege from increasingly demanding patients, from the state passing responsibility for the NHS to local organisations which are still largely run by clinicians, and from the requirement to conform to the rigours of evidence-based medicine and the new performance measures it is able to generate. At the same time as clinical risk has become of greater significance, organisational risk has also grown considerably.

Organisational Risk

Organisational risk is defined as the risk in relation to the extent to which local organisations are held accountable when things are held to have gone wrong in the NHS. At the creation of the NHS there was very little organisational risk; accountability was centrally-held in Parliament and, even during the scandals over mental health provision in the 1960s (Robb, 1967), organisations were not held to account. One of the problems experienced by those in government is that there were very few measures of organisational activity available to them for much of the NHS's history, and those few statistics that were available were unreliable and had been produced so long after the event as to be nearly worthless. Enoch Powell, one of the more energetic Ministers for Health in the 1960s, and the architect of the Hospital Plan, made very clear his concerns over the lack of information that the Department of Health held about the day-to-day activities of the NHS (Powell, 1966). Without any measurement of individual organisational activities, it was very difficult to hold NHS organisations to account in any meaningful way.

As suggested above, however, politicians grew tired of accepting responsibility for the NHS's failings, especially where they held little or no control over the day-to-day running of the service. The difficult financial environment of the 1970s, moreover, helped more managerialist approaches to running health organisations gain legitimacy in the 1980s. In 1983, the 'Griffiths' inquiry into NHS management (Department of Health and Social

Security, 1983) led to the appointment of General Managers in hospitals, later to become Chief Executives; and in 1989 the 'internal market' was created (Secretary of State for Health, 1989) to try and make healthcare organisations more business-like through the use of private sector-style disciplines. The 1990s saw a 'becalming' of health policy (Wainwright, 1998) in which politicians became, after a period of radical reform, more circumspect in attempting to drive health reform because of its electoral sensitivities (the NHS remains the nearest thing the UK has to a national religion), but by 2000, Labour were signalling more radical reform was on the cards.

In the NHS Plan (Secretary of State for Health, 2000) Labour proposed a performance management system that made it clear that individual organisations were to be held to account for failing to achieve government-specified standards for the delivery of care. Performance management was not new to the NHS, having existed sporadically since the 1980s (Pollitt, 1985). What was new was that managers could now face sacking if their organisations did not meet nationally-specified standards.

In addition to the performance management system, Labour recast the internal market so that PCTs held most of the NHS's budget, and were required to commission (purchase) care in a way similarly to the way that the Conservative internal market of the 1980s had proposed, but never implemented. Labour, to increase competition for care, brought in private sector treatment centres and encouraged not-for-profits such as the Nuffield Foundation to expand their NHS work. By 2007 the use of market mechanisms had cost the NHS about an extra £1bn (Healthcare Commission and National Audit Office, 2008), but with little definable result.

What had happened, however, was that the NHS had attempted, through the delegation of budgets and the use of the centrally-imposed performance management system, to find ways of blaming local managers for any problems that appeared in their organisations. This would seem to make a good deal of sense intuitively – if local managers are not doing their jobs they should be held to account. However, whereas a rhetoric of decentralisation and localisation has come from successive Secretaries of State for Health, the performance management system has led to a marked increase in the degree of central control over health services. When combined with the use of inspections from the Healthcare Commission and the use of clinical standards such as National Service Frameworks, this has significantly reduced the amount of local 'decision space' for managers to work within (Peckham et al., 2005). It also remains the case that it is odd to blame NHS managers entirely for the performance of their local organisations when examinations of the measures used by government show substantial problems, both in terms of their reliability, and in terms of the extent to which managers can be said to be responsible for the variables they are being measured against (Street, 2000).

Perhaps the most visible example of the establishment of organisational risk came in 2006/7 when the NHS, as a whole, ran into substantial budgetary problems. Again, it is a tenant of good management to work within the budget available, so it would seem sensible to hold managers unable to do this to account. However, the budget deficits occurred in an environment where centrally imposed pay increases for doctors led to local organisations facing substantial increases in their costs (Kings Fund, 2006); where PFI builds (which had become the only way of getting NHS capital investment) had created substantial increases in capita costs for the organisations benefiting from them; and where a new, centrally-imposed market for care was being imposed upon local health organisations who now faced competition from treatment centres that held the potential to undermine their cost base. Local managers needed to take account of these factors, but central policymakers had been careless in subjecting managers to these risks, and in refusing to take any responsibility for them.

As such, the present reforms have meant a substantial movement in health risk, political risk clinical risk and organisational risk. The next section considers the implications of these transfers and asks if there might be a more appropriate way to reform healthcare.

DISCUSSION: WHAT ARE THE IMPLICATIONS OF CONSIDERING RISK IN THIS WAY?

Health risk, as suggested above, has increasingly been formulated by the state as part of an attempt to make individuals more and more responsible for their lifestyles. The central problem with this strategy is that, despite widespread coverage of health campaigns around lifestyle issues, obesity and alcohol consumption still appear to be rising, while smoking cessation is hitting something of a plateau. Part of the explanation for this is that individuals are being asked to behave responsibly at the same time as they are expected to behave in a new role as healthcare consumers (Greener, 2008b). Giving patients greater choice about where and when they will be treated, as well as whether they would like complementary and alternative medicine (which may often have little or no evidence base), puts the public in a relationship with health services where the NHS exists to meet their needs, rather than to instruct them on how to have a healthier lifestyle. The public expect that, no matter how self-inflicted their condition is, the NHS is there to help them pick up the pieces and provide care for them. As people live longer, they require more care over their lifetimes, and, given their increased awareness of the range of diseases they might suffer from, are more likely to want to make use of health services. Demand for health services, in other words, is rising, but the standards of care expected from it are rising too.

This creates an uncomfortable local logic for care. Health organisations are required to produce more care at a higher standard, and at the same time reduce waiting periods for that care. The not-for-profit and private sectors have provided extra capacity to the NHS to meet the need for increased demand and to reduce waiting lists, but still decisions need to be made about which care should be prioritised. This raises a central question in health delivery – who decides what care we should receive?

At the creation of the NHS, care decisions were entirely taken locally, but with little or no accountability for those decisions. Substantial differences in the availability and quality of care arose, giving policymakers that wish to impose central targets and performance management systems a reason for adopting those approaches. The use of these systems, as noted above, it also politically useful as it allows policymakers to pass risk to the organisational and clinical levels, and to couch healthcare decisions in terms of clinical guidelines to alleviate clinical risk. Given these problems, it is little wonder that, following Taylor-Gooby's claims with which the paper began, that public trust in healthcare systems is being undermined. However, this decline in trust is only part of the story of the transfer of risk within the NHS, and one of the key questions is whether there is an alternative.

Allocating over 85% of the budget to PCTs is meant to make them more responsive to local healthcare needs, but the raft of performance management systems coming from the Department of Health make this near impossible (Greener and Powell, 2003). PCTs are therefore mostly centrally-accountable, with little local accountability for their decision-making. Little wonder that they are easily blamed by central policymakers when things go wrong, or by local media and the public when they lack the funds to prescribe new drugs.

To deal with the problem of central paternalism and local accountability, PCTs should now be moved into the sphere of responsibility of local government. That way a greater local engagement in the running of health services might be achieved, and far more opportunities for local discretion in health decision-making be allowed. Some limited minimum standards could still be set by the Department of Health, but far greater local responsiveness allowed.

An argument against this is that local government, after thirty years of resource starvation and responsibilities being stripped from it, is no longer able to take on such a role. However, it is surely time to reverse policymakers' belief that they are able to run health services from London whilst increasingly refusing to be accountable for their decisions. Moreover, the invigoration of local democracy would be greatly facilitated by giving it as important a role as healthcare commissioning to be responsible for.

Allowing a more local health service would also allow the perversities of a competitive market for healthcare to be alleviated, putting the plurality of care providers not in a competitive relationships, but instead in a more collaborative one where care decisions, under the scrutiny of local people, could be made to benefit local people. The risk trade-offs between care decisions could be more carefully made through local participation in decision making, recognising the expertise of medics, but recognising that the NHS needs to become more transparent and more democratic in its decision making processes.

A local health service would therefore allow a recasting of risk relationships to attempt to pool risks of all types at the local, collectivised level, rather than individualising risk at the personal level (in the case of health), by blaming medics (in the case of clinical risk) and by allowing organisations to work together to meet health needs rather than being placed in competitive relationships (when nothing other than blind dogma appears to suggest that this can possibly work to improve health services). Political risk would therefore be aligned with political accountability, at the local level, creating the potential to enrich local democratic processes and remove the presently perverse combination of a strong centralisation and local blame through the use of healthcare markets.

Considering how to more sensibly allocate risks has the potential of allowing the construction of a genuine alternative the present health reforms, and the possibility of a more engaged and informed citizenry.

REFERENCES

Asenova, D., Beck, M. 2003. The UK Financial Sector and Risk Management in PFI projects: A Survey. *Public Money and Management*, 23: 3, 195-202.

Baggott, R. 2006. *Understanding Health Policy*. Bristol, Policy Press.

Beck, M., Asenova, D., Dickson, G. 2005. Public Administration, Science and Risk Assessment: A Cause Study of the UK Bovine Spongiform Encepalopathy Crisis. *Public Administration Review*, 65(4): 396-408.

Beck, U. 1992. *Risk Society: Towards A New Modernity*. London, Sage.

Beveridge, W. 1942. *Social Insurance and Allied Services*. London, HMSO.

Carter, N., Klein, R., Day, P. 1992. *How Organisations Measure Success: The Use of Performance Indicators in Government*. London, Routledge.

Department of Health and Social Security. 1983. *NHS Management Inquiry*. London, HMSO.

Giddens, A. 1994. Living in A Post-traditional Society, in Beck, U., Giddens, A., Lash, S. (eds) *Reflexive Modernisation*. Cambridge, Polity, 56-109.

Greener, I. 2005. Health Management as Strategic Behaviour: Managing Medics and Performance in the NHS. *Public Management Review*, 7(1): 95-110.

Greener, I. 2008a. *Healthcare in the UK: Continuity and Change*. Bristol, Policy Press.

Greener, I. 2008b. Markets in the Public Sector: When do They Work, and What do we do When They Don't? *Policy and Politics*, 36(1): 93-108.

Greener, I., Powell, J. 2003. Health Authorities, Priority-setting and Resource Allocation: A Study in Decision-making in New Labour's NHS. *Social Policy and Administration*, 37(1): 35-48.

Greener, I., Powell, M. 2008. The Changing Governance of the NHS; Reform in a Post-Keynesian Health Service. *Human Relations*, 61(5): 617-636.

Healthcare Commission and National Audit Office. 2008. *Is the Treatment Working? Progress With the NHS System Reform Programme*. London, Audit Commission.

Kings Fund. 2006. *NHS Reform: Getting Back on Track*. London, Kings Fund.

Klein, R. 1990. The State and the Profession: the Politics of the Double-bed., *British Medical Journal*, 301: 700-702.

Klein, R. 1993. The Goals of Health Policy: Church or Garage? In *Health Care UK 1992/3*. London, Kings Fund, 136-138.

Klein, R. 2006. *The New Politics of the NHS: from creation to reinvention*. Abingdon, Radcliffe Publishing.

Le Grand, J. 1997. Knights, Knaves or Pawns? Human Behaviour and Social Policy. *Journal of Social Policy*, 26(2): 149-169.

Lewis, J. 1990. Mothers and Maternity Policies in the Twentieth Century. in Garcia, J., Kilpatrick, R.,Richards, M. (eds) *The Politics of Maternity Care: Services for Childbearing Women in Twentieth Century Britain*. Oxford, Oxford University Press, 15-29.

Mannion, R., Goddard, M., and Smith, P. 2001. On the Limitations and Pitfalls of Performance Measurement Systems in Health Care. In Davies, H., Tavakoli, M. , Malek, M. (eds) *Quality in Healthcare: Strategic Issues in Health Care Management*. Aldershot, Ashgate, 158-169.

Maynard, A. 2006. On Restructuring and Redundancy. *Health Service Journal*, 16.

McKeown, T. 1976. *The Role of Medicine: Dream, Mirage or Nemesis?* New York, Academic Press.

Mohan, J. 2002. *Planning, Markets and Hospitals*. London. Routledge.

Monbiot, G. 2001. *Captive State: The Corporate Takeover of Britain*. London, Pan.

Munro, R. 1999. Power and Discretion: Membership Work in the Time of Technology. *Organization* 6(3): 429-450.

Peckham, S., Exworthy, M., Greener, I., Powell, M. 2005. Decentralizing Health Services: More Local Accountability or Just More Central Control. *Public Money and Management*, 25(4): 221-228.

Peterson, A., Lupton, D. 1996. *The New Public Health: Health and Self in the Age ofRrisk*. London, Sage.

Pollitt, C. 1985. Measuring Performance: A New System for the National Health Service., *Policy and Politics* 13(1): 1-15.

Powell, J.E. 1966. *Medicine and Politics*. London, Pitman Medical.

Public Finance. 2007. PFI Hospitals 'Costing NHS Extra £480m a Year'. http://www. cipfa. org. uk/publicfinance/news_details. cfm?News_id=30216

Robb, B. (ed). 1967. *Sans Everything: A Case to Answer*. London, Trevor Nelson and Sons.

Salter, B. 2004. *The New Politics of Medicine*. London, Palgrave.

Secretary of State for Health. 1989. *Working for Patients*. London, HMSO.

Secretary of State for Health. 1996. *The NHS: A Service with Ambitions*. London, HMSO.

Secretary of State for Health. 2000. *The NHS Plan: A Plan for Investment, A Plan for Reform*. London, HMSO.

Secretary of State for Health. 2006. *Our health, our care, our say: a new direction for community services*. London, HMSO.

Street, A. 2000. Confident about efficiency measurement in the NHS? *Health Care UK*, 47-52.

Tallis, R. 2005. *Hippocratic Oaths: Medicine and its Discontents*. London, Atlantic Books.

Taylor-Gooby, P. 2006. Trust, Risk and Health Care Rreform. *Health, Risk and Society*, 8(2): 2.

Wainwright, D. 1998. Disenchantment, Ambivalence and the Precautionary Principle: The Becalming of British Health Policy., *International Journal of Health Services*, 28(3): 407-426.

Wanless, D. 2002. *Securing our Future Health: Taking A Long Term View - Final Report*. London, HM Treasury.

Welshman, J., Walmsley, J. (eds). 2006. *Community Care in Perspective: Care, Control and Citizenship*. London, Palgrave.

In: Understanding Risk
Editor: Matthias Beck
ISBN: 978-1-62618-686-6

Chapter 14

ARSENIC AND OLD WOOL: AN EARLY EXAMPLE OF THE PRECAUTIONARY PRINCIPLE IN THE RISK MANAGEMENT CYCLE OR A SHEEP IN A TOXIC WOLF'S CLOTHING?

Andrew Watterson*
Occupational and Environmental Health Research Group,
University of Stirling, Scotland

ABSTRACT

The paper explores arsenic as an active ingredient in the cycle of dipping substances used to control sheep parasites in the UK in the 19th and 20th centuries. Technological optimists prevailed over a small number of prudent decision-makers in agriculture and used untested, unknown, suspect or even known carcinogens such as arsenic for supposed economic gain and, at the same time, marginalised worker health. Early unsuccessful efforts were made by some in industry to apply the precautionary principle primarily for consumer protection reasons; but action only occurred when 'better' products appeared on the markets. A similar pattern was to be repeated in later decades with other active ingredients. The risks were inevitably almost always born by the farm worker and small farmer. Sheep dipping demonstrated cyclical developments depending on which risks were assessed and what political and economic pressures were at work. Such pressures included perceived economic gains as well as compulsory regulatory dipping controls. Meanwhile, the evidence base of toxicology and occupational medicine developed in particular ways, whereby different adverse health effects of arsenic sheep dip were documented at different time periods. Focusing on the uneven and cyclical nature of these processes, this paper highlights how the dominance of chemistry over the biological and medical disciplines ultimately led to a neglect of the subtle and chronic effects of arsenic dips on human health. The paper concludes by drawing potential lessons from these developments.

* E-mail: aew1@stir.ac.uk

INTRODUCTION

Arsenic occurs naturally and is a metalloid with both properties of a metal and non-metal. Arsenic pigments, dyes and mordants were used in the 19th century. In the 21st century water pollution by arsenic presents a major public health threat in countries such as Bangladesh, while in 'developed countries' wood treated by arsenic has also come to represent a serious health threat. Arsenic is usually found in the environment combined with oxygen, chlorine and sulphur: that is in the form of 'inorganic arsenic'. Arsenical pesticides are mainly inorganic and were used to control parasites such as ticks, scab, keds and blow flies that attacked sheep. Arsenic proved effective in controlling some, but not all, of these parasites. The pesticide formulations of arsenic are the ones that have most documented ill-health effects in humans. In the 19th century sheep and animal dips contained sodium and potassium arsenite, arsenious oxide, arsenic sulphides and thioarsenates. The pervasive toxicity of these compounds is evidenced by the fact that old sheep dip sites in Australia contaminated by arsenic are now considered a threat to public health. Organic arsenic is produced when arsenic combines with carbon and hydrogen. A few organic arsenic pesticides are still used (ATSDR, 2007; Oliver, 1902; Hunter, 1962).

Other uses of arsenics have included labels, cardboard boxes, children's books, Christmas decorations, printed and woven fabrics, children's toys, carpets, lino, coloured soaps and sweetmeats all in the 1880s. Arsenical compounds occur in smelting and ore refining. They also take the form of white arsenic which occured in sheep dip production (as sodium arsenite); in the insecticide Paris green, used on fruit trees (as copper aceto-arsenite); and in Scheele's green (as cupric arsenite). White arsenic was further used as a preservative of hides, skins, and furs.

Arsenical compounds in industry were light and hence represented a dust hazard (Q. J. M. New Series Ho. 48). By 1879, Henry Carr publicised a paper on the toxicity of arsenical colours entitled 'Our Domestic Poisons'. This was followed in 1880 by Oliver, who noted the injurious effects of arsenic in dye workers. By the 1900s, Oliver observed that sheep dip makers and those washing clothes of sheep dip manufacturers suffered from effects on 'their extremities and nervous system' (Oliver, 1902).

This paper explores arsenic usage in dipping to control sheep parasites in the UK in the 19th and 20th centuries and the underpinning approach to hazard identification and risk assessment. It examines how risks were perceived, assessed, recorded and reported during that period. This analysis forms the basis for a discussion of the potential lessons that can be drawn from these risk perceptions, assessments and related risk management strategies for the future regulation of hazardous substances.

THE ECONOMIC AND AGRICULTURAL FRAME FOR DIPPING

Historically, 'ecological' sheep farming came first. Farmers bred only those sheep that were 'adapted' to their environment and resistant to diseases created in that environment because no technological or chemical alternatives existed. This limited the breeds and numbers and location of grazing available. Such sheep did not necessarily produce the most or best wool and meat, but they were ideally suited to subsistence and 'organic farming'. In the middle and late 19th century and early twentieth century, the markets for sheep grew and spread to the colonies. This coincided with the growth of industrial chemistry, growing knowledge of biology and significant mechanical engineering advances; whereby only the former significantly influenced pest control at the time.

'Large' sheep farmers' economic interest in producing meat, wool and leather dominated approaches to sheep farming during the period in question. This tended to shape governmental regulations, requiring dipping at certain times and with certain dips, and supposedly ensured markets for large sheep producers without necessarily establishing the most effective method(s) for controlling parasites. It also created additional costs and labour burdens for small sheep farmers. Intermittently this hegemony was threatened by consumer interests such as the hosiery industry's concerns about arsenic contaminated wool products, or consumer reluctance to purchase leather goods from sheep damaged by parasites. Meanwhile, minimal attention was paid to health risks created for those making arsenic dips, contract dippers and small farmers who dipped their own, and their neighbours', sheep. The following section examines the causes of this disjunction.

Sheep Farming Cycles and Dipping Cycles

Sheep dipping products and techniques have 'evolved' over centuries in the UK. The evolution has been spasmodic and uneven; and at times the developments appear to be cyclical (see Figure 1).

In the 'Ecological' stage, farmers only kept—or keep— those sheep breeds, such as the Hebridean sheep, that were— or are— 'adapted' to their environment in the absence of pesticides. This approach often relates to subsistence farming and ensures the survival of small rural populations dependent on their sheep as a major part of their meat diet and as a resource for clothes through wool. leather and other materials.

In ensuring resistance to diseases created in these environments, the choice of sheep is limited in terms of breeds, numbers and locations of grazing. While there were no other alternatives to the ecological approach in mediaeval times, in modern organic farming, such sheep provide a niche commercial market; albeit that certain veterinary medicines are approved for use on 'organic' sheep with regard to parasite control if the welfare of the sheep may be affected by those parasites. The ecological approach also relied on good husbandry methods and very regular inspections of flocks. With growing markets and the economic imperative to raise very large flocks, and with higher labour costs, such methods were not attractive to commercial farmers.

With the historical development of a lucrative market for wool, sheep farming first used non-toxic dipping. This dunking of sheep was simply to ensure the sheep's wool was cleaned in the water from streams and rivers to increase wool saleability. No parasite control was used.

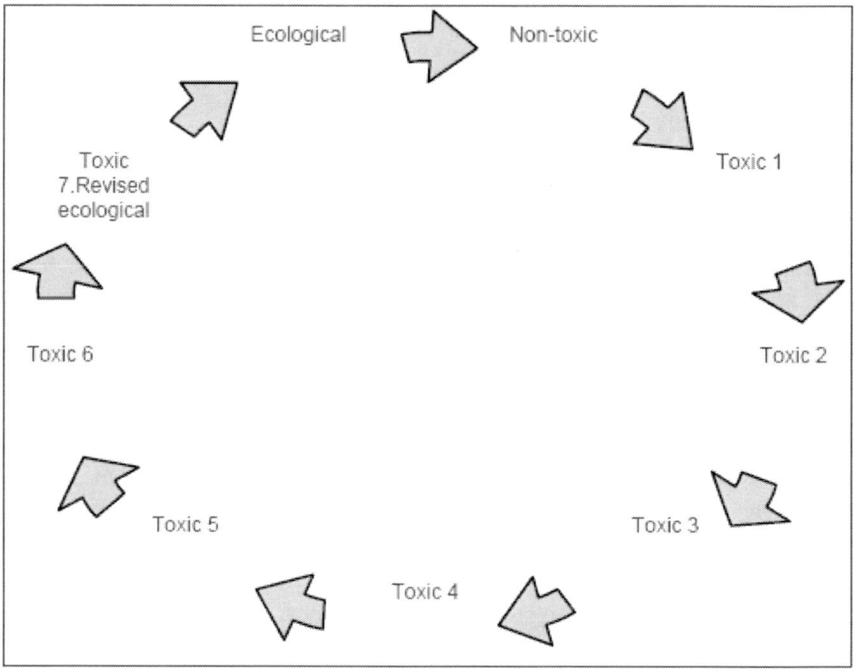

Figure 1. Approaches to Sheep Farming.

Scientific advances then led to greater choices for sheep farmers wishing to control parasites that damaged fleeces, weakened sheep and affected the quality of leather available from the hides. This led to the gradual adoption of different approaches (see Figure 1):

(1) Toxic: Controlling sheep parasites to ensure sheep production with products assumed safe for sheep; but no evidence for such assumptions either available or, if available, used. Efficacy was assumed, but not fully proven, to flow from usage of veterinary pesticides and economic factors drove developments. Sheep and human safety in the dipping process were never explored in the early stages of product use. Arsenic and sulphur were key active ingredients in dips initially followed later by organochlorines (as the limited persistence of arsenic rather than its neurological, dermatological and carcinogenic effects were recognised by manufacturers and farmers).

(2) Toxic: Controlling sheep parasites that threaten not wool or meat production but leather quality. Organophosphates were key active ingredients here. These replaced organochlorines because the latter's persistence and environmental toxicity was recognised. Evidence about arsenic's toxicity to workers was not ranked as highly as organochlorines' adverse impacts on UK raptor populations.

(3) Toxic: Controlling sheep scab, largely in the absence of data on sheep morbidity or mortality which resulted from these applications. This applied at various stages to sulphur, arsenic, organochlorine and organophosphate sheep dips. The usual pattern for product development was to assume that no animal or human toxicity existed; and, only over time, would such evidence emerge. Hence new products were by definition thought to be safer because the evidence base on their effects did not exist.

By the time evidence of toxicity did emerge, new products would have been developed and workers exposed to the old products would either have retired or, if adversely affected by the old products, have great difficulty in gaining recognition of occupational illnesses and compensation.

(4) Toxic: Controlling of parasites which may affect sheep and workers. This involved moves to improve application technologies.

(5) Toxic: Substituting chemicals that adversely affect workers with ones that are safer from an occupational health perspective but may damage, through incorrect high dose applications or disposal, the environment because of water pollution. This part of the cycle led to the reduced use of organophosphates and the introduction of synthetic pyrethroid dips (Watterson 1997).

(6) Toxic: Usage of injectables which reduce risks to workers and the environment, but potentially increase risks to consumers. Injectables have eliminated worker exposure to dips and put an end to direct water pollution; but they have created potentially increased risks to consumers who eat lamb and mutton and may ingest the injectables.

(7) 'Revised' Ecological: This returns to the earliest sheep farming practices. It depends on raised animal husbandry standards, lower stocking density, selection of breeds suited to specific region, minimal use of veterinary medicines - pesticides not available in the original ecological stage - and greater labour input.

Chemical, Commercial and Toxicological Developments Linked to Arsenic Sheep Dips

With larger markets and flocks, chemistry drove innovations in sheep parasite controls abetted by some engineering technology advances. Biological and medical disciplines contributed far less to sheep dip developments; and hence the means available to monitor and measure the risks to human health were limited. The subtle effects of arsenic dips often went undetected, the crude effects in terms of mortality went unrecorded, and the chronic effects remained obscure or unknown. This is a familiar pattern in the history of occupational diseases and is partly based on the deliberate social construction of ignorance amongst politicians, regulators and scientists who failed to inform workers of the risk to their health that they ran. Workers often identified the hazards and related diseases themselves (Legge, 1934; Watterson, 1993).

By the 1800s, there were already reports of arsenical use in UK dips (Hendricks 1937). The Georgians and early Victorians lacked any toxicological or epidemiological knowledge that they could draw on to make risk assessments. Hence the assumption always was that any new materials that appeared to work were safe to use. The 'Complete Grazier' of 1807 discussed an arsenical sheep dip preparation as an example of 'leading edge' and untypical chemical sheep tick control which was at the time used by Lord Somerville in Norfolk. This involved "four pounds of soft soap and two pounds of arsenic be steeped in thirty gallons of water and the animals be immersed in the suffusion.... " (quoted in Hendrick, Trans Roy High Ag Soc, 1937)

Between 1843 and 1852, a vet, William Cooper developed a mixture of arsenic and sulphur in experimental sheep dips. In 1852 he began the large scale factory-based production of this dip. A description survives of the process, although almost all the family members involved in the production at this time died in their 30s and 40s (The Story of Coopers of Berkhamsted, Dacorum Heritage Museum):

> The arsenic and sulphur were dressed using a machine called 'the Joggler'. This consisted of a long flat sieve in a deep box which was moved backwards and forwards at high speed by a wrench. The mixture was then boiled in the Kiln which was attached to the Grinding Mill. It was then cooled for several days until it had the consistency of treacle. The powder was then placed on the kiln floor and mixed with the liquor by men using shovels. When thoroughly mixed, it was spread out evenly on the kiln floor and pressed down tightly by men walking over it. Initially, the men wore their own shoes but eventually were provided with boots. William Cooper noted, 'It is a serious affair if the 'dipping' gets into their feet'.

By 1857, the British medical journal 'Lancet' was carrying reports of skin effects on the hands, arms, thighs and scrotums of shepherds who dipped sheep for nine hours in one day; which was a common occurrence at the time (Lancet, 1857). Other reports of arsenical sheep dip poisoning were also well known to physicians and publicised in definitive works on poisons and medical jurisprudence (Taylor, 1859).

The acute risks to those manufacturing arsenic were considerable, but chronic risks do not appear to have been fully identified by the medical profession until studies in the first part of the century by Sir Thomas Legge were reported (see Table 1 below; and Neubauer, 1947). This is despite the fact that the 1895 Workshop Act required every medical practitioner to report cases of arsenic poisoning in factories and workshops that they attended (Legge, 1934: 4). It seems unlikely that many medical professionals at the time would have been able to diagnose such illnesses and the law did not apply to agricultural uses. At the same time, similar reports about the hazards to dippers emerged in Governmental enquiries by the Board of Agriculture and Fisheries 1904. By 1913, UK medical professionals were reporting arsenic cancer affecting sheep dip factory workers in the Lancet (Harwood et al., 1913).

In Australia, the Australian Workers Union in the 1920s noted the skin irritation caused by arsenical sheep dips specifically to shearers and called for their banning. These calls had little success because of the employers' arguments that such bans would damage the industry, and because their views were supported by leading scientists (Penrose, 1999: 259). No similar protests emerged in the UK or none were reported (the numbers of UK shearers would, of course, have been much smaller). This was the case despite the fact that UK studies had been cited to support the Australian workers' arguments in the 1920s and 1930s. Legge's discovery of cancer cases among arsenic sheep dip manufacturing workers, published in his standard occupational medicine text of 1934, must have reached a large medical readership. However, it produced no immediate regulatory response in the UK.

In the 1930s it was increasingly recognised that arsenical dips, though very effective against external adult parasites, could be washed off. Hendrick (1937), accordingly, reported that:

- Sheep ticks. Worked for one hit only;
- Keds. Adults killed but not pupae and they miss second dips as they hatch 21 days after being laid;
- Lice. Some are killed but not all unlike more successful carbolic and nicotine dips.

Arsenical soaps, moreover, could lead to prolonged exposure of animals (sic) to arsenic which resulted in serious poisoning. Hence, despite the effectiveness of arsenicals, they were gradually abandoned. However, there was no move to remove them from the market on account of their carcinogenicity.

Standard UK medical texts on occupational medicine in the 1940s by Collier (1943: 252-255), and in the 1950s by Lloyd Davies (1957: 178), recognised the acute and chronic toxicity hazards including lung cancer presented by arsenic and noted its prescribed industrial disease status. But both textbooks argued that these problems could be controlled by industrial hygiene measures; even in agricultural situations and sheep dip manufacturing. Moreover, neither suggested that the toxicity of the metal necessitated its removal from the workplace. In Collier's case, this was possibly prompted by the report of only one case of arsenical poisoning notified to the Chief Inspector of Factories in 1936.

The toxicity of arsenic had been reported with regard to different target organs throughout the 19th and early 20th centuries, as well as in earlier sources (Source, Neubauer, 1947). These reports covered:

- Dermal effects [Agricola, 1556; Arlidge, 1872; Morris, 1902; Dunlap, 1921] which included adverse effects to the public through stockings, handkerchiefs and gloves that had been dyed with arsenic;
- Cardiovascular effects;
- Respiratory effects which included laryngitis, bronchitis and rhinitis, (asthma) [Morris, 1902; Dunlap, 1921] as well as nasal septum perforation [Dunlap, 1921];
- Gastrointestinal effects[Morris, 1902];
- Neurological effects [Morris 1902];
- Cancer;
- Conjunctivitis [Dunlap 1921].

Arsenical dips were replaced firstly by organochlorines and then by organophosphates and synthetic pyrethroids. However, arsenic compounds were still listed in the UK Ministry of Agriculture, Fisheries and Food 'A Guide to Veterinary Pesticides' in 1984 with a variety of uses and with a UK supplier (1984: 89). Even in 2002, the UK Health and Safety Executive regulatory and enforcement agency was still producing leaflets referring to the use of arsenic in pesticides.

Inorganic arsenic, as well as being a known human skin and lung carcinogen (Ihrig et al., 2008) is also a well known reproductive health hazard. In 2008 it was linked to prostate cancer and endocrine disruption according (Benbrahim-Tallaa and Waalkes, 2008; Davey et al., 2008).

Table 1. Dates of knowledge on arsenical toxicity related to sheep dip, other manufacture and medicinal treatments

Source	Date	Dip/other activity	Site and effect
Lambe in Eggers 1932 and cited by Neubauer 1947	1809	Hypothesised that arsenic in drinking water was toxic	Malignant disease
WJ O'Donovan in Brit J Dermatology 1924 Vol 36:481 quoting John Ayrton Paris. Pharmacologia 1820 4th ed	1820	Non-dipping. Ayrton Describes pernicious impact of arsenic fumes in Cornish copper smelting	Describes tumours in animals near the works and scrotal cancer in smelter workers
Haerting and Hesse cited by Bradford Hill in 1948	1879	Inhalation of arsenic Dust	Arsenic as a major cause of Schneeberg lung. This was due , it now transpires, primarily to radiation exposure
Aschoff between 1887-1899 reported in 1902 and cited by Neubauer 1947	1880s 1890s	Cancer in gardeners. No specific reference to Arsenic	Cutaneous cancer
Dacorum Heritage Trust www. dacorumheritage. org. uk/coopers. htm	Pre-1885	Dip manufacturing Workers	Cooper quote ":it was a serious affair if the dipping (arsenic and sulphur) got into the workers' feet as men initially used own shoes to press the dip powder
Hutchinson. Trans Path Soc London 1888 39:352 quoted by Pershagen 1981	1888	inorganic arsenic medication	Associated with skin cancer
Legge cited by Neubauer 1947	1902/3	Arsenical dust in sheep Dip manufacturers Industry	Lung irritation linked to skin irritation
UK Departmental Committee On sheep dipping	1904	Application and wool Product	Skin exposure occurred in dippers who used grease on arms to protect themselves. Skin irritation in consumers of woollen hosiery treated with arsenic
Case notes of Dr Sequeria reported by Dr O'Donovan 1924	1911	Labourer who carried cases of sheep dip for 20 years	Fatal skin cancer first reported 1910 and death occurred in 1911
Nutt, Beattie and Pye Smith Lancet 1913 also cited by O'Donovan in 1924 p477	1913	Dip manufacture	Skin cancer due to sheep dip manufacture in 2 workers with 16 others related to arsenical medicines
Bayet and Slosse 1919 paper	1914	Factory arsenical dust Analyses	Strongly supported arsenic as a cause of many industrial cancers
	1920	Sheep dip manufacture	Process widely recognised prior to 1920s as being very dusty
Leitch and Kennaway	1922	Toxicology tests on Animals	Provided lab evidence of arsenic's skin carcinogenicity quoted by O'Donovan 1924

Source	Date	Dip/other activity	Site and effect
Morgan JG BJIM 1958	1920s	Welsh nickel refining Industry	Lung and sinus cancer
Henry cited by Bradford Hill BJIM 1948 5:1	1934	Sheep dip Manufacturers	Dermatological problems and suggested link between arsenic and one or lung cancer cases
Source	Date	Dip/other activity	Site and effect
Doerle and Ziegler 1930 Cited by Neubauer 1947	1930s	Arsenic insecticide use in gardeners, fruit farmers, wine growers	Chronic arsenicism
Bridge in British Factory Department report cited by Neubauer 1947	1939	Arsenical dust exposure In arsenical insecticide manufacture	First fatal lung cancer case reported followed by 2 in 1940 and 1 in 1943
Hill AB et al. BJIM	1948	Sheep dip manufacture	Lung and skin cancer

Source: Watterson – Collection of history of sheep dipping papers. University of Stirling, Stirling held at Stirling.

In 1981, the Swedish researcher Goran Pershagen noted that inorganic arsenic's poisonous properties had been well known for centuries, with recent reviews highlighting its chronic respiratory, cardiovascular, neurological and haematopoietic effects. He also noted that the health effects of organic arsenic compounds remained inadequately investigated, and importantly, that the carcinogenicity of arsenic had not materialised in some animal tests.

By 1980, the International Agency for Research on Cancer (IARC) (1987), eventually, concluded that arsenic was a proven human carcinogen. This drew on evidence from occupational studies, including pesticide manufacture and application, about work–related cancers published in the 1960s, 1970s and 1980s (Thiers, 1967; Pinto, 1978; Horiguchi, 1979; Mabuchi, 1980; Luchtruth, 1983; Buiatti, 1985; Leyh, 1985). However, as Table 1 above illustrates, evidence of arsenic's carcinogenic properties significantly predates the IARC decision.

Approaches to Hazard Identification and Risk Perception on Arsenic

The default position, dominant in science, is to assume the null hypothesis of 'no effect' until definitive evidence emerges to the contrary. This works well in some scientific settings, but it is the antithesis of the approach needed in public and occupational health, because it may be too late to protect the public health when exposures have occurred (Watterson, 1993). An alternative approach is the precautionary principle which accepts lower levels of evidence, or the similarities between chemicals and processes already known to be hazardous, as evidence for a need to protect public or occupational health. This approach has been adopted, for instance, by agencies such as the European Environment Agency (2001). In the case of arsenical sheep dips, however, there were several factors which prevented the timely recognition of these hazards.

Technological and Legislative Drivers Linked to Economic Development

Hand dipping was not possible with the large sheep flocks in the colonies and this led to the invention of the swim bath and, later in the 20th century, to jets and showers in such countries as Australia.

The political, if sometimes declining economic, dominance of landowners in the political systems of many countries meant that legislative approaches to perceived sheep pests that threatened markets were to ensure blanket requirements on dipping; albeit that the efficacy of such approaches had not always been established. Dipping was seen as a necessary quick fix, even though evidence of its effectiveness was lacking and there was ample and growing knowledge about the adverse health effects of dipping with a range of pesticides (Watterson, 1997). Those most at risk were, of course, agricultural workers on large estates who had few legal rights and little trade union organisation to protect them. Contract dipping workers were in a similar position, as were small hills farmers in vulnerable rural areas of the UK who would often do the dipping themselves.

Legislation requiring dipping, with a few lacunae, dates back many decades. The 1903 UK Diseases of Animals Act empowered the Board of Agriculture:

- To make regulations for 'prescribing, regulating and securing the periodic effective dipping of sheep' or the use of some other remedy for sheep scab;
- To ensure that sheep were dipped with a dip approved by the Ministry of Agriculture;
- To ensure that some sheep in certain areas were double dipped;
- To enforce the use of an arsenical dip for second dipping.

As the dipping had to be approved by the Ministry, and as they approved arsenic despite evidence about its limited persistence, sometimes poor results and known or suspected adverse effects on workers were detected as early as 1902.

In the 1930s, the British Ministry of Agriculture still required arsenical dips to be used with levels of arsenic present that related to impacts on parasites rather than safeguards for workers. This flew in the face of the significant body of epidemiological, clinical and toxicological evidence about adverse human health effects that existed in both the UK as outlined above (and in Australia as Penrose, 1999 described).

Diluted dip at this time had to contain:

- Not less than 0. 2% of total arsenic (as arsenious oxide);
- Not less than 0. 13% of soluble arsenic (expressed as arsenious oxide).

In 1935, there were 91 approved arsenic dips of which 49 contained tar acids. There were also 210 tar acid dips, 12 of which contained some arsenic (Hendricks, 1937). Despite mounting evidence of adverse effects, compulsory dipping of sheep continued, with some interruptions, throughout the 20th century.

DISCUSSION

Sheep dipping products and techniques have 'evolved' over centuries in the UK. The evolution has been spasmodic, uneven and, at times, complex. Ecological and biological controls of sheep parasites have lagged behind chemical controls and related application technologies. Sheep dipping practices demonstrate cyclical developments depending on which risks were assessed and what political and economic pressures were at work. 'Large' sheep farmers' economic interest in producing meat, wool and leather dominated during most of the period in question. This tended to shape governmental regulations requiring dipping at certain times and with certain dips; supposedly ensuring markets for large sheep producers without necessarily implementing the most effective method(s) for controlling parasites. Economic governance and regulation were strong throughout the period in question. Social governance to protect workers' health, meanwhile, was weak and rarely properly enforced. Dipping regulations also created additional costs and labour burdens for small sheep farmers. At other times, consumers' interests dominated the regulation of sheep dips, primarily on account of hosiery industry concerns about arsenic contaminated wool products, or consumer reluctance to purchase leather goods from sheep damaged by parasites. Additional animal welfare arguments were used even though the risk to sheep survival from dipping and dips was manifest. Minimal attention was paid to the health risks affecting those making arsenic dips, or contract dippers and small farmers who dipped their own and their neighbours' sheep.

Some of this disjunction can be attributed to the historical development of sheep farming. During the 'ecological' stage, farmers could only breed those sheep that were 'adapted' to their environment and resistant to diseases created in that environment. This limited breeds, numbers and locations of grazing available. Additionally, these sheep did not always produce the most or best wool and meat.

With larger markets and flocks, chemistry drove innovations in sheep parasite controls, abetted by some engineering technology advances. Biological and medical disciplines contributed far less to sheep dip developments and hence the means available to monitor and measure the risks to human health were limited. The subtle and chronic effects of arsenic dips often went undetected, the crude effects in terms of mortality went unrecorded and the chronic effects remained obscure or unknown. Although the toxicological and medical evidence base on the adverse effects of these dips grew rapidly, the UK scientific and scientific civil service community was slow to act on many of the early warnings of damage to workers' health. This pattern of government supported action in the application of these toxins resulted in a significant, and avoidable, loss of human life.

CONCLUSION

The history of sheep dipping in the UK exposes a pattern in which technological optimists prevailed over prudent decision-makers and used untested, unknown or suspect carcinogens such as arsenic. Early unsuccessful efforts were made by some in the industry to apply the precautionary principle to arsenic in order to protect consumers and markets. This pattern was repeated with other dips at other times. The greatest risks resulting from these approaches were born by the economically and politically weakest parties; namely farm workers contract sheep dippers and small farmers.

With concerns growing about global warming, carbon footprints, food miles, animal welfare, supply chain checks and fodder inputs, there is now mounting support for ecological approaches to sheep farming. However, global issues of food production and food security, which have re-emerged in 2008, have also created support for technicist solutions which are associated with the misnamed 'Green Revolution' of the 20th century.

The 'Green Revolution', a classic example of technological optimism and scientism, promised scientific fixes for agriculture that would produce food for all globally through extensive use of pesticides, fertilisers and new crop varieties not normally available to the developing world. The revolution failed to address the political and economic factors that created poverty and food scarcity and hence it failed spectacularly to end world hunger. What it did do was boost the profits of agri-capital enterprises which benefited from the sale of genetically engineered crops. In the context of risk cycles, it led to the spread of engineered crops that were resistant to pesticides especially herbicides, and thereby ensured future markets for the agro-chemical industry. The same revolution encouraged the genetic engineering of animals and now there are possibilities of producing breeds resistant to parasites, or breeds capable of being treated by veterinary pesticides without adverse effects–with side-effects we do not yet know about. This is indicative of another iteration in the risk cycle, and specifically one which is again prioritising technological optimism and producer interests over health and safety concerns. Whether this cycle will be as harmful as previous ones will depend to a large degree on how risks are assessed and addressed, and specifically whether precautionary or traditional approaches to risk management guide policy makers.

References

Agency for Toxic Substances and Disease Registry. 2007. *Toxicological Profile for Arsenic* (update). Atlanta, USDHS.

Benbrahim-Tallaa, L. and Waalkes, M. 2008. Inorganic Arsenic and Human Prostate Cancer. *Environmental Health Perspectives,* 116(2): 158-164.

Board of Agriculture and Fisheries. 1904. *Dipping and Treatment of Sheep*. Sheep dipping Committee. Cd 2258. London, HMSO.

Buiatti, E., Kriebel, D., Geddes, M., Santucci, M., Pucci, N. 1985. A Case Control Study of Lung Cancer in Florence, Italy. I. Occupational Risk Factors. *J. Epidemiol. Commun. Health,* 39: 244-250.

Collier, H. 1943. *Outlines of Industrial Medical Practice*. London, Edward Arnold.

Dacorum Heritage Museum. The Story of Cooper's of Berkhamsted. http://www. dacorumheritage. org. uk/coopers. htm (accessed June 2008).

Davey, J., Nomikos, A., Wungjiranirun, M., Sherman, J., Ingram, L., Batki, C., Lariviere, J., Hamilton, J. 2008. Arsenic as an Endocrine Disruptor: Arsenic Disrupts Retinoic Acid Receptor–and Thyroid Hormone Receptor–Mediated Gene Regulation and Thyroid Hormone–Mediated Amphibian Tail Metamorphosis. *Environmental Health Perspectives,* 111(2): 165-172.

European Environment Agency. 2001. *Late Lessons From Early Warnings: The Precautionary Principle 1896-2000.* Copenhagen, EEA.

Harwood Nutt M., Beattie, J. , Pye-Smith RJ. 1913. Arsenic Cancer. *Lancet* 26th July and 2nd August 1913.

Hendricks, J. 1937. Sheep Dips and Dipping. *Transactions of the Royal Highlands Agricultural Society Scotland,* 49:158-177.

Health and Safety Executive. 2002. *Arsenic and You.* MSA8 Reprinted 9/02. C25. Bootle, HSE.

Horiguchi, S. 1979. A Case of Lung Cancer Due to Exposure to Arsenical Compounds in an Insecticides Factory. (Studies on Lead Arsenate Poisoning, Part 4). *Osaka City Med. J.* , 25: 45-51.

Hunter, D. 1962. *The Diseases of Occupations.* London, The English University Press, Third edition.

Ihrig MM., Shalat SL., Baynes C. 1998. A Hospital-Based Case-Control Study of Stillbirths and Environmental Exposure to Arsenic Using an Atmospheric Dispersion Model Linked to a Geographical Information System. *Epidemiology,* 9(3): 290-4.

International Agency for Research on Cancer. 1987. *Arsenic and Arsenic Compounds.* IARC Summary and Evaluation, Supplement 7. Geneva, IARC.

Lancet. 1857. Case Report on Shepherds Dipping with White Arsenic. September 12th: 282.

Legge, T. 1934. *Industrial Maladies.* London, Oxford University Press.

Leyh, F. and Rothlaender, JP. 1985. Multiple Bowenoid Keratoses Due to Arsenic (Ger.). *Dermatosen,* 33: 99-101.

Lloyd Davies, T. 1957. *The Practice of Industrial Medicine.* London, J and A Churchill.

Lüchtrath, H. 1983. The Consequences of Chronic Arsenic Poisoning Among Moselle Wine Growers. Pathoanatomical Investigations of Post-Mortem Examinations Between 1960 and 1977. *J. Cancer Res. Clin. Oncol.*, 105: 173-182.

Mabuchi, K., Lilienfeld, A.M., Snell, L.M. 1980. Cancer and Occupational Exposure to Arsenic: a Study of Pesticide Workers. *Prev. Med.*, 9: 51-77.

Ministry of Agriculture, Fisheries and Food. 1984. *A Guide to Veterinary Pesticides.* Reference Book 245. ADAS. London, HMSO.

Neubauer, O. 1947. Arsenical Cancer: a Review. *British Journal of Cancer,* 1: 192-244.

Oliver, T. 1902. *Dangerous Trades.* London, John Murray.

Penrose, B. 1999. The Australian Workers Union and Occupational Arsenic in the 1930s. *Journal of Industrial Relations* 41(2): 256-271.

Pershangen, G. 1981. The Carcinogenicity of Arsenic. *Environmental Health Perspectives* 40: 93-100.

Pinto, SS., Henderson, V., Enterline, PE. 1978. Mortality Experience of Arsenic-Exposed Workers. *Arch. Environ. Health,* 33. 325-331.

Taylor, AS. 1859. *On Poisons in Relation to Medical Jurisprudence and Medicine.* 2nd American edition, 2nd and revised London edition. Philadelphia, Blanchard and Lea.

Thiers, H. , Colomb, D. , Moulin, G. , Colin, L. 1967. Arsenical Skin Cancer in Vineyards in the Beaujolais (Fr.). *Ann. Dermatol* , 94: 133-158.

Watterson, A. 1993. Occupational Health in the UK Gas Industry, in Platt S., Thomas H., Scott S. and Williams G. (eds) *Locating Health.* London, Avebury Press, 172-194.

Watterson, A. 1997. The Hazards of Organophosphates: UK Risk Assessments of Sheep Dips in Historical and Contemporary Context' in Donham KJ., Rautianien R., Schuman SH., Lay, JA. (eds) *Agricultural Health and Safety: Recent Advances.* New York, The Haworth Medical Press, 157-167.

In: Understanding Risk
Editor: Matthias Beck
ISBN: 978-1-62618-686-6

Chapter 15

A WORKER-DRIVEN AND COMMUNITY-BASED INVESTIGATION OF THE HEALTH OF ONE GROUP OF WORKERS EXPOSED TO VINYL CHLORIDE MONOMER (VCM)

Joanne Carlin[1], John Knight[1], Simon Pickvance[2] and Andrew Watterson[3*]
[1]TRUST, Chesterfield, Derbyshire, UK
[2]Sheffield Occupational Health Advisory Service, Visiting Researcher at Sheffield University.
[3]Occupational and Environmental Health Research Group, University of Stirling, Scotland

ABSTRACT

Global occupational health history contains numerous cases of employees who worked in hazardous industries, contracted work-caused or work related diseases and who were then neglected and abandoned when those industries closed. Often decades pass before agreement is reached among scientists and civil servants about the causation, impact and compensation of such diseases although a range of risks may well have been identified and control standards set. Evidence may exist, rarely recognised or used by official sources, that employees recognised some of the occupational diseases they faced with sentinel events indicating possible disease causation or the specific causes prior to the scientific community either investigating, revealing or agreeing that such diseases existed.

This health study was organised and carried out by former employees of one plant, now closed, and their representatives. 162 questionnaires from a survey were collected and analysed from former plant workers on selected ill-health reported and primarily relating to respiratory, cardio-vascular and mental health functions as well as recorded angiosarcoma cases. The survey revealed under-reported and unrecorded illnesses in the

* E-mail: aew1@stir.ac.uk.

ex-workers that were associated with VCM in the scientific literature since the 1970s. The paper also documents working conditions using papers and reports from the ex-employees. Government departments at the time of the study such as the HSE (Hereafter Health and Safety Executive: the UK enforcement body on occupational health and safety) and Department of Work and Pensions (DWP) did not and still do not appear to offer coordinated and comprehensive support to those who later develop diseases that may be caused or related to their past work.

INTRODUCTION

The history of global occupational health contains numerous cases of employees who work in hazardous industries, contract work-caused and work related diseases and who are then neglected and abandoned when those industries close. Decades pass before agreement is reached among scientists and civil servants about the causation, impact and compensation of such diseases and support for those who contract such diseases. Often evidence exists that employees themselves recognised the occupational diseases they faced with sentinel events indicating possible disease causation or the specific causes prior to the scientific community.

Vinyl chloride was first synthesised in 1835 (IARC 1979:378). Polyvinyl production began in 1927 and was industrially important by the 1930s. Vinyl chloride monomer gas (VCM) production then increased very steadily. In the 1970s about 96% of VCM produced in USA was used for polymer production and the rest for methyl chloroform production and in resin production. Similar patterns of VCM usage emerged in other countries. The largest use for PVC resins in this period was in plastic piping, floor covering and electrical applications. In the UK, PVC and copolymer production figures rose very rapidly between 1960 and 1970s the following figures show: UK PVC and copolymer production figures ranged from 108,000 tonnes in 1960 up to 315,000 tonnes by 1970 [Levinson 1974]. By 1982, UK production figures had reached over 400,000 tonnes. Commensurate activity in tracking the adverse health effects of VCM on workers did not occur.

Toxicology tests established that VCM causes brain tumours in lab tests (Rosenstock and Cullen 1994:600). By 1971-4 Maltoni in Italy had reported on the relationship between inhalation of vinyl chloride and brain tumours in rats (Rosenstock and Cullen 1994:601). In 1974 the first published reports on angiosarcoma cases in VCM workers appeared. From 1976 onwards, reports of increased risk of brain cancers especially glioblasta multiforme, in humans working with VCM appeared in the literature (Waxweiler 1976, Doll 1988, Simonato 1991). Cases of liver angiosarcoma have been reported among workers in PVC fabrication plants (Wagoner 1983). One case of angiosarcoma has also been reported in someone employed at a vinyl chloride factory during the late 1950s but not as a VC production worker (Elliott et al. 1997). Two studies at least have also suggested an association between VCM exposure, digestive cancers (Theriault et al. 1981; Smulevich et al. 1988) and cancers of the lymphatic and haemopoietic systems (Smulevich et al. 1988).

The USA ATSDR describe the long term lower level human effects of vinyl chloride exposure as ‘vinyl chloride disease’ which is characterised by severe damage to the liver, effects on the lungs, poor circulation in the fingers, changes in the bone at the end of the fingers, thickening of the skin and changes in the blood” (USA Agency for Toxic Substances and Disease Registry [ATSDR] August 1989:2). This US Agency report accepts that VCM had been linked with cancers of tissues other than the liver in humans. ATSDR in 1997 acknowledged that breathing in VCM for long periods of time could cause liver damage, immune reactions, nerve damage and liver cancer (ATSDR 1997:1)

Table 1. Dates of knowledge of toxicity of VCM 1927-1981

1927 VCM first used

1949 First reports of liver damage in 14 of 48 exposed VCM workers (Tribuch)

1961 VCM in lab tests affected the liver at 100, 200 and 500ppm (Torkelson)

1963 Reynauds phenomenon and dermatitis problems reported in 6% of a group of 168 Romanian PVC workers (Suciu)

1960s VCM workers were reported to have acro-osteolysis (Pushin 1965; Berk et al. 1976)

1967 Adverse neurological effects reported for VCM polymerisation workers

1969 Neurological effects of VCM were summarised at an International Conference (Schotteck)

1970 VCM caused cancer in animals (Viola)

1970 PVC linked to pneumoconiosis in one production worker: similar effects reported in over 90 other workers (Szende; Vertkin)

1972 Maltoni reported his first observation of an angiosarcoma in animals exposed to VCM (Levinson 1974:38)

1974 VCM carcinogenic effects were reported in the liver of animals (Maltoni) and BF Goodrich reported 4 angiosarcoma cases in VCM workers in its plants. Bleeding conditions associated with VCM exposure of workers (Veltman;Lilis) Chronic lung disease associated with human exposure to VCM (Miller 1975a) Immunological data from 19 of 28 patients with 'vinyl chloride disease' suggest an immune complex disorder (Ward)

1976 Angiosarcoma became a prescribed industrial disease in UK

1976 Hepatic fibrosis described in VCM workers IARC report on VCM carcinogenicity noted VCM was mutagenic and concluded that vinyl chloride was a human carcinogen and its target organs were the liver, brain, lungs and blood

1981 US researchers found studies suggested a link between VCM and lymphatic and haemapoietic system cancers (Infante 1981) and showed associations between VCM exposure and CNS cancers and lung cancer

IARC re-confirms vinyl chloride as a human carcinogen and noted inconclusive data on breast cancer and urinary cancer in female workers in plastics/PVC fabrication

Government departments such as the HSE and DWP do not offer coordinated and comprehensive support to those who later develop diseases that may be caused or related to their past work. The study presented here describes research designed and conducted by the former employees and their representatives. It demonstrates what might be termed type 8 lay, popular or worker epidemiology (See table below and also Watterson 1992; Watterson 1994; Popay and Williams 1996; Bloor 2000). Such methods have wide applications in public health generally as well as in occupational health (Hynes et al. 2003).

Types of Lay Epidemiology

(1) Epidemiologists design, carry out, analyse and present the study
(2) Epidemiologists design, study and train and use lay staff to carry out survey. Epidemiologists analyse and present data.
(3) Epidemiologists invite lay people to contribute to design of study protocol. Lay staff carry out questionnaire surveys, interviews. Epidemiologists analyse, present data.
(4) Epidemiologists invite lay people to contribute to study design. Lay people carry out surveys. Epidemiologists, with lay people, analyse and present results.
(5) Lay people identify problem and invite epidemiologists to investigate the problem. Back to (1)
(6) Lay people identify problems, involve epidemiologists. Joint protocol is drawn up. Back to (3) and (4)
(7) Lay people identify problem, involve epidemiologists. Joint protocol. Lay people and epidemiologists jointly investigate problem, analyse results. Joint presentation of results.
(8) Lay people identify problem. Develop tools with health professionals, lay people collect data, data analysed jointly by lay people and health professionals, joint report produced.

(based on Watterson 1999 and Watterson 2003)

Occupational Hygiene Standards Relating to Controlling VCM Exposures and Possible Plant Exposures at Vinatex

Exposure limits in the 1970s across the world illustrate the very different risk assessments made for vinyl chloride and were critical to the relatively high exposures of workers to VCM that were acceptable in the UK.

Table 2. Threshold Limit Values for vinyl chloride in 1977

Country	TLV 8 hour	Country	TLV 8 hour
UK	10ppm	Italy	50ppm
Sweden	1ppm	USA	1ppm

Source IARC 1979:380.

Adverse effects of VCM , in terms of animal carcinogenicity, were detected by Maltoni at 50ppm in the 1970s. In 1977 , NIOSH surveyed 3 VCM plants and found 8 hour TWAs for VCM of 0.7-27ppm (La Dou 1997:474). Remarkably in the UK in 1999 the maximum exposure standard for vinyl chloride was still 7ppm over an 8 hour time weighted average with an overriding annual exposure limit of 3ppm. (HSE 1999:21). In the USA in 1999 the ACGIH had a time weighted average for vinyl chloride of 1ppm (ACGIH 199:71)

Where no or incomplete or inaccurate monitoring of VCM occurred in VCM and PVC polymerisation plants, some crude exposure indicators may be available. In the 1940s and 1950s VCM exposures in some PVC plants often exceeded 1000 ppm (Lewis in LaDou 1997:517) In the US exposures in such plants between 1970 and 1974 ranged between 100 and 200 ppm. Without ventilation, typical VCM air concentrations were around 3,000 ppm; in scraping they were 600-1000 ppm; near polymer reactors in 1950s levels of 4000 ppm have been recorded. Factory workplaces where PVC has been produced have had air concentrations of 40-312 ppm with peaks in 1950s of up to 33,500 ppm (IARC 1979:380). In UK cable factories, VCM levels of 0.15-0.35 ppm were recorded in the 1970s (Murdoch and Hammond 1977:55).

The odour threshold of VCM for humans may vary but has been placed at around 500 ppm. This may serve as some indicator of levels reported by ex-workers in Vinatex. VCM levels recorded in autoclave cleaning during the 1970s were also recorded at around 3000 ppm (Barnes cited in Langard 2000). The Norwegians considered that 'Before 1970 it is likely that a surplus of monomer was present in the PVC when leaving the manufacturing plant which could have been 500 ppm of VCM (Landgard 2000). In Russia large epidemiological studies found that cancer risks to VCM workers were highest in workers exposed to 300mg/m^3 or more who worked at plants for 15 to 19 years (Smulevich et al. 1988)

Diseases Associated with VCM Reported in the 1970 or Recorded in Cohorts of Workers Exposed in the 1970s of Relevance to the Vinatex Workers

Hepatic angiosarcoma has been strongly linked to VCM exposure since the 1970s even when a powerful healthy worker effect was observed in cohorts studied (Langard et al. 2000; Fox et al. 1977; Heldass et al. 1984; Salmon 1985; Jones et al. 1988). In 1974 two angiosarcoma cases were reported in Italian workers (Maltoni 1974). In 1975 two possible angiosarcoma cases were reported in Swedish PVC workers (Byren et al. 1975); two in Yugoslavia in the same year (Zorica et al. 1975); and ten in Canada (Delorme 1978). Similar cases were reported in France (Makk et al. 1975). Recent studies have continued to detect excesses of primary liver cancer cases in 1259 Italian workers exposed to VCM through the 1970s and 1980s (8 observed cases) (Piratsu et al. 1998). Cohort mortality studies of VCM exposed workers showed significant mortality rates for liver cancer especially angiosarcoma. 1991 studies showed biliary tract cancer and liver cancer risks other than angiosarcoma to be increased in VCM workers (Wong 1991). Other liver changes have been reported in PVC workers with 10 – 25% of PVC workers in cross-sectional studies in the 1970s having liver function abnormalities although not all these effects were connected to VCM exposure (Rosenstock and Cullen 1994:789). Researchers concluded that relatively low levels of VCM cause liver damage (Cheng et al. 1999). Italian studies of 1259 VCM and polymerisation plant workers found non-significant increases of this disease in workers in two out of three plants.

Lung cancer has been associated with VCM exposure since at least the 1970s (Maltoni et al. 1981; Wagoner 1983; Langard et al. 2000). By 1979 VCM was designated as a known cause of human lung cancer (Rosenstock and Cullen 1994:550). IARC in 1979 noted 'several independent but mutually confirmatory studies have shown that exposure to vinyl chloride results in an increased carcinogenic risk in humans, involving the lung...." (IARC 1979:377). By 1989, vinyl chloride in plastics production was listed as a suspect cause of lung cancer (Wu et al. 1989). In one Italian VCM plant, observed mortality for lung cancer was higher than expected with an SMR of 146 based on 14 cases (Piratsu 1998). The researchers considered that their results pointed to VCM's 'possible role in lung cancer development' as indicated in previous studies in the Porto Marghera plants. In 2000, a 428 Norwegian worker cohort followed from 1953 to 1993 observed 11 cases of lung cancer against 8 expected (Langard 2000).

Laryngeal cancer has been associated with VCM since the 1970s-80s (Langard et al. 2000). Skin cancer has been associated with VCM since the 1970s-80s (Heldaas 1984:Storetvedt et al. 1987; Langard et al. 2000). In a recent study of a cohort of 428 workers in Norway in a study group followed from 1953 to 1993, 7 melanoma cases were recorded against 2.07 expected (Langard et al. 2000). In addition to the melanoma cases, a follow up study found 5 cases of spinocellular skin cancer when 1.7 were expected. Bladder cancer has been associated with VCM since the early 1990s (Simonato et al. 1991; Langard et al. 2000)

Brain cancer has been associated with VCM since the 1970s-80s (Wagoner 1983; Smulevich 1988; Langard et al. 2000). IARC in 1979 noted 'several independent but mutually confirmatory studies have shown that exposure to vinyl chloride results in an increased carcinogenic risk in humans, involving the brain." (IARC 1979:377) In 1991 Wong in a study for the industry of 1536 deaths in 10173 PVC workers across 37 plants in the USA found a significant increase in brain tumours especially of workers exposed to VCM for 20 or more years (Wong 1991). In the mid 1990s leading occupational physicians felt able to state with regard to human brain neoplasms that " an association with vinyl chloride is generally (though not universally) agreed upon as an occupational cause of brain neoplasms and may be considered as a suspected cause of the disease" (in Rosenstock and Cullen 1994:600). Adverse effects on the neurological system have also been associated with VCM. 5 out of 8 studies assessed in 1980 found excesses of CNS tumours in VCM exposed workers (Infante 1980)

Thyroid cancer has been associated with VCM since the 1970s-80s (Langard et al. 2000). Testicular cancer has been associated with VCM (Langard et al. 2000). Leukaemias associated with VCM exposure in humans (Smulevich et al. 1988). IARC in 1979 noted 'several independent but mutually confirmatory studies have shown that exposure to vinyl chloride results in an increased carcinogenic risk in humans, involving the haemo-lymphopoietic systems ." (IARC 1979:377).

Immunological data from a small study of 19 of 28 patients with 'vinyl chloride disease' suggest an immune complex disorder (Ward 1976). Occupational sclerdoma has been linked to VCM exposure. "a scleroderma-like syndrome has been well documented in workers exposed to vinyl chloride" (Rosenstock and Cullen 1994:347). Others consider that no conclusive association has been reported yet (Steen 1999). However, associations between autoimmune diseases in humans and exposure to VC have been reported (Powell 1999). VCM exposed male workers have shown 'decreased androgen levels, decreased libido but few studies have examined VCM reproductive effects on women workers (La Dou 1997:475).

Impaired pulmonary function in VC exposed workers has been reported (Miller et al. 1975b, Gamble et al. 1976). In 1976 20% of workers at one PVC plant were found to have opacities on chest X-rays (Lilis 1976). There appears to be a link between such opacities and pulmonary lung function abnormalities. Cases of pneumoconiosis in PVC dust exposed workers have been reported and some PVC production and fabrication workers exposed to more than $10/mg^3$ of PVC dust have reduced lung function and an increased incidence of chest X-ray abnormalities (LaDou 1997). In 1982 a UK study suggested that 'work in a PVC plant before 1975 may have involved exposure to a substance that caused more damage to the lungs in a small number of men' (Lloyd et al. 1982)

Skeletal effects were first reported in humans exposed to VCM in the late 1950s and defined as acro-osteolysis syndrome (Rosenstock and Cullen 1994:788). Around 3% to 6% of the PVC workers studied in the 1960s and 1970s had this syndrome and it was mainly linked to workers with high VCM exposure. Excesses of cancer of the bone have been associated with VCM workers in the period 1939-1977 (Smulevich et al. 1988).

Cardio-vascular and other related effects of chemicals including VCM on workers has been the subject of enquiry from at least the early 1970s (Capellini et al. 1974). 16 of 20 German PVC workers found to have thrombocytopenia (Marsteller et al. 1973). By 1977 researchers were confident in observing that 'thrombocytopenia is often one of the first signs of vinyl chloride disease': with changes in platelets and destruction of platelets (Heusermann et al. 1977). Changes in blood of VCM exposed workers were identified as a well known effect of that exposure (ATSDR 1989) as were other harmful effects to the cardio-vascular system (Maschewsky 1993). In 1996 commentators concluded that chemicals including vinyl chloride 'produced both hypertension and cardiac arrhythmias in most studies' (Taylor 1996)

In 1981 a study explored neurological changes in vinyl chloride exposed workers (Styblova et al. 1981). In 1983 neurological disturbances were found among 200 PVC production workers with 27% having astheno-autonomic syndrome and 44% with various neurological effects. 48% also reported headaches, 26% nervousness and 14% loss of memory (Langauer-Lewowicka et al. 1983). Similar results were found in a Polish study with various cerebellar syndromes and headaches, irritability and sleep disturbance also reported (Kurzbauer 1988).

One study at least has examined both neurological and psychiatric disorders involved in vinyl chloride disease based on literature searches and case studies. The results found in chronically exposed VCM workers: neurological disturbances including sensory-motor polyneuropathy, trigeminal sensory neuropathy, slight pyramidal signs and cerebellar and extrapyrimidal.. cerebellar... motor disorders. Psychiatric disturbances present as neurasthenic or depressive syndromes (Podoll et al. 1990).

The VINATEX Vinyl Chloride Plant

Data on the Plant

The Chesterfield vinyl chloride plant opened in 1968 and began production in 1969. It is understood that the plant had two reactor buildings, one operational in 1969 and another operational in 1970, each building containing 20 autoclaves. The workforce for the plant between 1968 and 1984 is estimated at 428. The majority of production workers apparently spent at least six months in the Dryer (bagging) building before moving to the autoclave buildings. In addition to the production workers, there were 12 to 15 fitters in the plant covering day and night shifts. The plant also contained some 4 or 5 technicians, 4 warehouse staff. For each shift there was also a foreman, production manager and plant manager. Later an additional supervisor post was created. 3 secretarial and administrative staff were on site as were a number of cleaners and canteen workers, a safety officer appointed in the late 1970s and 2 odd job ‘men’. On any one shift there would be approximately 35 people on site and there were 4 shifts in the 24 hour cycle.

VCM Exposures at the Plant

Employee accounts of very varied VCM exposure levels include the following figures. In 1970 workers reported some levels of 200ppm in the plant. In 1974 figures of up to 100ppm were recorded in the plant and in bagging and other areas figures of 1000 to 4000ppm were recorded. Some shift foremen were exposed to between 0.1 – 6.5ppm between 1975-1984 with one exposure up to 142ppm. Reactor lead operators between 1974 and 1984 were working in atmospheres where VCM levels ranged from 3.5 to 34.6ppm. Drivers in 1974 loading tankers had TWA VCM levels recorded in their work areas of between 1.8ppm and 9.9ppm.Warehouse staff were working in areas where VCM levels ranged from 10.5ppm TWA in 1975 to 0.5ppm in 1977 with levels dropping to 0.1ppm in the mid 1980s.

A General Municipal Workers Union (trade union) visit to Vinatex in 1981 noted that excursions above the TWA TLV of 10ppm had occurred with 11 excursions at 11.4ppm (GMWU Visit 26 October 1981). Concerns about VCM extractor units on reactors and high level alarms on VCM recovery tanks or rather their absence in the plant were also expressed by the HSE in reports of a visit in November 1979. 1973 VCM was recorded in the plant at airborne levels of 50,000 ppm (Morris 1998) post-1974 Levels of VCM of 3000ppm were recorded in the plant (TUSC Report 1997/8:3)

Health Problems Identified in the Vinatex Plant Through the 1970s and 1980s

In the 1970s a series of 9 gassing incidents were reported in the plant that indicate major problems with systems of work and basic health and safety management in the plant.

Early 1980s: the plant reportedly settled 35 claims for acro-osteolysis. The ex-Vinatex workers support group have details of 31 settled cases which include acro-osteolysis cases, other skeletal problems and also cases relating to respiratory, reproductive, circulatory, neurological effects. 27 claims were settled totalling £857,000. Settlements ranged from £1500 to £100,000.

1984 Norsk Hydro who took over the plant in 1980 when Vinatex, ceased production of PVC and the plant closed in 1986. Drivers previously employed by Vinatex apparently still worked at Staveley until 1991/2. 2 angiosarcoma cases have been reported in Vinatex workers by 1998 (Morris 1998). The ex-Vinatex workers group are aware of 1 definite angiosarcoma case and have come across a report of 1 other. 1 liver cancer case and a number of suspected liver cancer cases are also known to the group.

UK data on the morbidity and mortality of former VCM and PVC workers are relatively restricted, frequently incomplete and often fragmented. Processes if not companies and industries have moved on leaving many vinyl chloride workers behind with no jobs and concerns about their health. Supposedly some of the major sources of information in the UK on these workers come in the 2 angiosarcoma registers. The HSE kept such a register from the early 1970s until 1994. Problems relating to diagnosis among pathologists of angiosarcoma slides emerged.

The plastics industry set up a voluntary angiosarcoma register of its own initially through ICI in UK and this is also recognised as incomplete (ref). In 1999 the industry register contained 196 cases with an average latency period recorded of 20 years between first exposure and onset of the liver cancer. The shortest latency period was 11 years and the longest was 40 years. These data indicate that the HSE register should have been kept open for significantly longer than it was even with no angiosarcoma cases reported for those exposed after 1974. Those health professionals who deal with the industry register acknowledge that angiosarcoma incidence varies greatly between plants supposedly using the same technologies. This may relate to work allocation and other factors. The industry register apparently has no angiosarcoma cases recorded from Vinatex.

VCM Exposure Levels and Disease

The principal route of entry of VCM for production workers has been inhalation. However, in the past it was observed that 'dermal absorption may be significant during manual reactor vessel cleaning' (La Dou 1997:474). By 1983 occupational physicians in the EU were indicating that employees should have an examination, before started working with VCM, of the lungs, cardiovascular system and liver and they advised liver function tests, tests on hand and finger bones, blood counts and ventilatory function tests (Roi 1983:131-132).

Health Survey Methods and Results (171 Ex-Vinatex Employees)

The survey, designed and conducted by workers and their representatives, analysed 162 questionnaires from ex-Vinatex workers of 229 identified. Of the 229 identified, 30 are deceased, 8 were uncontactable and may also be deceased. 17 men did not wish to be involved in the study and 3 men came forward after the interview process was concluded. Those participating in the survey were contacted by word of mouth and through articles in the local press asking ex-Vinatex workers to participate in the survey. 5 pilot interviews were carried out and the initial questionnaire was modified. The survey consisted of a pre-circulated work history questionnaire sent out to each interviewee to be completed before the interview. At the interview, the interviewer filled in the health questionnaire. The two questionnaires explored the employees' work at Vinatex, some aspects of their general health and the type or types of job that they had done at Vinatex.

Employment

The starting date of employment at Vinatex was recorded as were the jobs undertaken at the plant during employment, the type and length of time in each job. Some effort was also made to assess what if any harmful chemicals the employee may have been exposed to, how they were exposed, what information was made available on these chemicals, what if any personal protective equipment (PPE) was available. Assessments of PPE effectiveness were made and those interviewed were asked about other factors connected to the job that may have influenced health.

Health

Questions about general health and medication were asked. Specific sections of questions using standard questionnaires from tried and tested questionnaires that have been designed to reduce errors. The cardio-vascular sections have been taken from the Health Survey for England Report of 1992 (Health Survey for England 1994:258-307) , the respiratory sections come from the European Union Iron and Steel survey (European Community for Coal and Steel Respiratory symptoms survey 1987 updating of 1962/1967 questionnaires) and the Mental Health Survey comes from the tool developed by Hanninen and Luukonen (Hanninen et al. 1985)

Areas of illness explored covered:

Cardio-vascular disease	Respiratory problems	Raynauds phenomenon
Bone/joint problems	Skin problems	Blood problems
Mental health problems	Reproductive problems	Other problems

METHODS

The health survey used 'a self-reported illness questionnaire' with all the associated strengths and weaknesses of that method. The group are also self-selecting and of 428 workers estimated to have been employed at the plant, data exist for 171. The response rate of almost 50% to the questionnaire, after exclusion of those known to be deceased or uncontactable, is excellent but it too does provide only a partial picture of the workforce.

The data analysis has been carried out using standard statistical packages (SPSS and Excel). The questionnaires were filled in and interviews conducted from June 1998 to August 1999.

The number of interviewers used were 10. One interviewer conducted 2 interviews, one conducted 4 interviews, the remainder conducted between 7 and 33 interviews each. All interviewers had previous interviewing experience. All interviewers undertook a one day training session on interviewing skills as well as being issued with guidance and instruction notes. The training assisted interviewers in standardising the interviewing process.

Only a very small number of women – 5 in total - filled in questionnaires as very few worked at the plant: therefore the analysis is restricted to male workers. The analysis provides data about the age of ex-workers, period of time spent working at Vinatex, Information about age, sex, length of time employees worked at the Vinatex plant, and smoking were collected and the relevant multivariate analysis was performed

Analysis of Ill-Health Reported

The study looks at the survivor populations. Ex-Vinatex workers may have died prematurely and so would not be included in the survey results. This would then skew the results to indicate a healthier population at the factory than in fact was the case. Several issues emerge about the nature of the data generated. For instance, the Vinatex workers often came from other and frequently heavy industries especially coal mining. Previous occupations may have contributed towards certain respiratory conditions and this may make data generated on these topics of limited value. Likewise the ex-Vinatex workers are also now older and data about cardio-vascular disease and mental health, in terms of memory etc, will also be influenced by such factors.

Results

TRUST manually recorded the following illnesses contained in the Health Study questionnaire. 162 case studies (157 men and 5 women) were analysed and the results are set out below. Two independent people according to agreed criteria calculated these figures.

113 out of 162 former workers identified as having symptoms associated with Raynaud's Phenomenon. According to the Raynaud's and Scleroderma Association (1999) women are affected nine times more than men. TRUST also found that six former workers had bladder cancer; four have skin cancer; one former worker involved in the interviewing has since died of lung and brain cancer; one had an undetermined cancer ; one had colon cancer and one prostate cancer.

VCM causes acro-osteolysis amongst PVC processing workers. Acro-osteolysis is characterised by bone absorption in the fingers, which become slightly shortened and clubbed (Grainger, Walker, Ward 1979). 41 out of 162 former workers indicated symptoms of Acro-osteolysis. Around 3% to 6% of the PVC workers studied in the 1960s and 1970s had this syndrome. However, the figures analysed by TRUST reveals that 25% of the former Vinatex workers indicated symptoms of Acro-osteolysis.

VCM also causes scleroderma amongst PVC processing workers. The condition is a disease of the immune system causing the skin usually on the hands and feet to become stiff, tight and shiny, thickening of the connective tissue becomes patchy or fibrotic). 35 out of the 162 former workers indicated symptoms of scleroderma. Scleroderma affects 20 in every million of the population per year and is three times more common in women than men (Raynaud's and Scleroderma Association 1999.

Other data were analysed using SPSS and produced the following results. Bronchitis is generally defined as having a productive cough for as much as three months each year. On this definition 32% had bronchitis. 48% reported productive cough (i.e. a cough which produced phlegm), and within this number current smokers were most likely to report productive cough, ex-smokers less so. Only 30% of those who had never smoked reported a productive cough of any kind, and only 20% had chronic bronchitis.

Symptoms of wheeziness showed a similar pattern to those of coughing with the highest levels of reporting amongst current smokers, least amongst never-smokers, and intermediate levels for ex-smokers. There did appear to be a consistent pattern to reported 'abnormal breathing', which was reported more frequently amongst those who had worked longer at the plant.

This pattern was not observed, however, in the reported symptoms of breathlessness. High levels of breathlessness were reported, with 30% of those who had never smoked reporting the higher level of breathlessness (difficulty when walking on level ground). Smoking made less difference to the reporting of breathlessness than to reported productive cough.

Cardiovascular Disease

The workers were asked questions about their history of heart disease and diabetes, and stroke. The reported levels were similar to those found in other studies, and there seemed to be little consistent relationship between the level of reporting of different kinds of cardiovascular disease and length of time working at the plant.

Psychological symptoms and Mental processes

There were high levels of reporting of symptoms related to mental activity and mood. For 10 questions relating to memory, concentration, thinking and tiredness over 45% reported problems, with 77% needing to take notes to assist them. For the four questions taken from a standard method of detecting depression a large proportion of those responding described depressed mood, or, for example, loss of pleasure from things they used to enjoy.

Discussion

Respiratory Illness

The established causes of respiratory illness are workplace pollution, environmental pollution, cigarette smoking, and previous medical history (family, childhood illness, etc). These interact with the effect that older people with exposure to pollutants and cigarette smoke are at highest risk. The levels reported in this survey for chronic bronchitis are in line with those from the Health Survey of England (HSfE). However the results for abnormal breathing and breathlessness on level ground are much higher than those reported in HSfE

This is consistent with what is already known about the effects of vinyl chloride monomer and PVC. Breathlessness results from changes in the body of the lung tissue reflected in reported severe breathlessness, rather than from changes in the main lung airways which would be reported as wheezing and bronchitis.

Breathlessness

HSFE			
Age	45-54	55-64	Vinatex (all)
None	84	72	32
Level 1	11	15	20
Level 2	5	13	48

Cardiovascular Symptoms

This section deals with high blood pressure, angina, heart attacks, other heart trouble, stroke, diabetes and other effects. The reported cardiovascular disease is in line with that found in the Health Survey for England and the Sheffield health survey (SHAIPS) when age, sex, and social class are taken into account. While there is evidence for changes in blood chemistry from studies carried out on Vinatex workers and elsewhere, and some evidence of cardiovascular disease in the literature, this survey did not confirm the findings.

Mental Processes

This section includes data on memory, concentration, discussions, feeling upset, irritability, disordered thinking, adapting, hobbies, tiredness, alcohol toleration, air toleration, sadness, pessimism, loss of pleasure, loss of interest, state of mind. The questionnaire used has been used as a screening tool in Scandinavian studies of solvent exposed workers. In a study carried out on solvent exposed workers matched with controls in Sheffield, there was a marked difference between the cases of solvent syndrome and the controls, which paralleled differences in score when carrying out psychological tests. The level of reported symptoms in the Vinatex study is comparable with that in other studies.

While these results on mental processes follow what has been reported in the literature, some caution must be exercised in their interpretation. We do not have standard values for comparison for men in this age group who are no longer working. It is possible that other factors are playing a role in the pattern of reporting. The relationship with length of time worked at Vinatex is not what would be expected if length of exposure was a factor. Reanalysis using period of exposure (before and after improvements in protection of workers were introduced) or intensity of exposure might help to clarify this.

The fact remains that very high levels of psychological symptoms are reported and the reported problems are consistent with what has been reported in the past.

CONCLUSION

Very high levels of reporting, above those expected from comparable surveys, for respiratory and psychological symptoms have been identified. Some of the psychological symptoms may be secondary to unemployment, which is itself a consequence of the long-term limiting illness which the legacy of working at Vinatex. These results are not inconsistent with findings in some of the literature on VCM exposure.

The failure of industry and HSE to follow up and properly investigate the health status of UK workers exposed to vinyl chloride monomer has been very serious albeit not unique in Western Europe. Major questions are also raised about the weak UK control standards for VCM from the 1970s through to the 1990s.

The survey fills in some gaps in our knowledge about the health status now of former Vinatex workers but there are significant methodological limitations. Nevertheless it provides data that has not hitherto been collected or recently explored by either industry or HSE on a similar scale. It is an indictment of both HSE and industry in the UK that these matters have not been more fully investigated and from a much earlier date. Only in January 2000 did the HSE search the HSE angiosarcoma register for cases involving Vinatex workers: this is a remarkable omission. The HSE could not then identify any angiosarcoma cases from the Vinatex plant but found one angiosarcoma of the soft tissue in the HSE study of 428 Vinatex workers that may or may not have been an incorrectly diagnosed liver angiosarcoma. The apparent cluster of bladder cancer cases will be the subject of further analysis.

Further action is needed to address the health needs, research expectations and equity concerns of the former workers. The location of HSE angiosarcoma register should be determined by the ex-employees as well as industry and HSE. Full and complete disclosure of data in appropriate and ethical form should occur of all HSE and company data to the ex-Vinatex workers and their representatives on VCM exposures and industry and HSE knowledge of health hazards from the early 1970s onwards.

ACKNOWLEDGMENT

The Authors would like to thank M Cairns and M Wingfield for assistance in data entry and analysis.

REFERENCES

ACGIH. 1999. *1999 TLVs and BEIs*. Cincinnati, ACGIH.

Anon. 1976. Vinyl Chloride: Can the Worker be Protected? *N. Engl. J. Med.* Mar 18; 294(12): 653-7.

Anon. 1981. Conference to Re-evaluate the Toxicity of Vinyl Chloride Monomer, Regulatory and enforcement standards. Russian and Italian toxicology data in 1930s, 1940s and 1950s. Poly(vinyl chloride) and Structural Analogs. Bethesda, Md., March 20-21, 1980, *Environ Health Perspect* 1981 Oct; 41:1-231

ATSDR. 1989. *Vinyl Chloride: Public Health Statement, August*. Washington ATSDR.

ATSDR. 1997. *Vinyl Chloride: Tox FAQs*, September. Washington, ATSDR.

Berk PD, Martin JF, Young RS, Creech J, Selikoff IJ, Falk H, Watanabe P, Popper H, Thomas L. 1976. Vinyl Chloride-Associated Liver Disease, *Ann. Intern. Med.* Jun; 84(6): 717-31.

Bloor M. 2000. The South Wales Miners Federation, Miners' Lung and the Instrumental Use of Expertise 1900- 1950, *Social Studies of Science* 30(1); 125-40.

Bonneton G, Champetier J, Sotto JJ, Guidicelli H, Letoublon C, Pahn M. 1975. Case of Spontaneous Rupture of a Hepatic Angiosarcoma in a Worker exposed to Vinyl Chloride, *Chirurgie* Dec; 101(12): 936-42.

Breeze E, Maidment A, Bennett N, Flatley J, Carey S. 1994. *Health Survey for England 1992*. London, HMSO.

Buffler PA, Wood S, Eifler C, Suarez L, Kilian DJ. 1979. Mortality Experience of Workers in a Vinyl Chloride Monomer Production Plant, *J. Occup. Med.* 1979 Mar; 21(3): 195-203.

Byren D, Holmberg B. (1975). Two Possible Cases of Angiosarcoma of the Liver in a Group of Swedish Vinyl Chloride-Polyvinyl Chloride Workers, *Ann. NY Acad. Sci.* Jan 31; 246: 249-50.

Capellini A, Maroni M. 1974. Clinical Studies of Arterial Hypertension and Coronary Disease and Their Possible Relations to the Work Environment in Chemcial Workers, *Med. Lav.* 65(7-8): 297-305.

Cheng TJ, Huang ML, You NC, Du CL, Chau TT. 1999. Abnormal Liver Function in Workers Exposed to Low Levels of Ethylene Dichloride And Vinyl Chloride Monomer, *J Occup. Environ. Med.* 41(12): 1128-33.

Corn JK. (1984). Vinyl Chloride, Setting a Workplace Standard: An Historical Perspective on Assessing Risk, *J. Public Health Policy* Dec; 5(4):497-512.

Couderc P, Panh MH, Pasquier B, Pasquier D, N'golet A, Faure H. 1976. Osseous Angiosarcoma Symptomatic of Liver Tumor in Worker Exposed to Vinyl Chloride, *Sem Hop* 1976 Sep 10-20; 52(31-32): 1721-2.

Delorme F. 1978. 10 Canadian Cases of Angiosarcoma of the Liver in Vinyl Chloride Workers, *Ann. Anat. Pathol.* (Paris) 1978;23(2): 97-104.

Doll R. 1988. Effects of Exposure to Vinyl Chloride. An Assessment of the Evidence, *Scand J. Work Environ. Health* 1988 Apr; 14(2): 61-78.

Duck BW. 1975. Proceedings: Vinyl Chloride Carcinogenesis, *Br. J. Cancer* 1975 Aug; 32(2): 260.

Elliott P, Kleinschmidt I. 1997. Angiosarcoma of the Liver in Great Britain in Proximity to Vinyl Chloride Sites, *Occup. Environ Med.* Jan; 54(1): 14-8.

European Community for Coal and Steel Questionnaire on Respiratory Symptoms. 1987. updated from 1962 and 1967 MRC Bronchitis questionnaire.

Falk H, Heath CW Jr, Carter CD, Wagoner JK, Waxweiler RJ, Stringer WT. 1974. Letter: Mortality Among Vinyl-chloride Workers. *Lancet* Sep 28;2(7883): 784.

Falk H, Waxweiler RJ. 1976. Epidemiological Studies of Vinyl Chloride Health Wffects in the United States, *Proc. R. Soc. Med.* 1976 Apr; 69(4): 303-6.

Forman D, Bennett B, Stafford J, Doll R. 1985. Exposure to Vinyl Chloride and Angiosarcoma of the Liver: a Report of the Register of Cases, *Br. J. Ind. Med.* 1985 Nov; 42(11): 750-3.

Fox AJ, Collier PF. 1977. Mortality Experience of Workers Exposed to Vinyl Chloride Monomer in the Manufacture of Polyvinyl Chloride in Great Britain, *Br. J. Ind. Med.* Feb; 34(1):1-10.

Gamble J, Liu S, McMichael AJ, Waxweiler RJ. 1976. Effect of Occupational and Non-occupational Factors on the Respiratory System of Vinyl Chloride and Other Workers, *J Occup Med*, 18:659-670.

Gokel JM, Liebezeit E, Eder M. 1976. Hemangiosarcoma and Hepatocellular Carcinoma of the Liver Following Vinyl Chloride Exposure. A report of Two Cases, *Virchows Arch A Pathol Anat Histol* 1976 Dec 27; 372(3): 195-203.

Grainger RG, Walker AE, Ward AM. 1980. Vinyl Chloride Monomer-Induced Disease: Clinical, Radiological and Immunological Aspects in *Preger L and Steiner RE* : 191-213.

Griciute L. (1978). The Carcinogenicity of Vinyl Chloride, *IARC Sci Publ* (22): 3-11.

Hanninen H, Luukkonen R. 1985. *Behavioural Methods in Screening Early Neurotoxic Effects: Methodological Considerations*. Copenhagen, WHO Environmental Health Series Document 3.

Hattis D. 1981. Needs For Public Health Intervention and Needs for New Research on Vinylhalides and Their Polymers: A Public Policy Perspective, *Environ Health Perspect* Oct; 41: 227-31.

Heldaas SS, Langard SL, Andersen A. 1984. Incidence of cancer among vinyl chloride and polyvinyl chloride workers. *Br. J. Ind. Med.* Feb; 41(1): 25-30.

Heusermann U and Stutts HJ. 1977. Aetiology of the Thrombocytopenia in Vinyl Chloride, *Blut* 35(4):317-22.

HSE. 1999. *EH40/99 Occupational Exposure Limits 1999*. London, HMSO.

Hublet P, Lefevre MJ, Decuyper L, Hanin C, Hamels J, Fievez M. 1977. A Case of Angiosarcoma of the Liver in a Worker With Long Exposure to Vinyl Chloride Monomer, *Arch Belg Med Soc* Nov-Dec; 35(9-10) :601-22.

Hynes HP, Brugge D, Osgood N, Snell J, Vallarino J, Spengler J. 2003. Where does the damp come from? *Journal of Public Health Policy* 4(3-4): 401-426.

Infante PF. 1981. Observations of the Site-Specific Carcinogenicity of Vinyl Chloride to Humans, *Environ Health Perspect* 1981 Oct; 41: 89-94.

International Agency for Research on Cancer. 1979. Some Monomers, Plastics and Synthetic Elastomers. Lyon, Volume 19 IARC: 377-438.

International Agency for Research on Cancer. 1987. *Monographs. Supplement 17.* Lyon, IARC.

Jones RD, Smith DM, Thomas PG. 1988. A Mortality Study of Vinyl *Chloride Monomer Workers Employed in the United Kingdom in 1940-1974, Scand. J. Work Environ Health* Jun; 14(3): 153-60.

Kurzbauer H. 1988. Effect of Vinyl Chloride and its Polymers on the Nervous System, *Neurol Neurochir Pol* 22(5): 404-409.

LaDou J. (ed) 1997. *Occupational and Environmental Medicine*. Connecticut, Appleton and Lange, 2nd ed.

Lancet. 1976. Letter: Vinyl chloride and Mortality? *Lancet* Aug 21; 2(7982): 416-7.

Langard S, Rosenberg J, Andersen A, Heldaas SS. 2000. Incidence of Cancer Among Workers Exposed to Vinyl Chloride in Polyvinyl Chloride Manufacture, *Occup. Environ. Med.* 57: 65-68.

Langauer-Lewowicka H, Kurzbauer H, Byczkowska Z, Wocka-Marek T. 1983. Vinyl Chloride Disease – Neurological Disturbances, *Int. Arch. Occup Environ. Health* 52(2):151-7.

Laplanche A, Clavel F, Contassot JC, Lanouziere C. 1987. Exposure to vVnyl Chloride Monomer: Report on a Cohort Study, *Br. J. Ind. Med.* 1987 Oct; 44(10): 711-5.

Levinson C. 1974. *Vinyl Chloride: a Case Study of the New Occupational Health Hazard.* Geneva, ICF.

Lilis R, Anderson H, Nicholson WJ et al. 1975. Prevalence of Disease Among VC and PVC Workers, *Ann. NY Academ. Sci.* 246:22-41.

Lilis R, Anderson H, Miller A. 1976. Pulmonary Changes Among Vinyl Chloride Polymerization Workers, *Chest* 69: 299S-303S.

Lloyd JW (1975) Angiosarcoma of the liver in vinyl chloride/polyvinyl chloride workers, *J Occup. Med.* May;17(5): 333-4.

Lloyd MH, Gauld S, Copland I. 1982. *IOM Technical Memorandum*. Edinburgh, IOM.

Makk L, Delorme F, Creech JL. 1975. Angiosarcomas of the Liver In Workers Having had Prolonged Contact With Vinyl Chloride: Epidemiology and Program of Research in the Workers, *Union Med. Can.* Dec; 104(12): 1833-5.

Maltoni C. 1974a. Liver Angiosarcoma in Workers Exposed to Vinyl Chloride. Report on the 1st 2 cases encountered, *Med. Lav.* Nov-Dec; 65 (11-12): 445-50.

Maltoni C, Lefemine G, Chieco P, Carretti D. 1974b. Vinyl Chloride Carcinogenesis: Current Results and Perspectives, *Med. Lav.* Nov-Dec; 65 (11-12): 421-44.

Maltoni C, Lodi P. 1981. Results of Sputum, Cytology Among Workers Exposed to Vinyl Chloride Monomer and to PolyVinyl Chloride. *Environ. Health Perspect* Oct; 41: 85-8.

Marsteller HJ, Lelbach WK, Miller R, Juhe S, Lange CE et al. .1973. Chronisch -toxische Leberschaeden bei Arbeitern in der PVC-Produktion, *DTsch Med Wschr* 98: 2311-14.

Maschewsky W. 1993. Do Workplace Chemicals Harm the Heart? *Soz Praventivmed* 38(2): 71-6.

Miller A. 1975a. Pulmonary Function Defects in Non-smoking Vinyl Chloride Workers, *Env Health Persp.* 11: 247-250.

Miller A, Teirsten AS, Chuang M, Selikoff IJ. 1975b. Changes in Pulmonary Function in Workers Exposed to Vinyl Chloride and PVC, *Ann. NY Academ Sci.* 246:42-52.

Morris J. 1998. Grim Numbers, *Houston Chronicle*, 26/6/98.

Murdoch IA and Hammond AR. 1977. A Practical Method for the Measurment of Vinyl Chloride Monomer in Air, *Ann. Occ. Hyg.* 20: 55-61.

North Derbyshire Trade Union Safety Committee. 1998. *Annual Report 1997-8.* Chesterfield, TUSC.

Panh Meng H, Faure H, Pasquier D, Couderc P. (1977. Liver Aangiosarcomas Occasioned by Exposure to Vinyl Chloride, *Acta Pharmacol. Toxicol* (Copenh) 41 Suppl 2: 331.

Piratsu R, Bruno C, De Santis M, Comba P. 1998. An Epidemiological Study of Workers Exposed to Vinyl Chloride in the Pplants of Ferrara, Rosignano and Ravenna, *Epidemiol. Prev* 22(4): 226-236.

Podoll K, Berg-Dammer E, Noth J. 1990. Neurologic and Psychiatric Disorders in Vinyl Chloride Disease, *Fortschr Neurol Psychiatri* 58(11): 439-43.

Popay J and Williams G. 1996. Public Health Research and Lay Knowledge, *Social Science and Medicine*, 42 (5): 759-768.

Powell JJ, Van De Water J, Gershwin ME. 1999. Evidence for the Role of Environmental Agents in the Initiation or Progression of Autoimmune Conditions, *Environ. Health Perspectives* 107(Supplt 5): 667-672.

Preger L and Steiner RE (1980) *Induced Disease: Drug Irradiation, Occupation.* Grune and Stratton, Harcourt Brace.New York

Puschin GA. 1965. *Soviet Medicine 28:132.*

Roi, R, Town WG, Hunter WG et al. 1983. *Occupational Health Guidelines for Chemical Risk.* Luxembourg, JRC, ISPA.

Rosenstock L and Cullen MR. (eds) 1994. *Textbook of Clinical Occupational and Environmental Medicine.* Philadelphia, WB Saunders and Co.

Simonato L, L'Abbe KA, Andersen A et al. 1991. A Collaborative Study Of Cancer Incidence and Mortality of Vinyl Chloride Workers, *Scand. J. Work Environ. Health* 17: 159-169.

Salmon AG. 1985. Vinyl Chloride: the Evidence for Human Carcinogenicity in Different Target Organs, *Br. J. Ind. Med.* Feb; 42(2): 73-4.

Schotteck W (1969) Zur Toxikologie des Vinylchlorids. *Chem. Tech.* 21:708.

Smulevich VB, Fedotova IV, Filatova VS. 1988. Increasing Evidence of the Rise of Cancer in Workers Exposed to Vinyl Chloride, *Br. J. Ind. Med.* Feb; 45(2): 93-7.

Steen VD. (1999). Occupational Sclerdoma, *Curr. Opin. Rheumatol.,* 11(6): 490-494.

Storetvedt Heldaas S, Andersen AA, Langard S. 1987. Incidence of Ccancer Among Vinyl Chloride and Polyvinyl Chloride Workers: Further Eevidence for an Association with Malignant Melanoma, *Br. J. Ind. Med.* Apr; 44(4): 278-80.

Stblova V, Lambl V, Chumcal O, Kellerova V, Paskova V, Vitovcova J, Zlab L. 1981. Neurological Changes in Vinyl Chloride-exposed Wworkers. *J. Hyg. Epidemiol. Microbiol. Immunol.* 25(3): 233-243.

Suciu L, Drejman I , Valaski M. 1967. Contributions to the Study of Affections Cused by Vinyl Chloride, *Medecina Interne*,15:967.

Szende B. 1970. Vinylchloride. *Med di Lavaro,* 61:433.

Taylor AE. 1996. Cardiovascular Effects of Environmental Chemicals, *Otolaryngol. Head Neck Surg.* 114(2): 209-211.

Theriault G, Allard P. 1981. Cancer Mortality of a Group Of Canadian Workers Exposed to Vinyl Chloride Monomer, *J. Occup. Med.* Oct; 23(10): 671-6.

Torkelson TR, Oyen F, Rowe VK. 1961. The Toxicity of Vinyl Chloride as Determined by Repeated Exposures of Laboratory Animals, *Am. Indust. Hyg. Assoc. J.* 22:354.

Tribuch SR et al. 1949. cited in *Puschin. Gig. Sanit* 10:38.

Veltman G, Lange CE, Juhe S et al. 1975. Clinical Manifestations and Course of Vinyl Cchloride Disease, *Ann. NY Acad. Sci.* 246:6-17.

Vertkin JL, Mamontov JR. 1970. PVC Pneumoconiosis, *Gig Trud Prof Zabol* 14:29.

Viola PL, Bisotti A, Caputo A. 1971. Oncogenic Response of Rat Skin, Lungs and Bones to Vinyl Chloride, *Cancer Research*, 31:516.

Wagoner JK. (1983). Toxicity of Vinyl Chloride and PolyVinyl Chloride: a Critical Review, *Environ. Health Perspect* Oct; 52: 61-6.

Wagoner JK, Infante PF, Apfeldorf RB. 1980. Toxicity of Vinyl Chloride and Polyvinyl Chloride as seen Through Epidemiologic Observations, *J. Toxicol Environ. Health*, Sep-Nov;6 (5-6): 1101-7.

Ward AM, Udnoon S, Watkins J, Walker AE, Durk CS. 1976. Immunological Mechanisms in the Pathogenesis of Vinyl Chloride Disease, *British Medical Journal* I: 936-938.

Watterson A. 1993. Occupational Health in the UK Gas Industry'. in Platt S., Thomas H., Scott S. and Williams G. (eds) *Locating Health,* 172-194. London, Avebury Press.

Watterson A. 1999. Why We Still Have Old Epidemics and Endemics in Occupational Health: Policy and Practice Failures and Some Solutions, in Daykin N and Doyal L (eds) *Health and Work: Critical Perspectives*, 107-126. London, Macmillan.

Watterson A. (ed). 2003. *Public Health in Practice*. Basingstoke, Palgrave Macmillan.

Waxweiler RJ, Stringer W, Wagoner JK et al. (1976). Neoplastic Risk Aamong Workers Exposed to Vinyl Chloride, *Ann NY Acad Sci* 271: 40-48.

Weber H, Reinl W, Greiser E. 1981. German Investigations on Morbidity and Mortality of Workers Exposed to Vinyl Chloride, *Environ Health Perspect* Oct; 41:95-9.

Weinbren K. 1976. Histopathology of Liver Lesions Associated With Exposure to Vinyl Chloride Monomer, *Proc. R. Soc. Med. Apr*; 69(4): 299-303.

Wong O, Whorton MDZ, Foliart DE et al. 1991. An Industry-wide Epidemiologic Study of Vinyl Chloride Workers 1942-1982, *Am. J. Indust. Med.* 20: 317-334.

Wu W, Steenland K, Brown D et al. 1984. Cohort and Case Control Analyses of Workers Exposed to Vinyl Chloride: an Update, *J. Occup. Med.* 31:518.

Zorica M, Saric M, Konstantinovic M, Kovac I. 1975. 2 Ccases of Angiosarcoma of the Liver Following Exposure to Vinyl cCloride: Serbo-Croatia, *Arh. Hig. Rada Toksikol.* 26(4):275-81.

In: Understanding Risk
Editor: Matthias Beck
ISBN: 978-1-62618-686-6

Chapter 16

VIOLENCE TOWARDS MENTAL HEALTH NURSES IN ENGLAND AND THE NATURE OF THE POLICY RESPONSE: A FRAME ANALYSIS

Brodie Paterson*
School of Nursing, Midwifery and Health, University of Stirling, Stirling, Scotland, UK

ABSTRACT

Nurses working in services for people with mental health problems are twice as likely to be assaulted as nurses working in general hospital settings (Health Care Commission 2007). The emergence of the issue of violence towards nurses as a social problem has however been accompanied by a contest to date unexamined, between conflicting 'frames' of the problem, which this paper seeks to make transparent. Two distinct 'master' frames are discussed the 'individualising' and the 'co-creationist'. It is concluded that the influence of these frames has influenced the nature of responses to the problem but the recent dominance of the individualising frame is being challenged by the emergence or perhaps re-emergence, of the ideals and values of the therapeutic community.

INTRODUCTION

This paper will firstly, place the method of frame analysis in context as a sub type of discourse analysis whose origins lie in social psychology and with the work of Erving Goffman (1974) before discussing more recent applications of the concept in the social policy literature which inform this study. An individualising frame that locates responsibility for violence primarily within the individual will then be contrasted with a co-creationist frame. Pathology in terms of the origins of violence for the latter is seen as residing in the staff

* E-mail: b.a.paterson@stir.ac.uk

involved, the organisation, the perpetrator and the pattern of their interactions, which are collectively co-created.

Discourse analysis encompasses an influential methodological tradition related to a number of different disciplines ranging from linguistics to ethnomethodology and social psychology (Potter and Wetherell 1994). This study used a subtype of discourse analysis called frame analysis developed by a number of authors since the 1980's including Snow and Benford (1992) in their work analysing social movements, Gamson et al. (1992) examining political communication and more recently, by Triandafyllidou and Fotiou (2006) to examine the processes involved in policy making. The concept of frames in the social sciences has a long history. Erving Goffman (1974) contended that we use 'frames' in order to make sense of our life experience. In his description, frames are internal cognitive structures consisting of systems of classification and rules of interpretation. Such frames allow us (Goffman 1974:21) to "locate, perceive, identify and label" the diverse phenomena we may encounter throughout the course of our lives. Framing theory posits that we make sense of our experience on an ongoing basis by continually relating it to patterns, which are already known. This tendency to refer to stable and recurring patterns in order to recognise new stimuli has been confirmed by a number of psychological studies. Heider (1958) affirms that people perceive reality and form expectations with respect to it by linking temporary attitudes with pre-existing stable patterns of behaviour. Thus, diverse new stimuli are interpreted for meaning by being linked to a known and enduring background, which serves as a point of reference.

However, the concept of framing has also found application in the study of social policy. Here, the process of framing is described as involving the selection of some aspects of a perceived reality that in turn, promotes a particular definition of a putative problem, in such a way as to construct a particular causal interpretation, moral evaluation and consequently specific recommendations regarding the type of solution that needs to be adopted (Entman 1993:52). Snow et al. (1986) propose that we can usefully distinguish between two levels of frame that they describe as 'master frames' and 'domain-specific interpretative frames'. Master frames signify meaning on a broader scope and serve to organise sets of 'domain-specific frames', such as those, which both depict and inform how we should understand violence to mental health nurses.

How the available master frames 'organise' the domain specific frame around any particular issue cannot readily be predicted. Two or more, different master frames can coalesce to produce a novel domain specific frame. Further what sometimes occurs is a competition to frame an issue within a given domain in a particular way congruent with one master frame or set of frames, as opposed to another (Snow et al. 1996). It is this position on frames that will be used to inform a critical exploration of the framing process in relation to the 'problem' of violence to nurses working with people with mental health problems.

In the case of workplace violence in mental health the influence of a series of master frames can be identified. First, is the classic 'discourse of deviancy', a frame of some antiquity. Its assumptions are that deviants real or imaginary, are easily identifiable, the reasons for their deviance reside within the individual and social actions to control or punish them are therefore justifiable. Moreover, because such actions serve to clarify the moral boundaries between 'the good' and 'the bad' that must always be maintained, a failure to punish the deviant would be remiss (Leadbetter et al. 2005).

This frame interacts however with those of mental health and mental illness. The frame of mental illness can in certain circumstances absolve a perpetrator of culpability both morally and legally of what would otherwise constitute a crime. However, the possession of a psychiatric diagnosis has never meant that punishment may not play a role in treatment. Control in extremis in contemporary services by means of coercion is often justified by reference to the need to maintain a safe environment (Paterson and Duxbury 2006). However,, the perception of service users is sometimes that coercion is being used to punish rather than enable treatment (Duxbury 2002). The use of systematic punishment to induce compliance, as a form of treatment was though once orthodox practice (Foucault 2006). The belief that 'fear (*is*) the most effectual principle to reduce the insane to orderly conduct' appalled Tuke (1882:90) however, to assume that such long established discourses no longer exert any influence on practice would be naive. Perhaps instead as Shapiro observes (1988: xi) it is precisely because such discourses are so familiar that they are able 'operate transparently' upon those affected who are effectively blinded to such influences on both their thinking and behaviour (Keywood 1995).

When such older frames interact with more current preoccupations of risk one consequence is the development of a particularly narrow understanding of the sources of risk where only the risks attached to individuals and their behaviour become the focus of examination and action. This fundamental attribution error (Heider 1958) can lead to the exclusion of consideration of risks arising from wider factors whether in the immediate or wider social context. The novel discourse that results can be described as an 'individualising frame' and is unfortunately that which seems to have informed what has been characterised as the 'security' or 'high tariff' approach to violence prevention in health and social services in the UK (Leadbetter et al. 2005). This approach is exemplified in the 'Zero Tolerance' policy on violence adopted by the National Health Service (s) of the UK in 1998 due in part to campaigning by the Royal College of Nursing. This promote intolerance of aggression by service users and/or provide for greater punishment or exclusion for perpetrators.

Snow and Benford (1988) observe that in order for frames to be successful they must either resonate with the sentiments of the population concerned. The individualising discourse with its location of the reasons for deviancy within the individual has several advantages in this respect. Research into the explanations for the violent acts of in-patients suggests a tendency amongst nurses to stress aspects of the service users' personality as causal (Duxbury 2002). However, service user's explanations for violence tend to differ stressing instead the situational dimensions of violence particularly that it was often a response to controlling behaviour by staff (Hinsby and Baker 2004). The apparent preponderance of individualistic explanations by nursing staff for service users' violence in studies may mean that the security high tariff framing of the problem resonated with the beliefs of many practitioners regarding the origins of violence (Duxbury 2002).

The seeming success of the individualising frame may though also stem from the form of the frame it uses to construct the problem of workplace violence. Gamson (1992) argued that three kinds of issue frames delineate how problems are framed. What he terms 'Aggregate' frames effectively define putative issues as 'social problems' but the burden of responsibility for action to resolve the issue is placed with individuals. 'Consensus' frames, in contrast, whilst also defining an issue as a social problem, represent it as one that can only be solved via collective action but leave unspecified who must act. 'Collective action' frames differ in three key respects from aggregate or consensus action. Firstly, they define the problem as one, which is intrinsically 'unjust'. Secondly, 'agency' i.e. responsibility for the problem is placed with an identifiable actor. Thirdly, and perhaps crucially, the frame establishes an adversarial relationship between 'us' in terms of identity as members of the in-group and ‘the other’ i.e. whomsoever the imputation suggests is responsible for the problem (Gamson 1992).

Evidence of the use of the latter frame is exemplified in the title of the Zero Tolerance resource pack sent to every NHS Trust in England in 1999 (Health Service Circular 199/226). Entitled ‘we don’t have to take this anymore’ the identification of ‘in’ group and an implied ‘other’ is clearly evident and an adversarial if not counter aggressive dimension is suggested. In the individualising frame the problem of violence to the worker is defined as an injustice’ perpetrated upon an ‘innocent’ (or sometimes unskilled) victim and responsibility for the behaviour is placed with the perpetrator. Of more significance in terms of social policy the resulting discourse is productive more specifically deontic, in creating an obligation on those charged with protecting nurses from such a threat to address this injustice.

This evoked what appears to have been a search for solutions to this construction of the problem which was found in Control and Restraint, (‘CandR’) an intensive physical restraint training program developed within the English prison service. The conventional explanation for the extraordinarily rapid adoption of CandR training across mental health services is that it followed the recommendation of an inquiry into the death of a patient while being restrained in Broadmoor high secure hospital in 1984 (Ritchie 1994). However, given the failure to adopt many of the other recommendations of the inquiry and a lack of concern about such deaths outside the special hospital sector over this period attributing causality for what was a radical change in policy to a single event seems highly questionable. As Michel Foucault (1980:114) reminds us, “there are actually a whole order of levels of different types of events differing in amplitude, chronological breadth and capacity to produce effects”. Foucault (1991:76) suggests that we should therefore approach the question of the role played by events by means of an analysis of the multiple processes which constitute them, a process he terms “eventalization”. The implications of adopting this approach are that what must be understood becomes not only ‘where the seed comes from’, that is, what event appeared to prompt a reaction in terms of social policy but more importantly ‘what makes the soil fertile’, that is, why is a particular sector may be uniquely responsive to a suggested initiative at a particular time (Kingdon 1995:77).

From this perspective the adoption of CandR provided a means of responding to growing concerns over the problem of violence towards mental health nurses that was congruent with the dominant individualising frame of the problem. It resonated strongly with the assumption contained within the individualising frame that violence results from individual pathology whether ascribed to madness demanding control or badness demanding punishment (Crichton 1997). The former is addressed in terms of prevention via ‘treatment’ directed towards goals specified by the service (although the extent and nature of the ‘treatment’ is not specified) whilst dangerous manifestations of the disorder are managed, via restraint if necessary. The latter is addressed via the deterrent affect of restraint conveniently maximised by the use of ‘pain compliance’ an integral dimension of CandR as then practised (Paterson 2005).

Why Was There No Opposition?

All frames are 'temporally variable and subject to reassessment and renegotiation' (Snow et al., 1986: 476). The individualising frame of the problem was successful at least for a time, not only because of its resonance with internal attributions of responsibility for violence or that it was articulated by means of a collective action frame, but also because it faced comparatively little coordinated opposition. Given the long history in the UK of the non-restraint movement with its emphasis on moral treatment this is puzzling. The reductionist explanations for violence offered by the individualising frame should have been countered by the discourses of social psychiatry and the insights provided to psychiatry by social psychology and sociology.

Perhaps at least in the UK, this did not happen because these discourses were marginalised during the nineteen eighties and nineties by the dominance achieved by bio-medical psychiatry. Ironically the ascendance of biological psychiatry as *the* dominant treatment paradigm may have been at least in part a response by psychiatry to critics in seeking to reassert its historical dominance by claiming equal status to its oft times distant cousin medicine. Exposed to criticism from within by Szasz (1994) and Laing (1964) and without by sociological studies such as 'on being sane in insane places' (Rosenhan 1973) psychiatry could have sought to engage with such critics, and initiate a creative dialogue. Instead with a few honorable exceptions, it promptly discarded it's former raison d'être psychoanalysis and any pretensions regarding milieu therapy (Pilgrim and Rogers 2005). The dominance by the discourse of bio psychiatry was so complete that it almost led to the demise of social psychiatry and a decades long estrangement by psychiatry from sociology (Pilgrim and Rogers 2005). Consequently psychiatry or at least many services experienced a form of collective amnesia that served to obscure their memory of previous treatment regimes based on moral treatment and the ideals of the therapeutic community (Bloom 2006).

Unfortunately psychiatry in its retreat from the social dimensions of causation was accompanied on its journey over this period by clinical psychology whose dominant paradigms over the period were of behaviour modification and cognitive behavioural psychotherapy. Such perspectives, or rather common misunderstandings and misapplications of them, located pathology almost wholly within the individual. As a result the emphasis in many settings was primarily on ameliorative interventions focused on trying to find solutions to violence within individuals rather than transformative interventions that sought to uncover and address the causes of violence in the social context (Duxbury and Paterson 2005).

The interaction between the individualising master frame and the frames of biomedical psychiatry and cognitive behavioural psychotherapy resulted in the creation of what Michel Foucault (1986) has described as an episteme. Epistemes exercise an all pervasive influence saturating and governing thinking rather than being held consciously and their power is exercised insidiously by delimiting how we can think about a given issue (Bevir 1999). As a result of the dominance of this episteme the conceptual frameworks offered by alternative paradigm essential if the social dimensions of causation were to be recognised and addressed became devalued in many settings for almost a generation. Sadly, an early if rarely recognized casualty of psychiatry's whole hearted embrace of biomedicine was mental health nursing itself (Hunter 1956). Stripped of any pretence regarding parity of esteem with psychiatry, the previous partnership of equals dissolved at least in relation to violence prevention, by the privileging of biological and thus scientific knowledge over the centrality of the therapeutic relationship, nurses became the handmaidens not just of the psychiatrist but of bio-psychiatry.

The result was unfortunate, self esteem diminished, knowledge base devalued and in some settings such as London latterly near overwhelmed by decreases in the number of acute beds and rising acuity and co-morbidity in those admitted to antiquated and understaffed services, nurses retained however their almost complete power over the day to day lives of those they cared for (Patrick et al. 1989). This juxtaposition of a lack of power and status in one dimension with almost complete control in another produced a situation eloquently captured in a phrase used by Wardhaugh and Wilding (1993) with reference to a similarly problematic dynamic in residential childcare, as one of 'dangerous ambivalence'. All too readily nurses could unconsciously displace their unmet needs for self-esteem, power and control in their professional lives into their relationships with service users.

Where such displacement took the form of over controlling behaviour by staff it increased the risk of service user non-compliance and the likelihood of counter aggression in turn (Paterson and Duxbury 2007). When repeatedly exposed to violence nurses coping strategies are typically characterised by avoidance or counter aggression (Maier 1999). These reflect the emotions of fear and/or anger produced by exposure to violence (Colson et al. 1986). Where the dominant emotional response was of counter aggression, control and restraint may have served to facilitate if not legitimate the expression of such hostility. Consequently control and restraint may have chimed not only with how nurses understood the problem of violence but with how nurses felt about the problem or rather its source as they perceived it, in 'the service users'.

It is though important to recognise that not all settings, services or practitioners adopted the individualising frame That there were many gaps in the dominance of the frame supports Snow et al's (1986) observations that while we are susceptible to influence by frames we can simultaneously be capable of reflection and opposition to the frames we encounter. Opposition to the dominance of the individualising frame has grown persistently over the last decade representing the emergence or perhaps more properly re-mergence of an alternative discourse that has been described as a co-creationist perspective by Paterson and Miller (2006).

The new/old frame operates from very different assumptions in adopting a focus that extends beyond the pathology of the individual (Bloom 1997). It assumes that a safe environment cannot be created without the active participation of the patients. Violence is seen as arising from the interactions between individuals operating within complex social systems whose interaction gives rise to violence. In this frame the problem of violence to the worker is defined not as an injustice' but as a failure to adequately understand and address the root causes of violence. Pathology in terms of the origins of violence is seen as potentially residing in the staff involved, the organisation, the perpetrator and the pattern of their interactions, which are collectively co- created. These are of course, the ideas integral to the concept of the therapeutic community and they remain equally valid some fifty years on. Our developing understanding of the impact of exposure to trauma has however served to add emphasis to the need to adopt such principles. As an approach to violence prevention co creationism's emphasis is on primary prevention in asking what 'kind of human environments we are creating in our workplaces' (Braverman 1999:4). In order for a environment to be truly 'safe' it must be physically, psychologically, socially, and morally safe for everyone in the community. The achievement of that level of safety can though only be reached by means of a shared process over time (Bloom, 1997).

Of interest perhaps, is why this counter discourse and the frame it utilises have seemingly been successful after the long standing dominance of the individualising discourse. A number of developments are of particular note each involving research. Research into deaths amongst patients being restrained has contributed to the reframing of such events as part of a potentially preventable social phenomena rather than isolated individual tragedies (Paterson et al. 2003, Blofeld 2003). This has made the nature of the methods used to control behaviour in many mental health services and injuries and deaths related to their use subject to a level of scrutiny previously absent (Frueh et al. 2005). The inclusion of service user voices in research studies has led to increasing scrutiny of the reasons why interventions such as restraint and seclusion are used because of findings that suggest service users perceive that such interventions are used not to manage dangerous behaviour but more often as forms of punishment (Duxbury 2002). Research into the antecedents to violence in in-patient mental health settings has also identified conflict linked to needs frustration as a common precipitant. This has led to increasing scrutiny of service cultures and staff attitudes and behaviour as key variables in the prevention of violence (Forquer et al. 1996, Whittington and Wykes 1996, Duxbury and Whittington 2005, Estryn-Bchar ct al. 2007).

Research has also identified high levels of trauma among users of mental health services and has led to demands for services to routinely screen for and treat the multiple potential consequences of trauma including aggression (Jennings 2004). Finally research has demonstrated that multilevel systemic organisational interventions can reduce the use of restraint and by so doing also reduce violence towards staff even where staff believe they neither can be reduced further (Lebel et al., 2004, Schreiner et al., 2004, Murphy and Bennington-Davis 2005). The reduction of violence towards staff as a consequence of efforts directed to reduce the use restraint is of course not a novel observation with such an effect consistently asserted by some of the much earlier proponents of restraint reduction including Conolly (Page 1904).

It may seem that a co-creationist framing of the problem cannot be refuted. The co-creationist perspective framing of violence is though vulnerable to a number of potential threats. It is not an exclusive strategy but an inclusive one, which challenges the categorical differentiation between the mentally ill and care providers that serves to justify the inequalities of power that embedded within the mental health system (Laurance 2003). Lacking a villain thc co-crcationist framc rcjccts simplistic moral judgcmcnts but this may not resonate with the master frames of our society or the sensitivities of practitioners because it challenges explanations for service user violence that attribute responsibility to character or personality deficits in the service user. If there is no villain there can be no punishment and punishment fulfils important symbolic functions in our society. The individualising frame is not dead rather it lurks in the policy corner waiting for the opportunity perhaps to be provided by events yet to happen, in order to reassert itself.

CONCLUSION

A 'battle among discourses and through discourses' (Foucault (1975:x) has been described in relation to how the problem of violence towards nurses in UK mental health services should be framed and the nature of the response determined. In these battles individuals and alliances have strived to construct the issue of violence in particular ways unconscious it appears, of the potential influence of societal master frames to that debate. An awareness of the cultural resources and master frames drawn upon in this debate may not alter its outcome but can at least illuminate one dimension of the conflict. It is though no small matter, that Zero Tolerance was quietly dropped by the English National Health Service as an inappropriate response to violence in mental health services (Department of Health 2004).

This analysis has focused on an examination of the role played by discourses in the policy process rather than that played by national and local policymakers in their struggle (Bendor 1995). This is not to suggest that such individuals did not exert an influence in the direction that policy took. However, the effect of the episteme suggested was so all encompassing that whilst policy makers may at one level consciously have known why they did what they did at another their decisions were determined by the dominant frame.

REFERENCES

Bauman, Z. 1988. *Freedom.* Milton Keynes, Open University Press.

Bendor J. 1995. A Model of Muddling Through, *The American Political Science Review*, 89(4): 819-40.

Bevir, M. 1999. Foucault, Power and Institutions, *Political Studies* XLVII: 345-359.

Blofeld, J. (chair) 2003. *An Independent Inquiry Set Up Uunder HSG (94)27 into the Seath of David 'Rocky' Bennett.* Cambridge, Norfolk, Suffolk and Cambridgeshire Strategic Health Authority.

Bloom, S. 1997. *Creating Sanctuary: Toward an Evolution of Sane Societies.* New York, Routledge.

Bloom S. 2006. *Organizational Stress as a Barrier to Trauma-Sensitive Change an System Transformation,* www.sanctuaryweb.com accessed 20.09.08.

Braverman, M. 1999. *Preventing Workplace Violence A Guide for Employers and Practitiones.* London, Sage Publications.

Colson, D.B., Allen, J.G. and Coyne, L. 1986. An Anatomy of Counter Transference: Staff Reactions to Difficult Psychiatric Hospital Patients, Hospital and Community Psychiatry, 47: 923.

Crichton, J. 1997. The Response of Nursing Staff to Psychiatric In-patient Misdemeanor, *Journal of Forensic Psychiatry,* 8: 36–61.

Duxbury J. 2002. An Evaluation of Staff and Service User Views of Strategies Employed to Manage In-patient Aggression and Violence on One Mental Health Unit: a Pluralistic Design, *Journal of Psychiatric and Mental Health Nursing,* 9(3): 325-37.

Duxbury, J. and Whittington, R. 2005. Causes and management of service user aggression and violence: staff and service user perspectives, *Journal of Advanced Nursing,* 50(5): 469–478.

Duxbury, J. and Paterson, B. 2005. The use of Physical Restraint in Mental Health Nursing: An Examination of Principles, Practice and Implications for Training, *Journal of Adult Protection,* 7(4): 13-24.

Entman, R.M. 1993. Framing: Towards clarification of a fractured paradigm, *Journal of Communication,* 43(4): 51-58.

Estryn-Behar, M., Duville, N., Menini, M.L., Camerino, D., Le Foll, S., ans le Nezet, O. 2007. Factors Associated with Violence Against Healthcare Workers Results of the European Presst-Next study, *Presse Medicale*, 36(1):21-36.

Forquer, S., Earle, K., Way, B., and Banks, S. 1996. Predictors of the Use of Restraint and Seclusion in Public Psychiatric Hospitals, *Administration and Policy in Mental Health and Mental Health Services Research,* 23(6): 527-532.

Foucault, M. 1980. *Power / Knowledge: Selected Interviews and Other Writings*, New York, Pantheon Books.

Foucault, M. 1991. Questions of method, in Burchell, G., Gordon, C. and Miller, P. (eds) *The Foucault Effect: Studies in Govermentality.* Chicago: University of Chicago Press.

Foucault, M. 1975. Foreword, in Foucault, M. (ed) *I, Pierre Riviere: Having Slaughtered My Mother, My Sister, My Brother: A Case of Parracide in the 19th Century*, vii-xiv. Lincoln, University of Nebraska Press.

Foucault, M. 1986. *The Order of Things: an Archaeology of the Human Sciences.* London, Routledge.

Foucault, M. 2006. Psychiatric Power: Lectures at the Collège de France, 1973-1974. Basingstoke, Palgrave Macmillan.

Frueh, C.B. Knapp R.G., Cusack, K.J., Grubaugh, A.L., Sauvageot, J.A., Cousins, V.C., Eunsil, Y., Robins, C.S., Monnier, J. and Hiers, T.G. 2005. Special Section on Seclusion and Restraint: Service User Reports of Traumatic or Harmful Experiences within the Psychiatric Setting, *Psychiatric Services,* 56: 1123–1133.

Gamson, W., Croteau, D., Hoynes W. and Sasson T. 1992 Media Images and the Social Construction of Reality, *Annual Review of Sociology*,18: 373-93.

Goffman, E. 1974. *Frame Analysis: An essay on the Organization of Experience.* New York, Harper and Row.

Heider, F. 1958. *The Psychology of Interpersonal Relations.* New York, Wiley and Sons.

Health Service Circular 1999/226. 1999. *Campaign To Stop Violence Against Staff Working in The NHS: NHS Zero Tolerance Zone.* London, Department of Health.

Health Care Commission. 2007. *Mental Health and Learning Disability Trusts: Key Findings from the 2006 Survey of Staff.* London, Health Care Commission.

Hinsby, K. and Baker, M. 2004. Service user and Nurse Accounts of Violent Incidents in a Medium Secure Unit, *Journal of Psychiatric and Mental Health Nursing,* 11: 341–347.

Hunter R.A. 1956. The Rise and Fall of Mental Nursing, *Lancet,* 270(6907):98-9.

Jennings, A. 2004. *Models for Developing Trauma Informed Behavioural Health Systems and Trauma Specific Services.* Virginia, National Association State Mental Health Hospital Program Directors.

Keywood, K. 2005. Psychiatric Injustice? The Therapeutic Ppresumption of Behaviour Management in Mental Health Law. *The Journal of Adult Protection,* 7(4): 25-30.

Kingdon, J.W. 1994. *Agendas, Alternatives, and Policy Alternatives*, Boston, Little Brown.

Laing R.D. and Esterton W. 1964. *Sanity, Madness and the Family.* London. Tavistock.

Laurance, J. 2003. *Pure Madness: How Fear Drives The Mental Health System.* London, Routledge.

Leadbetter, D., Paterson, B. and Crighton, J. 2005 Physical Intervention In Human Services: From Moral Panic To Moral Action, Paper Presented At *Examining The Safety Of High Risk Interventions With Children And Young People An International Symposium For Researchers Policy Makers Advocates And System Providers*, New York, Cornell University.

Lebel, J., Stomberg, N., Duckworth K., Kernzer J., Goldstein, R., Weeks, M., Harper, G., LaFlair, L. and Sudders, M. 2004. Child and Adolescent Restraint Reduction: A State Initiative to Promote Strength- Based Care, *Journal of Academic Child and Adolescent* Psychiatry, 43(1): 37-45.

Maier, G.J. 1999. Psychological Issues In Treatment: Transference and Counter transference, in ardiff K. (ed) *Medical Management of the Violent Patient: Clinical Assessment and Therapy,* 277-209. New York, Dekker.

McMillan I. 2005. Unrealistic NHS Policy on Violence Ditched, *Mental Health Practice*, 8(6):8.

Morrall, P. and Hazelton, M. 2000. The Restoration of Asylumdom in Mental Health Care? *Australian and New Zealand Journal of Mental Health Nursing* 9: 89–96.

Murphy, T. and Bennington-Davis, M. 2005. *Restraint and Seclusion: The Model for Eliminating theirUse in Healthcare*, hcPro, Marblehead, Ma.

Page, C.W. 1904. Mechanical Restraint and Seclusion of Insane Persons, *Boston Medical and Surgical Journal,* 590-595.

Paterson, B., Bradley, P., Stark, C., Saddler, D., Leadbetter, D. and Allen, D. 2003. Deaths Associated with Restraint Use in Health and Social Care In the United Kingdom: The Results of A Preliminary Survey, *Journal of Psychiatric and Mental Health Nursing,* 10: 3-15.

Paterson, B. 2005. Thinking the Unthinkable: A Role for Patient Compliance and Mechanical Restraint in the Management of Violence?, *Mental Health Practice,* 8(7):18-2.

Paterson, B. and Miller, G. 2006. *Promoting Safe and Therapeutic Services, National Health Service Security Management Service, Trainers Handbook,* Security Management Services, London.

Paterson, B. and Duxbury, J. 2006. Developing a Perspective on Restraint and the Least Intrusive Intervention, *British Journal of Nursing*, 14(22): 1235-1241.

Paterson, B. and Duxbury, J. 2007. Restraint. A Question of Validity? *Nursing Ethics,* 14 (4): 535-545.

Patrick, M., Higgit A., and Holloway, F. 1989. Changes in an Inner City Psychiatric inservice User Service Following Bed Losses: a Follow up of the East Lambeth 1986 survey, *Health Trends* 21: 121-123.

Pilgrim, D. and Rogers, A. 2005. Social Psychiatry and Sociology, *Journal of Mental Health,*14(4): 317 – 320.

Potter, J. and Wetherell, M. 1994. Analyzing Discourse, in Byrman, A. and Burgess, R. (eds). *Analyzing Qualitative Data,* 47-66. London, Routledge.

Ritchie, S. 1995. *Report to the Secretary of State for Social Services*, London, Special Hospitals Authority.

Rose, D. (1996) *In the Name of the Law: The Collapse of Criminal Justice.* London, Jonathan Cape.

Rosenhan, D. 1973. On Being Sane in Insane Places. *Science*, 179: 250-8.

Schreiner, G.M., Crafton CG, Sevin J.A. 2004. Decreasing the use of Mechanical Restraints and Locked Seclusion. *Administration Policy Mental Health* 31: 449-463.

Shapiro, M.J. 1988. *The Politics of Representation: Writing Practices in Biography, Photography and Policy Analysis.* Wisconsin, University of Wisconsin Press.

Snow, D.A., Rochford B. Jr., Worden S.K. and Benford R.D. 1986 Frame Alignment Processes, Micromobilization and Movement Participation, *American Sociological Review*, 51(4): 464 - 81.

Snow, D.A. and Benford, R.D. 1988 Ideology, Frame Resonance, and Participant Mobilization, in Klandermans, B., Kriesi, H. and Tarrow, S. (eds) *International Social Movement Research*: Volume 1, 197-219. London: JAI Press.

Snow, D.A, and Benford R.D. 1992 Master Frames and Cycles of Protest, in Morris, A.D. and McClurg-Mueller, C. (eds) *Frontiers in Social Movement Theory*. New Haven, Yale University Press.

Szasz, T. 1994. Mental Illness is Still a Myth, *Society:* 31(4), 34-9.

Triandafyllidou, A. and Fotiou, A. 1998. Sustainability and Modernity in the European Union: A Frame Theory Approach to Policy-Making, Sociological Research Online, 2(1) *http://www.socresonline.org.uk/socresonline/3/1/2.html.*

Tuke, D.H. 1882. *Chapters in the history of the insane in the British Isles.* London, Kegan Paul.

Wardhaugh, J., and Wilding, P. 1993. Towards an Explanation of the corruption of Care. *Critical Social Care* 37(13): 4 – 31.

Whittington, R. and Wykes, T. 1996. Aversive Stimulation by Staff and Violence by Psychiatric Service Users, *British Journal of Clinical Psychology,* 35(1): 11-20.

Young, J. 1999. *The Exclusive Society: Social Exclusion Crime and Difference in Late Modernity.* London, Sage.

In: Understanding Risk
Editor: Matthias Beck
ISBN: 978-1-62618-686-6

Chapter 17

FIRE AND RISK: THE CONTROVERSY OVER THE ROLE OF FIRE-RETARDANTS IN THE WORLD TRADE CENTER DISASTER

Geoffrey Tweedale[*]
Business History, Manchester Metropolitan
University Business School, Manchester, UK

ABSTRACT

In the aftermath of the World Trade Center (WTC) conflagration in 2001, a debate began about the role of fire-retardants. Some commentators argued that the decision to dispense with asbestos during the construction of the Twin Towers played a key role in their subsequent collapse. It was further argued that the disaster was a consequence of the 'asbestos hysteria' that had supposedly gripped New York in the 1960s and 1970s. This article, based on contemporary documents and recent investigations of 9/11, shows that there is no evidence linking asbestos (or the lack of it) to the collapse of the Towers and that the debate about asbestos in the WTC has been largely 'manufactured'.

INTRODUCTION

'I am sure [asbestos] spraying contractors find it difficult to imagine their towering monuments will one day crumble beneath the wreckers' ball, but that is the history of our every rebuilding city. All the built-in hazards will again be freed to float into the surrounding atmosphere ... [and so] ... we are certainly building an environmental hazard into the future' (Rickles, 1970).

This warning, made by a New York City environmental commissioner, has proved eerily prescient in relation to the World Trade Center (WTC) – though certainly not in a way that the official could have foreseen. One unforgettable sight of the 9/11 attack was the collapse of

[*] E-mail: G.Tweedale @mmu.ac.uk

the Towers amidst a billowing dust cloud that enveloped lower Manhattan (Claudio, 2001). Metaphorically that cloud has never quite settled, because the dust has remained a source of considerable debate. The fire-retardants that had been used when the WTC was constructed included a significant quantity of asbestos. Because of the toxicity of asbestos, this had potential perils for rescue workers and also for those who inhaled dust afterwards (Landrigan, 2004). The nature of the fire-retardant materials in the Towers also had implications for key questions relating to their collapse. Did the structures disintegrate so swiftly because their fire protection was deficient; or was the reason to be found in their original design? (Seabrook, 2001) What added an extra dimension to these questions was the fact that during the construction of the WTC in the early 1970s a decision had been made – based on a growing awareness of the health hazard – to switch from asbestos to man-made mineral fibres. It was the latter which made up the bulk of the fire-retardants in the WTC. It was soon suggested that the buildings might have stood for longer had asbestos not been discontinued.

This debate began even while the rubble was smouldering. It was launched by Steven Milloy, a commentator for *Fox News*, on 14 September 2001, only days after the terrorist attacks. In an article entitled 'Asbestos Could Have Saved WTC Lives', Milloy wrote that the WTC might have stood longer, preventing many casualties, had the use of asbestos fire-resistant materials not been curtailed. Milloy cited experts, who questioned the efficacy of the asbestos-free insulation that was applied to the steel on the upper floors. He also quoted the late Herbert Levine, who according to Milloy invented sprayed asbestos fireproofing in the late 1940s. Apparently Levine frequently would say that, 'if a fire breaks out above the 64th floor, that building will fall down.' If Levine was the prescient hero of events, then for Milloy the chief villain in the decision to abandon asbestos was Professor Irving J. Selikoff, a physician at Mount Sinai Hospital in New York, who had first publicised the dangers of asbestos insulation. Milloy concluded that 'Selikoff was wrong to press the panic button about … asbestos. We may now be paying a horrible price for junk science-fuelled asbestos hysteria' (Milloy, 2001).

Within days, Milloy's article was picked up both by *The Times* in London (Henderson, 2001) and by *The New York Times*, which ran a feature that asked a 'Haunting Question: Did Asbestos Ban Lead to Loss of Life?' (Glanz and Revkin, 2001). The article quoted a range of opinions and also provided details on the extent of asbestos use during the construction of the WTC. One of those interviewed, Dr Arthur Langer, director of an environmental sciences laboratory at Brooklyn College, stated: 'In retrospect, considering the recent events at the World Trade Center, I wonder if the performance characteristics of the replacement material were as good'. By the end of 2001, Langer and a colleague had written a journal article that answered that question: 'The ban of asbestos-containing spray fireproofing was probably a reasonable conclusion for the time, only if the substitute material performed as well as the material which it replaced. However it did not.' (Langer and Morse, 2001). Having discounted the health risk, these authors presented evidence that, in their view, showed that sprayed asbestos was a more reliable product in terms of its density and cohesiveness than asbestos substitutes. This was published in a special issue of a journal, *Indoor and Built Environment*, in which it was further argued that the WTC disaster might foster a 'more balanced approach' to the risk of asbestos in buildings (Lange, 2001).

When that approach was not forthcoming, the debate was reinvigorated by Andrew Schlafly (2003) in an article in a medical journal. In trenchant language, Schlafly attacked what he perceived as the 'flawed science' behind the decision to ban asbestos in the WTC, with Selikoff again as the culprit. 'Litigation-fed hysteria' was behind the collapse of the WTC, as it was behind the Challenger and Columbia space shuttle disasters (which were also alleged to have been due to the lack of asbestos). Sympathisers with this view now felt able to proclaim the emergence of a 'new policy' towards asbestos as a result of the WTC tragedy – one that was based on 'actual scientific facts, with less influence from social and political factors' (Lange, 2004). These views struck a chord elsewhere. English medical historian Peter Bartrip, in an article that described Selikoff as a medical fraud, suggested that the American 'might be remembered as the man who caused the World Trade Center ... to be constructed without the benefit of asbestos to safeguard it from fire damage' (Bartrip, 2003). The issue of asbestos in the WTC was also raised by Rachel Maines (2005) in a study of the technological history of asbestos as a fire-retardant, which praised the benefits of the mineral.

This debate is important, because it relates not only to society's use of asbestos but also to the problem of providing adequate fire protection in skyscrapers, both for occupants and those involved in the original construction work. Until now no detailed historical account has been presented of the role of asbestos in either the construction or the collapse of the WTC. However, new documents and official studies can be used to shed fresh light on this episode.

CONSTRUCTING THE WTC

The WTC was part of an urban renewal project that was launched by the Port Authority of New York in 1966. The ribbon-cutting took place in 1973. The project involved the erection of a complex of WTC buildings, but the chief ones were two 110-storey skyscrapers: WCT 1 (the North Tower) at 1,368 feet (417m) and WCT 2 (the South Tower) at 1,362 feet (415m). These buildings eclipsed the height of the Empire State Building and were the tallest buildings in New York until 9/11. The WTC was also briefly the tallest building complex in the world.

The skyscrapers marked an important point in the evolution of high-rise buildings and the development of their fireproofing (Wermeil, 2000). Since the nineteenth century, such structures had progressed from iron frame-designs (with heavy exterior walls), through steel beams (with columns, beams and concrete), to designs where a core and perimeter wall carried the load and allowed the removal of interior columns to provide more office space. The Towers were reportedly the first super-tall buildings built without any masonry – a feat accomplished by using a lightweight 'hollow tube' design, with steel columns set only 22-inches apart on the perimeter. This steel lattice was connected to floor supports radiating to a central core, which enclosed the elevators and stairs. The floor construction was prefabricated trussed steel, only 33 inches in depth, that spanned the full 60 feet to the core, and this also acted as a diaphragm to stiffen the outside wall against buckling from high winds.

The fire risk had received careful consideration, even to the extent of designing the WTC to withstand a jet strike (in those days the worse-case scenario involved a Boeing 707). Fire protection measures included sprinklers, fire detection apparatus, and fire-retardant materials. The building had to comply with contemporary fire regulations, which demanded a three-hour fire-resistance rating formulated and tested according to the 1970 New York City Building Code. From the viewpoint of later developments, a key feature of the fire protection was that the exterior faces of perimeter columns, besides the spandrels, and the floor-joists and framing were to be coated in *sprayed* asbestos fibre.

Spraying asbestos required a mixture of asbestos and cement (delivered to the site in bags) and a bin-like machine on wheels (Tweedale, 1999). Once the mixture had been tipped into a hopper, a fan propelled the mixture through a large hose. A water spray was simultaneously fed to the head of the hose, where the spray operator stood directing the wet jet at the target surface. It proved an effective method of plastering floors, ceilings, girders, and ships bulkheads with a layer of asbestos and cement. The process had been devised in England in 1931 by asbestos multinational Turner & Newall (T&N). That company licensed it world-wide, but by the 1950s variants of the spray process were in use by other firms. The first high-rise use of sprayed mineral fibre was in 1958 in the 60-storey Chase Manhattan Bank. By 1970, over half of American multi-storey buildings had sprayed asbestos.

Two contracts were involved in the spraying of the Towers. The main one was awarded to Alcoa and another was subcontracted to Mario & DiBono Plastering Company (NIST, 2005). Both contractors used an asbestos coating named Cafco Blaze-Shield Type D. The spray mixture itself, which probably contained about 20-30 per cent asbestos fibre, was manufactured by US Mineral Products Corporation, a manufacturer of asbestos building materials. Another company appears in accounts of the construction of the WTC. That was W.R. Grace, which also manufactured buildings products and operated a vermiculite mine in Montana. Grace manufactured a product named Monokote, which contained asbestos, and was also used in the WTC. However, the extent of Grace's involvement in the WTC's construction is unclear both from the documents and later published accounts (Bowker, 2003; Peacock, 2003; Schneider and McCumber, 2004). It seems that the main WTC retardant was Blaze-Shield, with vermiculite plaster (presumably Grace's) only used on exterior wall panels (NIST, 2005, p. 74). Whatever the truth of the matter, it has been estimated that about 5,000 tons of asbestos were used in the WTC, with the metal and concrete-fill floors receiving ½-inch of sprayed fibre and the trusses ¾-inch.

The Dispute over Asbestos

During the erection of WCT 1 (the North Tower) a dispute arose concerning the health hazards facing the construction workers. Spraying asbestos was inherently dusty, but when it was conducted within confined spaces (such as a skyscraper) providing adequate ventilation was difficult and wearing respirators continually was impossible. Ironically, spraying asbestos had been introduced in the UK in 1931 – the year when the British government had legislated for asbestosis (the chronic lung scarring caused by the kind of high dust levels experienced during spraying). Spraying, however, was exempted from regulation until the end of the 1960s – a move that reflected government pragmatism and the opposition of manufacturers such as T&N, who fought fiercely against the introduction of safety measures (Tweedale, 2001). The lack of a safety culture in spraying asbestos was apparent overseas, where T&N licensed the process. Photographs taken in the USA in 1940s and 1950s confirm the dangerous work conditions (Lilienfeld, 1991).

The gross dust exposures suffered by sprayers and other insulation workers were a major factor in the rising mortality from asbestos-related diseases (ARDs) in the 1960s and 1970s.

By now the carcinogenicity of asbestos fibre in causing lung cancer and mesothelioma (a lethal and painful cancer of the lining of the lung or gut) was well recognised. Worryingly, too, an environmental hazard existed. By the early 1960s, mesothelioma was associated with relatively short and transient inhalation of asbestos fibres by individuals who had never worked in the asbestos industry – brake repairmen, tradesmen, engineers, construction workers, architects, nurses, office workers and teachers. New Yorkers, in particular, were put on notice of the hazard. In 1964, Professor Irving Selikoff from his base at Mount Sinai Hospital had organised a major conference in New York City, which publicised the hazards of asbestos and highlighted the problem of mesothelioma (McCulloch and Tweedale, 2008). In 1968, Paul Brodeur, a staff writer for the *New Yorker*, wrote a series of articles entitled 'The Magic Mineral' that sold so well it was later reprinted as a booklet (Brodeur, 1968). In a striking passage, Brodeur recounted how on Sixth Avenue he had watched sprayed asbestos escaping from building tarpaulins and blowing over the pavement like thistledown. In New York on any given day in 1970, there were six to eight buildings taller than thirty stories being sprayed.

With asbestos in the headlines in New York, it is not surprising that sprayed asbestos at the WTC began attracting attention. Inevitably, Selikoff – who became a world authority on ARDs – and his Mount Sinai team were at the centre of events. But they were not the only important participants. Johns-Manville, the leading asbestos manufacturer in the USA, monitored developments closely. In 1968, the company had helped launch an Insulation Industry Hygiene Research Program (IIHRP) that was based at Mount Sinai Hospital (Selikoff, 1970). Another key player was the Department of Air Resources, which had been established in New York by the newly-established Environmental Protection Administration (EPA). Inevitably, manufacturers' trade associations, trade unions, engineers, and architects became involved. Some of the documents from the meetings between these individuals have survived and enable us to piece together the main events.

'Sprayed asbestos continues to worry Dr Selikoff', noted a Johns-Manville director, after one meeting (Raines, 1968). Selikoff was disturbed not only by the occupational hazards, but also by the environmental risks caused by asbestos dust circulating through plenums (the false ceilings in buildings). Johns-Manville believed plenums would probably have to be eliminated and unless greater control could be achieved, 'the building of the World Trade Center could, in effect, raise a real alarm and perhaps lead to an injunction to cease using [spray]'. By 1969, a task force to look at spray jobs had been formed under the aegis of the IIHRP. The initial intention was to improve safety standards, which pleased Hill & Knowlton, the industry's public relations advisers. They wrote to Johns-Manville: 'This is a good story and important because the sprayed asbestos is a potential source ... of bad publicity' (Thompson, 1969). Unfortunately, the bad publicity was to increase. In June 1969, Austin N. Heller, Commissioner of the Department of Air Resources, met Selikoff and reported his concern about community pollution from spray. Selikoff had no cheerful news to report: his colleague Dr Bill Nicholson had found that most of the sites he had visited were hazardous (IIHRP, 1969). In the following month, Johns-Manville and Hill & Knowlton met Selikoff to discuss problems at the WTC (Raines, 1969). Selikoff tried to emphasise the progress made by Herbert Levine (the president of Asbestospray Corporation and chairman of the Sprayed Mineral Fiber Manufacturers' Association) in reducing dust, but said his team would soon take dust counts.

Selikoff wanted dust control measures to be given a chance and never argued for a ban, but he was also uncompromising in his depiction of the risks. In November 1969, he lectured to the *Contracting Plasterers' and Lathers' International Association* (CPLIA) and highlighted the dangers of both spraying asbestos fibre and the unchecked 'snow' that was drifting downtown from the WTC. According to an industry observer:

> Selikoff stated they estimate 100 tons of fiber will be airborne in New York from this job. He closed by stating the work practice was the worst he could imagine and from his observation not one man spraying fiber today would be alive in 20 years. The officials of the international unions were there along with contractors and I know it landed like a bomb (Egan, 1969).

Actually, Selikoff referred to young workers exposed to dust at fifty times the safe level, but his statement certainly had an impact. By the end of 1969 events began to accelerate. Several meetings were held, either at Mount Sinai Hospital or at the Building Trades Employers' Association headquarters on Third Avenue, specifically to discuss the problem of the WTC. Notes and minutes of these meetings, which often involved over 30 participants, have survived. They show that Selikoff provided epidemiological studies, dust counts, and physical examinations of workers. But increasingly the driving force was the Department of Air Resources. At Mount Sinai Hospital in December 1969, Heller stated that a zero exposure limit was the objective for the protection of the public (Johns-Manville, 1969). Like Selikoff, Heller had been appalled at the dust created by spraying. When squabbles broke out with the spray contractors, Heller warned that he would hold public hearings, convene a two-day conference at Rockefeller University, and could take legal action against spraying.

By now, Selikoff's team had visited and monitored sites in Europe and New York. Work safety was poor, unskilled (and often young) operatives were often employed, few respirators were used, and often the most dangerous types of fibre (blue and brown) were being sprayed. Mount Sinai's scientists began conducting dust counts. As yet no safety threshold had been set in America, but the British government had agreed on a dust threshold of 2 fibres per cubic centimetre of air (2 f/cc) that was supposed to protect against asbestosis (though not cancer). Disturbingly, Selikoff's team would show fibre counts for sprayers between 30 f/cc and 100 f/cc, with hopper fillers exposed to 5 f/cc to 22 f/cc. Moreover, counts had only been taken with an optical microscope, which was incapable of resolving the tiniest and thinnest fibres that were suspected of being the most carcinogenic (Reitze et al., 1972). Aside from occupational exposure, environmental counts outside the construction site had also exceeded safe levels.

At a meeting at Mount Sinai on 8 December 1969, Selikoff recommended the formation of a committee of all the interested parties. This meeting, chaired by Selikoff, took place on 9 and 10 January 1970. Ed Fenner, a Johns-Manville director (who was later to die of mesothelioma), watched a 'real battle' between Selikoff and Herb Levine and his associates (Fenner, 1970). The spray companies argued that the problem was exaggerated, while Selikoff berated them for their lack of progress and poor work practices. Selikoff believed that the future occupational level would be set at 2-6 f/cc – though he wanted 2 f/cc – with the ambient air criteria at 0.01 f/cc. Murray Shapiro, a consulting engineer, wanted sprayed asbestos banned. Architect Harold Rosen (representing Skidmore, Owings & Merrill) bluntly told the meeting: 'Our firm will not design any more buildings to be sprayed! The article in the *New Yorker* alerted us!' (Fenner, 1970).

At this point, the Department of Air Resources took control. Heller had been succeeded by Robert N. Rickles, a thirty-four-year-old chemist and committed environmentalist. Under Rickles, a set of regulations was issued in April 1970 that aimed to control dust at the WTC (and the city's other twenty asbestos spray sites). Aside from measures to control dust on site (such as personal protection and vacuum cleaning), jobs would have to be sealed off with plastic tarpaulins. Incredibly, these were the first known orders anywhere in the USA relating to the handling and application of asbestos materials on construction sites. When it began monitoring the regulations, the city authorities found that five sites were violating virtually every clause of the rules, while three others had to be shut down because of environmental emissions (Rickles, 1970). One of the summonses was issued on the WTC site to subcontractors DiBono. On 20 April 1970, all spray operations at the WTC site were suspended and spraying then stopped across the city.

No 'hysteria' was apparent. What was clear was that asbestos spraying had very few defenders. Monitoring the regulations was taking more resources than the Department of Air Resources had available. For the manufacturers, too, the regulations would prove expensive and cumbersome. It was obvious that asbestos dust could never be reduced to acceptable levels, aside from the environmental risk. Even the country's biggest asbestos producer quietly pulled the plug. Matthew Swetonic, Johns-Manville's public relations adviser, had attended one of the spray meetings. He recalled how he had looked out over Bryant Park at the construction site of the W.R. Grace building:

> From a tarpaulined floor about 10 stories up, a virtual snow shower of sprayed asbestos was slowly drifting down to the street below ... I called everyone to the window. 'That', I said, pointing to the street, 'is why we have to take a walk on those people'. We quietly informed Dr Selikoff, the city of New York, and the EPA ... that while we wouldn't attack the practice [on] health grounds, neither would we defend it (Swetonic, 1993, pp. 301-2).

The WTC reaction to Rickles's directive was immediate. In April 1970, when the Port Authority's WTC construction manager, Rino M. Monti, visited the New Jersey offices of US Mineral Products, they already had a substitute material – Cafco type D/CF – to show him. He was told that the new fireproofing material, based on ceramic fibre, was 'without asbestos ... and equivalent to their previous Cafco type D with asbestos in all aspects' (Monti, 1970). That was soon confirmed by the Underwriters' Laboratory, which stated that substitute Cafco was 'at least as good ... [and] ... may even be slightly better' as regards fire resistance (Bell, 1970). Alcoa decided to change the product anyway, because they did 'not want to get involved with the bad public relations that would be associated with their continuing the two towers with an asbestos material' (Monti, 1970). Mario & DiBono agreed to use the new product and also apply sealant to all areas already sprayed with asbestos. W.R. Grace also responded. After hearing Selikoff speak in 1969, a Grace executive had told its products division: 'We must go all out to get asbestos out of Mono-Kote at once. If it means changing assignments or putting additional people on the job, I recommend it' (Egan, 1969). Within months Grace had formulated a new version of Monokote.

By September 1970, when T&N's representatives arrived in New York in an attempt to rescue their technology and to belittle asbestos substitutes, the battle for the continuance of spraying had already been lost. Rickles told them bluntly that 'the banning of spray was still [the Department's] objective ... because the spray contractors in New York were irresponsible and could not even be trusted to apply the emergency controls ...' (Howe and Holmes, 1970). Even Levine agreed that the spray contractors were negligent. By mid-1971, Selikoff's team was ready to publish their findings. They predicted a 'most unhappy fate' for sprayers and also highlighted the risk for pipe fitters, welders, electricians, plumbers, carpenters, whose deaths would not be evident until 1980s and 1990s. They believed that such occupational hazards were 'intolerable' (Reitze et al., 1972). By the time that paper went to press, on 25 February 1972 New York City had banned all asbestos spraying in the city. Within a year that ban was nationwide. At the WTC, asbestos spraying had reached the 38th floor, but henceforth the Cafco asbestos-substitute material would be used for the bulk of the fireproofing. The WTC opened the following year.

WTC under Fire

Fire-proofing in a skyscraper is not static: it can be modified and tested by events. The first test of the WTC's fire-retardants and the escape procedures for its staff occurred in 1975. A fire started on the eleventh floor of the North Tower and burned for three hours, spreading flames along cable shafts and sending smoke to several floors above. This fire first raised the issue of the effectiveness of the fire-protection in the WTC. New York Fire Commissioner John T. O'Hagan, in particular, voiced concerns – not about asbestos – but about sprayed fire-retardants generally. He argued that more traditional materials, such as concrete, offered a greater margin of safety than sprayed-on materials (whether asbestos or mineral fibre), which could deteriorate and fall off (O'Hagan, 1977). These criticisms of sprayed fibre were true. Much depended on the competence of the sprayers, the preparation of target surfaces, and inspection procedures. Sprayed asbestos was notorious for being carelessly applied by semi-skilled sprayers and then flaking away and creating dust. For example, in August 1970 – only a few months after spraying ceased in New York – a fire broke out in One New York Plaza, a skyscraper a few blocks south of the WTC that was protected by sprayed asbestos. The fire was soon extinguished, but there were two fatalities. A subsequent investigation found that much of the insulation on the key floors had fallen off soon after its application or had been disturbed by later construction work (Abrams, 1979). In the Twin Towers themselves, it had been known since the 1980s that some of the buildings either lacked a fireproof coating or that coating had been sprayed very thinly. Repairs, buildings swaying in the wind, and the impact of elevator cables on beams also dislodged the coatings (Glanz and Moss, 2001).

This partly explains why a repair and modification program was underway almost as soon as the WTC was completed. In the aftermath of the fire in 1975, more fire-resistant material was added where cabling and plumbing penetrated floors and walls. Asbestos fibre that was already in place was either sealed or 'abated' (in other words, removed). Later the Port Authority would begin legal action against its insurers in an attempt (which was unsuccessful) to recoup the removal costs. Nevertheless, in 1981 the Asbestos Corporation in Canada used the WTC in a striking advertisement that proclaimed the life-saving properties of its product. The slogan was 'When Life Depends On It You Use Asbestos'. The advertisement highlighted that it took only two hours to evacuate the building after the alarm went off. It was an ironic advertisement because most of the floors did not contain asbestos. On the other hand, it should be remembered that during the 1980s WTC 7 was still being built (and was not opened until 1987). W.R. Grace had won the contract for this building and used their Monokote 5 sprayed insulation. This vermiculite-based product was to have a controversial history, because (as Grace knew) it contained small percentages of a dangerous type of asbestos known as tremolite (Peacock, 2003; Schneider and McCumber, 2004).

A more severe test of the WTC's resilience came in 1993, when terrorists first attempted to blow it up. A truck bomb was detonated in the underground garage at the base of the North Tower, killing six people. Power was lost in the Tower and smoke rose through it, but the building was soon evacuated. The Tower was repaired, cleaned, and reopened in less than a month. However, further modifications to the WTC's fireproofing followed. The Port Authority decided in the mid-1990s to increase the layer of Cafco fire-retardant on the trusses from ¾-inch to 1½-inch. Thirty-one stories had been upgraded when the Boeing 767s, heavily laden with fuel, hit the Towers on the morning of 9/11. After the impact, WTC 2 collapsed in 59 minutes and WTC 1 in 102 minutes. The death toll, including occupants, jet passengers, and New York safety personnel, was over 3,000. However, 25,000 escaped. Later that day, in an event that received scant publicity, the fire-damaged WTC 7 also collapsed.

Conclusion

The debate over asbestos in the WTC was only one strand among many that emerged as commentators began to grapple with the events of 9/11 (Eagar and Musso, 2001; Sellers, 2003). Inevitably, official reports followed. In May 2002, the Federal Emergency Management Agency (FEMA) completed a Building Performance Study for the World Trade Center and nearby buildings (FEMA, 2002). It concluded that the design of the WTC was sound and attributed the collapses wholly to extraordinary factors beyond the control of the builders. While it called for further study, it suggested that weakening of the floor joists led to the floors falling upon each other in a 'pancake' collapse.

In August 2002, the National Institute of Standards and Technology (NIST) announced a multi-year investigation into the collapse of the Towers, besides WTC 7. The NIST investigation was to look at structural fire protection, life safety, and engineering practice. It included extensive investigations, ranging from heat tests on the structural steel, computer simulation, and modelling of smoke and fire movement, besides interviews with survivors. The NIST *Final Report* (2005) also vindicated the design of the WTC, noting that the damage caused by the jets was unprecedented. But it emphasised that their impact caused fireproofing to be detached from the structural steel, making the columns more vulnerable to the heat from the resulting fires (heat that drastically weakened the steel). That factor, combined with so much immediate physical destruction of external and core columns, caused the sagging floors to pull the outer walls of the buildings inwards until they buckled. At WTC 7, which was a more typical high building and had not been hit by jets or doused in kerosene, the investigation concluded that the collapse was due to the prolonged fire (triggered by WTC 1) and the design of the building.

Although fire protection receives close attention in these reports and in their voluminous drafts and appendices, it is striking that the word 'asbestos' hardly ever occurs. For example, in the NIST (2005) report the word 'asbestos' is mentioned in passing on only five pages in a report of nearly 300 pages. NIST's WTC 7 (2008) report, though it recommended enhancement of fire protection systems, did not single out the sprayed Monokote for criticism and, again, never mentioned asbestos. The mineral itself was simply not regarded as an issue. However, sprayed-on fireproofing of whatever type *was* an issue. The fact that these reports fail to emphasise asbestos highlights a very important point. As a fire-retardant in buildings, asbestos is not unique. Its legendary fire-resistant properties can be duplicated by other mineral fibres – products, moreover, that do not damage the health of their applicators. The history of the WTC shows how easily manufacturers could devise – even before a ban was introduced – alternatives that not only replaced asbestos, but also delivered better fire ratings. Although one might point to WTC spray fire-retardants as being far from perfect, it is clear that the lack of asbestos made little difference to the fate of the Towers.

To be sure, one might regard the government accounts as no more than a sanitised view of events. But none of the protagonists of the idea that asbestos contributed to the disaster have provided convincing scientific analysis or contemporary documents. The Milloy and Schlafly contributions are full of exaggerations and misleading statements. Their favourite quote is by Herbert Levine who, as this article has shown, was an ardent proponent of a process that proved lethal to his workforce. The apparent source of this quote is a reported conversation between Levine and Professor Richard Wilson at Harvard University. The latter is the main expert cited by Milloy to support his case, but Wilson is a risk analyst who does not publish in the field of asbestos. Langer and Morse (2001), in their more substantial contribution, have argued that sprayed asbestos is a superior product and would have better protected the WTC. But as we have seen, other evidence shows that sprayed asbestos was far from satisfactory. Maines, too, has described asbestos as a 'perfect material' and has implied that serious fires in American buildings have increased as asbestos use has declined (Maines, 2005, p.134). However, fire statistics do not support this conclusion. US fire fatalities have steadily declined and, in particular, deaths from fires in high-rise American office buildings had become exceptional by the 1990s (in many years no one died in this way); and until WTC 7, no high-rise office structure had ever collapsed through fire (National Fire Protection Association, 2008).

The above accounts have usually linked what is essentially a construction problem with contemporary litigation issues and ad hominem attacks on critics of asbestos, such as Selikoff. The coincidence of 9/11 with the crescendo of asbestos litigation in the USA is surely relevant. The credentials of most of those who have praised asbestos have left them open to the charge of writing from an ideological rather than scientific perspective. Steven Milloy, the apparent originator of this WTC debate, is presented by *Fox News* as an independent journalist. However, he is also a consultant for tobacco companies Philip Morris and R.J. Reynolds and oil giant Exxon Mobil. Milloy's main claim to fame is as a self-appointed critic of 'junk science' and opponent of the idea of global warming. From the 1990s until the end of 2005, he was an adjunct scholar at the 'libertarian' Cato Institute, which has a track record of hostility to asbestos litigation. Richard Wilson also has links with the Cato Institute and appeared at a US Senate hearing in 2007 to state his opposition to the banning of asbestos. Schlafly is a conservative lawyer and founder of *Conservapedia*, which has been described as the US religious right's version of *Wikipedia*. The publication in which his article appeared, the *Journal of American Physicians and Surgeons*, is not regarded as a valid peer-reviewed journal. Langer, perhaps the only expert of substance on asbestos to have become involved in this debate (he once worked at Mount Sinai with Selikoff), has received (and has declared) asbestos industry funding. Most of Peter Bartrip's work has been commissioned by defendant asbestos attorneys; and both he and Rachel Maines have testified in litigation at the request of asbestos companies.

Some of the key articles on this issue have appeared in *Indoor and Built Environment*, a journal that has claimed the moral high ground in the asbestos debate. However, recently-released documents suggest that the launch of this journal was orchestrated by the tobacco industry as a way of presenting research that questioned the health risks of environmental tobacco smoke (Michaels, 2008, p. 53). Currently, the journal's content reflects the outlook of a small coterie of mineralogists, toxicologists and industry consultants, who support the continued use of asbestos. Its editor, John Hoskins, has consistently supported the Canadian government and its asbestos industry in their quest to extend asbestos manufacture in the developing world. A literature that supported the idea that the WTC collapsed because it had been denuded of asbestos would obviously be extremely useful in rehabilitating asbestos and furthering these aims.

However, if this debate was an attempt to 'manufacture doubt', then it has been unsuccessful. No convincing evidence has been presented that substitutes did not perform as well as asbestos. The WTC disaster has made no difference to the types of fire-retardants used in current buildings (though it may influence building design and building codes). Designers of high-rise buildings are continuing to rely on man-made mineral fibres and no moves are afoot to relaunch asbestos fire insulation. The fire-retardant that has been used in the recently rebuilt WTC 7 is none other than the latest version of Grace's Monokote. It contains no asbestos.

ACKNOWLEDGMENTS

I would like to thank Dr David Higgins at the University of York for providing copies of some of the more obscure publications.

REFERENCES

Abrams, M.S. 1979. Behavior of Inorganic Materials in Fire. In H. Smith, Edwin Earle Smith, T. Z. Harmathy (eds), Design *of Buildings for Fire Safety: A Symposium*. Boston, MA, American Society for Testing and Materials International: 14-75.

Bartrip, P. J. 2001. Irving John Selikoff and the Strange Case of the Missing Medical Degrees. *Journal of the History of Medicine and Allied Sciences*, 58: 3-33.

Bell, S.W. 1970. Underwriters' Laboratory Inc. letter to Port of NY Authority. 24 April.

Bowker, M. 2003. *Fatal Deception: The Untold Story of Asbestos. Why It Is Still Legal and Still Killing Us*. Emmaus, PA, Rodale.

Brodeur, P. 1968. *A Reporter at Large: The Magic Mineral*. New York, *New Yorker*.

Claudio, Luz. 2001. Environmental Aftermath. *Environmental Health Perspectives*, 109: A529-A536.

Eagar, Thomas W. and Musso, Christopher. 2001. Why Did the World Trade Center Collapse? Science, Engineering, and Speculation. *JOM*, 53: 8-11.

Egan, J.F. 1969. Letter to R.W. Sterrett, Zonolite Construction Products Division. 28 November.

FEMA. 2002. *World Trade Center Building Performance Study: Data Collection, Preliminary Observations and Recommendations*. FEMA 403, May.http://www.fema.gov/rebuild/mat/wtcstudy.shtm (accessed November 2008)

Fenner, Ed. 1970. Miscellaneous notes dated 12 January re. meeting, 9 January.

Glanz, James and Moss, Michael. 2001. The Towers: Faulty Fireproofing is Reviewed as Factor in Trade Center Collapse. *New York Times*, 13 December.

Glanz, James and Revkin, Andrew C. 2001. A Nation Challenged; Haunting Question: Did the Ban on Asbestos Lead to Loss of Life?. *New York Times*, 18 September.

Henderson M. 2001. Ban on Asbestos Cladding Cost Lives. *The* [London] *Times*, September 18.

Howe, M.F. and Holmes, S. 1970. Memo re. Sprayed Asbestos in New York, 7 September.

IIHRP. 1969. Minutes of Meeting Advisory Council, 11 June.

Johns-Manville Corporation. 1969. Mount Sinai Meeting on Asbestos Spraying. Typescript notes, 5 December.

Landrigan, Philip J. et al. 2004. Health and Environmental Consequences of the World Trade Center Disaster. *Environmental Health Perspectives*, 112: 731-9.

Lange, J.H. 2001. Has the World Trade Center Tragedy Established a New Standard for Asbestos? *Indoor and Built Environment*, 10: 346-49.

Lange, J.H. 2004. Emergence of a New Policy for Asbestos: A Result of the World Trade Center Tragedy. *Indoor and Built Environment*, 13: 21-33.

Langer, Arthur M. and Morse, Roger. 2001. The World Trade Center Catastrophe: Was the Type of Spray Fire Proofing a Factor in the Collapse of the Twin Towers? *Indoor and Built Environment*, 10: 350-360.

Lilienfeld, David E. 1991. The Silence: The Asbestos Industry and Early Occupational Cancer Research – A Case Study. *American Journal of Public Health*, 81: 791-800.

McCulloch, Jock and Tweedale, G. 2008. *Defending the Indefensible: The Global Asbestos Industry and its Fight for Survival*. Oxford, Oxford University Press.

Maines, Rachel. 2005. *Asbestos and Fire: Technological Trade-Offs and the Body at Risk*. New Brunswick, N.J., Rutgers University Press.

Michaels, David. 2008. *Doubt is Their Product: How Industry's Assault on Science Threatens Your Health*. New York, Oxford University Press.

Milloy, Steven. 2001. Asbestos Could Have Saved WTC Lives. *Fox News*, 14 September. http://www.foxnews.com/story/0,2933,34342,00.html (accessed November 2008)

Monti, R.M. 1970. Port Authority Memo, 15 May 1970.

National Fire Protection Association. 2008. Web site. http://www.nfpa.org/ (accessed November 2008)

NIST. 2005. *Final Report on the Collapse of the World Trade Center Towers*. Washington, D.C, NIST. http://wtc.nist.gov/NISTNCSTAR1CollapseofTowers.pdf (accessed November 2008)

NIST.2008. Final *Report of the Collapse of World Trade Center Building 7: Draft for Public Comment.* Washington, D.C, NIST. http://wtc.nist.gov/media/NIST_NCSTAR_1A_for_public_comment.pdf (accessed November 2008)

O'Hagan, John T. 1977. *High Rise/Fire and Life Safety.* New York, Dun-Donnelley Publishing. Corporation.

Peacock, Andrea. 2003. *Libby, Montana: Asbestos and the Deadly Silence of an American Corporation.* Boulder, Colorado, Johnson Books.

Raines, W.P. 1968. Letter to F.J. Solon re. meeting with Dr Selikoff, 11 April.

Raines, W.P. 1969. Report of Meeting with Selikoff, 11 July.

Reitze, W.B., Nicholson, W.J., Holaday, D.A., and Selikoff, I.J. 1972. Application of Sprayed Inorganic Fiber Containing Asbestos: Occupational Health Hazards. *American Industrial Hygiene Association Journal*, 33: 178-191.

Rickles, R.N. 1970. Testimony [at] Public Hearings of the Health Effects of the Spraying of Asbestos-Containing Materials. Astor Place, NYC, 27, 28 May.

Schlafly, A. 2003. Did Flawed Science and Litigation Help Bring Down the World Trade Center? *Journal of American Physicians and Surgeons*, 8: 89-93.

Schneider, Andrew, and McCumber, David. 2004. *An Air that Kills: How the Asbestos Poisoning of Libby, Montana, Uncovered a National Scandal.* New York, G.P. Putnam's Sons.

Seabrook, John. 2001. The Tower Builder: Why Did the World Trade Center Buildings Fall Down When They Did? *The New Yorker*, 19 November.

Selikoff, I.J., 1970. Partnership for Prevention – The Insulation Industry Hygiene Research Program, *Industrial Medicine*, 39: 21-25.

Sellers, Christopher C. 2003. September 11 and the History of Hazard. *Journal of the History of Medicine and Allied Sciences*, 58: 449-458.

Swetonic, M.W. 1993. Death of the Asbestos Industry. In Jack Gottschalk (ed.), *Crisis Response: Inside Stories of Managing Image under Siege.* Detroit, Gail Research Inc.: 289-308.

Thompson, Carl. 1969. Hill & Knowlton Memo to F.J. Solon et al., 22 January.

Tweedale, G. 1999. Sprayed 'Limpet' Asbestos: Technical, Commercial, and Regulatory Aspects. In G. Peters and B.J. Peters (eds.), *Sourcebook on Asbestos Diseases*, Charlottesville, VA, Lexis Law Publishing, 20: 79-109.

Tweedale, G. 2001. *Magic Mineral to Killer Dust: Turner & Newall and the Asbestos Hazard.* Oxford, Oxford University Press.

Wermeil, Sara E. 2000. *The Fireproof Building: Technology and Public Safety in the Nineteenth-Century American City.* Baltimore, Johns Hopkins University Press.

In: Understanding Risk
Editor: Matthias Beck
ISBN: 978-1-62618-686-6

Chapter 18

SOME ARE MORE EQUAL THAN OTHERS: ON HOW HEALTH WORKERS COPE WITH IDEAS THAT SEEM IMPOSSIBLE TO PRACTICE

Rour Stokken
Patient Education Resource Centre, Sunnmøre Hospital Trust, Volda, Norway
and Faculty of Social Sciences and Technology Management,
Norwegian University of Science and Technology, Trondheim, Norway

ABSTRACT

In Norway, recent health political documents adhere to the idea of rendering patients and health professionals equal. In this article, discussions between health workers, lay representatives and academic actors concerning equality within patient education is investigated. The aim of the article is to reveal how health professionals cope with the idea of equality that in many ways seams impossible to practice.

The discussions were analyzed in a theoretically informed inductive process inspired by grounded theory. A theoretical framework based upon Brunsson's organized hypocrisy and Habermas' division between system and lifeworld guided the analysis. Three categories of double-bind situations originating from the demand for rendering lay representatives and health professionals equal were identified: considering knowledge payment and collaboration.

The dilemmas are coped with by decoupling those values evoked when attuning to the health care system, and those values evoked when attuning to patient education as practice. The article concludes that the decoupling between idea and practice is made possible by equality being an idea in the system world and a practice in the lifeworld. This nails equality to the lifeworld and makes it fragile to quality assurance.

INTRODUCTION

In Norway recent health political documents (HMN, 2004; HOD, 2005; NKLMS, 2004; SHdep, 1998) adhere to the idea of helping people to help themselves. In these, the health service is conceived as a partner for the prosumer-patient. In such a relationship, the aim is to combine the knowledge and experience of health workers and patient, at the same time as the patient is supposed to have a high degree of control (Barry, Stevenson, Britten, Barber, and Bradley, 2001; Coulter, 2002; Lorig, 2002; Morgan, 1991). This call for a modern health professional-patient relationship where these two parties team up as equal.

Within the field of patient education, equality between lay and professional should also be rendered during conduction. Even if this is a wonderful idea that maintains a strong foothold, it tends to turn out problematic to put into practice; for lay and professionals rest their legitimacy upon two diverse logics. While legitimacy of the lay rest upon experiences and stories with verisimilitude, the legitimacy of professionals rest upon formal education, employment and knowledge of a generic character.

In this article, we first take a brief look at patient education as a concept. Then we discuss patient education as a public service before we look into how health professionals discuss how they relate to the demand for equality in practice. At the end, the article argues that there is a decoupling between patient education as idea and practice, rendered possible by equality being an idea in a government logic and a practice a governance process. This is related to how an organization can withstand contradictory demands.

PATIENT EDUCATION

Patient education is legislated as one of four tasks that Norwegian hospitals have a special responsibility for. The legislation is connected to one of the major changes in public planning: the turn from *government* to *governance*. 'Government' refers to the formal institutional structure and location of authoritative decision-making in the modern state, like ministries, agencies, municipalities and counties. 'Governance' concerns governmental and non-governmental organizations working together in partnerships between public, private and voluntary sectors; and between national, regional and local level (Amdam, 2009).

The existence of both government and governance approaches denotes that two seemingly different health promotion discourses co-exist and have evolved into two distinct and somewhat exclusive approaches (Laverack and Labonte 2000: 256):

(a) The conventional discourse that emphasises top down disease prevention through lifestyle management and vector control.
(b) The more radical discourse that emphasises social justice through bottom up community empowerment, advocacy and partnership.

In Norway patient education surfaced within the more radical discourse, from a common interest in savvy patients among health professionals, patient organizations and politicians. This interest was adopted by the governmental framework, and became fed downwards within the hospital structure. Here it was well received among both health professionals and patient organizations, and the idea spread quickly throughout the country. An important reason for this seems to be that it suited the government logic well, since the strategy of the newly appointed Minister of Health in 1995 was to 'create' as few patients as possible (Hernes G, 2006 pers. comm. 22 March).

In 2001 a national patient education resource centre was designated to promote implementation. This centre has manifested itself as a close collaborator with patient organizations, and has adopted many ideas from the voluntary sector into its foundation. One of these ideas was that, if patient and health professional were to be equal, they should also be equal with regard to patient education.

Until 2001 this centre had been a local patient education resource centre pilot at a local hospital. When it took on its new and national role, they first tried to impart course templates and other tools they had developed for their own use during the pilot phase. They soon gave this up, simply because the tools did not make their way either into practice or into understanding.

The failure to impart templates and tools was followed by an effort to spread the founding idea of user involvement and self-help. In this process they chose an approach that suited the idea of equality: they delegated format, ingredients and quality measures to local knowledge. This corresponded perfectly to those values found in self-help, daily life, and within the framework of governance.

The most important tool for dissemination of the idea of equality between lay and professional within the field of patient education has been '*the standard method for quality development of patient education*'. This method is a mix of democratic values, the idea of self-help and quality circles (Deming, 1986). *Standard method* was disseminated as a practical method. This gave predecessors in the field room to project their own views and practices into the concept of patient education, by acting a prescription of how to do old things in a better way. In that way the National Patient Education Resource Centre simultaneously embraced existing practices and demonstrated how lay representatives could be treated as equal to professionals, by treating local units as equal to themselves.

The model disseminated from the national resource centre entails that patient educative initiatives have two levels of implementation: the first level involves health workers in arranging collaboration with lay representatives, and the second level involves collaboration which puts patient education into practice. At the first level, health workers operate within a government logic, whilst at the second level the governance process takes over.

The idea of equality between lay and professional reflects important values in Norwegian health care policy and is in general applauded by health workers in the field (Steihaug and Hatling, 2006, 2007; Steihaug, Hatling, and Bringager, 2008). This, in combination with the flexible nature of standard method has made the field both avoid the tyranny of principles (Toulmin, 1981), and fostered a wide variety of practices. This can to a certain degree explain why equality is demanded, but it does not explain how the demand for equality can exist within the health care. To do so, we turn to organizational theory.

Hospitals Are Political Organisations

Patient education exists within what Brunsson (1988/2002) defines as a political organization. In opposition to an action organization that legitimizes its existence through efficient production of coordinated action, the political organization legitimizes its existence by reflecting a world containing values, ideas or people that are in conflict with one another – that is by embedding the conflicts.

The political organization embeds conflicts by delivering both actions and ideologies, where the latter come in two different shapes: talk and decisions. The difference between these two modes is that decisions are important enough to warrant classification as a separate category (Brunsson, 1988/2002, p 26). The third category of outcome is action. By decoupling talk, decision and action, a wider range of stakeholders get something, and no one gets it all.

The ability to decouple talk, decision and action rests upon the difference between ideas and actions. The difference is not only due to action being a here-and-now phenomenon as opposed to talk and decisions, which concern the future. It is also due to a significant difference between the world of ideas and the world of action. There are after all several things that can be said but not done, and done but not said. This is both due to social barriers, for instance in terms of taboos, and the fact that action demands more resources than ideas (Brunsson, 1993, 2006).

At street-level, where health workers do their job, policy becomes practice (Lipsky, 1980), and lacking coordination between talk, decision and action can be both observed and felt by both patients and health professionals. To the health worker that ought to put talk and decision into action, decoupling induces double-bind situations. To understand the nature of these concerning equality between lay and professional, we need to examine the foundations for collaboration between these two parties.

Lay-Professional Collaboration

The requirement of collaboration between lay and professional places patient education on both sides of the border between employed and voluntary work. In Habermas-ian terms (1984), the collaboration then is to be found on the border between lifeworld and system.

The lifeworld is our public and private spheres, the framework that culture, social integration and personality are sustained and produced from. It is our background and horizon and vehicle for all knowing (Hellesnes, 2002; Scambler, 2001). The counterpart to the lifeworld is the 'system', that is, our notions of economy and state, regulated by money and power.

The relation between the lifeworld and the system is regulated between traded medias produced in four subsystems. Two subsystems exist within the system, called economy and state, and two exist within the lifeworld, called public sphere and private sphere. These subsystems produce different outcomes, but they are dependent upon each other for what is not produced. The state produces power; the economy produces money; the private sphere commitment; and the public sphere influence. These media have diverse capacities, and the media of the system tend to dominate those of the lifeworld (Habermas, 1984).

Another important difference between the lifeworld and the system, concerns their logic. This is denoted by the medias produced. Whereas the lifeworld focuses on optimization of commitment and influence through consensus, the system strives for optimisation of power and money in a pragmatic ways.

The system's domination over the lifeworld can potentially replace the logic of the lifeworld with the logic of the system. This is what Habermas calls 'colonization', which can occur from systematically distorted communication. This means that communication is imbued with power hidden to the partakers. It can become impossible to conduct a discourse where the best argument wins – because arguments are imbued with power in a way hidden to those judging the argument. Hence, systematically distorted communication captures the same kind of power which Lukes (1974/2005) defines as power of third dimension.

Despite the system's power over the lifeworld, it is from the lifeworld that the system acquires its legitimacy; by blending in. For when the system does not blend in, we see it, and we see that it does not support our lifeworld. This reduces the chance for colonization (Habermas, 1984).

While ideas are abstract, referring to intentions and the future, practices are concrete and concerning the here and now (Brunsson, 1988/2002; Czarniawska-Joerges, 1988). This makes ideas more adaptive to our lifeworld than practices, since reality does not interfere with intentions and hopes in the way that practices do (Brunsson, 2006). Hence, equality between lay and professional are much easier to speak of than carry out.

METHOD

To acquire knowledge of how health professionals think about patient education, the author attended a discussion group arranged by the patient education resource centre at a hospital in Central Norway. The primary target group were those conducting patient education at the hospital, but lay and academic representatives were also asked to participate to add perspectives to the discussions. The aim was to increase knowledge and reflection concerning patient education.

To study how equality is coped with through a case study has its limitations when it comes to generalization. Still, the concept of equality is general, and from discussions and documents originating from other contexts, it is evident that challenges originating from equality between lay and professional are more than a local problem of academic interest. It is a rather general concern among health professionals within the field of patient education. It is also is also a general concern in that it is expected to be practiced by street level bureaucrats (Lipsky, 1980) who therefore experience the contradiction between an idea and practice.

All sessions analyzed had a topic, i.e. motivation, learning or coping, and were often started by an introduction from one of the participants. No actual patient cases were been discussed, but the topics discussed were often enlightened by reference to stories of actual and anonymous patients. This was been done without violating the professional secrecy

The make-up of the group was not been consistent during the whole period, but the core had been six health care workers where at least four had participated in each session. Two laypersons occasionally participated. The number of occasionally participating health workers varied. The group fluctuated from about 20 participants at its peaks to 7 during the smallest discussion groups. All in all, there was a decline in the number of participators over the period studied, which stabilized the make-up of the group.

The group sessions were taped and the content was analyzed in a theoretically informed inductive approach inspired by grounded theory (Glaser and Strauss, 1967). Saturation was based upon consistency between discussions, a body of 30 individual and focus group interviews on patient education, documents describing patient education and theory. Eight sessions from January 2006 to November 2007, making up a total of 14 hours, were included. The theoretical framework discussed earlier guided the analysis.

Several topics relating to patient education were covered in the group. Challenges related to the fact that patient education should be conducted in a collaboration that renders lay and professional equal were one of the most discussed topics, and a topic that have kept on across all analyzed sessions. The topic was linked to many other issues, like health as concept and experience, health workers' working conditions and trends and changes in society.

In the group, the participant Dina (a diabetes nurse) acted as a storyteller; and we will return to the role played by her. Often discussions played out like this: First a topic is encircled, then Dina tells a story, and further discussion is related to her story. In later group sessions, Dina's story becomes the symbol of the topic and connected discussions. This makes Dina's stories both important to the group and in the forthcoming text. However the discussions in the group are embedded in the text connected to the story.

DILEMMAS

The inductive analysis identified three kinds of dilemmas. These included the dilemma of knowledge, dilemma of payment and dilemma of collaboration. At least from an academic perspective, these are interwoven. Still, the way the dilemmas were discussed warrant for treating them as three different concepts.

In the forthcoming text, the dilemmas are investigated to reveal how the health workers coped with ideas that seemed impossible to practice; for lay representatives cannot be both paid and unpaid, lay knowledge cannot be both equal and subordinate, and power cannot be distributed between two equal parties when only one is in charge.

Reasons for collaboration between health professionals and lay representatives were discussed thoroughly in the group, and the arguments were many; spanning from more people to share the workload upon, via increased knowledge resource and increased legitimacy, to simply being the right thing to do. Still, the health professionals experienced dilemmas when equality was to be put into practice. The reason was that 'equal collaboration between lay and professionals' contradicted with values of the health care system.

According to Brunsson (1988/2002), inconsistency can legitimize organizations by making them satisfy a wider set of demands; but only as long as the inconsistencies do not present themselves as repulsive. To achieve this, Brunsson finds four decoupling mechanisms: by sequence, by subject matter, through enacting diverse environments and through distribution between organizational units. In this case, I will advocate the presence of a fifth decoupling mechanism: distribution between two Habermasian worlds (Habermas, 1984).

The imbued contradictions is not made covert through distance in time or space, as in the four decoupling mechanism put forward by Brunsson, but though the diversity between the Habermasian worlds. Through decoupling between these, lay representatives can be both paid and unpaid, lay knowledge can be both equal and subordinate and power can be distributed between two equal parties when only one is in charge. This is made possible by evoking two different sets of values and practices in the two different Habermasian worlds within the same sequence, subject matter, environment and organizational unit by the same actor. In the forthcoming text, this kind of decoupling will be explained through the three dilemmas expressed in the discussion group.

Decoupling through Habermasian worlds rests itself upon the same diversity that makes the meeting between the health professional and the patient into a double meeting: one meeting in the system between a patient and a health worker, and one meeting in the lifeworld between two human beings (Stokken, 2009), the value of medias produced in the two worlds, and their trivial impact upon the other.

DILEMMA OF KNOWLEDGE

As diabetes nurse, Dina was to ensure that education initiatives concerning diabetes were of high quality. This denoted that according to the *standard method*, initiatives should both rest upon both professional and lay knowledge.

In a discussion concerning the difference between lay and professional, Dina sighs and utters: 'Some times it becomes troublesome. There are many views on many topics.' Then she tells a story of a patient educative initiative concerning the use of insulin.

> Dina spends a long time emphasizing the well-documented importance of hygiene, especially the importance of needle change prior to each injection. When she is about to wrap up the topic, her lay co-instructor opposed her message by telling the participants that he seldom changes the needle and frequently injects through his clothes, and it causes no problems.
>
> Dina did not know what to do in this situation, as from a professional standpoint it is great numbers that count, while it is close experience that count to the lay. This makes professional knowledge bound to the system and explicit, while lay knowledge is closely connected to the lifeworld and the tacit. As a leader for an initiative resting on both lay and professional legitimacy, she experiences double-bind situations when the logic of the system and the logic of the lifeworld does not team up. Hence lay and professional knowledge were incompatible in the system, while they complemented each other in the lifeworld.

Health professionals in the discussion group noted that lay knowledge in patient educative initiatives was of great value, partly due to its deviation from professional knowledge. This is a lifeworldly logic that denotes that the demand for optimization of influence and commitment through consensus justifies being a little lenient with the professional knowledge. On the other hand, in a system that is imbued with evidence based knowledge and quality assurance, lenience with professional knowledge can be problematic.

This gives two social worlds, one lifeworldly caring for governance processes, and one in the system governed by the logic of a government approach. While the rules within the latter render lay knowledge to be of low credibility compared to the professional, governance processes renders them equal. This induces a burden on the governance processes during patient educative practice, and to the government logic within the health care system. But the two systems handle issues, such as quality, differently.

In the lifeworld, 'good' is about good experiences, while within the system, 'good' is about measured quality. In our lifeworld, coffee, apples, music, humans and art are 'good' if we like them. And often that is the end of the matter. In general we can give reasons, but seldom entirely. For to like, or dislike, is often about the tacit. By contrast, the system measures quality through ticking check-boxes for each characteristics of an entity that is able to satisfy predefined needs. This implies that 'needs' ought to be defined before something within the system can be considered as good.

DILEMMA OF PAYMENT

Another much discussed theme within the group was payment. To the paid party that represents the system, getting help for free from lay representatives can be an ethical challenge. In the discussion group, this issue was discussed and approached from many angles, and differences between lay and professional perspectives often surfaced.

> Leila is an experienced lay representative that participates in several settings where most participants are managers and well paid, while she is not. 'This is the nature of being lay and it is chosen.' she says.

The lifeworldly nature of voluntary work implies that it is commitment and influence that keeps the layperson in place, not money and power, which is the medias that keeps the employed in place. Hence cooperation between lay and professional involves great diversity regarding how their participation is appreciated.

> Dina arranges patient educative initiatives for diabetics. In general she conducts them together with Valerie as lay representative. Dina experiences that Valerie does a good job, and helps her out. This she is grateful for. But Dina also feels that she ought to thank Valerie for her work.
>
> As a representative of the system, Dina feels that she should show appreciation through medias produced by the system, for instance in terms of payment or gifts of real value, but no funds exist for this purpose. And giving away the symbols the system provides, like postcards in a clip frame, she considers as inappropriate. Therefore, Dina has bought Valerie jewellery, from her own pocket, to thank her.

Even though participation is regulated and appreciated by medias produced in diverse worlds, both lay representatives and health professionals are present in both system and lifeworld. This makes the gift from Dina to Valerie a deed, coined by Dina as a person for gratitude, and not by an employed nurse as payment for the work done. This makes the gift, despite of its objective value, a symbol traded in the lifeworld. Not some kind of payment – as it would be in the system world.

The governmental logic is based upon the logic of the system and regulates the health professional. The governance framework rests upon the logic of the lifeworld and regulates the conduction of patient education as collaboration between parties that share a commitment.

In governance processes within the logic of the lifeworld, the division of labour is between two equal parties, while it is between one in charge and one voluntary worker within the system and the government logic. Furthermore the demand for equality is expressed by the same system that provides unequal resources and power to the same parties. This creates an inner contradiction within the government logic.

The inner contradictions within the government logic, and between the government logic and the governance processes, make it easier to practice governance processes than maintain a government logic. On the other hand the governance processes limit legitimacy in the health care system due to its lifeworldly logic. By enacting a lifeworldly logic in the group that conducts patient education, and a government logic when interacting with the health care system, the problematic practice of equality within a governmental logic never becomes relevant.

DILEMMA OF COLLABORATION

Collaboration between one party regulated by medias produced within the system, and one party regulated by medias produced within the lifeworld might pose challenges. Obviously, lay representatives often represent a patient organization in the health care system, and they are thereby not entirely free from the system. But the lay representative is not held in position by money and power in the same way as the employed.

> Valerie participates as a lay representative at regional level. Her experience is that the intentions behind user involvement are good, but in practice it is hard to exert any influence. For it is impossible to gain access to all those arenas where decisions are made, which in turn means that the logic of professionalism or money easily gain the upper hand.

This is not a concern only for lay representatives. In the group, there has been an awareness of the connection between knowledge and power, first and foremost advocated by the manager at the local patient education resource centre. Due to this, a recurring concern within the group has been the risk of shaping lay representatives too much into what suits the health care system best, first and foremost when it comes to agenda and values.

Participants in the discussion group pinpoint a dilemma between helping lay representatives to gain influence, for instance by providing knowledge of the system, and at the same time giving lay representatives the freedom to set their own agenda. This dilemma is considered as parallel to the dilemma of helping patients out and at the same time rendering them helpless. Also, the health professionals have their reasons for being concerned about not shaping lay representatives too much, because they themselves have also felt the power of the health care system.

Despite challenges, health professionals perceive lay participation as important, and lay representatives are often seen as ‘allies’ in the ‘fight’ against the bad sides of the health care system.

Local patient education resource centres have met the challenge of getting access to lay perspectives in three ways: through employment, organizational and individual collaboration. Employment makes lay representatives more available to the system at the same time as the representative’s work becomes appreciated through the media produced in the system: money and power. But then lay become regulated by the system.

Another way of overcoming challenges is to cooperate with organizations. Then the autonomy of the voluntary sector is maximized, at least if the patient organizations themselves educate the representatives. But this model also has its downsides, because the health workers that administer a patient educational initiative have less control over whom to cooperate with, and disagreements and conflicts between professional and lay are more likely to occur.

The third way is to collaborate with individuals. This is the way preferred by those participating in the discussion group. This is argued to give less tension in the cooperation, after all; there is an educative initiative that should be conducted in a good manner. But for health care and patient organizations, there is a demand for control of the actors. If things are solved between a health professional and a lay representative directly, this can become problematic because both patient organizations and health care lose control.

In practice it seems possible to combine individual and organizational collaboration, where the person appointed by the organization works well with the health professional; but this call for combining top-down and bottom-up processes. No matter which model is adopted, cooperation between lay and professional ought to overcome great differences concerning responsibility and power, at least from a system-perspective. From this perspective, the professional is doing a job on behalf of the hospital, and as long as the lay party not is paid, she or he is just helping out.

An alternative view of equality is to understand it as concerning influence, and hence belonging to the lifeworld. Then the system perspective can be suspended. Here are also two worlds: One in the government logic where health professionals have more power and are more responsible than the lay representative; and one in a governance logic where the health professional is equal to, and teaming up with, the lay representative. In the government logic, the governance process is a challenge and therefore easily becomes suspended. Meanwhile, it is active as representation of the educative initiative towards the health care system; for at idea-level, contradictions are less apparent and troublesome.

Discussion

While the system cares for pragmatic use of power and money, the lifeworld cares for communicative action, commitment and influence. This is possible due to the separation of two different worlds; one where idea, system and government logic team up perfectly, and one where practice, lifeworld and governance processes team up. Due to the diversity between these, the two worlds interfere minimally with each other – and a decoupling between them can be established.

These two worlds utilize the diversity between how concepts present themselves to hide the hypocrisy (Brunsson, 1988/2002) demanded when equality is to be practiced within a system that gives one of the parties a raw deal. For, by evoking the system when attuning to, or representing the health care system, and the lifeworld, when attuning to lay representatives, the contradiction between the system's demand for rationality and the lifeworld's demand for communicative action becomes covered up. Despite this, participants in the discussion group express frustration over the dilemmas that force them to choose between being loyal to the governance processes or to the government logic.

Which side health professionals choose seems to be determined by whether it is the system or the lifeworld that demand most loyalty in combination with contradictions within the government logic. Since the medias coined in the system tend to dominate those coined in the lifeworld (Habermas, 1984), the system should have good chances to gain the upper hand. Still, health professionals revealed a strong loyalty to the lay system, and a shortage of loyalty, to the health care system. The health professionals do not feel that the agenda of the system, that ought to optimize outcome, supports and blends into their lifeworld. But they experience that the agenda of the laypersons does. Hence they pay more attention to the demands from the governance process practiced in lifeworld, than to the medias produced in the system.

On the other hand, this way of acting is approved by the system in at least two ways. The first is that equality between lay and professional reflects important values in the Norwegian health care policy. The second is the set of practical guidelines disseminated by the National Patient Education Resource Centre. Together, these values and guideline legitimise suspension of the system's demand for rationality, and let the health professional be loyal to the demand for equality. A third reason is the nature of education, which does not fit the positivistic approach of medicine. In this way the system does to some degree legitimize suspension of its own logic.

All in all, these factors facilitate equality between lay and professional in a way which is able to withstand the risk of colonization by leaving validation, rationality and logic to the lifeworldly parts of governance processes. The consequence is that the system cannot grasp equality. It is bound to the lifeworld, and is most likely to be colonized and destroyed if any attempt at quality assurance is made 'the government way.' Hence the main challenge, when decoupling through two diverse Habermasian worlds exists, is to accept a translation from lifeworld to system and vice versa that is built upon trust between governance processes and government logic. Then the two approaches can care for diverse aspects.

Acknowledgments

First of all, a debt of gratitude goes to members of the discussion group who have generously shared their lifeworld and stories with me. Thanks are also owed to those who have read the text and passed on their comments – mostly as a lifeworldly gift. Finally, I would like to thank the Central Norway Regional Health Authority that has financed the project. Because, it is the lifeworld that comes first, and the system afterwards…

References

Amdam, R. 2009. Empowerment Planning in Regional Development. *European Planning*, Accepted fall 2008.

Barry, C. A., Stevenson, F. A., Britten, N., Barber, N., and Bradley, C. P. 2001. Giving voice to the lifeworld. More humane, more effective medical care? A qualitative study of doctor-patient communication in general practice. *Soc Sci Med*, 53(4), 487-505.

Brunsson, N. 1988/2002. *The Organization of Hypocrisy: Talk, Decisions and Actions in Organizations,* Copenhagen Business School Pr.

Brunsson, N. 1993. Ideas and Actions: Justification and Hypocrisy as Alternatives To Control. *Accounting, Organizations and Society*, 18(6): 489-506.

Brunsson, N. 2006. *Mechanisms of Hope: Maintaining The Dream of the Rational Organization.* København Oslo Malmö, Copenhagen Business School Press Universitetsforl. Liber.

Coulter, A. 2002. *The Autonomous Patient: Ending Paternalism In Medical Care.* London: Stationary Office (for The Nuffield Trust).

Czarniawska-Joerges, B. 1988. *Reformer och Ideologier Lokala Nämnder på väg.* Lund: Doxa ekonomi.

Deming, W. E. 1986. *Out Of The Crisis Quality, Productivity And Competitive Position.* Cambridge: Cambridge University Press.

Glaser, B. G., and Strauss, A. L. 1967. *The Discovery of Grounded Theory Strategies for Qualitative Research.* Chicago: Aldine.

Habermas, J. 1984. *The Theory of Communicative Action.* Boston, Mass.: Beacon Press.

Hellesnes, J. 2002. Den galne grisen hans Lars Liabø og dei tre verdene hand Jürgen Habermas, eller om formalpragmatikkens grunnlag. *Grunnane:* 93-115: Aschehoug.

HMN (2004). *Handlingsprogram for pasient- og pårørendeopplæring for Helse Midt-Norge.* Stjørdal: Helse Midt-Norge.

HOD (2005). *Fra stykkevis til helt - En sammenhengende helsetjeneste.* from http://www.regjeringen.no/Rpub/NOU/20052005/003/PDFS/NOU200520050003000DD DPDFS.pdf.

Labonte, R. and Laverack, G. 2000. *A Planning Framework for Community Empowerment Goals within Health Promotion. Healthy Policy Plan*, 15(3): 255-62.

Lipsky, M. 1980. Street-Level Bureaucracy: Dilemmas of the Individual in Public Services. *Politics and Society*, 10(1): 116.

Lorig, K. 2002. Partnerships Between Expert Patients And Physicians. *Lancet*, 359(9309): 814-815.

Lukes, S. 1974/2005. *Power: A Radical View*, Second Edition. London: Palgrave Macmillan.

Morgan, M. 1991. The Doctor-Patient Relationship. In G. Scambler (Ed.), *Sociology As Applied To Medicine* (3rd ed., pp. xiii, 303 s.). London: Baillière Tindall.

NKLMS. 2004. *Ideologi og metode for Lærings- og mestringssentre.* Oslo: Nasjonalt kompetansesenter for læring og mestring ved kronisk sjukdom.

SHdep. 1998. Ot prp nr 10 (1998-99). In *Sosial- og Helsedepartementet* (Ed.). Oslo: Odin.

Scambler, G. 2001. Introduction: Unfolding Themes of an Incomplete Project. In G. Scambler (Ed.), *Habermas, Critical Theory and Health.* New York: Routledge.

Steihaug, S., and Hatling, T. 2006. *Evaluering av Nasjonalt kompetansesenter for læring og mestring ved kronisk sykdom* (Vol. A6). Trondheim: SINTEF helse.

Steihaug, S., and Hatling, T. 2007. *Evaluering av LMS-aktiviteten i Helse.* Nord Trondheim: SINTEF Helse.

Steihaug, S., Hatling, T., and Bringager, N. 2008. *Evaluering av familieprosjektet.* Trondheim: SINTEF Helse.

Stokken, R. 2009. The Patient Educated Patient - A Health Care Asset Or Problem? *Social Theory and Health*, 7(2), 81-99.

Toulmin, S. 1981. The Tyranny Of Principles. *The Hastings Center report*, 11(6): 31-38.

INDEX

#

A

D

E

H

I

J

K

L

N

O

P

Q

R

S

T

Y

Z